Tennessee Senators 1911-2001

Portraits of Leadership in a Century of Change

William H. Frist
with J. Lee Annis, Jr.

MADISON BOOKS
Lanham • New York • Oxford

Published by Madison Books
4720 Boston Way
Lanham, Maryland 20706

12 Hid's Copse Road
Cummor Hill, Oxford OX2 9JJ, England

Distributed by National Book Network

Library of Congress Cataloging-in-Publication Data

Frist, William H.
  Tennessee senators, 1911–2001 : portraits of leadership in a century of change / William H. Frist with J. Lee Annis, Jr.
    p.   cm.
  Includes bibliographical references and index.
  ISBN 1-56833-120-7 (cloth : alk. paper)
    1. Legislators—United States Biography. 2. United States. Congress. Senate Biography. 3. United States—Politics and government—20th century. 4. Tennessee—Politics and government. I. Annis, J. Lee (James Lee), 1957–   . II. Title.
  E747.F75 1999
  328'.092'2768
  [B]—DC21   99-29281
                                                                  CIP

∞™ The paper used in this publication meets the minimum requirements of American National Standard for Information Sciences—Permanence of Paper for Printed Library Materials, ANSI/NISO Z39.48–1992. Manufactured in the United States of America.

Dedicated in loving memory
to my parents
Dorothy Harrison Cate Frist
(1910–1998)
and
Thomas Fearn Frist, M.D.
(1910–1998)

and to Lee's father
James L. Annis
(1929–1996)

Also dedicated with great love to my wife
Karyn Frist
whose love and support is my mainstay
and to our children
Harrison, Jonathan and Bryan
who are the joy of our lives

Contents

Preface

I'd never served in public office; I'd never run for public office. I was a forty-two-year-old heart surgeon. Yet there I was, in the middle of a tough campaign in 1994 challenging a fellow Tennessean who had been in the United States Senate for eighteen years.

After a fitful night of tossing and turning, unconsciously digesting the rigors of the campaign trail of the day before and trying to anticipate what rapid-fire surprises the next day would bring, I was abruptly awakened by the dream. The setting was the office of a U.S. Congressman, the time 1972.

"Bill, Washington is full of career politicians," the senior and courtly political figure said in a fatherly tone as I, a twenty-year-old intern, listened in awe.

"If you really want to serve your country well, go do something else—and it doesn't matter exactly what you do—but do it outside Washington and do it successfully. After twenty years of that something else, come back to Washington, and use what you've learned to dedicate a part of your life to the greatest of all careers, public service."

I'd totally forgotten, or maybe repressed, those words and the events of that day until they resurfaced early that morning twenty-two years later. The summer day in 1972 was typical for Washington, hot and muggy, and as I left the Georgetown basement apartment I shared with four other students I was thinking how I should phrase the question that had been on my mind for weeks. I'd spent July and August of 1972 working as an intern in the office of Tennessee's Fourth District Congressman Joe L. Evins. As I'd be returning to college the following day, I knew this would be my last chance to thank him for my summer experience and, more importantly, to ask him the question that I could ask no other.

I still vividly recall the worn leather chair, the expansive desk, the dark red rug, and even the queasy nervousness I felt in speaking one-on-one with a man of his stature.

"If someone my age," I asked hypothetically, not wanting to seem presumptuous that I would ever be qualified enough to serve in federal public office, "wanted to serve in the U.S. Congress someday, what advice would you give?"

At the time I was in college about to begin a course of study in public and international affairs, but I was also in the middle of those premedical courses that set the stage for a career as a physician. In half my classes were friends who single-mindedly were on track to become compassionate physicians, and in half were friends who wanted nothing more than to spend the next ten years of their lives in Washington, D.C. Thus the counsel the Congressman would give just might influence my own decision as to which path to follow. And though I never again thought consciously about that conversation until the dream in 1994, his words undoubtedly confirmed my own instinct to follow in the footsteps of my dad and two brothers, all physicians, and to put on hold any consideration of serving in Congress.

While I've been in the Senate now for just four years, my belief in the correctness of the Congressman's advice has only been strengthened. His words underlie my own conviction, reinforced almost daily in my life in the Senate, that the citizen-legislator has a unique and vital role to play in American democracy. Our Founding Fathers clearly understood the value of people who have held real jobs in real communities serving in Washington for a period of time and sharing their experiences. They understood the importance of keeping government close to the people by the constant rotation in office of citizens whose real-life experiences could help shape the legislation that so directly affects the daily lives of all Americans. This is what the Congressman was telling me so many years ago.

So why does one U.S. Senator write a book about his predecessors? The answer rests in why one seeks to become a U.S. Senator in the first place.

My entire life was focused on the public service of being a physician. My earliest memories as a child are of Dad leaving the table as we were finishing dinner, his worn black doctor's bag in hand, to make his nightly rounds at the hospital. On occasion I would accompany him as he drove to neighboring communities to deliver medicines and an encouraging word to patients too ill to leave their homes. And I fondly remember listening to Mother compassionately tending to patients over the phone when they called for simple medical advice or sometimes just consolation and support and Dad wasn't around. I grew up thinking all families revolved around such service to others. Wasn't this commitment to others what life was all about?

Thus it was only natural that I gravitated to medicine as a profession. To me public service was serving others one-on-one, physician to patient, through the practice of medicine. The art and the craft consisted of listening carefully to assess and make a diagnosis, then addressing the problem by developing and fulfilling a treatment plan. Fixing the heart so one could return to work, removing the diseased lung so one could take a deep breath, opening the stenotic windpipe so respirations could flow more comfortably, or transplanting a new heart into a sixteen-year-old so she could lead a full life—this was what brought joy to service. However, from my earliest college and medical school days, I also quietly hoped that I someday would have the opportunity to serve others at a broad policy level, where I could advance, in a way not really that different from medicine, the health and quality of life of a community just as I had advanced the health of individuals as a doctor.

My medical practice of heart and lung surgery impressed upon me what genuine leadership is all about. A leader clearly understands where he or she is going. His goal must be what he believes is right and good for the persons he is leading. Equally important, a leader must have the ability to convince those he leads that it is in their interest to follow. When a patient comes to a physician with simple symptoms of fatigue, and the physician knows that only a heart transplant will save his patient's life, that physician must sensitively lead the patient to the understanding that only such a radical procedure can change the intractable course his condition will otherwise take. Such servant-leadership seemed to me to be what genuine service in political office should be all about.

In the early 1990s, I decided to explore how best to serve the health of a community, but I had no idea where to begin. Every waking hour, seven days a week, was spent focusing on the welfare of my patients. As a transplant surgeon, I was on call twenty-four hours a day, managing the care of the patients whose hearts and lungs I had transplanted and trying to keep those waiting for a transplant alive until organs became available. The dual commitment to family and profession left little time to devote to social or political activities, and I didn't know any politicians to whom I could turn for advice as to how to make a transition from medicine to public service.

So I began a journey which lasted approximately two years, the purpose of which was to seek the advice and counsel of as many public servants as I possibly could. I spoke with university presidents, foundation directors, medical missionaries, the governor of Tennessee, various Congressmen, former Ambassador Joe Rodgers, Senators Jack Danforth and Howard Baker, and many others. My questions were focused. Essentially I was looking for the best fit that would allow me to serve effectively, recognizing both the potential strength of my past experiences as a physician as well as my own too numerous limitations. My search gradually inclined me toward elective office. But what office? Should it be the school board, the Statehouse, or the U.S. Congress?

Although I did not personally know Howard Baker, again and again I was told that he was someone whose advice I could trust. My good friend John

Van Mol, who had been so helpful to me in my efforts to educate people across the state about organ donation, quietly arranged a meeting with Senator Baker in Knoxville. The March 6, 1990, meeting was the first of several. I asked direct questions and Senator Baker, I'm sure responding to the same questions that hundreds of others had asked about a life in politics, patiently explained the mechanics of running for statewide office. Another meeting several months later, this time in Washington and set up on my instigation, included me, Senator Baker and his longtime friend Jim Cannon. I left that meeting sure of one thing: elective office was the path I should pursue. Yet I was more than a little confused as I witnessed what must have been an ongoing sincere debate between Cannon and Baker as to the merits of the office of Governor versus the office of U.S. Senator. Jim, former chief of staff to Governor Nelson Rockefeller, argued his preference for the Statehouse, while Howard persuasively made the case for the Capitol.

Content that I'd made progress in my journey toward public service, I sought to clarify some of the confusion I felt after listening to the Cannon-Baker debate. Back in Nashville, I wandered into Elder's Book Store on Elliston Place, a favorite local rare book store that specializes in Tennessee history. I asked Randy Elder for references that might help me understand the lives, motives, and contributions of those who had chosen to serve Tennessee in statewide office. At the time, I knew little about the politicians of the past. I knew that Tennessee had produced three Presidents, Andrew Jackson, Andrew Johnson, and James K. Polk. I wondered if they had served in the Senate.

I left that day with a red volume that served as the inspiration for this work, *Tennessee Senators as Seen by One of Their Successors*, by former Senator Kenneth McKellar, published in 1942. I read the book cover to cover, and then and there decided to dedicate the next period of my life to the people of Tennessee through the institution of the U.S. Senate. Thus, the words of this former Tennessee Senator, reflecting the past contributions of his predecessors, crystallized my own decision to enter public service by seeking the position of Senator. I told myself that if I made it to the Senate, I'd try to do for the twentieth century what McKellar in his writing did for the nineteenth century.

The McKellar treatise provides short biographies of thirty-nine Tennessee Senators, "who had already crossed the great river" at the time the book was written in 1942. McKellar's impact on me is what I hope to accomplish for others. My goal is simply to open a door into the lives of the seventeen U.S. Senators since McKellar's time who dedicated a portion of their lives to the service of Tennessee. Each chapter presents a portrait. The compilation presents a tapestry of Tennessee history against the backdrop of the history of our nation. Each life story is based on original and published research and focuses on both the Senator's motivation for public service and his place in history within the context of Tennessee, national and world history and politics. Taken together they are a fascinating group, replete with examples of courage, intrigue, behind-the-scenes maneuvering, and some less admirable qualities like greed. The portrait of each is admittedly incomplete. And what I've chosen to include is for the most part arbitrary, though I've done my best to select occasions and occurrences that typify the man and his times. For more expansive treatises, I encourage the reader to explore the references in the sources section at the end of this volume.

Tennessee Senators 1911–2001 surveys an astonishing time and place in American politics. I'm frequently asked, "Do they put something in the drinking water down there in Tennessee to breed so many accomplished politicians?" My answer draws upon the political history covered in this volume. Over the past century, the people of Tennessee have sent to the U.S. Senate a dynamic and remarkable group of leaders, who contended with Presidents, counseled Presidents, and sought to be Presidents.

It is my hope that this book will serve as both an inspiration to future public servants and a valuable reference not only of individual biographies of Tennessee leaders serving in our nation's upper legislative body but also of the political and social changes of the twentieth century that helped shape their lives and careers. Especially inspiring to me are those glimpses of courage that emerge as these individuals exercised their judgment on behalf of their constituents. Holding fast to one's convictions is not always easy in the face of well-organized and well-financed pressure, nor is subordinating one's own personal ambitions to the greater good. It takes giants to rise above the moment, and Tennesseans have been fortunate to have had more than our share of giants in the Senate. Who else but Howard Baker would have extinguished his own presidential aspirations to rescue Ronald Reagan's presidency after the debacle of Iran-Contra? Who else but Estes Kefauver would have taken on the kingpins of organized crime in full knowledge that his investigation of their lawlessness might alienate big-city bosses whose support he would need if his bid for the presidency were to be successful? Who else but Cordell Hull in the minutes after Pearl Harbor would have so boldly refuted the assertions of Japanese diplomats that their intentions had always been peaceful? I am reminded most of the words of my colleague Fred Thompson, who told the jury in summing up for Marie Ragghianti how important it was for those of us in public office to hold fast to our principles and take a stand when necessary. In taking those often unpopular stands, we signal future generations that they, too, can act on their principles knowing that they won't be standing alone.

Finally, I've written not just about the most enduring and well-known of our leaders but also about the more obscure, for all merge into the collective portrait of Tennessee as one of our nation's more politically influential states. The book was written with the able and diligent assistance of Lee Annis, whose work in researching the histories included visiting libraries, combing though official papers, and conducting interviews across the length and breadth of Tennessee. His insight and scholarly approach have richly enhanced my own appreciation of the historical significance of these figures.

While I'm a physician and a U.S. Senator, I am not a historian. So right up front I ask forgiveness of any reader who may be critical of my treatment of either these influential men or of the events of their time. The task of placing contemporary figures in historical perspective is a challenging one. For those Senators in the early part of this century, I have benefited from the interpretation of historians who have spent years digesting and interpreting their papers and contributions. For more recent Senators, I suffer from the lack of historical perspective that only time can provide. For this reason, the book is separated into two parts. Part I includes those Senators from Luke Lea (1911–1917) to Ross Bass (1964–1967), for whom I've had the leavening advantage of time and access to scholarly studies. Part II presents those modern era Senators, from Howard Baker (1967–1985) to current office holders. It's impossible to write the final words on their careers. That will be left to future commentaries and to future historians.

I do hope that my personal reflections and interpretations will contribute in some small way to the appreciation we should all feel for those who have given so much to our state and to our nation.

Acknowledgments

No project of this sort can be undertaken without the input and assistance of many wonderful people. For their reminiscences, we are grateful first and foremost to three of our subjects—Howard Baker, Bill Brock and Harlan Mathews—who have been generous with their time. But we also want to thank for their reminiscences Bill Allen, Reverend Horace Bass, Jim Cannon, Paul Clark, my good friend Congressman Bob Clement, Charles Crawford, Tony and JoAnn Edmonds, Harrison Fox, Lois Hessler, Fricks Stewart, Tom Stewart, Jr., Mary Louise Lea Tidwell, Bill Timmons, and Mark Tipps. We were honored by the guidance of a host of historians including Stephen V. Ash, Tennessee State Historian Wilma Dykeman, Steve Meyer, Jim Neal, Jo Quatannens, James Summerville, and Ridley Wills II, whose generosity we deeply appreciate.

And for making our research so much easier, we want to thank the librarians at a horde of libraries and a number of others, especially Gayle Annis-Forder, John Brock, Debbie Durkin, Carol Harford, Kiki Kienstra, Steve Lodge, Mike Prince, Shannon Prothro, and Jeff Stewart who have helped us along the way. Richard A. Baker, the U.S. Senate Historian, opened his archives to us and provided us with the keen historical insight that only he is capable of. Gregory Harness, U.S. Senate Librarian and Karin Sedestrom, U.S. Senate Reference Librarian, provided expert guidance to our research. And finally, we thank Jed Lyons, Peter Cooper, Alyssa Theodore and all our friends at Madison Books whose commitment, encouragement and patience made this work possible.

To my wife, Karyn, your tolerance of my late, late nights at the computer has been generous. Your support of our journey to serve fuels the spirit!

A Sense of Place and Time

Throughout the twentieth century, Tennesseans have sent to Washington U.S. Senators who have not only contributed significantly to the history of their own state, but dramatically influenced the development of our nation as well. Indeed, they have permanently secured for Tennessee a position of national historical significance and given its citizens a distinct sense of place and time, as I hope this walk though history will illustrate.

Like their predecessors, twentieth-century Tennesseans possessed the same courage, tenacity, and ingenuity of their earlier forebears. And Senators from every decade have reflected these qualities in both the legislation and the principles they championed and pursued.

The ensuing chapters paint portraits of seventeen U.S. Senators who have represented Tennessee during this century. To understand these men (and so far they have been men only) and their contributions, one must appreciate them within the context of the times in Tennessee, in Washington, and in the nation as a whole. It is with this in mind that I offer a backdrop, much more impressionistic than definitive, of our century and Tennessee's place in it.

Among other things, Tennessee Senators were directly responsible for the first federal highways and the interstate highway system, the Tennessee Valley Authority, women's suffrage, airmail delivery, the reciprocal foreign trade agreements of the 1930s, removal of a railroad freight rate structure that discriminated against southern producers, the atomic research site at Oak Ridge, regulation of potentially harmful drugs, the warnings on cigarette packages about the hazards of smoking, the elimination of discrimination against women in acquiring credit, the Fair Housing Act, the monumental Clean Air and Clean Water Acts of 1970, the availability of highway funds for mass transit, the congressional budget process, the allocation of organs for transplantation, the establishment of a "Superfund" to treat toxic wastes, and a basing system for the MX Missile.

And while each April many of us might reasonably berate Cordell Hull for introducing America to the federal income tax, it must be remembered that the previous system took more from most Americans in hidden costs. Similarly, although Howard Baker's rescue of President Jimmy Carter on the Panama Canal Treaties was severely criticized by some Republicans, President George Bush, who originally opposed those pacts, was able to use their language to remove dictator Manuel Noriega and help restore democracy to Panama.

The most famous congressional hearings chaired by a Tennessean in this century were those held by Estes Kefauver on the activities of organized crime. However, Tom Stewart and Fred Thompson both chaired, and Howard Baker and Luke Lea both distinguished themselves on, committees that probed violations of campaign laws, those rules that protect the core of our democracy. During his tenure as Democratic National Committee (DNC) chairman, Cordell Hull presided over the rebuilding of his party from its lowest depths since Reconstruction. Bill Brock did the same for Republicans after Watergate. I challenge my Senate colleagues from the other forty-nine states in our Union to present a similar record of such solid achievement by those who have preceded them in this century.

More often than most realize, Tennessee has been at the center of national attention during much of the twentieth century. What was once called "the trial of the century," the Scopes "Monkey Trial," occurred in Dayton, Tennessee, in 1925. A few years later, the tensions implicit in our national transition from a rural, agricultural nation to an urban, industrial, and commercial society—which became obvious in this trial—thrust into America's cultural consciousness an intellectual collective from Nashville. At the opposite ideological pole from these so-called Agrarians, the New Deal once again brought attention to our state. One of Franklin D. Roosevelt's most successful initiatives brought electricity, flood relief, and the first glimmer of prosperity to much of the Tennessee Valley. Tennessee played an integral role in the Allied victory in World War II, although at the time few Americans were aware of the significance of Oak Ridge. Then, as our nation struggled to redress the error of centuries of racial discrimination, the state and its people often found themselves at the center of the controversy. Many young African-American leaders led our people to probe their consciences and consider the promise of Abraham Lincoln. Those we've elected to the Senate since 1948 have always stood with African Americans in their quest for voting rights and were generally ahead of much of the rest of the South in prompting compliance with laws opening all public accommodations to African Americans. It was also a Tennessee case that prompted the Supreme Court to require that city-dwellers and country folk be represented equitably in Congress and all state legislatures. During the Watergate investigation, Tennesseans were among the most effective and conscientious probers of the misdeeds of the Nixon administration.

Modern politics in Tennessee emerged from the uncertain and volatile era that extended from Reconstruction to the agrarian revolution of the 1890s. The period, characterized by high voter turnout and competitive political instability, was controlled for the most part by shifting factions of Democrats, with some serious episodic competition from the Republicans of mountainous East Tennessee during the 1880s.

The twentieth century has been one of remarkable change. An adult living in the 1890s would hardly recognize the United States of today. While historian Frederick Jackson Turner noted the closing of the "frontier" as early as 1893, most Americans and most Tennesseans of that time were still tied to the soil. In fact, it wasn't until 1920 that the Census Bureau discovered that more Americans lived in urban areas than rural ones. Even then, an "urban area" was defined as one with 2,500 people or more. Fifty-four of Tennessee's ninety-five counties had no urban population at all in the 1920s. While agriculture remains a central feature of Tennessee's economy, the state has adopted a largely industrial and commercial economy, and the great majority of our people today live in cities and suburbs.

The pace of our modernization spawned political and cultural conflict at each stage of new development. The first bloc in Tennessee to organize against the new industrial order was a group of small farmers of generally humble, devoutly Protestant stock, who found it increasingly difficult to make ends meet in the otherwise prosperous decade of the 1880s. Because Tennessee farmers, unlike many farther south, had for the most part diversified and relied on more than one staple crop, most were able to keep their cherished independence. However, tenancy was becoming a looming reality for many once-proud yeoman farmers in other parts of our Southland, and out of their anxiety grew an entity called the People's Party. It soon became better known as the Populist Party.

Populists attributed part of their plight to the high tariffs imposed by Yankee legislators that aided northern industry yet made it harder for farmers to sell their produce abroad and forced them to pay higher prices for increasingly necessary farm machinery. As knowledge of the wealth being amassed in the North became common, Populists grew increasingly convinced that federal and state *laissez-faire* policies were crafted to benefit industrial magnates to the detriment of agricultural interests. In their zeal to restore equity, Populists fielded candidates for the presidency and many legislative seats throughout the South and Midwest in 1892. Their platform was clear. They demanded that the federal government regulate railroads and the facilities where farmers stored their produce. They wanted rural free delivery routes for their mail. They sought to extend democracy by instituting a secret ballot and mandating the direct election of U.S. Senators. While these planks all became law after the Populists went the way of the Federalists and the Whigs, the Populists are best remembered for their unrealistic scheme to reduce poverty by inflating prices. Infighting among Populist leaders and their fusion with the Democratic Party after 1892 brought an end to the Populist movement, but its influence persisted well into the twentieth century. Even now we talk of populist principles whenever a politician suggests using the government to regulate business or redistribute wealth or casts aspersions on big business on behalf of "the people." It is entirely fitting that the historian Kyle Longley plans to subtitle his forthcoming biography of Albert Gore, Sr., *The Last Populist.*

In the early 1900s, Democratic domination was the rule in every southern state. In the elections of 1894 and 1896, the Republican Party suddenly became the nation's majority party, a shift which left the Democratic South a majority component of the nationwide minority. This dramatic shift in power effectively ended GOP attempts to compete seriously in the South. Yet East Tennessee remained Republican in spite of Democrat dominance in Middle and West Tennessee, and this GOP presence in the east served a useful balancing function when statewide Democratic leadership became too fractious or too unpopular.

During the early part of the century, political and social reform campaigns spread across the country. In Tennessee, a loose congregation of more urban-oriented reformers known as Progressives adopted many Populist-inspired initiatives. Progressivism was in fact the first broad-based political movement that sought to counteract the excesses of the American industrial revolution. Progressives, who included both Democrats and Republicans, were political pioneers and reformers at heart. Some, such as prominent Progressive Tennessee GOP Governor Ben W. Hooper (1911–1915), were quick to refuse free railroad passes that their predecessors had accepted as a matter of course. Others at the national level were the first to enforce antitrust laws that had been on the books since 1890.

Progressives also introduced a number of their own initiatives. Their Democratic spirit led them to extend suffrage to women in 1920 and institute devices such as the secret ballot, the referendum, and the ballot initiative that gave ordinary citizens more of a voice in government. Their search for efficiency prompted them to contemplate more effective modes of local government, and their interest in public health spurred them to seek the end of child labor and institute quality controls on meat and drug producers. Their belief in fair competition led them to establish the Federal Trade Commission and the Federal Reserve Board to regulate business and currency. Progressives had a moralistic streak as well, one forever enshrined in public memory through what Herbert Hoover called the "noble experiment," prohibition. All facets of Progressive thought were well-represented in Tennessee. As will become clear in later chapters, most Tennesseans embraced Prohibition, but unlike their northern compatriots, they also fought to keep international markets open.

Southerners were especially interested in the presidential election of 1912 after Woodrow Wilson, a native Virginian, became the Democratic nominee.

In Wilson, Southern Democrats had the opportunity to influence not only the national party but also the entire federal government. This period of domestic reform and international involvement felt the influence of southern dominance in the U.S. Congress. Cordell Hull, at the time a member of the U.S. House Committee on Ways and Means, spearheaded the adoption of the federal and income tax provisions of the Underwood-Simmons Tariff Act of 1913.

Tennessee can be especially proud that in 1920 it became the thirty-sixth state—the last one needed—to ratify the Nineteenth Amendment and thus establish forever the right of American women to vote. However, not all Progressive reforms were quickly embraced by all Tennesseans. In a model study of eleven counties on the Upper Cumberland plateau, historian Jeanette Keith notes Tennessee farmers' considerable resentment of the dominance of merchants and professionals in Progressive campaigns to build better roads and schools. Even such basic reforms as the creation of graded classes, the construction of the first public high schools in the region, and the extension of the elementary school year beyond two months aroused opposition from farmers who feared both higher taxes and the supplanting of the home as the center of instruction for youth. Once the new schools arose, the eyes of a new generation were opened to subjects such as geography, which brought awareness of a larger world, and mathematics, which if mastered promised an array of new careers in a market-oriented world. To mitigate the apprehension of farmers, Progressives agreed to allow schools to engage in some form of religious training. In doing so, they laid the foundation for one of the most explosive court cases in our history.

Meanwhile, in 1920 the Republican Party in Tennessee had a very brief resurgence when it elected Alfred A. Taylor governor, five GOP members to the U.S. House of Representatives, and gave its electoral votes to Republican presidential candidate Warren G. Harding. Two years later Democrats recaptured the office of the governor with the election of Middle Tennessean Austin Peay, who is credited with transforming and modernizing Tennessee state government in the 1920s. Former Senator Luke Lea, publisher of the *Nashville Tennessean*, proved to be a valuable political ally to Peay and later became one of the most powerful individuals in the state.

Scientific progress hastened the rise of one of the central social issues of the early twentieth century, the debate between creationism and Darwinism. Several religious leaders tried to reconcile the idea of man evolving from the apes with the biblical dictates of Genesis. Staunchly conservative religious groups not only dismissed Darwin's theories as blasphemous, but pushed to eliminate the theory from public debate. By the early 1920s, discussion between the two groups, the Modernists and the Fundamentalists, had erupted into open conflict.

The Fundamentalists took as their leader William Jennings Bryan, the renowned, three-time Democratic presidential candidate who had established his reputation in the 1890s as a Populist and advocate of reform. A fiery orator, Bryan will forever be remembered for his "Cross of Gold" speech at the 1896 Democratic National Convention that resulted in his nomination for President. Bryan took up the Fundamentalist mantle with equal gusto, and by 1920 was recognized across the South and Midwest as the leader of the resistance to Darwin's theory.

Because of the work of Bryan and other Fundamentalists, thirty-seven states considered laws restricting the teaching of the theory of evolution in public schools. In Texas, Governor Miriam "Ma" Ferguson ordered that textbooks espousing Darwin's theory be removed from the classrooms. The state of Oklahoma outlawed the teaching of evolution in 1923, and two years later Tennessee passed a similar law. According to historian George C. Webb, Governor Austin Peay signed the Butler Act into law, believing that something was "shaking the fundamentals of the country, both in religion and morals," but hoping that the anti-evolution law would never become an "active statute." Peay's hopes were dashed. The American Civil Liberties Union chose to create a test case to challenge the law and hired the liberal agnostic Clarence Darrow, the most celebrated defense attorney of the time, to represent its position against his onetime friend Bryan. During the summer of 1925, the Scopes "Monkey Trial" became a *cause celebre* that captured the entire nation's attention. Details of the trial are related in the chapter on one of its central participants, A. T. "Tom" Stewart.

The struggle against the theory of evolution was just one example of the battle over American culture during the "revolutionary" period known as the Roaring Twenties. At Vanderbilt University, twelve intellectuals called the Agrarians achieved such distinction that the historian George Brown Tindall called them "the most influential group in American letters since the New England Transcendentalists." In the literary journal *The Fugitive*, published during the 1920s, and in the manifesto *I'll Take My Stand: The South and the Agrarian Tradition* published in 1930, the Agrarians sought to stem the tide of industrialization and progressivism. "The agrarian discontent in America," they wrote, "is deeply grounded in the love of the tiller for the soil. . . . In proposing to wean men from this foolish attachment, industrialism sets itself against the most ancient and the most humane of all the modes of human livelihood."

The Agrarians called for a "counter-revolution." In doing so, they presented a moral counterweight to and many valid criticisms of the loss of traditions and the alienation that resulted from an increasingly impersonal industrial society that relied on rootless modernity and empty technology. Their critique, which drew its sustenance from the land and the farmer's virtue, was certainly thoughtful, but they somewhat confoundingly admonished southern politicians, particularly those working in Washington, for displaying their loyalty to the South by "scrambl[ing] vigorously for a Southern share of the federal pie." In purely economic terms, *I'll Take My Stand* was an unrealistic rearguard action. Southern farmers, whose way of life the Agrarians so celebrated, were already in the midst of one of their worst depressions in history. High tariffs further limited their markets abroad. To many, the South continued to languish as a northern colony, in part because it suffered from regional discriminations such as the freight-rate differentials on cargo carried by trains. Due entirely to the strength of our people, we have maintained the sense of spirituality and independence that the Agrarians feared we might lose. Yet the intractable march of history determined that we would do so in different, more populous surroundings.

During the presidency of Franklin D. Roosevelt, Southerners once again assumed leadership positions in the U.S. Congress. Representative Joseph W. Byrns from Nashville, chairman of the powerful U.S. House Appropriations Committee, in 1933 became Majority Leader and two years later Speaker of the House. Senator Kenneth D. McKellar became chairman of the Post Office Committee with its associated patronage opportunities and was the second-ranking member of the Committee on Appropriations. Thus even as the Agrarians were pressing their ideas, McKellar was cutting a particularly substantial share of the federal pie for our state. Most Southerners had not enjoyed the prosperity that so much of the nation had in the 1920s. Like most of the South, which Franklin D. Roosevelt declared the "Nation's Number One Economic Problem" in 1938, Tennessee was particularly hard-hit by the Great Depression. Many parts of the state remained remote, lacking economic opportunity and many of the things that we take for granted today, such as hydroelectric power, improved navigation and flood control, and conservation of natural resources. So it was that Senator McKellar pushed for a colossal development project for Tennessee and its neighbors, approved in 1933. The details of the purpose, creation, and administration of the Tennessee Valley Authority (TVA) are told in our McKellar chapter. Thanks to Senator McKellar and others, TVA has brought immeasurable benefit to our state and continues to pay dividends in industrial and agricultural development, as well as the environmental protection, of the Tennessee River watershed.

One project that TVA helped bring to the state remained largely unknown to the public until after its impact was felt worldwide. Scientists in Germany had split the uranium atom in 1939, a remarkable event that presented mankind with tremendous opportunities. The power unleashed during nuclear fission, if harnessed safely, could provide electricity in quantities never before imagined. It also represented the possibility of nearly unfathomable destructive force. The Nazis began working on a bomb generated by nuclear fission, and scientists in the United States pursued the same course in the late 1930s. When the United States entered World War II after the Japanese attack on Pearl Harbor, the issue of creating an atomic bomb took on new urgency.

Through the Army Corps of Engineers, the United States established the Manhattan Engineer District to build a bomb.

Space, secrecy, and power were essential to the success of the Manhattan Project. A site in East Tennessee offered all three. Some fifty thousand acres of land in a thinly populated, remote area on the Clinch River could be purchased inexpensively, and TVA could provide all the power needed. As readers of the McKellar chapter will learn, the craftiness of the senior Senator also played a part in the choice. In September 1942, the Army Corps of Engineers in Oak Ridge, Tennessee, began to produce the explosive element for an atomic bomb, a weapon that helped bring an end to the war with Japan and changed history forever. For those interested, I turn your attention to the delightful "saga of a people who share in history," as told by George O. Robinson in *The Oak Ridge Story.*

Roosevelt's impact on Tennessee was significant; he remained popular in the state and his proposals were broadly supported. The New Deal affected the state more indirectly than directly, fostering debate on the welfare and regulatory role of government, imposing national issues into state politics, and stimulating with Cordell Hull a new spirit of internationalism in Tennessee. In the years after World War II, the Tennessee political landscape began to shift away from the one-party domination toward two-party competition, and the state and region achieved a heightened role in defining national politics. The era of Estes Kefauver, Albert Gore, Sr., and Governor Frank Clement reflected a spirit of youth, national ambition, and party independence from former bosses, prompting our current state historian, Wilma Dykeman, to entitle her 1955 article in *Harper's Magazine,* "Too Much Talent in Tennessee?" In 1952 Kefauver won a series of the presidential primaries, including New Hampshire, and in 1956 won the vice presidential nomination which both Gore and Clement had sought.

World War II also had unexpected consequences for American social relations. The war against the racist theories of the Nazis brought to light what the eminent Swedish sociologist Gunnar Myrdal called the "American dilemma" of racial prejudice. African Americans had performed valiant service during World War II, first in supply operations such as the famed "Red Ball Express" and later on the front lines of combat. Thanks to pressure generated by leaders such as A. Philip Randolph, founder of the Brotherhood of Sleeping Car Porters, a union for black railroad car attendants, other blacks gained employment in the plants that built the arsenal that ultimately defeated the Nazis and the Japanese. Still, everyday humiliations remained common for blacks. Funding for black schools remained disproportionately low in all parts of the South. Few restrooms were open to them along roadsides. Blacks were denied access to most white-owned public accommodations, except on a "separate but equal" basis. After the war, it became clear that race relations must change. The struggle for racial justice that had begun during the Civil War and Reconstruction grew into a widespread, grass-roots movement.

It might be said that what some call the Second Reconstruction began and ended in Tennessee. Rosa Parks, whose refusal to give up her seat on a bus in Montgomery, Alabama, spurred a boycott of that city's buses that lasted more than a year and sparked the modern civil rights movement, was tutored in the art of civil disobedience and nonviolent protest at the Highlander Folk School in Monteagle, Tennessee. Carl T. Rowan, the talented journalist whose tastefully understated exposé of segregation, *South of Freedom*, became a best-seller in 1952, is a native of McMinnville. A future head of the National Association for the Advancement of Colored People (NAACP), Dr. Benjamin Hooks of Memphis, has explained to me how he got his start in government service when Governor Frank G. Clement appointed him as the first African-American criminal court judge in Tennessee history. Other noted civil rights activists, including John Lewis (now representing the Fifth District of Georgia) and Marion Barry (the former mayor of Washington, D.C.) attended Fisk University in Nashville. And tragically, the most effective and prominent leader of the civil rights movement, Dr. Martin Luther King, Jr., was assassinated in Memphis on April 4, 1968.

One of the areas where African Americans fought for their civil rights was education. The NAACP began their challenge of public school segregation in the courts in the 1930s. First, they pushed to open state universities to black students; then they turned to elementary and high schools. The court struggle culminated in a case originating in Topeka, Kansas. In 1954 the Supreme Court unanimously struck down the doctrine of "separate but equal" in the case of *Brown v. Board of Education,* saying that segregation in public schools was unconstitutional because separate schools were inherently unequal. Segregation thus failed to give African Americans equal protection of the laws as mandated under the Fourteenth Amendment. In 1955 the high court insisted, in what became known as *Brown II,* that states had to desegregate schools "with all deliberate speed" to remedy the past unequal treatment of blacks. But that phrase was vague and seemed to leave the pace of desegregation up to each state. Several southern states undertook a policy of "massive resistance." Some southern governors even sanctioned mob threats against those attempting to enforce the high court's rulings.

Instead of belligerently fighting the federal orders to desegregate schools and provide some equality of civil rights to African Americans, as had happened in Alabama, Mississippi, and Arkansas, most white Tennesseans obeyed the decrees. However, racial violence did flare up in our state after federal Judge Robert Taylor ordered that blacks be admitted to Clinton High in 1956. "Desegregation in Clinton and Anderson County would have occurred in an orderly manner," historian Wali R. Kharif noted, "had the people of that East Tennessee city been left to handle their own affairs," but it was not to be. While a group of Tennesseans, unreconciled to desegregation, sought an injunction blocking integration, a handful of outside agitators led by New Jersey native Frederick John Kasper (then based in Washington, D.C.) incited whites to intimidate the blacks into staying out of Clinton High. Courageously, Governor Clement sent troops to quell the uprising, and several young African Americans attended Clinton High that school year.

Even so, Kasper would not give in. A year later, on September 9, 1957, he staged demonstrations at several schools in Nashville, as the public school system there was integrated with the registration of thirteen black children in first-grade classes. My aunt Margaret Randolph Cate was principal of Hattie Cotton Elementary School where one African-American child had enrolled with no picketing on that day. But her school was dynamited and suffered the destruction of one wing in the early hours of September 10. Fortunately, no one was in the building at the time of the blast, and Hattie Cotton reopened the following week.

While Kasper was soon convicted of contempt of court for his role in the 1956 protest in Clinton, the demonstrations and terror continued in that Anderson County town. Despite the leadership of a courageous white Baptist minister, Reverend Paul Turner, who walked with the black students, the commitment of the newspaper editor, the majority of the community working toward a peaceful transition, and the bravery and grace of the black students and their families, three dynamite blasts nearly destroyed Clinton High on October 5, 1958. Thankfully, unlike the cowardly act that killed four young black girls attending church in Birmingham, Alabama, nearly five years later, the Clinton blast injured no one. Understandably, the incident brought national notoriety to Tennessee. That attention, while a mark of disgrace, ultimately had the positive effect of producing a fund that rebuilt Clinton High School in time for the fall term of 1960.

In the face of the *Brown* decisions, a group of congressional legislators from the Deep South drafted a document known as the "Southern Manifesto." This declared the *Brown* ruling a "clear abuse of judicial power [that] climaxes a trend in the Federal judiciary undertaking to legislate, in derogation of the authority of Congress, and to encroach upon the reserved rights of the states and the people." Signers pledged "to use all lawful means to bring about a reversal of [the] decision . . . and to prevent the use of force in its implementation." Our Senators, Albert Gore, Sr., and Estes Kefauver, and Congressmen Howard Baker, Sr., J. Percy Priest, and B. Carroll Reece honored our state when they refused to sign the manifesto. No other state among the eleven that once comprised the Confederacy had such a high percentage of members of Congress intent upon facing the future.

That Tennessee responded to such courageous leadership can be seen in the overwhelming victories of Senators Gore and Kefauver against segregationist opposition in the 1958 and 1960 Democratic primaries respectively. Tennessee Senators and Senators-to-be continued to lead the South throughout the 1960s. In 1962 then-congressional candidate Bill Brock joined his father in leading a march through Chattanooga to spur compliance with a court order to desegregate. Tennessee's Ross Bass was one of two southern Senators to support both the Civil Rights Act of 1964 and the Voting Rights Act of 1965. And Howard Baker helped produce the compromise draft that led to the enactment of the Fair Housing Act of 1968.

As a physician, I'm especially proud that Tennessee has led our country in the education of African-American physicians. In 1910, three of the seven U.S. medical schools for African Americans were in Tennessee, one of which was Meharry Medical College. Meharry, named for an abolitionist family who helped to start it, began as the medical department of Central Tennessee College in 1876, the year of our nation's centenary. The teachers and students of those first years built hospitals and treated black people as they took their skills across the South. When Abraham Flexner surveyed American medical schools in his famous report of 1910, he recommended that philanthropists support two African-American medical schools—those at Howard University and Meharry. Andrew Carnegie and John D. Rockefeller helped build a new physical plant at Meharry, but the drive for a modern medical school rose out of local leadership in the 1920s, 1930s, and 1940s. Over much of its first century, Meharry Medical College graduated over half the black physicians in the United States, and in our day, Meharry has given to our nation such leaders as Dr. Henry Foster and Surgeon General David Satcher.

Trends in music in Tennessee mirrored our movement toward a multiracial society. Nashville, of course, has been known as "Music City USA" ever since WSM Radio began broadcasting the Grand Ole Opry in 1925. The country music originating there, historian Bill C. Malone wrote, "evolved primarily out of the reservoir of folk songs, ballads, dances, and instrumental pieces brought to North America by Anglo-Celtic immigrants." Yet its secondary influences included not just the standards played in all parts of the United States, but contributions from African-American artists. While the banjo, the instrument most identified with early country music, is thoroughly African in origin, the brands of music most identified with black Tennesseans are the blues and rhythm-and-blues. Memphis has long been a center of the blues and rhythm-and-blues recording industry. It is said that Elvis Presley, who made his home and first recordings there, fused the influences of blues, rhythm-and-blues, and country music into what we know today as rock and roll. Yet the journalist Pat Watters found even more social significance in the first appearance of black country singer Charley Pride at the Grand Ole Opry. "It was unlikely," he wrote in 1969, "that all the combined forces of civil rights organizations, church, government, or even integrated athletics had worked as much good for race relations on the whites of the South most in need of it as had Country Charlie."

Like these musicians, tens of thousands of people had been leaving our rural areas in search of opportunity in our cities. Largest in number were blacks, whose "great migration" to Memphis and points north began just before World War I. Opportunities on such a large scale would not be seen again until the 1940s. After World War II, many large corporations began opening regional offices in our cities, and their employees found it easier to buy homes because of newly established Federal Housing Authority and Veterans Administration loan programs. While our metropolitan areas were growing tremendously, they held barely half the seats their numbers warranted in our General Assembly. Although these inequities were replicated in many southern and midwestern states, it took the Supreme Court case initiated in Tennessee known as *Baker v. Carr,* unquestionably one of the landmark cases of the twentieth century, to bring our system of apportionment back to a "one man, one vote" basis.

Baker v. Carr originated in Memphis in 1959 when Charles Baker and a group of qualified voters sued Tennessee Secretary of State Joe C. Carr alleging that they had been deprived of equal protection of the laws under the Fourteenth Amendment "by virtue of debasement of their votes." The Tennessee Constitution, in fact, provides that representation in the state legislature be based on population and that legislative districts be apportioned every ten years according to the federal census. Unfortunately, our General Assembly had neglected to reapportion those seats since 1901. While the Supreme Court had previously avoided ruling on "political" cases, the Court led by Chief Justice Earl Warren determined that the focus of this case was equal protection, not politics. In 1962 it remanded *Baker v. Carr* to the federal district court, which ordered that voting districts be redrawn to conform to new population patterns. The impact of *Baker v. Carr* on state and federal elections justifies its inclusion in any catalogue of the most important high court verdicts of the last forty years.

Baker v. Carr also portended the rise of the Republican Party in Tennessee. While the GOP had maintained strong footholds in East Tennessee and parts of Middle Tennessee since the Civil War, Republicans were heavily outvoted by Democrats in statewide elections. By allowing for the equitable representation of city-dwellers and suburbanites (who, since the Eisenhower years, had begun to leave the Democratic past of their forefathers and vote in increasing numbers for candidates of the party of Abraham Lincoln), *Baker v. Carr* gave a boost to the GOP. Although Bill Brock's 1962 election to the Third District seat (serving Chattanooga and its environs) in the U.S. House signified the strength of GOP pockets in the state, it was not possible for Republicans to be represented in their true numbers until *Baker v. Carr* forced the General Assembly to redraw its lines to conform to the population patterns of that time.

During the early 1960s, Senators Kefauver and Gore, both highly regarded as liberal and influential Senators, were popular and strongly supported, as were Democrats throughout the state. Abruptly, however, the political center of gravity shifted. The long-standing truce between East Tennessee Republicans, who some believe for years had conceded statewide elections to the Democrats in exchange for regional control, and Democrats, who stayed away from the regional elections of the minority party in the East in return for statewide domination, had begun to fracture in the 1950s. The statewide popularity of GOP General Dwight D. Eisenhower and later 1960 Republican nominee Richard Nixon, the growing disenchantment of Tennessee Democrats with their national party's leadership and policies, and GOP inroads in suburban and urban centers in middle and west Tennessee all indicated that the days of total Democratic domination of the state was coming to an end.

The turning point was the 1966 Senate election of Howard Baker, Jr., who defeated Frank Clement. The legislative reapportionment resulting from *Baker v. Carr*, disciplined organizing across the state, and the emergence of attractive candidates culminated in the growing influence of the Republican party. By 1970, Republicans held both U.S. Senate seats and in that year won the governorship with the election of Winfield Dunn from Memphis. Tennessee became the first southern state since Reconstruction to elect two Republican Senators. In 1972 Republicans achieved a five-to-three majority in the U.S. House of Representatives, and many pundits were hailing Tennessee for creating the first competitive two-party state in the South. Though many of the GOP gains of this time ensued in part from divisions within the ranks of Democrats, the presence of able Republicans in high offices forced Democrats to work harder both in Washington and in our capital city, Nashville, and return home more frequently to learn what was on their constituents' minds.

This added competition between the parties has served Tennessee well. Both regularly have produced leaders from the sensible center of public opinion who have shunned the politics of racial division and looked to the betterment of all our citizens. Not only have we become the model for the New South, but recent national leaders like Howard H. Baker, Jr., and Al Gore, Jr., have made us its envy. Senator Baker was the first Republican U.S. Senator to be elected directly by the people of Tennessee. As all of us remember, he distinguished himself as vice chairman of the Senate's probe of Watergate, the central political scandal of our time, by his integrity and his intelligence. It was Baker who posed the central question of that investigation: "What did the president know and when did he know it?" Had Richard Nixon been truthful in his answer to that query, much probably would have been forgiven. Had Nixon taken Baker's earlier advice to disclose everything fully, the break-in might still be seen as a "third-rate burglary." It took true courage for Baker to look into every facet of the Watergate scandal that consumed a president of his own party, including the cover-up that eventually led to President Nixon's resignation. That is the kind of courage I'd like to see more of in Washington today.

Though Democrats were successful in regaining one Senate seat when Nashville lawyer Jim Sasser defeated Senator Bill Brock in 1976, the corruption of the Governor Ray Blanton administration shook the roots of the Democratic Party, and Lamar Alexander, a protégé of Howard Baker, won the governorship for the Republicans in 1978. The team of Alexander, who won re-election four years later, and Baker, who ascended to Senate Majority Leader after the Republicans captured the Senate in 1980, represented the moderately conservative center which came to distinguish modern Republicanism in Tennessee.

The swing back to Democratic strength came with the 1984 election of Al Gore, Jr., to the Senate, though Ronald Reagan won the state overwhelmingly in the presidential election that same year. Six of the nine Tennessee House seats were Democrats, and two years later Democrat Ned Ray McWherter was elected governor. This Democrat dominance persisted until 1994 when Republicans swept both Senate seats, the governorship, and five of the nine House seats, reflecting nationwide rejection of big government, high taxation, and the policies of the first Clinton administration.

Tennessee has had a unique political history over the last century, having undergone substantial political and social transformation. Political science professor Michael Nelson has observed that during the first sixty years of the twentieth century, Tennessee's competitive character made it the least Democratic state in a solidly Democratic South, while during the last forty years it has been the least Republican state in the generally Republican South. Throughout the century, he noted, Tennessee voters have behaved more like those in the rest of the country than any other southern state's, supporting the winning candidate for the presidency in twenty of twenty-five elections.

Many attribute the success of Tennesseans at the national level to the three distinct geographical divisions represented by the three stars on the Tennessee state flag. The mountainous region of East Tennessee has been consistently Republican for more than a century and a quarter. The hills and farm lands of Middle Tennessee have been consistently Democratic, and the flat cotton lands east of the Mississippi River have over the century evolved from Democratic to Republican. Over the years Democrats have grown increasingly competitive in the east, though their foundation remains most solidly in Middle Tennessee. The case can be made that these three grand divisions, so diverse in outlook and geography, demand statewide politicians who are well-grounded, facile, and strong—qualities that characterize those who have served Tennessee in the U.S. Senate over the past one hundred years.

Chapter 1

Luke Lea

1911–1917

*Attempted Capture
of the Kaiser*

*Founder of
The Nashville Tennessean*

(1879–1945)

Of all those who have served Tennessee in the U.S. Senate, none has made a bigger splash in life at an earlier age than Luke Lea. He earned a B.A., an M.A. and a law degree by the age of twenty-four. He presided over the convention of Tennessee's largest political party at twenty-seven, founded one of our great newspapers, *The Nashville Tennessean*, at twenty-eight, and won election to the U.S. Senate at thirty-one. Before this bold and daring Tennessee native reached forty, just after World War I, he tried with only a few associates to do what every American "doughboy" dreamed of doing in the midst of that conflict, capturing His Majesty, the Kaiser of Germany. Certainly the swiftness of his rise alarmed many contemporaries. In hindsight, there may be more appealing characters in Tennessee annals, but none who lived more colorfully or more fully.

Luke Lea was born on April 12, 1879, the third of four children of Ella Cocke and Overton Lea. His pedigree was quite distinguished. His mother was a descendant of William Cocke, one of Tennessee's first two senators. One great-grandfather, another Luke Lea, was a U.S. Congressman (1833–1837), and another was Judge John Overton, a business and political

1

associate of President Andrew Jackson. Luke Lea's grandfather, John M. Lea, served as mayor of Nashville and judge of the Davidson County circuit court in the 1840s and 1850s and, during the Civil War, helped Andrew Johnson (then Military Governor of Tennessee) secure Tennessee's ratification of a state constitutional amendment voluntarily freeing the slaves. Luke Lea's father, Overton Lea, also began adulthood as an attorney, but faltering health prompted him to leave his practice and turn instead to farming Lealand, the family homestead five miles south of Nashville.

The thousand acres of Lealand must have been an ideal place for young Luke to grow up. The land had housed the headquarters of General John B. Hood during the Battle of Nashville in December of 1864, and by the 1890s it held a tennis court and a golf course alongside immense spans of pasture and cropland. In these surroundings, Lea developed a dynamic personality that blended his mother's refinement with Overton's practical business acumen. As a youth, he showed a talent for focusing on a subject of study and mastering it quickly. His ready command of whatever topic he was espousing at the moment may have gained added authority coming from a husky, dark-haired, blue-eyed man of six foot two.

Luke Lea's college career was distinguished in every respect. Previously educated by tutors at home, at sixteen, he entered the University of the South in Sewanee in March of 1896. During his four and a half years there, he served as president of his class and several clubs while earning B.A. and M.A. degrees. What Tennesseans will always remember, however, was his work as business and equipment manager for the miracle Sewanee football team of 1899, which outscored its opponents by a combined score of 322–10. Lea was the scheduler for the squad, which over a six-day period toppled five rivals, including such contemporary and current powers as Georgia Tech and the Universities of Tennessee and Georgia. And he saw to it that this talented group from the Cumberland Mountains of Tennessee remained healthy, for it was he who secured two barrels of Sewanee spring water for every road trip.

After a short trip to Europe, Lea moved to New York City and right into Columbia University Law School where he became editor of the law review and again was elected president of his class. He returned to Nashville and opened a law practice in 1903. During his first two years in private practice, he also taught law classes at Sewanee. He began representing clients such as the Long Distance Telephone and Telegraph Company and organized his first business venture, the Home Telegraph Company, which built a line between Franklin and Goodlettsville. Not long after, he met Mary Louise Warner, the quiet, demure daughter of Percy Warner, the president of Nashville Railway and Light Company. Mary Louise's mother, Margaret Lindsley Warner, was a descendant of Felix Grundy who served Tennessee in the U.S. Senate

(1829–1838, 1839–1840) and as Attorney General to President Martin Van Buren (1838–1839). They were married after a two-year courtship. The union was a loving one and produced two sons, Luke, Jr., and Percy. Sadly, Mary Louise contracted tuberculosis less than three years after their wedding and nearly died during a miscarriage three years later. Only Luke's demands that doctors go through with the then rare procedure of transfusing his blood to her saved her life. So much blood was drawn from him during the three-hour procedure that he had to be hospitalized for ten days. The next year, she suffered a mild heart attack. It said something about the drive of Luke Lea that he carried on with all of his activities in the midst of so many near-tragedies. He frequently took time off to be at her side.

It was in 1906 that Luke Lea became a force in Tennessee politics. That May, he attended a Democratic gubernatorial nominating convention as a supporter of Malcolm Patterson, a relatively "wet" Democrat who was challenging incumbent John Cox. A Prohibitionist and a moralist like many other Progressives, Lea liked Patterson's ideas of limiting the governor's powers to appoint election commissioners, instituting direct primary elections, and building schools and roads. But Davidson County Democrats were divided. When the clerk called the roll on a preliminary vote, a regular delegation backing Patterson and a dissident group backing Cox both responded. A fight broke out on the other side of the floor and the presiding officer fled. At this point, a Memphian rose and moved that Lea, who had raised several points of order, be made chairman. When the motion carried, Lea strode to the podium, seized the gavel, and brought the convention to order. He could not bring the delegates to vote that day, but did manage a truce that bought time for representatives of both candidates to secure an agreement on a permanent chairman for the duration of the convention. Later in the week, Democrats nominated Patterson on a platform that allowed local communities to ban the sale of alcohol if the majority of voters so desired. The position did not go as far as Lea would have liked, but it was sufficient to keep him heartily within the ranks of the Democratic primary.

In light of Lea's fervent Prohibitionism, it was inevitable that he would break with Governor Patterson. The split came in early 1907 when Lea became convinced that Patterson had become a captive of the whiskey and railroad trusts. What could he do? Noting that men he knew to be connected with the Louisville and Nashville Railroad owned both daily newspapers in Nashville, he opted to form his own, which he dubbed *The Nashville Tennessean*. At first, he had trouble making ends meet, even with support totaling $58,000 in loans from his father. The *Tennessean* began to fare better when Lea made it the organ for the 1908 gubernatorial candidacy of former Senator Edward W. Carmack, a fervent Progressive and Prohibitionist like himself. When Carmack lost the election, Lea hired him to edit the *Tennessean*.

If editorial bite is a measure of a paper's success, Carmack was an ideal choice for the *Tennessean*. He was scathing in his references to Patterson and even more derisive in his treatment of Colonel Duncan B. Cooper, a Patterson aide whom Carmack likened to the governor's Svengali. Annoyed, Cooper warned Carmack against editorializing against him again. This prompted Carmack's friends to give him a pistol for his own protection, which Carmack agreed to carry until Cooper's anger had dissipated. Only days later, on November 9, 1908, Cooper spotted Carmack walking home from the *Tennessean* building. He shouted to the editor, causing Carmack to jump behind an elderly female friend. Carmack reached for his gun and fired two shots. One entered the shoulder of Cooper's son, Robin, who had leapt in front of his father. Robin Cooper pivoted, then turned, and fired three shots into Carmack's heart and neck, killing him instantly.

Carmack's violent death transformed Tennessee politics and Luke Lea's career. Public revulsion at Robin Cooper's acquittal on a retrial and Governor Patterson's pardon of the colonel led Carmack's followers, among them Lea, to organize themselves as Independent Democrats. In 1910, Lea helped put together a slate of candidates for the judiciary to challenge a group favored by Patterson. The absence of any Republicans in the race led many GOP regulars to vote in the primary for the Independents, thus producing a 40,000 vote majority for Lea's slate. The cooperation of Republicans in this instance led Independents to look kindly on them and then shock Tennessee by endorsing Republican gubernatorial nominee Ben W. Hooper, a Prohibitionist like Lea and most Independents. In turn, Republicans endorsed former Democratic Congressman B. A. Enloe for railroad commissioner. This "Fusion" strategy produced a strong coalition, one that incumbent Patterson realized he could not beat, particularly after September 1910, when Lea bought the *Nashville American*, the one urban daily that had remained loyal to the governor. The governor withdrew from the race, leading regular Democrats to turn to old party war-horse Bob Taylor. But voters saw this as an act of desperation, and they gave Hooper a 12,000 vote victory and his fellow Fusionists control of the railroad commissionership and the State House of Representatives.

One of the first decisions of the General Assembly as it opened in 1911, in the days before the Seventeenth Amendment, was the choice of a U.S. Senator. In the first nine days of balloting, Democrats produced sixty-four votes for ten-term Congressman and former Governor Benton McMillin. It took sixty-six votes to be nominated, though, and Fusionists were determined to elect one of their own. They tried a number of candidates, but B. A. Enloe, the one who ran best, could muster but sixty-three at his apogee. On the thirteenth day, Luke Lea went to Governor-elect Hooper and told him that he could be elected with the support of a few recalcitrants from Memphis if the Fusionists, who had been backing Enloe, would stand behind him. Were he unsuccessful on the first ballot in which his name was forwarded, he would back out in favor of Enloe. It took some doing for Enloe to agree. Once he did, sixty-eight members voted for Lea and thereby elected him to a six-year term. Again, Lea, only thirty-one, had shown a flair for the dramatic and a rare sense for the opportune time to move into the limelight.

Lea was easily the youngest Senator in the chamber when he arrived in Washington in the spring of 1911. He earned his spurs as a Progressive quickly, being one of the few members at the time with the integrity to refuse a free railroad pass. In time, believing the Louisville and Nashville Railroad exerted too much control in Tennessee and other states, he persuaded the Senate to order the Interstate Commerce Commission to investigate its holdings and those of a number of other carriers.

Like all other Senators, Lea was restricted to some degree in his foci by the jurisdictions of the committees to which he had been assigned. One panel on which he served was the seemingly dead-end Committee on Privileges and Elections, which in 1910 had rejected a report by Indiana Republican Albert Beveridge calling for the decertification of the election of Illinois Republican William Lorimer. Lea and two other freshmen determined that Beveridge had been correct, that several Illinois legislators had been bribed to vote for Lorimer, and that his election should be invalidated. Although they did not prevail in committee, Lea took the floor to declare the "utmost importance in preserving the integrity and perpetuity of our institutions that an innocent man not be driven in disgrace from this chamber, or that a guilty man not be permitted to remain here as a monument to the power of money and to the callousness of this Senate to corruption." Whether it was the power of Lea's words, or the meticulousness of the written case these three young Turks made for the need to preserve the integrity of our body, the Senate sustained them by a 55–28 vote, a rare case of our members reversing themselves over the course of just two years.

Lea rose quickly within national Democratic councils. Soon after entering the Senate, he hosted a meeting at his Massachusetts Avenue home where Democrats chose Indiana freshman John Worth Kern as their leader. Determined to see his party elect a Progressive in 1912, Lea attended the Baltimore convention with the instruction to vote for Alabama Congressman Oscar Underwood. However, along with most other Tennessee delegates, he soon bolted to the camp of Woodrow Wilson. It would be a while before the rest of the Union caught up with Tennessee's lead, as Democrats still required their nominees to win by two-thirds. *The Cleveland Press* reported that many were raising Lea's name as a compromise choice until they were reminded that he was not yet thirty-five, the minimum age the Constitution prescribes for one to hold the highest executive office in the land. Lea held firm until the Wilson boomlet finally found the requisite two-thirds vote on the forty-sixth ballot.

Once Wilson entered the White House, Lea proved a staunch supporter of his New Freedom program. He voted for the Underwood bill's low tariffs, the Clayton Antitrust Act, and the creation of both the Federal Trade Commission and the Federal Reserve System. He supported constitutional amendments imposing an income tax, extending suffrage to women, and mandating the direct election of senators and the president. He also was an ardent advocate of Prohibition, backing the Webb-Kenyon bill, which allowed dry states such as Tennessee to bar liquor imports. Still, Wilson never completely trusted Lea, in part because he had been elected with GOP support and in part because he had initially backed Underwood rather than Lea.

By 1914, Lea concluded that his interests lay in mending fences with Regular Democrats. He became the principal advisor to District Attorney General Thomas Rye, the Regulars' candidate for governor. That fall, he even sprang for the cost of a Democratic whistle-stop tour for Rye headlined by Secretary of State William Jennings Bryan, still the lion of agrarian virtues. But he had not brought all the Independents with him; in fact, *Nashville Banner* publisher E. B. Stahlman held firm with his support of two-term Republican incumbent Ben Hooper and began to ridicule Lea with an unprecedented degree of invective. Wounds hardly healed after Rye's narrow victory. Regulars who believed that Lea had betrayed them in 1910 found common cause with Independents such as Stahlman and Memphis Mayor Ed Crump. At the instigation of Congressman Cordell Hull, Regulars scheduled the primary for the first direct senatorial election in Tennessee history a full year before the November 1916 general election, thus denying Lea an opportunity to consolidate his strength. Former Governor Malcolm Patterson entered the race and his quarrels with Lea reached such a pitch that Congressman Kenneth McKellar, who was also a candidate, found it easy to declare that the only way to restore Democratic harmony was to do "away with these constant troublemakers." McKellar was the only fresh face to the people of Tennessee and he had a solid record of achievement. Unlike Lea, he had not yet developed a habit of intervening in other Democratic races. He also had a solid record of attendance in Washington, one that Lea could not match because of his dutiful attention to his ever-ailing wife Mary Louise. Although Lea remained popular among rural Democrats, McKellar's strength in Memphis allowed him to prevail narrowly over Patterson and by almost 10,000 votes over Lea. Tennessee law in 1915 provided for a runoff between the top two contenders in the primary. McKellar easily defeated Patterson with the help of many who had previously supported Lea.

As a Wilson loyalist, Luke Lea initially resisted cries by former President Theodore Roosevelt and others for the United States to intervene in World War I. As peace initiatives proved increasingly fruitless, Lea, like Wilson, concluded that America might have to enter the conflict. After Germany resumed unrestricted submarine warfare, thereby threatening American merchant ships, Lea rallied loyally behind the President's preparedness program, voting in the last week of his tenure to allow those ships to be armed. Lea determined that should Congress declare war, he would raise a regiment of Tennessee volunteers and tender them to the federal government for service in France. Even in the absence of a large standing army, which America did not have until after World War II, high-ranking military men were not always enthusiastic about such help. During the Civil War, political generals had frequently been failures, and the War Department had declined a similar offer from Theodore Roosevelt. But Lea was a loyal Democrat and the brass were glad to assent to his commission first as a lieutenant colonel, then as a full colonel in the 114th Field Artillery.

In 1918, the quickly trained American Expeditionary Force reached Europe. Lea and the 114th arrived in Scotland on June 6, then sailed to France a week later. They would play a vital role in the Meuse-Argonne offensive in which fellow Tennessean Alvin York so distinguished himself. The 114th advanced into Riaville, Pitchville, and Marcheville the morning of November 11, 1918, until Lea received orders to cease firing, as an armistice was about to be signed. Here was a terribly difficult order to heed, for the Germans continued to shell the 114th until 11:11 A.M., the moment the armistice went into effect.

The operation for which Lea will always be remembered came after the armistice. In June 1918, he and other officers had cringed when the Duke of Connaught boasted over tea that he was uncle to both the King of England and the Kaiser of Germany. This to Lea indicated that the Allies, if victorious, might opt against punishing the Kaiser and others they held responsible for the war. His suspicions were confirmed when the Allies allowed the Kaiser to take up exile in the Netherlands after abdicating in November 1918. Lea recognized that it had been Woodrow Wilson's intention to pursue "peace without victory." After nearly six months in France, however, he sensed that the French, having lost millions of their youth, would insist upon extracting some kind of vengeance. Were the German people rather than their leaders to be punished, Lea guessed correctly, their resentments might develop into a nationalistic fervor even more dangerously expansionist than it was under the Kaiser. Any ordinary citizen anticipating such impending anarchy would feel a sense of helplessness, but not Luke Lea. How did he propose to block the folly he saw likely to ensue from the Versailles Peace Conference? He would round up a few Tennesseans, drive to the castle of Count Bentinck in Amerongen where the Kaiser was housed, kidnap him, and then cart him off to Paris to present him to President Wilson.

In the past eighty years, it has become customary for historians to deride Lea's plan as a "hare-brained scheme," but, in fact, this virtually unprecedented display of bravado very nearly succeeded. On New Year's Day 1919, Lea secured leave for himself and seven others, promising only to avoid any site prohibited by Allied High Command. His crew left its base in Luxembourg in a beat-up Winton that exploded just twenty miles away. Luckily, a regimental truck passed by shortly thereafter and picked up one of the men. Lea's comrade returned at midnight with a new Cadillac. In that car and the repaired Winton, Lea and his party drove to Brussels. They secured a passport from U.S. Ambassador Brand Whitlock and a laissez-passer from the Dutch legation. Snow slowed their pace, but the laissez-passer allowed the group to cross the Rhine on a ferry. Only then did Lea inform his men of his aim and offer each a chance to return. All proceeded.

The force arrived at Amerongen on January 5, 1919. Lea left the car, walked up to a guard and ordered him in German to take his party into the castle. The sentry did as he was told and took Lea and his men into the library where they were met by Count Godard Bentinck, the son of the owner. Lea asked to see the Kaiser. "Why?" Bentinck replied. Lea retorted that he would tell only the Kaiser. As Bentinck moved into the adjoining room, Lea could hear him addressing someone as "Your Majesty." Bentinck and the local burgomaster returned twice, the latter time to say that the Kaiser would meet them if Lea swore he was a representative of President Wilson, General John J. Pershing, or Colonel Edward House, a close associate of Wilson's and a leading peace negotiator. Here, Lea backed down, but not before Captain Leland S. "Larry" MacPhail, the future owner of the Brooklyn Dodgers and the New York Yankees, had pilfered a bronze ashtray. Once he discerned that the Kaiser's hosts were not going to budge and were showering them with cigars to buy time, Lea and his men left. Outside were two companies of Dutch infantry and hundreds of locals. As Lea's men got into their cars and prepared to leave, they noticed the Dutch forming an armed passageway for them. They sped off and made it back to camp with but five minutes left on their leave.

What went wrong? Future Tennessee Governor Gordon Browning, who had wanted to join the party but could not because superiors thought that too many officers would be leaving camp, always maintained that Lea's mission might have succeeded had the party merely entered the Kaiser's office by force. It is possible. One, however, can only contemplate how the future of the world might have been changed if the Kaiser had been punished, as Luke Lea seemed to hope, rather than the German people. At the very least, as 1912 presidential hopeful Champ Clark suggested, Luke Lea might have been elected president.

Lea's superiors did not take the matter lightly. Three weeks after his return from Amerongen, he was ordered to return to Chaumont, France, to meet with the inspector general. This, Lea knew, meant that a court-martial was being instituted against him. He prepared his defense. During the initial proceedings, the authorities suggested that regulations barred soldiers from entering neutral countries without permission. Lea countered, pointing out that the ban extended only to enlisted men. When they charged that he had no right to use a government car on leave, Lea threatened to call as his first witness General Pershing, who had recently visited Nice on leave in a U.S. vehicle, and then, as his second, the inspector general who had taken another U.S. car joy-riding the previous day. The inspector general smiled and conceded the point.

The proceedings grew almost comic the next day. A brigadier general told Lea that the Kaiser had charged that Lea and his men had arrived at his castle and had made him nervous. Smiling, the general added that Lea could only be court-martialed by a general court and that Lea had the constitutional right to face his accuser. Knowing that such an instance would not likely come to pass, Lea hatched a plan. He went to the inspector general and offered to plead guilty and serve a sentence on this count, saying he intended then to go on the vaudeville stage at a high salary as the only soldier proved to have achieved every American soldier's ambition—to make the Kaiser nervous—and that he would split the money with the brigadier. That would not be necessary, Lea's superior replied.

There remained the question of Count Bentinck's bronze ashtray. The inspector general asked Lea what he knew about the purloined item. Hearsay only, Lea replied, which was a true statement given that he had never pressed MacPhail for details of what he suspected his subordinate might have done. The inspector general then cleared Lea. Lea proceeded to go to lunch with MacPhail, and offered to serve as his counsel. MacPhail assented and told Lea that he had taken the ashtray. That afternoon, the inspector general asked Lea again what he knew about the ashtray. Lea responded that the information had become privileged as between attorney and client. When MacPhail was summoned he asserted his Fifth Amendment right against self-incrimination on each question. The investigation was finally closed, though General Pershing did officially reprimand Lea for his "amazingly indiscreet" exploits. But what did Blackjack Pershing really think about the expedition? "I'm a poor man," our only five-star general at the time told a friend, "but I'd have given a year's pay to have been able to have taken Lea's trip into Holland and to have entered the castle of Count Bentinck without invitation."

Lea had little time to regale people with such tales. On his voyage home, he learned that Mary Louise had suffered an aneurysm and died before the doctor arrived at her bedside. He walked the deck tensely, sometimes in silence, sometimes telling a friend of his love for her and of his inability to face the future without her. Upon his return, he was met by Luke, Jr., and Percy

Warner. His father-in-law insisted that Lea and his boys stay with him at his Royal Oaks home once he left the service. Lea agreed and soon found some solace by throwing himself into the operation of the *Tennessean*, which had gone deeply into debt during his absence. In time, he became smitten with his tall, attractive sister-in-law Percie, who had adored him since she, as a nine-year-old, had helped him woo Mary Louise. The following year they were married. It was appropriate that they would name their first child after Mary Louise and even more fitting that she would pen his most thorough biography. Later in the 1920s, Percie bore him another daughter, Laura, and a son, Overton.

Always, Lea remained absorbed in his work. Having become convinced after World War I that "pacifism and unpreparedness are the twin incubators of war instead of guarantors of peace," Lea served on the first executive committee of the American Legion and as chairman of organization and nominations for its first Tennessee state convention. But he spent the bulk of his time running the *Tennessean*. The only publisher in Nashville to maintain a union shop, Lea hired a stellar staff that included such luminaries as sportswriter Grantland Rice, Vanderbilt fugitive Donald Davidson, political columnists Joe Hatcher and Percy Priest, and even his old rival Malcolm Patterson, now beset by financial problems. Lea made his paper a mouthpiece for Progressive causes such as women's suffrage and Prohibition and a strident critic of the practices of the political machines of Mayor Hilary E. Howse of Nashville and Boss Ed Crump of Memphis.

Lea and the *Tennessean* reached the zenith of their influence within state government during the administrations of Governors Austin Peay (1923–1927) and Henry Horton (1927–1933). On a personal level, he was closer to Peay, a lawyer, businessman, and tobacco farmer from Clarksville. An independent man of strong character, Peay was what historian George Brown Tindall describes as a "business progressive," who strove to make government more efficient while building schools and roads and paying for them with taxes on corporate profits, gasoline, and tobacco. With rural areas more likely to benefit and urban areas bearing more of the costs, Peay won renomination in 1924 and 1926 by shoring up his base in the countryside. This was Luke Lea's territory, and the *Tennessean* proudly trumpeted Peay's virtues at every opportunity. Just six weeks prior to his death, Peay likened Lea to a brother. Here was a relationship of mutual respect between two strong men that neither would exploit for undue gain. In fact, Lea's support for Peay's tobacco tax led cigarette manufacturers to withdraw their ads from the *Tennessean*.

Henry Horton, Peay's successor, was not such a strong personality. Lacking a political base, he came to rely on Lea almost immediately upon his accession. It became easy for Lea's opponents to link him with Horton and most were quick to enter the fray. Just four months after Horton took office, the *Nashville Banner* blasted him, and by association Lea, for firing the state highway commissioner. Horton had done so because the Kentucky Rock Asphalt Company, owned by Lea's business associate Rogers Caldwell, had not been awarded a contract for Kyrock, its brand of rock asphalt. In truth, it was less expensive to buy Kyrock, for its sources were closer, thus rendering its freight charges cheaper. Yet the connection of Lea and Caldwell led the *Banner* to deride Caldwell in cartoons as "Kid Kyrock" and Lea as the "Governor-in-Fact" and as "Musso-LEA-ni." What the *Banner* editorials did arouse was envy of the growing wealth and interests of Lea.

Lea's civic work remained constant. He was elected to the Board of Trustees of Fisk University in Nashville in 1912 and sought to improve education for black Americans. In the 1920s, he lobbied for the creation of Great Smoky Mountains National Park, the Conservatory of Music, and the War Memorial Building in Nashville. He deeded the initial 868 acres of Percy Warner Park to Nashville in 1927 and served as a director of the Federal Reserve Bank in Atlanta. He was generous to fellow Democrats, in one instance donating $6,500 toward the campaign of 1928 presidential candidate Al Smith. Though he turned down the Senate vacancy that went to Will Brock in 1929, few could fail to notice his growing number of acquisitions. He bought the *Knoxville Journal*, and, with Rogers Caldwell, the *Memphis Commercial Appeal*. Again with Caldwell, he bought a quarter interest in the Holston National Bank of Knoxville and heavy blocks of stock in other depositories.

Under ordinary circumstances, Lea and Caldwell might have been hailed as among the state's most valued benefactors, but the force of the 1929 stock market crash and the ensuing Great Depression destroyed thousands of businesses and wiped out Lea's fortune. Before the crash, there was no bigger mercantile institution in Tennessee than Caldwell and Company. Caldwell-Lea banks lost $6,659,000 in state funds, and Lea, often described as the "Governor-in-Fact," became an obvious target. Several longtime critics pursued Lea with a vengeance. Two sets of indictments in Tennessee and one in North Carolina were brought against him and then dropped. In 1931 the court in Asheville, North Carolina, found Lea and his son, Luke Jr., guilty of defrauding the Central Bank and Trust Company of Asheville, North Carolina.

Many questions remain about the trial. Those who wish to consider the issues for themselves are directed to John Berry McFerrin's *Caldwell and Company*, which sides with Lea's critics, and Mary Louise Lea Tidwell's *Luke Lea of Tennessee*, which provides a vigorous defense of her father and brother. What is certain is that much of the legal ammunition used against the Leas before and after the trial was provided by Nashville attorney K. T. McConnico, a longtime political foe of Lea. As renowned defense attorney Arthur Garfield Hays argued at the time, it was next to impossible to find a jury unbiased against anyone connected with bank management in the climate of opinion prevalent in 1931. That was particularly true in Haywood County, North Carolina, for many of those residents who made up the jury pool, and even some of those impaneled, had their deposits tied up in the area's largest bank, which had been closed for a year. Indeed, two of the jurors had pronounced Lea guilty prior to the verdict. Even more astoundingly, a bailiff later boasted of his role in prodding the jury to find Lea guilty.

After using up all appeals, the Leas entered the North Carolina state prison in April 1934. It had always confounded Lea how his twenty-three-year-old son, never more than his assistant, had been convicted. He was heartened when Luke, Jr., was paroled in late July, but Lea's relief turned to sorrow when he learned within a week that his son Percy had been killed in an automobile accident. Lea's financial woes were compounding as well. Not only had the *Tennessean* been placed in receivership, but also $40,000 in bonds he had bought to sustain his family turned out to be forgeries. Percie Lea had to move in with her mother and go to work selling insurance.

It is a testament to Luke Lea's character that he remained a model prisoner. He worked as a secretary for the prison physician and often served as a father confessor and nurse to those in pain or despondency. All the while, friends worked assiduously for his release and even secured the cooperation of some who had helped convict him. The chief prosecution witness wrote the governor of North Carolina as early as September 1934 asking for Lea's pardon because evidence unknown at the time of his trial exculpated him. Similar conclusions were reached by an independent auditing firm that had access to the previously closed records of Caldwell and Company. By December 1935, even the original prosecutors had joined Lea's defenders, and the trial judge had agreed not to oppose clemency. Only in April 1936 would Lea be paroled; fourteen months later, he received a full pardon from Clyde Hoey, the new governor of North Carolina.

Lea returned to Nashville determined to make something of the rest of his life. Although some urged him in good faith to make another bid for the governorship, he recognized that such a course was no longer feasible. He did manage the successful campaign of Richard Atkinson for the House seat left vacant in 1936 by the death of Speaker Joseph Byrns. In 1939, he began publishing the *Dixie Farmer*, a small newspaper that reached 150,000 farmers. Always a man of ideas, he forwarded proposals for prison reform and networks of superhighways to span the United States and indeed the Americas to anyone who cared to consider them. Such plans came to fruition in the years after Lea's death, but certainly were well ahead of their time in the cash-crunched 1930s.

In later years, Lea made his living as a lobbyist and dreamed of reacquiring the *Tennessean*. He worked for firms such as the Tri-State Independent

Oil Association, the Texas Pre-Fabricated House and Tent Company, and the Nashville Auto Diesel College. In 1945, he got old foe Senator Kenneth McKellar, who had often been stung by the acerbic tone that the *Tennessean*'s new publisher, Silliman Evans, took toward him, to launch an investigation of the means Evans and his allies used to take control of the herald he had created. Lea died unexpectedly on November 18, 1945, of pancreatitis, which at that time was inoperable. His demise was also the death knell of the Senate investigation of the sale of the *Tennessean.*

Luke Lea was an idealist. This trait showed most vividly in his altruistic if wild-eyed scheme to kidnap the Kaiser. Certainly his wealth aroused envy among Tennessee Democratic pols who were born in humbler circumstances and were jealous of his influence. In truth, Luke Lea was the champion of rural and small town Tennessee in an age when the populace was beginning to gravitate toward the cities. Some of the changes he helped bring about transformed the face of our state. But ironically, they also tilted power in the state to leaders in more urban areas who took the opportunity provided by the Great Depression to act upon ancient enmities and end any chance that he might reemerge as a rival. Luke Lea refused to be defeated by the reversal of fortune and he never lost his joy in living. He took his losses courageously and returned to build a decent life for those he loved. Perhaps among his greatest achievements was his managing against terrific odds not only to support his family but also to create for them a happy home life. There is an old saying that institutions span the length and breadth of a great man. For a Populist-tinged Democrat like Luke Lea, the *Nashville Tennessean* is a most fitting monument.

Chapter 2

Kenneth D. McKellar

1917–1953

Rich Uncle of TVA

Building Modern Tennessee

(1869–1957)

No one has served Tennessee longer in the U.S. Congress than Kenneth McKellar. Through three terms in the House and his first four in the Senate, he left a rarely matched legacy of achievement that in myriad ways improved the lives of all Americans. An extraordinarily shrewd man of husky dimensions with a long memory and a short fuse, McKellar was reputedly the model for Charles Laughton's movie portrayal of the character Seab Cooley of Allen Drury's Pulitzer-prize winning novel *Advise and Consent*, as well as the characters of Senator Beauregard Claghorn on the Fred Allen radio program and Foghorn Leghorn of Warner Brothers cartoons. Unfortunately, when he is remembered today, it is often for the less fruitful final twelve years of his career when he seemed more prepared to avenge old affronts than to attend to the hopes and aspirations of all of us.

Kenneth Douglas McKellar was a product of central Alabama of the immediate post–Civil War era. He was born on January 29, 1869, in Richmond, Alabama, a "suburb" of Selma, the eighth and last child of lawyer James Daniel McKellar and the former Caroline Howard. The McKellars had owned slaves prior to the Civil War, and like many other families in the vicin-

15

ity, they found themselves cash-starved thereafter. Even so, they gave their former slaves their cabins and many took the opportunity to work a portion of the McKellar plantation. Perhaps this was the source of K. D. McKellar's paternalistic brand of segregationism, a strand readily distinguishable from the virulent variety practiced in the first two-thirds of this century by avowed white supremacists in the states of the Deep South.

The McKellars were of Scottish Presbyterian stock, and like many other Calvinists, they impressed on each of their six boys and two girls a desire for an education. Caroline McKellar schooled her children herself in a one-room cabin with backless benches. By the age of thirteen, K. D. resolved that he would attend the University of Alabama and set out to make enough money to cover his costs. At the McKellar homestead, he baled hay, picked cotton, mended horse-collars, doctored chickens, and cured hams. Having read about the virtues of commercial fertilizer in a magazine, he was the first in Dallas County to concoct a similar mixture and surprised everyone with the enormous crop he grew on his test site. Working at a nearby store, the owner was sufficiently pleased by the end of his three-year stint to offer him a stake in the business.

McKellar enrolled at the University of Alabama at Tuscaloosa in 1887. His lack of formal schooling meant that he would be placed on academic proba-tion in all subjects except history and English, yet he fared well in everything he undertook. He joined a literary and debating society and the Delta Kappa Epsilon fraternity, played on one of the first Crimson Tide football teams, and rose to the rank of cadet captain at what was then an all-male military insti-tution. Surprising nearly everyone from more prominent backgrounds, he finished fourth in his freshman class of 238, a class that included future Sen-ate colleague John Bankhead, and was subsequently elected valedictorian and orator of the class of 1891. The university thereupon hired him as a tutor in history, a job that paid his tuition through its law school. Once again, he finished first in his class. At the same time, he received a master's degree, awarded at the time to virtually anyone who completed additional studies.

Able young men always seem to seek out challenges, and K. D. McKellar had heard that opportunities would be especially lucrative in California. He asked his brothers, all of whom had since moved to Memphis, to secure him a free railroad pass to Los Angeles. They sent him a pass to Memphis and wired him that they would have one for him to the West Coast when he ar-rived. K. D. reached Memphis with a quarter in his pocket. Already in debt $600 to his brothers, he opted to stay in Memphis for a while. Within a day of his arrival in the summer of 1892, he had secured a job with the city at-torney at $25 a month preparing a digest of Memphis city ordinances.

By 1894 McKellar had settled into a legal practice in a firm whose senior partner was Colonel William H. Carroll, the grandson of one of Tennessee's early governors who was also a past state Democratic chairman and onetime campaign manager of Senator Isham G. Harris. McKellar proved an adept trial attorney in a practice that was almost exclusively devoted to civil law. Within a few years, he was earning more than $25,000 a year, and by 1911 his net worth was estimated at $300,000, no small sum for those times.

The case that distinguished McKellar outside of Memphis involved a challenge to the election of Edward W. Carmack to the House of Representatives in 1896. As a write-in candidate, Carmack had defeated the incumbent, Josiah Patterson, by little more than 400 votes. Carroll, who was related by marriage to Carmack, looked at the case, then leveled with Carmack, telling him that the House Republican majority would likely side with Patterson, a fellow "gold bug," rather than an advocate of the "free silver" ideas of defeated 1896 presidential nominee William Jennings Bryan. McKellar got the case because, according to Carroll, "He [had] no legal reputation to lose." A year of legal wrangling ensued before a settlement was reached. House Republicans agreed to seat Carmack if Democrats would abstain from interfering in a New York challenge involving two GOP claimants to a disputed seat.

By the turn of the century, McKellar was a political force in Memphis and the Democratic Party. He served as an elector for Democratic nominees William Jennings Bryan and Alton Parker in 1900 and 1904, respectively, and as a delegate to the 1900 and 1908 Democratic National Conventions. He also served as Democratic chairman for the tenth congressional district. He became counsel to the Memphis Power Company and helped found the Memphis Bar Association. Throughout the decade, he attached himself to several movements to reform the Memphis city government. In 1903, he and Carroll won a suit before the Tennessee Supreme Court that compelled the city government to open its financial records to the public. Later, he crafted a new city charter for Memphis, a revised version of which the General Assembly approved, and built a slate of progressives that would unseat the city's reactionary old order in 1905.

Over time, McKellar worked with any number of Democrats of various stripes and he remained on good terms with most. His name figured in speculation whenever rank-and-file Democrats were asked whom they deemed viable candidates for the future. At first, McKellar appeared uninterested in a political career for himself. He begged off an effort by Shelby County Democrats in 1910 to draft him for governor, urging them in that year of Democratic disarray to rally around old party war-horse Bob Taylor. When he learned while golfing in Atlantic City in 1911 that incumbent Congressman George Gordon had died, he told someone who urged him to seek the vacant seat that he was "not interested." But when he learned while vacationing that T. C. Looney, the apparent front-runner, was telling fellow Memphians that McKellar was the only one who could cause him concern and that

McKellar was "afraid to run against [him]," McKellar hurried back to the river city to throw his hat into the ring. As campaigns go, the special election of 1911 was uneventful, but Looney's fears were warranted. McKellar defeated him in the primary by a healthy four-to-three margin and at the age of forty-two was elected to the U.S. Congress.

McKellar entered the House as the most junior member of the Democratic minority on the Military Affairs Committee. There, he sided with those who wanted to limit military spending, even after World War I broke out in Europe. His only divergence while in the House came in 1914, when he introduced a bill calling for the federal government to provide military training for one hundred men in every state at a designated university. Tuition for the trainees would be paid in full. In return, each would become part of the reserve officers corps and be subject to call for seven years after their graduation. The bill attracted some support, but was never acted on by the full House.

McKellar's reserve officer education bill indicated the progressive philosophy he was frequently associated with during his early days in Congress. The bill's chief virtues, he believed, lay both in its bolstering of the reserve officers corps—thus limiting the possibilities of both the rise of a large standing army and the institution of a draft—and its provision for the education of thousands of young men who might not otherwise be able to go to college.

When Woodrow Wilson entered the White House in 1913, McKellar was quick to support the President's "New Freedom" program. He backed efforts to create the Federal Trade Commission and the Federal Reserve System, strengthen antitrust laws, institute a federal income tax, reduce tariff rates, limit the work week to forty hours, and bolster credit to farmers by depositing federal funds in rural banks. He embraced legislation tightening federal controls over liquor trafficking and ultimately, the Eighteenth Amendment which initiated Prohibition. If anything, McKellar's progressive streak ran even deeper than Wilson's. Upon eating eggs that tasted stale at a Washington hotel and learning from his waiter that those eggs had been kept in cold storage for two years, he drew the conclusion that packers were likely hoarding the eggs to raise prices. He therefore introduced a bill limiting the time manufacturers could store virtually any food product. His measure won support from many consumer groups, but he did not yet have influence on the committees with jurisdiction over the issue and little on Wilson. The House never acted on McKellar's plan. In addition, McKellar, who had toured a New England textile town in 1911 and been moved to tears as he watched small, poorly clothed children leave a mill at quitting time, was quick to embrace federal limits on such practices. Although such a stand was heralded in Theodore Roosevelt's Bull Moose platform of 1912, Wilson remained convinced that such restrictions were state prerogatives until the election year of 1916.

If Kenneth McKellar had done nothing else during his three terms in the House, he would have earned the gratitude of all Americans for his role in creating the federal highway system. The dearth of good paved roads had perturbed him since 1911 when he set out with friends on a long East Coast vacation. Before he got out of Shelby County, his big new $7,000 Packard had gotten mired in the muddy dirt roads of West Tennessee. On his election to the House that same year, he had to ship his car by train to Washington so he might use it. Not long thereafter, he introduced a bill, a variation of which President Taft signed into law, creating a commission to study the feasibility of additional post roads to facilitate mail delivery. After the report came out recommending the road construction, McKellar presented his plan to Congress. He won House support for the measure, but could not convince the Senate, whose Democrats seemed to agree with President Wilson that such a program was the responsibility of the states.

By 1916, McKellar had still not given up on the post-roads construction plan. He and Alabama Senator John Bankhead, his college classmate, introduced a bill providing $5 million for a few roads. Bankhead could not convince Wilson and privately derided the President as a lawyer of no great distinction and a "Scottish skinflint." He informed his partner of the defeat and McKellar promptly arranged for the two to meet with Wilson. Ask for $5 million, Bankhead counseled McKellar on the way to the White House, in the hope that they might get $4 million. Wilson heard the two out, then told them he believed their measure was unconstitutional and that he needed every dollar possible for defense as Germany appeared likely to "make war on us."

"Mr. President," McKellar cut in, "did you see in the newspapers that a German submarine rose in Baltimore harbor the other day and 110 submariners got off . . . and ate lunch in Washington?" Suppose Germany landed troops in the Great Dismal Swamp of southeastern Virginia. How could any troops defending that land be supplied?

"That would make these highways legal," Wilson replied. How much money would be needed?

McKellar astounded Bankhead by suggesting a then astronomical sum of $100 million. To his surprise, Wilson agreed to fight for $75 million. The subsequent enactment of the somewhat misnamed Bankhead Good Roads Act of 1916 thus provided the first major infusion of funds into our national highway system.

Early in his political career, McKellar set his sights on the Senate. In 1913, he allowed his name to be placed in nomination before the Tennessee General Assembly. At the time, his support was limited to the Shelby County bloc; he could only hope that the legislature would deadlock and then turn to him. Close McKellar associates threw their votes to John K. Shields after six votes, and the move ended up benefiting McKellar. The votes of his backers gave Shields the nomination, but they also made McKellar far more acceptable to Shields's fellow East Tennesseans, including Republicans who voted in the Democratic primary thinking they would have no voice in the election otherwise.

Thanks to the Constitution's Seventeenth Amendment, the 1916 Senate election would be the first in Tennessee in which the people themselves would decide the outcome rather than the General Assembly. Congressman Cordell Hull feared the growing power of incumbent Luke Lea and saw to it that a primary would be held a full year before the general election. It was hardly lost on Hull and other yellow-dog Democrats that Lea had been one of the engineers of the "Independent Democrat" movement that had bolted from the regular party to back—and elect—fellow Prohibitionist Ben Hooper, a Republican, to two terms as governor earlier in the decade. In addition, former Governor Malcolm Patterson, who did not run for reelection in 1910 but whom Hooper succeeded with Lea's help, had not forgotten. Determined to wreak vengeance, Patterson entered the race; but he was the once-"wet" governor who, as told in the chapter on Luke Lea, had pardoned Colonel Duncan Cooper, the convicted murderer of former Senator Edward Carmack. Those Prohibitionists unhappy with both candidates certainly would entertain someone else, and McKellar was a fresh face and ideally situated. While Lea and Patterson concentrated their fire on each other, McKellar added the backing of most of his congressional colleagues and the editorial clout of the *Chattanooga Times* and the *Nashville Banner* to his solid Shelby County base. He and Patterson ousted Lea in the initial primary. In the runoff, he topped the increasingly hapless former governor with more than 60 percent of the vote. The general election a year later was an anticlimax. Attaching himself firmly to the coattails of Woodrow Wilson and shunning controversy, McKellar defeated former Governor Hooper by more than 25,000 votes.

McKellar was nearly forty-eight when he entered the Senate. He was both a lifelong bachelor and a teetotaler, having as a child observed the ill effects of alcohol on a relative. Nevertheless, he was a very social gent who liked to go to parties, usually carrying a bag of bonbons to offer to friendly sorts. He would greet women by bowing, and most he would tease by saying that he had proposed to one hundred women, all of whom had turned him down. Actually, his one true love had been Louise Turley, the daughter of Senator Thomas Turley, and he had lost her affections when he took a grand tour of Europe without her. According to his biographer Robert Dean Pope, McKellar engaged in "numerous liaisons," but most of them were short-lived. On occasion he attended football games and horse races with associates like Ed Crump. After the advent of talking films, McKellar often spent Saturday afternoons at the movies, always sitting in the front row with the children and reporting that his favorite stars were Roy Rogers, Gary Cooper, and Clara Bow. In his spare time, he read the Bible, Shakespeare, and history—the knowledge of which he put to good use in the predecessor to this volume. McKellar first published *Tennessee Senators as Seen by One of Their Successors* more than half a century ago in 1942. It covers the Senators not included in this volume and remains a valuable and inspiring resource of history and an enduring tribute to Tennessee and the U.S. Senate.

In truth, K. D. McKellar's life was the Senate. He routinely put in a ten-hour and sometimes a seventeen-hour workday, often intruding on weekends. He answered wires immediately, personally handled most casework with federal agencies, and dictated responses to most constituent mail. He was a frequent participant in floor debates, and on days he planned to make a major address, McKellar donned a dark suit with a bow tie, pin-striped breeches, and a white-edged vest out of which sprang a gold chain and watch. His blue eyes were often hidden by cheeks that reddened naturally from a skin condition, but flared even more when he got excited. Those around the Capitol knew of a sensitive side to K. D. McKellar that was often hidden by a gruff exterior and a temper they incited at their peril. When, for example, Republican Daniel Hastings decried a $25,000 Memphis dog pound, replete with showers for many of the canines, as emblematic of the waste in Franklin D. Roosevelt's Works Progress Administration, McKellar rose in indignation. Hundreds of Memphians, he said, had been bitten by mad dogs and six had died of rabies. "As vitriolic as the senior senator from Delaware is," McKellar concluded, "I would not have him bitten by a mad dog for anything."

McKellar's talents as a legislator were recognized from the beginning. He was the only one of seven freshman Senators named to chair a standing committee, the Civil Service and Retrenchment Committee. On this panel and others, McKellar followed the Wilson line, a natural choice for a southern Progressive. He voted with Wilson on many controversial issues, most notably the Versailles Treaty of 1919 that ended World War I and created the League of Nations. When Wilson resisted the bids of Foreign Relations Committee Chairman Henry Cabot Lodge to add fourteen reservations to the pact, McKellar worked with Rhode Island Republican LeBaron Colt to devise a solution that addressed the stated concerns of both Senator Lodge and President Wilson. They produced one that garnered much support from both parties, but, sadly, satisfied neither principal.

McKellar's brand of progressivism, like his character, had an ornery streak. It emerged any time he sensed the overextended hand of northern businessmen into the affairs of our government. He vehemently resisted a bill authorizing the Interstate Commerce Commission to adjust rates to allow railroads a 6 percent profit, thinking northern magnates would use it to extract a bit more from the people of Tennessee. He also was quick to berate the wealthy "dollar-a-year" businessmen whom Wilson brought in to direct war agencies, suspecting they might use their positions to benefit the firms they had left temporarily. Though depicted by a reputable 1922 primary opponent as a "dangerous radical," he was quick to deplore any political ideology further left than his own. In 1919, he described "anarchism, radicalism, IWW-ism and Bolshevism" as the most serious threats to America. The same year, he introduced a bill requiring aliens to learn English within five years after their arrival or face deportation. He introduced another that authorized the government to deport native-born radicals to penal colonies to be established in Guam or the Philippines. In his early days, the radicals he denounced were the usual suspects. As time passed and McKellar consolidated his base among whites outside of Memphis, his view of what constituted radicalism came to include anyone he thought was advocating an accelerated desegregation of his Southland, including Aubrey Williams, whose nomination to be head of the Rural Electrification Administration he blocked in 1945. McKellar condemned the lynching of blacks, yet filibustered bills designed to eradicate such horrors. Deeming such bills as shots at the South and intrusions on state and local prerogatives, he often chided northern legislators for their inattention to racial injustices in their own domain, citing the Chicago and East St. Louis riots of 1919 and other incidents as examples.

K. D. McKellar was one of the more effective champions of women's suffrage. He believed that women's voting would "purify" politics. In 1916, he saw to it that Tennessee Democrats placed a suffrage plank in the party platform and continued his support throughout the war. Congress put the question to the states in 1919 in the form of a constitutional amendment, and McKellar took to the road to lobby for its adoption. While at the Democratic convention in San Francisco in 1920, McKellar received a wire from the President informing him that ratification of the Nineteenth Amendment was at hand if Tennessee voted "yes" and thus became the thirty-sixth state to approve the amendment. McKellar rushed to Nashville to manage the fight for ratification. He found the sides closely divided. Liquor interests and one misguided Nashville IRS collector lobbied hard to keep politics a male prerogative. When McKellar informed Wilson of the IRS collector's suggestions that there might be jobs for the nay-sayers, the President wired the taxman, telling him that he would have no job if he persisted in his lobbying. The collector desisted, but still, one vote was needed. That vote came when McKellar got former GOP Senator Newell Sanders to call in a pledge from GOP state representative Harry Burn, who had vowed to vote aye if his vote would be determinative. The two deciding votes came from Republicans, and the Nineteenth Amendment became part of our Constitution, thanks to Tennessee.

McKellar was a fierce critic of the GOP administrations of the 1920s, but despite this Republican President Calvin Coolidge often allowed him to escort his wife, Grace, to events he did not wish to attend. A free-trader, McKellar recoiled at the Protectionist policies of those years and joined with the Plains-based Democrats who sought to provide relief to the cash-strapped farmers of that decade. He introduced legislation to initiate federal aid to education and, twenty-five years before the enactment of the 1944 G.I. Bill of Rights, to extend educational benefits to returning veterans. While quick to condemn those responsible for Teapot Dome and other Harding administration scandals, McKellar was even more relentless in his attacks on GOP nominees who he deemed too closely tied to Wall Street. He was one of very few Senators to oppose the elevation of former Secretary of State Charles Evans Hughes to Chief Justice of the United States, thinking that Hughes's past work for corporate clients might influence his decisions. He also joined with frequent allies in the American Federation of Labor in their successful bid to block Senate approval of Supreme Court nominee Judge John Parker, who they believed had been too quick to issue injunctions against strikers. An even more frequent target of his wrath throughout the 1920s was Secretary of Treasury Andrew Mellon. In part, his stances reflected a desire to arouse populist suspicions of great wealth. McKellar was also genuinely convinced that the removal of luxury and excess profits taxes imposed during World War I and a 1921 move to reduce the maximum income tax to one-third were unfair to the average taxpayer, and he was rarely afraid to say so.

The antipathy that McKellar displayed toward President Herbert Hoover was more personal. Hoover had been one of the dollar-a-year men he had so despised during World War I, and McKellar even in later life demonstrated an inexplicable disdain toward Hoover that bordered on hatred. As an archpopulist, he lambasted Hoover for not prematurely releasing bonuses that were scheduled to be paid to World War I veterans beginning in 1945. Hoover's decision led to a march on Washington by the "Bonus Army." McKellar termed the Reconstruction Finance Corporation, a program far more elaborate than any ever before created to help our nation recover from a depression, the "greatest pork barrel . . . ever established" because it was lending money only to banks, railroads, and insurance companies. He even blasted Hoover for the extraordinarily successful food relief programs that he ran during World War I, programs that saved thousands, even millions, of lives in Western Europe and Russia.

McKellar cast his lot with the Roosevelt candidacy early in 1932. With then-Senator Cordell Hull, he built a strong organization in Tennessee to support the New York governor. In the Senate, he highlighted FDR's calls for economy in government by pushing resolutions cutting House levels of outlays by 10 percent. At the Chicago convention, he and Hull worked to reconcile differences over cultural issues that had long divided Democrats, such as Prohibition. After the third ballot, he and Hull worked the Texas delegation and helped sway several members away from House Speaker John Nance Garner, a fellow Texan, and toward FDR. Perhaps their efforts led FDR to name Garner as his running-mate.

When Roosevelt took office, McKellar was the seventh most senior Democrat in the Senate. He had risen to ranking majority member on the powerful Appropriations Committee and chaired the Committee on Post Offices and Post Roads. From this perch, he joined with Hugo Black of Alabama to get a bill passed taking airmail away from the army, limiting the routes available to any carrier to three and salaries of carrier company executives to $17,500. The bill responded to public concerns about unsafe delivery and Black's finding that preferential treatment had been given to favored firms that fixed prices at high levels. It also reflected McKellar's populist values and his long-standing commitment to airmail: McKellar had played a major role in creating the first experimental airmail route between Washington and New York a full fifteen years earlier.

McKellar proved one of the most reliable New Deal loyalists throughout the 1930s. In fact, he could even be credited with coming up with the term. "I believe the country wants a new deal," he told Memphians in October, 1930, thus predating Roosevelt's first use of the phrase by almost two years. McKellar supported the Agricultural Adjustment Act after seeing that it protected the interests of Tennessee cotton and tobacco planters. He sided with FDR's plans to reinvigorate America's faltering banking system, to provide relief for those the depression hit hardest, and to create a bevy of public works programs. He even rallied behind FDR's controversial court-packing plan, and his support was appreciated in the highest councils of the Roosevelt administration.

McKellar used his influence to benefit himself politically and our state economically. Harry Hopkins, FDR's alter ego, and Postmaster General Jim Farley saw to it that there would be plenty of money spent in our state and that much of it would be channeled through McKellar. The Senator insisted that anyone getting an appointment must be both a Democrat with an impeccable reputation for integrity and one loyal to him, and in Memphis, loyal to Boss Ed Crump. The number of jobs he found for Tennesseans was enough to make Wisconsin Republican Alexander Wiley declare that McKellar had "obtained more out of the Treasury of the United States than any half-dozen senators." McKellar always deemed his fight during his first year in the House to authorize a bridge from Memphis to Arkansas as his most satisfying. In the 1930s, he got money to build seventy-two new post offices in Tennessee. Over time, he secured funds for the Shelby County Forest, the Great Smoky Mountains National Park, and the Arnold Engineering Development Center in Tullahoma. A few days after Pearl Harbor, the Joint Chiefs of Staff learned that McKellar was angry because there were no Tennessee bases, and they quickly revealed plans to open Camp Forrest near Tullahoma. By the end of the war, our state was what historian William Majors called "an armed camp." Army posts were opened at Paris and Clarksville, and air bases at Halls and Smyrna. Millington housed the world's largest inland naval training station and military hospitals were reopened in Memphis and Nashville.

McKellar also showed himself to be willing to take on the New Deal's enemies. For instance, Senator Huey Long, the brilliant but mercurial Louisianan, loved to taunt McKellar, knowing that he could exasperate him. He made it a point to be on the floor when McKellar was speaking, to stand next to him, ask him to yield, and then ask, "The last thing you just said—What does it mean?" Known to all in the Bayou state as the "Kingfish," Long once alluded in the course of a filibuster to the wage scale for work-relief projects in TVA. McKellar interrupted and demanded that Long "confine himself to Louisiana." Noting that Long had sponsored no successful legislation while in Washington, he declared that Long "can be the 'Kingfish' in Louisiana," but was not "the 'Kingfish' in Tennessee" or in the Senate. The galleries roared and the presiding officer threatened to empty them. Future Vice President Alben Barkley appealed, saying, "When people go to the circus, they ought to be allowed to laugh at the monkeys." Ever quick, Long cut in with mock indignation, "Now, Mr. President, I resent that statement about my friend from Tennessee."

McKellar responded more impetuously when he thought his honor was challenged. In 1938, he took the floor to laud an army witness who denied the alleged need cited by New York Democrat Royal Copeland for a $40 million outlay for an antiaircraft defense of his state's coast. When Copeland retorted that "it may be that some others tell the truth, too," McKellar charged Copeland's desk and lunged at him, thinking Copeland had impugned his integrity. Bennett Clark of Missouri hurried over to Copeland and shoved him out of the chamber to keep McKellar away from him. A headline in the next day's *Washington Post* touted Tennessee's senior Senator as "One Round McKellar, the Memphis Kid." Clark also embellished the tale, suggesting that McKellar had chased Copeland with a Bowie knife; Clark's was a fanciful description, if one oft-repeated in Senate lore, for the only knife McKellar carried was one of the pocket variety that hung from his watch chain.

Throughout his career in Washington, McKellar devoted most of his attention to developing the Tennessee River Valley. He first indicated interest in such a program in 1916, when he introduced a bill providing for the building of a dam and a nitrate plant in Muscle Shoals, Alabama. Although a similar bill passed that provided for the conversion of the plant in peacetime for use in the manufacture of fertilizer, neither the dam nor the factories were completed by the end of World War I, and Congress provided no additional funds. McKellar spent more than a decade searching for a legislative vehicle to develop those facilities. He was initially attracted to a plan of auto manufacturer Henry Ford to lease Muscle Shoals and buy the nitrate plants and a nearby steam plant if the government would finish the Wilson Dam and build another nearby. Ford rescinded his offer in 1924, the year Oscar Underwood of Alabama introduced a measure authorizing the secretary of war to lease the site for fifty years, but allowing a federal corporation to take over the site if no suitable lessee could be found. McKellar feared that the plan might enable Alabama Power, a firm largely owned by British stockholders, to control the site and amended Underwood's bill by limiting any possible control by Alabama Power. Still, McKellar concluded that Tennessee would not get any of the power generated at Muscle Shoals under the Underwood approach. Accordingly, he threw his support behind a bill drafted by George W. Norris, a maverick Republican from Nebraska, that would finish the two dams, sell the surplus power, and require the federal government to manufacture 40,000 tons of fertilizer each year.

The House did not act on any Muscle Shoals bill until 1928. That year, the Senate approved a Norris-drafted, McKellar-amended bill calling for public power development and a fertilizer plant at Muscle Shoals. The House, however, cut the funding for the fertilizer plant and added money for a dam at Cove Creek, the future site of the Norris Dam. Because Tennessee had not asked for federal assistance and would derive no funds from it, McKellar called the House measure a "rape of Tennessee's rights" and launched a filibuster. He could not stop the conference report, but his defense of state rights buttressed the determination of the notoriously frugal Calvin Coolidge to veto the bill. In 1929, Norris produced a measure giving Tennessee and Alabama 5 percent of the revenues from power sales at Cove Creek and Muscle Shoals plus 2.5 percent from additional sales at Wilson Dam. McKellar defended the proposal, saying that Tennessee's interests were now protected. The new approach cleared the Congress in 1931, but Herbert Hoover vetoed it. McKellar had expected that and took great care to see that Franklin Roosevelt endorsed a similar bill in his 1932 campaign.

Roosevelt made his plans known when he toured Muscle Shoals with McKellar and Norris in January 1933. "George," the President-elect said, putting his arm around the Nebraskan's shoulder, "I want *you* to introduce the bill." It made sense politically that the sponsor of such a bill should be a Republican and a non-Southerner. McKellar may even have recommended that course initially, but it always bothered Tennessee's senior Senator that someone else would be known as the "father of TVA." As time passed, his ire grew toward Norris, whom he deemed a bit lazy. The two were different breeds of political animals. Norris was a progressive who wanted a "yard-stick" to measure the performance of public, as opposed to private, utilities. McKellar saw TVA, writes Robert Dean Pope, "not only as a desperately needed source of jobs but also as a source of abundant and cheap power to stimulate economic growth and break the power of Northern . . . companies doing business in the South."

Because he had been essential to the creation of TVA, McKellar wanted to oversee its organization. He convinced Roosevelt to pick one Tennessean to be among TVA's three original directors and he was pleased with the selection of former University of Tennessee President Harcourt Morgan. He soon grew angry with the initial chairman, Dr. A. E. Morgan (no relation), an idealist who warned of a "patronage evil" that threatened the authority from politicians with "slimy hands." His words were ill-considered for he would need the help of some of those very pols. Like many others, McKellar deemed Dr. Morgan one of those "arrogant Yankee intellectuals" who wanted to lift up "those poor benighted ignorant people of East Tennessee." At the time, he typed a vituperative letter to Morgan chiding him for "willful, deliberate and malicious falsehood."

It irked McKellar that the act creating TVA had banned political tests in its hiring practices. Appointments belonged not to him or anyone else from the region, but to Morgan. On a personal level, this outraged the Senator because he was the Appropriations Committee member who was carrying the ball for TVA. In 1935, he found that Morgan was double-dealing. In McKellar's office, Morgan promised to agree to finish Norris, Wheeler, and Pickwick Dams and to begin five others in a program designed to provide a nine-foot channel for the Tennessee River. Morgan soon wrote another Senator to urge additional study on all five of the dams, thus hampering McKellar's efforts to win additional revenues. McKellar managed later in the decade to carry bills authorizing construction on the Kentucky and Watts Bar Dams only by the narrowest of margins. Even after FDR fired A. E. Morgan in 1937, McKellar resented the treatment the TVA hierarchy had given him and perhaps regretted even more its doting upon George Norris.

Despite his vital role in creating TVA, McKellar more frequently is remembered for a feud with TVA Chairman David Lilienthal that consumed much of his time. Prior to 1941, McKellar and Lilienthal, while never close, were allies against A. E. Morgan, and they always seemed to work in tandem to secure more funding for TVA. But 1941 was a trying year physically for McKellar, then seventy-two years old. In April, he had fainted while visiting Memphis, and soon thereafter had his gallbladder removed. Side effects continued through the summer and McKellar's staff was only partially successful in prodding him to slow down. It is almost certain that they did not inform him that the Office of Production Management was pressing TVA to build one large power-dam on the French Broad River near Dandridge, rather than two dams on the Holston River as McKellar and Lilienthal had agreed. In light of McKellar's illness, Lilienthal opted to recommend the French Broad project, now known as the Douglas Dam, before consulting with McKellar.

Lilienthal's decision unleashed all of McKellar's resentments against George Norris, the TVA chief's mentor. To Lilienthal's letter informing him of his rationale behind keeping McKellar out of the Douglas Dam project decision, the Senator replied by chastising the TVA administrator for his discourtesy and insisting that he was "entitled to some consideration" because of all of his work for TVA. In truth, McKellar, like many other Tennesseans, had been swayed by arguments that the Douglas Dam would inundate 30,000 acres of valuable farmland and deprive East Tennesseans of 5,000 jobs in the canning industry. These representations had been articulated by a lawyer close to the Stokely Canning Company, who added that TVA had miscalculated the relative wattage that would emerge from both the Lilienthal and the McKellar approaches. Soon, facts went out the window and McKellar began portraying the issue to colleagues as one of personal loyalty. Members who had traditionally yielded to him on TVA concerns increasingly identified with him against Lilienthal, a man they saw as a bureaucratic ingrate. McKellar called in chits and got the House Appropriations Committee to reject the Douglas Dam proposal and persuaded his Senate Appropriations Committee colleagues to line up against it. Only Roosevelt's personal plea that the dam was necessary to the war effort caused McKellar to submit in January 1942.

Unfortunately, the McKellar-Lilienthal feud had only just begun. In March 1942, McKellar introduced one bill forcing TVA to return its power earnings to the U.S. Treasury rather than return them to operations and maintenance, and another requiring Senate confirmation of all TVA employees earning more than $4,500 a year. These measures were crafted to subject TVA to strict congressional scrutiny. It was lost upon no one that McKellar, as *de facto* chairman of the Appropriations Committee, would come to dominate all TVA hiring and funding. A majority of Senators sided with him in each of the next three years during the "McKellar spring offensives," partly out of friendship, partly out of recognition of his work for TVA, and even more out of a fear that he might exert a great deal of influence over their future programs. But, House members noted the opposition of Tennesseans such as their colleagues Albert Gore, Estes Kefauver, and Percy Priest, and killed McKellar's amendments each year.

In Tennessee, Lilienthal waged his own battle, taking his case to the people and freely feeding friendly journalists information about his disagreements with McKellar. After he warned a Chattanooga crowd about the dangers of "political management" of TVA, newspaper editors began to decry the substitution of political tests for merit. The most eager was Silliman Evans, Sr., the new publisher of the *Nashville Tennessean*, a paper that had long battled Boss Crump and his allies including McKellar. Under Luke Lea, the *Tennessean* had excoriated Crump for manipulating elections by paying the poll taxes for black Memphians, thus allowing the River City to dominate statewide elections. Evans, seeing himself and his allies, Gore, Kefauver, and Lilienthal, as the true New Dealers, attacked supporters of the poll tax as enemies of democracy and anxiously awaited other evidence to make their case. Attacks on the Douglas Dam or Lilienthal were painted as attacks on TVA itself.

As the feud raged near the point of destruction, Boss Ed Crump got involved. Aware that his power was being challenged and that his mastery of statewide elections depended on considerable tallies from McKellar's friends in East Tennessee, Crump gently but firmly warned McKellar that his feuds were self-defeating. After 1944, McKellar dropped his moves to limit TVA, but not his feuds. He and Senator Tom Stewart provided the only opposition to Lilienthal's nomination as chairman of the Atomic Energy Commission in 1947. And the first time Evans, whom McKellar called "Sillyman," introduced himself and extended his hand, McKellar cold-cocked him square on the jaw.

The Douglas Dam controversy, in fact, was the only instance in over nineteen years in which McKellar aligned against TVA. For the remainder of his career, he shepherded TVA bills through the often complex appropriations process meticulously and conscientiously, sometimes even delaying all other funding requests until he got what he wanted for TVA.

By his fifth term, McKellar seemed far less the big-spending New Dealer than he once had. As a member of the Joint Economic Committee chaired by the frugal Virginia Democrat Harry Byrd, he came to question all expenditures he did not believe were essential to the war effort. In light of the full employment brought by World War II, he saw no justification for continuance of the National Youth Administration or the Civilian Conservation Corps. He carried legislation eliminating them and reducing funds for the Works Progress Administration by two-thirds. He also became more determined to block the renomination of Vice President Henry Wallace because of Wallace's association with persons whom McKellar deemed radical. He and other Tennessee delegates rallied behind Governor Prentice Cooper, their favorite son, on the first ballot at the 1944 Democratic convention. As the contest moved to one between Wallace and Harry Truman, McKellar persuaded Boss Crump to put aside his curious objections to Truman's ties to Boss Tom Pendergast of Kansas City and yield to the larger good of keeping Wallace out of the vice presidency (and as it turned out, the presidency).

On questions related to the war itself, McKellar deferred to his President, and he pushed the bills incorporating FDR's wishes on the floor. Only one bill really troubled him, and this story is told in Alben Barkley's delightful memoirs. It originated with Secretary of War Henry Stimson, who hinted in a meeting with several Senators that he needed McKellar to hide $2 billion in an appropriations bill for a secret project that might bring the war to an early end. That night, McKellar could not sleep. He returned to Stimson's office the next day to inquire further.

"Can you keep a secret?" Stimson asked. "We are going to split the atom."

"Here we are in the middle of a big war," McKellar shot back, "and you are fooling around trying to split the atom."

Legend has it that McKellar took his concerns directly to the top and was actually with the President, who had summoned him to the White House to reiterate the request, when it finally dawned upon McKellar what Stimson had in mind.

President Roosevelt asked, "Senator McKellar, can you hide two billion dollars for this supersecret national defense project?"

Senator McKellar, not missing a beat, replied, "Well, Mr. President, of course I can. And where in Tennessee do you want me to hide it?"

Roosevelt's death on April 12, 1945, gave McKellar a new set of responsibilities. As the senior member of the majority party, he became the Senate's president *pro tempore.* Truman included McKellar in Cabinet meetings and kept him abreast of all developments, war-related and otherwise. In his two-year stint in the post (Republicans captured the Senate in 1946 and Alben Barkley was elected vice president in 1948), McKellar proved a reasonably compliant ally, except on matters in which he had a long-standing grudge. He backed much of Truman's foreign policy, from the creation of the United Nations to the containment strategy to limit Soviet expansion. But he opposed the nominations of David Lilienthal and Henry Wallace to head the Atomic Energy Commission and Department of Commerce, respectively. He also warned against the United States getting overly involved in worldwide relief efforts after the war, perhaps remembering that old foe Herbert Hoover had been lionized after World War I for his success in feeding tens of thousands of hungry Europeans.

The aging process was not kind to K. D. McKellar, and at seventy-seven he stood for his sixth term in 1946. He was too plagued by kidney problems to return to Tennessee even once during the primary campaign, the only one that mattered then. He threw best-selling chronicler John Gunther out of his office when he asked what he should see in Tennessee, "aside from TVA." Upon being blistered by columnist Drew Pearson, he denounced him on the Senate floor as a "low-lived skunk" and an "unmitigated liar and mercenary . . . crook." Not long thereafter, he grabbed Pearson's associate Jack Anderson and kicked him after Anderson inquired about his age.

Colleagues marveled about the professionalism with which he occasionally presented appropriations bills, but even the friendliest could not ignore signs of debility. In 1948, McKellar was too frail to even try to dissuade Ed Crump from dropping his ever-loyal colleague Tom Stewart. Once that year, McKellar fell out of his perch while presiding over the Senate. Twice after the Senate had been in session for many hours, he banged the gavel and asked for the morning prayer. In 1949, he broke several bones when he tripped into a tub full of hot water, and by 1950, even Democratic Leader Scott Lucas was heard ruing McKellar's ill health, as McKellar could not make it onto the floor without leaning on a heavy cane.

Rumors proliferated by 1952 that McKellar would be retiring. Reports from Washington indicated that Arizona's Carl Hayden and Georgia's Richard Russell were more and more frequently handling the day-to-day operations of the Appropriations Committee. Now in his eighties, Ed Crump privately tried to persuade his eighty-three-year-old partner that it might be time to give way to a younger man. He would be loyal if McKellar opted to run one last time, Crump said, but his organization had been sapped of much of its strength with the near unanimous defection of the black community and diminished union support. A determinative Shelby County majority was no longer certain. But McKellar's life had become the Senate, and he resisted the entreaties of Crump and others. Unfortunately for McKellar, forty-five-year-old Congressman Albert Gore was ready to move up, particularly since his seat had been eliminated by redistricting. McKellar opened his campaign in Cookeville and promised in a fifty-one-minute address to see that new post offices were built across Tennessee and that a four-lane highway would link the state. Observers characterized the Senator's voice as still strong, but noted that his hands were trembling as he grasped the rostrum. Honest to the end, he admitted that a touch of rheumatism had sprung upon him. What he did not know was that that malady would permit only four further speeches during the course of the campaign. Thus limited, his backers tried to accentuate the advantages of his seniority in the Senate by planting signs around the state that read "Thinking Feller, Vote for McKellar." Gore supporters, however, trumped them by placing in front of each the rejoinder "Think Some More, Vote for Gore." In a rare upset, all but Shelby County and Hub Walters's First District stronghold went for Gore, ending K. D. McKellar's illustrious career.

Historians might find a variety of explanations for Gore's victory. I turn to Albert Gore himself, who asked throughout the campaign, "Don't you think it is about time to give another young man a chance?" The query enabled voters both to recollect McKellar's many services to our state and country and to ponder the value of Gore's youthful energy in the immediate future. Gore, in part, was merely calling for a fresh approach with new ideas. He recognized that McKellar was an outstanding advocate for Tennessee in his youth. What better testimonials can there be to his long service than TVA, airmail, and federal highways? As time went on, however, health and the demands of Washington prevented McKellar from leaving Washington for any length of time. This kept him from gaining the kind of close communion with his constituents that I believe is so necessary for a member of Congress to maintain if he or she is to effectively represent their hopes and dreams. K. D.

McKellar came to Congress as a man with a bevy of good ideas about how to solve the problems plaguing in Memphis in the 1910s. Had he retired sooner, he would be remembered for the enlightened Progressive ideas of his youth. Instead, the McKellar who often appears in our history books is the epitome of a reactionary curmudgeon wedded to a distant past and committed to the persistence of some of its more odious elements.

McKellar retired to his small apartment in the Hotel Gayoso in Memphis. He started work on memoirs he never completed and corresponded frequently with old associates in other parts of the state. He maintained an interest in Democratic politics, letting allies know that, after health precluded any further participation, he would prefer that someone, anyone, other than Estes Kefauver be nominated for president in 1956. As his eighty-eighth year came to an end, McKellar seemed increasingly unable to recognize old friends. Death from kidney trouble overtook him on October 25, 1957.

At memorial services for K. D. McKellar, only Albert Gore and Estes Kefauver of the ninety-six Senators then sitting were present. This fact may remind us of the fleeting nature of glory. Even more poignantly, it served as a sign of their recognition of how much "Old Mack" had done for the people of Tennessee and highlighted the trace of common philosophical, if not factional, lineage that tied the work of the younger McKellar with their own. Common to all were a Populist-tinged, Wilsonian ideology that led each to be suspicious of concentrations of power and to build systems that more tightly linked neighbors to neighbors and farmers to their markets. It can be said that the interstate highway system that Albert Gore, Sr., was so instrumental in creating was merely a technological update of the model that K. D. McKellar had spawned some two generations earlier. Although Gore had defeated McKellar in 1952, he was quick to hail him in both his victory speech and his memoirs. So am I.

Chapter 3

William Emerson "Will" Brock

1929–1931

Brock Candy Company

Business Progressive and Civic Leader

(1872–1950)

Those who deride American entrepreneurs for an alleged lack of social responsibility might reassess their view upon contemplation of the career of William Emerson "Will" Brock. "Pap" Brock, says grandson Bill Brock, himself a former U.S. Senator from Tennessee, was "a country boy who achieved everything life offers." Although he cut a Horatio Alger-like path through the world, Will Brock never lost sight of those who started life in the same humble straits as he, but had not fared as well.

Will Brock was born March 14, 1872, to Richard Emerson Brock and Mary Hoe Brock of Mocksville, North Carolina, a hamlet twenty-three miles from Winston, the nearest town of any size. A disability from a wound his father had incurred while fighting for the Confederacy meant that young Will began to work on the family tobacco farm at a very early age. Will had only four years of formal schooling at a one-room schoolhouse in nearby Grasshopper, North Carolina. Instead of going to school, he said, he became "one of the best plowhands" in Davie County. It was fortunate for his five younger siblings that he was so diligent because his father's death in 1887 left Will as his family's principal breadwinner. The five younger Brocks completed their secondary schooling, but Will tended the family farm until age nineteen.

A lack of formal education did not keep Will Brock from being ambitious and aggressive, but he was also poised and had an engaging knack for self-deprecating humor. Before reaching the age of majority, he rode into Winston-Salem on a friend's wagon. He asked the owner of the first store he reached for a job and was hired on the spot at a salary of $30 a month, a sum that grew within three years to $50. The experience was especially valuable as it allowed him to refine his salesmanship skills.

One early customer was Mrs. R. J. Reynolds, who suggested that Will come to work for the future cigarette mogul as a traveling salesman. It did not matter to the Reynolds family that young Will did not smoke. What they wanted, Brock later joked, was the "greenest, countryest, ugliest boy they could find." As an adult, Will Brock bore a remarkably close physical resemblance to his hero, the urbane Woodrow Wilson, but the young, rustic Brock ideally suited the Reynolds mold. Although the job meant taking a $20-a-month pay cut, he saw an opportunity and took it. He especially liked the idea of taking trains, for he had never before ridden anywhere farther than from Mocksville to Winston-Salem. Brock was a highly successful salesman and sold the first carload and trainload of tobacco R. J. Reynolds ever sold. In 1892, his first year on the job, he earned a $500 bonus and used the money to make a down payment on a home for his mother.

By 1896, Brock had become the R. J. Reynolds sales manager for the entire southeast region. In the course of his travels, he met Miriam Acree, the daughter of a prominent and itinerant mule-riding Baptist minister then preaching near Clarksville, Tennessee. Within thirty minutes after meeting Miriam, Will proposed marriage and she accepted. It took her a bit longer to accept his Methodist Episcopal church; she thereafter often joked that she was "backsliding." The engagement lasted six years because he insisted on waiting until he felt prosperous enough to take a wife. Even so, Miriam remained Will Brock's anchor for the duration of their forty-seven-year marriage. Called the "most caring, generous person I've ever met" by her grandson Bill Brock, Miriam Brock (along with her husband) taught Sunday school classes in Chattanooga throughout her life. Her particular interest was the youth of Chattanooga and she aimed to get them active in the church at an early age. Miriam also directed Will's attention to the less fortunate in their community. Among the fifteen to twenty churches Will Brock helped build were several in the black community.

Will Brock was a truly phenomenal fund-raiser. He succeeded primarily because he gave so much of his own time and his own money. He was president of the Holston Conference of the Methodist Church for fifteen years, a delegate to the annual Methodist Conference for twenty-five years, and an integral force in the 1939 reunification of the southern and northern branches of the church that had split over the slavery issue nearly a century before. He also was a trustee of several Methodist colleges, serving more than a decade apiece as a trustee of Emory University, Emory and Henry College, Mary Washington College, Tennessee Wesleyan College, and Hiwassie College. During the same period, he spent thirty-seven years on the board of the University of Chattanooga, many of them as executive committee chairman. Twice, fellow trustees called upon Will Brock to lead million dollar fund-raising drives. He met his goal within a month both times. Appropriately, the university, now the University of Tennessee at Chattanooga, designated its science building as Brock Hall.

Will and Miriam Brock settled in Chattanooga in 1906. Then earning $300 a month as R. J. Reynolds's top salesman, he declined an offer to become a partner and took a job as a salesman for Trigg, Dobbs and Company, a candy wholesaler. Believing that his new firm would grow astronomically, Brock prodded its owner, without success, to install a kettle. Fortunately for him, the owner was preparing to retire and was willing to sell him the company if he could secure a $4,000 loan to buy the kettle. Brock got the loan.

Just as Roy Acuff liked to say that his real talent was in selling his songs rather than singing them, Will Brock often claimed that he could sell candy if he "could get someone to make it." An accomplished raconteur, he was an even better listener and had an instinctive feel for what would sell. The company, rechristened Brock Candy Company in 1909, quickly took off. By 1913, business had quadrupled and Brock Candy employed 250 people.

Will Brock was also an innovator. In the 1920s, he stopped producing items such as peanut brittle and fudge that many companies were making, and began sending to market new lines of jelly and marshmallow candies. In the 1930s, he introduced to the world the chocolate-covered cherry. That little item kept Brock Candy solvent during the depression. Sugar rationing limited what confectioners could produce during World War II, but Brock improvised with a coated peanut roll he called the Brock Bar. Thousands of Chattanoogans can still hum the tune of "Stop where you are. Buy a Brock candy bar," the jingle Brock commissioned to sell his new creation in the late 1940s.

Will Brock was a leader of the Chattanooga community from the day he arrived. He served as vice president of the Palmer-Sowers Clothing Company and as director of the Chattanooga Savings Bank, the First National Bank, the Chattanooga Gas Company, the H. G. Evans Lumber Company, the Chattanooga Stamping and Enameling Company, the Chattanooga Sash and Mill works, and the Century Company. In 1913, he presided over a fifty-year reunion of Confederate soldiers who fought in the campaigns around Chattanooga. During World War I, he was active in the Liberty Loan and War Savings drives. Thereafter, he organized the first Community Chest drive held in Hamilton County.

It was as president of the Chattanooga Chamber of Commerce in 1911 that Will Brock got his first taste of Tennessee politics. When he took the post, he startled some by declaring that the Chamber of Commerce should take a part in politics, as it was made up of the city's leaders. "Politics is just a name for a big business," Brock later asserted, "just as coal means coal business, steel means steel business, and sugar means sugar business. Therefore politic business needs, just as any other big business, safe and unselfish leadership." Brock increasingly became interested in local politics, not out of personal political ambition, but believing it was his duty "as a matter of conviction." In 1912, he managed the first of three successive reelection campaigns for Third District Congressman John A. Moon.

During the 1920s, Brock directed lower East Tennessee campaign operations for Governor Austin Peay, a close friend since his ventures into Clarksville on R. J. Reynolds business. Peay, a lawyer and tobacco farmer, exuded an image as a champion of rural interests, a posture that led Bosses Ed Crump of Memphis and Hilary E. Howse of Nashville to oppose him in his third and final bid for renomination. Despite the loyalties of a majority of traditional rural Democrats in Middle and West Tennessee, it took a 68 percent showing in the East for Peay to eke out a narrow 8,000 vote win statewide. Understandably, Peay was grateful to his leaders in the most Republican of the three Grand Divisions of Tennessee. On one visit to Chattanooga, Governor Peay vowed to Brock that "If I ever have a Senate vacancy to fill, I'm going to appoint you."

Brock's visionary outlook for Tennessee, like that of Governor Peay, was what the historian George Brown Tindall has described in his magisterial work, *The Emergence of the New South, 1913–1945*, as that of a "business progressive." Southern business progressives excited few with their calls for streamlined, more efficient government. Their overarching goal of economic development in their still largely impoverished region dictated that they espouse the creation of regional communications and transportation systems designed to support a tremendous expansion of trade. They also backed a vastly expanded system of public education that would train the youth of the region to take better advantage of the opportunities they were creating. Peay, a believer in "pay as you go" financing, instituted privilege taxes on corporations, a gasoline tax to pave old highways and build new ones, and a tobacco tax to lengthen the rural school year to eight months.

Jeffersonian purists might argue otherwise, but these ideas had deep southern roots. Their pedigree includes the American System propounded by the great Kentuckian Henry Clay and his fellow antebellum Whigs, as well as Atlanta publisher Henry Grady's New South philosophy of the 1880s. For Peay and Brock, the most appropriate ideological influence to cite was always the New Freedom of Woodrow Wilson, the most recent southern-born Democratic President.

Like most other lower East Tennessee Democrats, Will Brock was particularly interested in the development of his own region. As early as 1898, his friend U.S. Congressman John Moon had been calling on federal and state authorities to provide a systematic plan for the development of the Tennessee River. Concerned with high railroad rates, Moon and the Tennessee River Improvement Association intended to render the waterway navigable from Paducah, Kentucky, to Knoxville, Tennessee. A series of canals near Muscle Shoals, Alabama, helped matters somewhat, as did the 1913 completion of the Hales Bar Dam. As late as 1930, however, there still was not a nine-foot channel along the length of the entire river, and many Tennesseans were still losing thousands of acres of crops to periodic floods. By this time, Brock firmly supported a plan sponsored by the Nebraska progressive, Republican George Norris. It suggested using the dams at Muscle Shoals to produce hydroelectric power for the lower Tennessee Valley and adding another dam at Cove's Creek, Tennessee, to serve the upper Valley. Brock supported the idea even though he conceded that the electricity produced "would not be even enough to make toast" for all of those in surrounding counties.

Brock soon learned that President Franklin D. Roosevelt had even more ambitious plans for the Tennessee Valley. He counseled those businessmen who feared an ever-expanding federal role to "declare a moratorium at least on fault-finding and criticism" and to back their president. Upon learning of the Tennessee Valley Authority's creation, he helped form the Tennessee Valley Club and served as its first chairman pro tem. While Chattanoogans wanted in part to locate some of TVA's offices close to home, they aimed principally to secure funding for a dam on Chickamauga Creek. For a business progressive like Brock, the power created was important not only because it would provide cheap electricity to the lower Tennessee Valley, but also because it would attract new industries to the Chattanooga area.

Tucked within Will Brock's civic activity was a remarkable visionary dimension. Particularly prophetic was a letter that he sent to Brock Candy employees and hundreds of civic acquaintances in October 1926. Contrary to those who projected an ever-continuing boom that would last well into the 1930s, Brock advised his friends to prepare for a readjustment. "This restless, high tension, swift going, high living standard of the American people," he wrote, "is coming to an end sooner or later." Three years before the great stock market crash, he warned friends to be wary of "shrewd salesmen" who offered "liberal extension of credit" on "almost all mercantile lines" and to spend no more than they could afford on the spot, except in "securing a home." "Those who realize this the quickest, and can revise their way of living and spending money," he insisted, "will suffer the least."

By the time the bubble burst, Will Brock was a member of the U.S. Senate. Austin Peay had died in 1927 and thus could not keep his promise to Brock, but an offer came from Governor Henry Horton, Peay's successor, following the August 1929 death of Senator Lawrence Tyson. Brock was not Horton's first choice. Horton, not the strong, principled, workaholic that Peay had been, at first had wanted to honor his patron, former Senator Luke Lea, then the publisher of the *Knoxville Journal*, the *Memphis Commercial Appeal*, and the *Nashville Tennessean*. When Lea declined, Horton named Brock, a sturdy and reliable ally, to fill the seat.

Having warned his own employees to prepare for a coming recession, Brock could hardly prepare for a long Senate career. Knowing that he would have to navigate Brock Candy through the crisis he foresaw, he made plans only to seek reelection in the special election that would be held in November 1930 to fill the remaining four months of Tyson's term. That election, the only time Will Brock's name ever appeared on a ballot, he carried handily and by an even greater margin than the total polled the same day by Congressman Cordell Hull, the Democratic nominee for the full six-year term.

Prior to the television age, freshman senators were expected to be seen but seldom heard. Will Brock played the game the way people expected it to be played. He quietly helped the senior Senator, Kenneth McKellar, secure funding for several Tennessee projects, notably an expansion of the Great Smoky Mountains National Park. Brock also played a key role in securing funding for a number of state transportation improvements including a handful of badly needed river bridges. The few times he spoke on the floor, his words were cogent and still apply today. He told the Senate on June 9, 1930, that America needed "less politics in business and more business in politics," an opinion echoed by 1992 presidential candidate Ross Perot. The occasion was a debate over the pending Smoot-Hawley protective tariff, a measure— as Albert Gore, Jr., reminded us in the North American Free Trade Agreement (NAFTA) debate with Perot in 1993—that proved to exacerbate the hardships of the depression by depriving America of foreign markets. Noting that forty-two countries and more than three hundred commodity producers had issued statements urging the rejection of Smoot-Hawley, Brock warned that the increased fees on imports were the "equivalent to an embargo and justification for retaliation." Trade wars, he asserted, might bring temporary psychological satisfaction, but the export business was already falling off and a further reduction would lead to a loss of more American jobs. Noting the arguments of Protectionists who fueled xenophobia at home, he declared, "We must either lift others or they will pull us down."

Lifting others: here was the core of Will Brock's life. Whether in the Methodist church or on the boards of trustees of colleges and universities, or groups aiming to develop the Tennessee Valley, he led by example and inspired hundreds to follow. A "devoutly religious, fervently patriotic" man, according to his grandson Bill, Will Brock is best remembered for his undying interest in Tennessee's future. In his own words about his beloved home state, Will Brock "looked hopefully to that day when her vast resources would be developed, her industries prosperous, all her people happy, and her place secure as one of the greatest commonwealths of a great and glorious country."

In his later years, Will Brock came to believe that the federal government had assumed too large a role in our society. This was an idea, the historian Otis Graham has noted, that was common to many Progressives, particularly southern ones. While not forgetting the potential of government to help cure the ills of the impoverished, Brock resisted the temptation and the growing habit to extend government into every facet of life. Government programs, while useful to an extent, could never replace traditional American values as an instrument of change. Perhaps Will Brock's view arose from his belief that many had left the spiritual portions of their lives behind as they moved from farm to city. This dimension Will Brock never lost, ever optimistically regaling friends with self-effacing tales with shrewd observations about "how hard life was and how good it was."

Will Brock guided Brock Candy until his death from pneumonia on August 5, 1950. "A mighty oak has fallen in the forest," lamented the *Chattanooga Times,* expressing the sadness shared by the people of Brock's adopted and beloved hometown. Often mighty oaks spawn strong acorns, and Will Brock left a powerful legacy in his two sons. Richard Brock was a capable executive for Brock Candy for nearly two generations. William E. "Bill" Brock, Jr., his eldest son, ran the business after his father's death and proved one of the truly remarkable civic leaders in American history.

A strong but sensitive man, Bill Brock (1904–1979) is remembered in Chattanooga for scores of acts of generosity that often were unknown to their beneficiaries. His courage in spurring cooperation with a court-ordered desegregation plan in 1962 won him the national Human Relations Award of the National Conference of Christians and Jews a decade later.

Bill Brock was suffering from a severe heart condition in 1962 when Mayor Ralph Kelley asked him to take on the task of prompting the people of the Mountain City to accept the social changes with grace and Christian dignity. Lesser men would have politely declined, but not Bill Brock. With rumors of violence rife in the air, he called leaders from all segments of Chattanooga society into his office and asked them to keep always in mind the best interests of their children. Each day, he went to work early, came home at noon to rest his heart through a nap, then arose at 4 P.M. to work well past midnight, meeting with any number of groups to defuse their fears and concerns. He listened carefully, constantly counseling reporters to be careful with rumors of impending violence, lest they become a self-fulfilling prophecy. "I'm on the scene with good people you can trust for truth and accuracy," he would assure them. It was hardly the case that violence was not possible. A few cowards from the Ku Klux Klan even burned a cross on his lawn. It thus was a particular, if peculiar, joy for Brock when he got a valid tip that a few segregationist extremists had decided not to "barbecue the town." The meetings continued for many months, with the firm, sensitive hand of Bill Brock defusing a tense initial reaction, then orchestrating a harmony then unknown in much of the South. Classes opened in September 1962 without incident anywhere in Chattanooga, a tribute to the calm, courageous leadership of one Bill Brock.

Many people note that America always finds such leaders as Bill Brock in times of trouble and wonders how. In this case the answer is rather easy. Bill, Jr., was a chip off the old Brock!

Chapter 4

Cordell Hull

1931–1933

*Longest-Serving
Secretary of State*

*Father of the
Federal Income Tax*

Father of the United Nations

(1871 –1955)

There is no more resilient politician in Tennessee history than Cordell Hull. Perhaps the length and breadth of his public service is best demonstrated by the fact that his memoirs are a full 1,700 pages long in the smallest of print. Unlike many others, Hull's Senate tenure proved but a brief respite between a generation of service in the House of Representatives and the longest stint as Secretary of State of any person in our history. Yet in that two-year period, he exemplified many qualities that make an outstanding U.S. Senator: intelligence, diligence, integrity, and old-fashioned country spunk.

If partisan attitudes were shaped during Tennessee's Civil War century more by the way people's fathers and grandfathers shot than by the way they themselves thought, then Cordell Hull must have been the most intractable Democrat of them all. He was the third of five sons of William and Elizabeth Riley Hull, born on October 2, 1871, in a small rented log cabin in Overton (now Pickett) County's mountain country, on the divide separating Union and Confederate sentiment during the Civil War and where sentiments overlapped and pitted brother against brother. William Hull was an unabashed Confederate who had been bushwhacked near his home by unionist guerrillas. In the skirmish, a friend was killed, but Hull very luckily escaped with a bullet hole between his eye and nose. Despite the fact that the sight in his right eye was gone forever, he tracked down and killed his assailant in Monroe County, Kentucky.

Cordell Hull's youth was marked by hard work and economic struggle. The Hulls did not own their own home until Cordell was nearly five. As he and his brothers grew older, they assumed an ever-increasing share of the chores. Before daybreak, they would arise to feed and milk their cows. By the time they were ten, they worked the fields and hauled logs. Schooling for Hull came in two three-month intervals each year until 1884, when the Hulls moved to Willow Grove in Clay County. There, Hull found time to swing over to Byrdstown to observe a number of trials, and it was then that he resolved to become a lawyer. Outside of studies in school, he read history and philosophy, and surprisingly, surveying, which he thought would be helpful in land boundary cases. He joined a debating society and won a countywide contest so handily that his father decided to send him to Montvale Institute in Celina, the best school he could afford, for the first five months of 1886. Here Hull saw his first daily newspaper, the *Nashville American.* Also he made the acquaintance of two brothers of Congressman Benton McMillin, one his headmaster, Professor Joe McMillin, and the other a lawyer, John McMillin. These contacts came in handy. In the autumn of 1887, Hull read law in the Celina office of John McMillin, and by 1890, before he was old enough to vote, Hull was elected chairman of his county's Democratic Executive Committee.

Hull spent semesters in the normal schools (teachers' colleges) of Bowling Green, Kentucky, in 1886 and Lebanon, Ohio, in 1888 and 1889. In 1887, sixteen-year-old Hull took advantage of his first trip to Nashville as a rafthand on a raft of his father's hardwood logs to purchase his first law books with his wages, and he accumulated more books with every trip. In 1891, the fully grown, six-foot one-inch Hull began formal legal studies at the famed Cumberland University School of Law in Lebanon, Tennessee. Having prepared extensively, Hull had no trouble passing the exam for admission to the senior class, and he graduated ten months later. Fortunately for the twenty-year-old Hull, a state law allowed Cumberland graduates alone the right to be admitted to the bar before the age of twenty-one.

After admission to the bar, Hull joined a law partnership in Celina but found himself more drawn to electoral politics. On a hunch, he decided, again before he reached twenty-one, to wage a campaign for the Tennessee House of Delegates. To nearly everyone's surprise, he ousted an incumbent in the Democratic primary and went on to serve two terms. It was in the General Assembly that Hull mastered the art of political infighting. In 1894, he managed the successful campaign of John A. Tipton for Speaker and was called on to serve as ranking House member on the committee investigating the outcome of a close gubernatorial election. Republican H. Clay Evans had actually won more votes than Democrat Peter Turney, but many of his supporters had not paid the poll tax then required by Tennessee law. In later years, Hull, like most in both parties, would come to see the poll tax as undemocratic. In 1894, however, that undemocratic practice saved the Democrat when Hull and his Democratic colleagues threw out the ballots of those who had not paid their poll tax, thus swinging the election to Turney. Hull could have been reelected to the State House interminably, but he decided in 1896 to return full time to the practice of the law. It would have been out of character for Hull to refrain from Democratic politics altogether, and he spoke as often as time would allow for the 1896 Bryan-Sewall presidential ticket.

In 1898, war clouds appeared on the horizon and, like many other young Tennesseans of the nineteenth century, Hull prepared for military service. He began to recruit volunteers for Company H of the Fourth Tennessee Volunteer Infantry almost as soon as the U.S. battleship *Maine* exploded in Havana Harbor in February, and he was commissioned a captain. The Spanish-American War was over by the time the Fourth Tennessee arrived in Cuba, but Hull's company remained there until May of 1899 to supervise the legal staff in the province of Santa Clara as it worked to install a responsive local government. It must have seemed tedious work, but Hull found it valuable in later years, as it acquainted him with Latin America.

After the war, Hull experienced several career shifts. He returned to his law practice in Celina, but soon moved to Gainesboro in Jackson County to enter a larger law firm. He stayed only a short time before assuming the presiding judgeship of Tennessee's Tenth Judicial District in 1903. Although his circuit spanned ten counties, which often entailed traveling by horse and buggy over almost impassable roads, Hull gained a reputation for opening court promptly at 8 A.M. and studying case law late into the night. A tough judge who liked to smoke cigars while at the bench and to instruct grand juries to indict anyone they saw cavorting recklessly in town squares in the expectation of excitement from pending trials, he was proud to note in his memoirs a precipitous decline in midday drunkenness during his three years on the bench. In 1906, some friends suggested that he seek the Democratic nomination for the Fourth District congressional seat. Hull was amenable and he soon found himself traveling to all of the district's fourteen counties. The hours were long, but Hull was used to that. His hard work, more than his oratory, allowed him to eke out a primary win by a scant fifteen votes.

Once in the House of Representatives, Hull quickly established himself as a member of consequence. Like most freshmen, he was assigned to fairly insignificant committees, in Hull's case Pensions and Reform of the Civil Service. This was hardly what Hull had expected when he ran and he soon took solace in advice that he specialize in one or two subjects. For Hull, the most significant issues were broad questions of finance and taxation, and he soon was acknowledged as one of the foremost congressional authorities on those subjects. He rarely took the floor to speak, seldom more than a half-dozen times per year. When he did, however, members listened, for Hull had taken the time to scour domestic and foreign periodicals and to put together well-constructed arguments with numerous literary allusions. Although the Republican Congresses of the Roosevelt and Taft years were not receptive to his arguments for lower tariffs and an income tax, his rhetoric did carry the authority of careful research and study.

On a personal level, Hull fit easily into the men's club that the Capitol was at that time. While not a regular at Washington parties, he did establish friendly relations with many colleagues. He chose as his residence the Cochran Hotel, the home-away-from-home for dozens of members of Congress. Each night, Cochran denizens would co-opt part of the lobby to discuss the issues of the day or merely to regale each other with tales from home. Here and elsewhere, Hull became known for his ability to curse for an hour without repeating the same word or taking the Lord's name in vain.

Hull's life was his work, and he found only limited time for recreation. He went to only one movie in his life: the wonderful celebration of his friend *Sergeant York*. In later years, he would restrict himself to a biweekly game of croquet at the home of his friend Henry Stimson. Any woman who would marry Hull would have to be as committed to his work as he was, and he found her at the age of forty-seven. His bride was Rose Frances Witz, the daughter of a prominent businessman from Staunton, Virginia, who had fought under Stonewall Jackson. The couple was quite attached to each other, and never had children. Frances Hull subordinated all of her desires to her husband's, even receiving by herself visitors whom he preferred to avoid. She was the ideal wife for Hull, and their bliss lasted until her death in 1954.

Hull's influence mounted after Democrats recaptured the White House and both houses of Congress in 1912. Two years earlier, he had taken a seat on the powerful Ways and Means Committee, a perch he could use to maximum effect to push his idea that the lot of the average person would be improved if tariffs were lowered and an income tax imposed. Hull wanted people to know when they were being taxed; he was fond of quoting the eighteenth-century British statesman Edmund Burke, who said, "You can tax the shirt off a man's back by indirect taxation without serious complaint on his part." He also wanted taxes to be more progressive. By Hull's math, protective tariffs added $8 in costs to consumers for every dollar borne by big business. Like other Wilsonian Democrats, he voted for stiffer antitrust laws and the creation of a Federal Reserve System and Federal Trade Commission as means of better regulating competition among businesses. These steps, however, were hardly enough, in his view, to equalize the tax burden. It was always his aim to lessen the benefits given to protected industries and thus allow American farmers and other exporters a better chance to sell their products abroad. In 1913, Hull worked long and hard with Ways and Means Chairman Oscar Underwood to lower tariffs by nearly one-third, but it was his duty alone to draft the portion of that bill which introduced America's first permanent income tax. Hull resisted suggestions to empower the President to raise or lower tax schedules as he saw fit, knowing that this would strip legitimate constitutional prerogatives from Congress. He crafted a measure establishing a top rate of 3 percent for those making more than $100,000 a year and a 1 percent rate for those with incomes over $4,000, no small sum for that era. With Hull as its manager, the bill made it through the Congress with virtually no changes. His work earned him the designation "the father of the income tax," a title Hull wore proudly, certain that he had lifted the brunt of the tax burden from the middle class and the poor.

The outbreak of World War I prompted Hull to seek new ways to raise revenue. He was always careful to make sure that the burden fell on those most able to pay. He tore apart protectionist claims that the lower tariff rates he had authored were to blame for declining revenues, saying a "blind man or a driveling idiot" knew that it was only natural that overseas wars would produce a decline in American exports. As was his custom, he began a study of foreign tax laws and concluded that estate taxes were best-suited to produce his desired effect. He fashioned such a tax after a British model, then another tax that raised tax rates on the wealthy. Both were approved, once Hull promised that he would see to the reinstatement of normal schedules at the war's end.

Once America entered World War I in 1917, Hull threw himself into the battle to raise revenues to finance our effort. Throughout the conflict, he pushed for higher levies on all, always framing arguments in patriotic terms. "The achievements of hundreds of years in the higher, greater and better development of government, education . . . and civilization itself," he said in March 1918, "hang in the balance." A few months later, he characterized the Germans as "scoundrels and villains," "assassins and freebooters," "highwaymen and desperados," and led Congress to approve a substantially higher tax schedule for the duration of the war.

Hull was just as quick to work toward a permanent peace. Like Woodrow Wilson, he believed that the war had been brought on in part by long-standing European commercial and imperial rivalries. As early as 1916, he had advocated the convening of a postwar trade conference that would endeavor to lower commercial barriers. In Hull's mind, this was the antecedent of the third of Wilson's famed Fourteen Points, the one that called for the eradication of all trade barriers. When the Senate did not consent to ratification of the Versailles Treaty, Hull blamed Senate Republicans, who he said had tried "to discredit the president" and in the process had made the United States "a hiss and a byword in every civilized government." His attachment to Wilsonian conceptions of collective security never wavered.

Hull's alliance with the ailing president did prove harmful in the short run, but it won a loyalty among the Democratic leadership that would pay future dividends. Frustration ran high among voters after America's intervention fell short of producing a "world safe for democracy." Many women also blamed all Democrats for the ardor of some of their rural legislators in opposing suffrage and made plans to retaliate. That opportunity came in 1920, when voters turned many Democrats out of office, including Cordell Hull by just 292 votes. Hull's loss astounded even his GOP opponent Wynne Clouse.

Hull resolved to recapture his seat in 1922. He turned down Woodrow Wilson's offer to nominate him for Chief Justice of the Court of Appeals for Customs, deciding instead to return for a spell to Carthage, where he had bought a home. In November 1921, he attended a meeting in St. Louis of the Democratic National Committee, ostensibly as an observer. He found on his arrival that he was the only man present whom all sides would accept as their chairman. It seemed a thankless job, with his party $300,000 in debt and just off one of its worst defeats in history, but Hull reluctantly accepted. He then went about working to rebuild Democratic organizations in all forty-eight states and to retire the debt, even putting up $10,000 of his own Liberty Bonds at one point just to pay salaries. When he resigned the position in 1924, his party had a $30,000 surplus, even after the DNC repaid him for his Liberty Bonds. In Congress, the Democrats were substantially stronger as well, having retaken seventy-five House seats in 1922. Their resurgence came partially from the public blaming Republicans for an ongoing recession, but also from Hull's often unrecognized work to reinvigorate their party. Hull himself was again elected to serve Tennessee's Fourth District.

Hull returned to the Ways and Means Committee, where he had so distinguished himself in the 1910s. His potential for affecting policy was limited, as he was a junior member of the minority party, but he continued to use his seat to warn of the dangers of protectionism. "Economic peace," he told the House in 1925, "offers the greatest assurance of permanent world peace." Hull was just as certain that free trade was a guarantor of prosperity. After 1929, he liked to answer protectionist critics by quoting Herbert Hoover's statement hailing "international trade" as the "lifeblood of our civilization." At the time, he cited projections that American workers had produced a full 25 percent more than they could sell on the domestic market and lambasted the Harding and Coolidge administrations for acting in the spirit of Alexander Hamilton rather than Abraham Lincoln in maintaining the highest tariff rates of any non-Asian nation except Spain and the Soviet Union. The determination of the Republican Congresses of the late 1920s to hike already exorbitant tariff rates led Hull to concede defeat, if not his point. "The hog has returned to its wallow," he told the House in May 1929, "and the dog to its vomit."

Hull's inability to affect policy led him to contemplate retirement from Congress. What made him change his mind was the death of Senator Lawrence D. Tyson and Governor Henry Horton's appointment of Will Brock to succeed him. Hull had nothing against Brock personally, but knew him to be an ally of longtime foe Luke Lea, and therefore he announced that he would run for the full six-year Senate term that would begin in March 1931. His decision allowed Brock the dignity of a chance to be elected in his own right for the remaining four months of Tyson's term, then to retire undefeated. As Hull expected, Lea's organization fielded an opponent, former state legislator Andrew Todd. While Todd blasted Hull's record long and hard, most Democratic constituencies backed Hull and he prevailed by 61,000 votes.

Hull's experience in the House led Senate Democratic leaders to open seats for him on the Finance Committee and Banking and Currency Committee, and as he had in the House, Hull concentrated on the economy, and he assailed the Hoover administration for not cutting spending and not raising taxes on the wealthy. These policies, he believed, would have produced a balanced budget. As always, his central focus was the tariff and he was quick to deride the "Bourbon" rates of the Smoot-Hawley Act of 1930. Half the support for those schedules, he told the Senate in May of 1932, emanated from fear and half came from the selfishness of a few affected groups. All in all, Smoot-Hawley amounted to an "embargo tariff," which had reduced exports to Canada, our largest trading partner, by two-thirds since 1929. For Hull, the ideal economic stimulus for the depression conditions of the early 1930s would be a gradual lowering of tariff rates, an authorizing of the President to negotiate reciprocal tariff reductions, and the institution of a world economic congress that would resolve commercial disputes. Hull could not convince the Senate to adopt his program when he aired it on the floor in February 1932. He did, however, manage to get the Democratic convention to install it in its 1932 platform, over the heated objections of 1928 presidential nominee Al Smith.

With the election of Franklin D. Roosevelt, Hull's life would change in a way he had never imagined. A bevy of key Democrats from the South and the West counseled the President-elect to choose as his Secretary of State someone without ties to the international business community. Roosevelt himself wanted to take the lead in formulating foreign policy. He was looking for someone who would carry out his aims and add in other ways to his team. Colonel Edward House, Woodrow Wilson's closest associate on foreign policy questions, recommended Hull. Although Hull's experience in foreign policy was scant, according to House, his presence would bolster southern confidence in the New Deal and provide a bridge to Hull's former colleagues in Congress. Roosevelt reflected for a while, then agreed. Roosevelt's offer startled Hull because he had hoped, even at sixty-one, that he had just embarked upon a long Senate career. Hull pondered the offer for nearly a month before concluding that the job would afford him a far greater opportunity to institute the Wilsonian system of free commerce that he had long envisioned. On securing Roosevelt's assurance that his counsel would be heard, Hull accepted.

Hull's initial preoccupation at State, as in Congress, lay in reopening foreign markets to American producers. "We must eliminate twade baa-yuhs," he liked to say in his lisping, raspy drawl, "heah, theyah, and evewywheah." His hope was that a real opportunity would arise at the London Economic Conference of June 1933. As he sailed from New York, Hull carried in his coat pocket a copy of the reciprocal trade agreements bill that he and Roosevelt had drafted. He assumed that FDR intended to secure its enactment while he was away and thus strengthen his hand in negotiations with other governments. Hull was wrong, as he learned while at sea. Roosevelt was anxious for Congress to adjourn before it decided to take up measures such as paper money inflation and veterans' bonus legislation that were popular but unwise. Letting Congress stay in session, he cabled Hull, might buy time for members to raise such matters that would harm our recovery even more than reciprocal trade might help it. Three weeks later, Roosevelt sent another emissary, Assistant Secretary of State Raymond Moley, a member of his original "Brain Trust." Upon arriving, Moley effectively sabotaged the conference by negotiating an agreement on currency stabilization that neither the President nor Hull had authorized and which Roosevelt had to renounce. Hull sent Moley home, then prolonged his stay for three weeks, merely to cool a broad-based European anger toward the United States. It would be a year before FDR saw to the passage of the Reciprocal Trade Agreements Act. In time, Hull came to resent FDR's *modus operandi.* Indeed, he endured humiliations, as the historian Margaret Coit wrote, that "no man in private life could accept and keep his self-respect." Hull had a knack for political infighting, though, and saw to Moley's removal from the State Department.

Hull had far greater success in his long effort to lay a foundation for hemispheric cooperation. In part, this meant that the United States would have to abandon what Latinos saw as a long habit of intervening in their affairs. Hoover's Secretary of State Henry Stimson had signaled such a shift in U.S. policy when he withdrew Marines from several Latin nations, but it was Roosevelt who coined the term "Good Neighbor Policy" to connote the friendlier ties he hoped would ensue. It fell to Hull to devise the means to lessen the enmity Latinos had traditionally felt toward "the Great Colossus to the North" and to facilitate closer commercial and geopolitical ties.

Hull's seriousness about his mission led Roosevelt to designate him as the chairman of the U.S. delegation to the Pan American Union Conference in Montevideo in 1933. Hull thus became the first Secretary of State to attend any meeting of the Union, a gesture attesting to the sincerity of the Roosevelt administration in trying to reach a greater degree of mutual understanding. He prepared meticulously, reading boxes of materials before arriving at the conference. He took care to have other delegations sail with him and to spend time with them after introducing himself only as "Hull of the United States." His courtly manner and "Howdy-do" won the personal goodwill of those delegates on board.

Some anti-*Yanqui* sentiment lingered among other delegates, as evidenced by the "Down With Hull" signs that lined the streets of Montevideo. Hull knew that the leader of those governments hostile to the United States was likely to be Argentine Foreign Minister Carlos de Saavedra Lamas, a small man with a red-dyed mustache. Hull sought out Saavedra Lamas and suggested to him that the conference pass two resolutions, one regarding economics and the other, peace. Ever the free-trader, Hull wanted to introduce the economic resolution himself, especially after having docked at Santos, Brazil, and observed the burning of tons of coffee. The other resolution called on each delegation to commit its government to signing a series of treaties. Hull hoped the assembly's actions might prevent the outbreak of conflicts such as the Chaco War then raging in Paraguay and Bolivia. He presented Saavedra Lamas with a draft and played to the minister's vanity by encouraging him to introduce the peace resolution. Saavedra Lamas not only assented, but spoke at greater length than Hull for Hull's free trade accord.

To Latinos, a far more significant issue was one committing all nations present not to intervene in the affairs of any other country. When the conference began to consider a convention establishing the rights of nations, a fiery group of orators arose to berate the United States. Saavedra Lamas followed with an unusually mild supporting speech, knowing Hull was about to startle the crowd. The United States was glad to sign the convention, he said, thus rendering inoperative the long-resented Roosevelt Corollary to the Monroe Doctrine that had made the United States the policeman and bill-collector of the hemisphere. Though the conference ended in harmony, Hull knew that Latinos would judge the United States by its actions more than by his words at Montevideo. Within three years, the United States signed treaties with Cuba and Panama abrogating previous accords that allowed it to intervene in their affairs. In addition, U.S. Marines left Haiti, Congress voted to help fund the Pan-American Highway, and reciprocal trade pacts were signed with Cuba, Brazil, Haiti, Colombia, and five Central American republics.

Our stance as a good neighbor took on critical importance once Nazi Germany began to spread its influence in Latin America. Hull took it upon himself to propose a special inter-American conference for December 1936 and acquiesced to an Argentine demand that it be held in Buenos Aires. Hull intended for the conference to reinforce existing peacemaking machinery and saw to it that FDR underscored the importance of closer U.S. ties with its neighbors by having the President address the opening session. He stayed behind after Roosevelt sailed home and got the conference to adopt a convention committing those present to consult any time their security was threatened. While the Argentines watered down the convention somewhat by adding the words "if they so desire," the American republics had taken a major step toward the kind of Pan-Americanism that would serve the interests of all and prove so beneficial throughout World War II.

Hull's work with our neighbors to the south had only begun. By the time the Pan-American Conference convened in Lima in 1938, the Nazis had overrun Austria and the Sudetenland, and Nazi propaganda had begun to penetrate the Americas at an alarming rate. To help present a united front to the rest of the world, Hull made Alf Landon, the 1936 GOP presidential nominee, a delegate. He wanted to have the conference approve a declaration instituting biennial foreign ministers meetings and binding member nations to resist threats to their security from any country outside of the Americas. He was even more interested in the Americas presenting a united front, and he deferred to demands from Argentina, Uruguay, and Chile—countries with extensive trade with Germany—that any potential threat not be identified in writing. This provided the consensus that Hull sought and fostered goodwill for the future. A year later, the first conference of foreign ministers met in Panama and adopted a declaration establishing a neutral zone extending three hundred nautical miles from the American continents and barring nations from allowing belligerents to use their lands as bases for operations. In July 1940, a month after the Nazis completed their conquest of Western Europe, Hull led the U.S. delegation to the second Pan American conference, which adopted the Act of Havana, allowing members to take over any European colony, such as those belonging to France and the Netherlands, whose sovereignty was jeopardized by a third party. This act was intended to warn the Nazis that multilateral action against them could result if they tried to move into those dominions. Although it never had to be applied, its presence effectively forestalled any further German penetration of the hemisphere.

The Good Neighbor Policy, writes Wayne S. Cole, the leading historian on isolationism, allowed Roosevelt and Hull to lead "the American people . . . towards a more positive and active multilateral role . . . in world affairs." Prior to Havana, the latitude of the administration in responding to Nazi and Japanese aggression was hampered by our historic aversion to involvement abroad. In such a climate, Hull felt he had no alternative but to cooperate with the Senate's Nye Committee investigation of the role of munitions makers in bringing on World War I. The Nye Committee held a controversial and some would say irresponsible inquiry that fueled doubts about all American policymakers and created a prevailing attitude that limited Hull's options. In 1935, he felt he had no choice but to advise the President to sign neutrality legislation that required him to embargo arms to any belligerent in an instance of war, not just the aggressor. Once Italy invaded Ethiopia later that year, Hull drafted a statement for Roosevelt urging Americans to observe a moral embargo on trade with both countries, knowing that the country hurt would be the Fascist aggressor.

It was Hull's hope that future Congresses would allow the President more discretion in moving to deter aggressors, but isolationist sentiment was so strong in the 1930s that all he could do was to limit transgressions against the president's authority. The first real victory for FDR came in 1938, when the House voted narrowly to kill the Ludlow Amendment, a measure Hull warned would "hamstring the nation's foreign policy" by requiring a popular referendum after any congressional declaration of war. Yet this was a temporary victory, for isolationists continued to hold majorities in both houses of Congress. Even after the Nazi juggernaut overran Czechoslovakia in 1939, William Borah of Idaho, one of the isolationist leaders, was telling Roosevelt and Hull that his sources were more reliable than theirs and they said that Europe would remain at peace. Hull was taken aback, but held his counsel. There was no point in giving Borah the Tennessee tongue-lashing that he would have loved to administer; for Borah had the votes to block the repeal of the Neutrality Acts. That state of affairs changed on September 1, the day the Nazis invaded Poland. FDR, having long before concluded that Britain and France were America's first line of defense against the Nazis and that they needed our arms to survive, called on Alf Landon and Frank Knox, the 1936 Republican presidential ticket, and Henry Stimson, the last Republican Secretary of State, to respond to Borah's contention that the Neutrality Acts had to stay in place for America to remain at peace. The legislation that FDR and Hull presented in 1939 was rather weak. It allowed France and Britain to buy only those arms they could cart away on a cash-and-carry basis. Perhaps its limited nature was a virtue, however, for it made it easier to sell Congress on the idea of authorizing Roosevelt to aid victims of Nazi aggression.

The mounting world crisis also wreaked havoc on Hull's presidential aspirations. Under normal circumstances, FDR would have honored the two-term tradition and retired. In 1938, he had hinted to Hull that he was his preferred successor and reiterated that to several key Democrats. Hull was flattered, but thought that his position necessitated that he devote all of his time to his work. A diabetic, Hull at age sixty-eight was not as energetic as he once was, and unbeknownst to FDR, he had contracted tuberculosis. Hull refused to encourage well-wishers who prodded him to organize a campaign, even after polls taken in the spring of 1940 showed him defeating any Republican opponent by a greater margin than Roosevelt. By not organizing, Hull was vulnerable to the attacks of several liberals who sensed, accurately, that he was not a knee-jerk ally of theirs, especially on FDR's controversial court-packing plan. It is likely that FDR tacitly concerted their attacks, if only to keep his own options open if he decided to run again. While Roosevelt told Hull that he was his choice as late as June 20, 1940, it was clear to Hull that FDR's attitude had changed when they had lunch less than two weeks later. Once the President opened the political portion of the conversation by alluding to friends who suggested that he run again, Hull knew that FDR would run again, especially given the crisis atmosphere of 1940 that almost dictated the choice of an experienced hand. Hull was flattered that Roosevelt offered him the vice presidency three times over the course of the next week, once begging him for three hours, but he declined, thinking the vice president's role inconsequential. For him, it was enough to know that Roosevelt knew his value to the administration as a bridge to the South, the Congress, and the public, and as an invaluable member of his foreign policy team.

Hull was busy in 1940. With the fall of Western Europe, it became imperative to shore up our defenses. It was Hull who worked out the details of the exchange whereby America transferred fifty aging destroyers to Britain in return for eight Caribbean bases that were essential to the defense of the Panama Canal. Like most other Americans that summer, Hull marveled at the courage of the British people in resisting nightly Nazi bombardments. Once the election was won, he began working with the Treasury Department to devise some other means of aiding the British. They arrived at a formula whereby money and equipment would be provided to the British that they could repay at war's end, the "Lend-Lease" program. The President likened the plan to a neighbor lending another his garden hose to put out a fire. Such a program was necessary to block "forces which are not restrained by considerations of law or principles of morality" from gaining control of the oceans, Hull told the Senate Foreign Relations Committee in January 1941. By that time, Hull was certain that those Nazi forces had other expansive designs. He had always suspected that the Nazi-Soviet entente forged in August 1939 would be short-lived. Even with the Soviet invasion of Finland in December 1939, Roosevelt and Hull tempered their rhetoric, suspecting that the Soviets at some point might be detached from the Nazis. By January 1941, Hull had a report that the Germans were preparing to invade the Soviet Union. The evidence was circumstantial but Hull was suspicious enough to turn it over to FBI Director J. Edgar Hoover. Once Hoover determined the report credible, Hull had it forwarded to the Soviet ambassador and U.S.-Soviet relations began to thaw.

America's deteriorating relations with Japan occupied even more of Hull's attention. From the beginning of his service at State, Hull had seen the Japanese record as "that of a highway robber." He recognized early in the 1930s that militarists led by future Foreign Minister Yosuke Matsuoka, a man he deemed "as crooked as a basket of fishhooks," and a group of young officers were in the ascendancy in the Japanese government. It was always his hope that Japan might fall under the control of elements not so committed to a concept of "law and order" that amounted to Japanese hegemony over all of Asia. Yet while many were horrified by the ongoing Japanese slaughter of Chinese civilians, there was little resolve among the American people to help the Chinese until the Japanese signed a three-power pact with Germany and Italy in September 1940. Here, the administration actually led the people, since it had banned the export of most war materials to the Japanese. The one exception was petroleum, which was exempted strictly to deny the Japanese an excuse to move into the oil-rich Dutch East Indies. While the Japanese avoided the Indies for the moment, they did exploit the Nazi takeover of France by moving into her colony of Indochina.

It fell to Hull to meet with Japanese emissaries. As early as January 1941, he had learned from Ambassador Joseph Grew that the Japanese had a plan to attack Pearl Harbor if they did not get what they wanted from the United States. Hull was skeptical that any amicable settlement could be worked out, but he met with Ambassador Kichisaburo Nomura throughout the year, often inviting him to his seven-room apartment at the Carlton Hotel for late night discussions. In April, Hull let Nomura know that an agreement could be reached if Japan pledged to respect the territorial integrity and sovereignty of all nations, if it supported the principles of noninterference and equality, and promised not to disturb the status quo except by peaceful means. What Nomura did not know was that the United States had already deciphered the Japanese diplomatic code and Hull knew that Japan would not agree to anything that infringed on its agreements with Germany and Italy. Japan's official response called on America to accept what Hull termed a European-type "peace on Nazi terms" and called on China to submit to Japanese demands in the Orient. This was out of the question, but Roosevelt and Hull decided not to reject it out of hand in the hope that they might pry Japan away from Hitler. As time passed, Hull noted that the Japanese would not budge from their intent to remain in China nor accept language that would bind them in any way. He preached to Nomura about the perfidy of Japan's Nazi allies and the intent of the United States to act only in self-defense. On July 21, Japan moved further into Indochina. Hull was recuperating at the time in White Sulphur Springs, Virginia, but he designated Undersecretary Sumner Welles to tell Nomura that Hull and Nomura would not meet privately for a while. Three days later, Roosevelt ended what some called a policy of appeasing Japan by freezing all Japanese assets in the United States.

Hull continued to listen to Japanese proposals, but their tenor never changed. The one exception was a suggestion that Japanese Premier Fumimaro Konoye meet the President at a summit in Hawaii, but Hull rejected this categorically unless some agenda resembling the American proposal of April was adopted beforehand. None was forthcoming and the relatively mild Konoye government was replaced in mid-October by the thoroughly militaristic War Cabinet of Hideki Tojo. By November 5, Hull knew that Japan intended to attack the United States unless he and the president caved in to their demands by November 25. He continued to meet with Nomura, but found him increasingly evasive. By mid-November, the two were joined in their meetings by Ambassador Saburo Kurusu, the man who had signed Japan's alliance with Germany and Italy. Hull instinctively suspected that Kurusu aimed to press him for an immediate settlement. Having dealt with many a Tennessee bully, he was hardly one to budge. On November 20, he received from the two emissaries a proposal that he knew from the "Magic" code-breaking operation would be Japan's last. There could be peace, the document said, if the United States released Japanese assets, supplied Japan with oil and other war materials, ended aid to China, and limited its presence in the western Pacific. This was out of the question, and Hull and FDR drafted a counterproposal that they deemed reasonable, but which they knew would have no value except as public relations. Hull called in the two emissaries on November 26, knowing that the Japanese had extended their deadline until the twenty-ninth. Then, Kurusu told Hull that Japan would not withdraw from China or sign a multilateral non-aggression pact, even if America unfroze its assets or expanded trade with them. The next day, Hull told Secretary of War Henry Stimson that the matter was in the hands of the military. He was hardly shocked to learn on December 6, 1941, that a Japanese fleet was heading from Indochina toward the Dutch East Indies, Thailand, Malaya, and the Philippines. Roosevelt read the same reports and concluded, "This means war."

On December 7, Hull headed for his office fearing a catastrophe and he was not surprised. By mid-morning, he had read an intercept of the Japanese response, which called the American reply disparaging of Japan's honor and prestige and accused the United States of conspiring with Britain to block its efforts to establish peace and a new order in East Asia. Nomura and Kurusu were instructed to present the message to Hull at 1 P.M. Slow in translating their directive into English, the two were actually more than an hour late, by which time Hull had learned of the Japanese attack at Pearl Harbor. He received the two standing up and went through the motions of scanning their document. Then, he looked at Nomura and lectured him indignantly, saying, "In all my fifty years of public service, I have never seen a document that was more crowded with infamous falsehoods and distortions . . . on a scale so huge that I never imagined until today that a government was capable of uttering them." Hull nodded the embarrassed ambassadors toward the door, then phoned Roosevelt. The reports from Pearl Harbor were accurate, but a larger attack on Malaya had actually preceded Pearl Harbor by two hours. Hull knew that the Pearl Harbor attack, although deemed secondary by the Japanese, had awakened a sleeping giant and brought unity to a people who had been divided over foreign policy for nearly a generation. Although near exhaustion, he spent the rest of the day setting down on paper his account of the interview with Nomura and Kurusu and drafting the address the President would give the next day asking Congress to declare war on Japan.

Hull's influence receded considerably thereafter. In part, this stemmed from Roosevelt's wartime preferences for working more closely with his generals and for delegating the most sensitive foreign assignments to close personal associates such as Harry Hopkins, his alter ego, and Harvard classmate Sumner Welles, the Undersecretary. Hull resented Welles especially, and his jealousy led him to abet a plot to remove him. Hull's actions did not endear him to FDR, yet the ever-shrewd President recognized that Hull was far too popular a political property to be sacrificed out of loyalty to Welles. It was Welles who had to go, even if Hull's value by 1942 was more related to his prestige and past accomplishments than to the work then in progress. By this time Hull's health had begun to fade; he was spending more and more time away from his office being treated for his tuberculosis. After passing seventy, he tried to work as hard as ever whenever possible. His preoccupation now was the creation of an international agency charged with maintaining world peace. Having lived through the League of Nations fight, he knew the potential pitfalls and was determined to avoid them, but even after a generation, he remained idealistic and certain that such a body offered the greatest hope to mankind for limiting the perils of war.

Hull's first public call for such an organization came in July 1942. "There must be international cooperative action," he said, "to set up the mechanisms which can thus insure peace." The British were interested, but they knew that the United States had to participate if such an organization was to deter aggression. The Senate would have to approve a treaty involving the United States, and Hull counseled House members in March 1943 to defer a resolution endorsing such a course until he was certain that the Senate would sign on overwhelmingly. Over that summer, Hull met frequently with key Senators of both parties to resolve potential points of contention. When a final vote came on the resolution, only five Senators voted in the negative, a stark contrast with America's experience after World War I.

Hull began to build support for the concept of collective security at the Moscow conference of foreign ministers in October 1943. The trip was the first and only airplane trip of Hull's life and he spent much of the flight spitting up blood. When he arrived, he and his British counterpart Anthony Eden assured the Soviets that their governments intended the next spring to open a second front in northern France, long the most substantial sticking point for the Soviets. Hull and Soviet leader Joseph Stalin got along well in their one private meeting, trading notes on the different means of rafting and wheat planting used by the people of Tennessee and Soviet Georgia. Hull got Stalin's vow to strongly consider his proposal for a post-war organization to promote world peace. By the end of the conference, he had secured Stalin's signature on the Four-Nation Declaration establishing such a forum and his promise that the Soviets would enter the war against Japan once the Nazis were defeated. Hull saved his preaching for Foreign Minister Vyacheslav Molotov. "After the war," he said, "you can follow isolationism if you want and gobble up your neighbors, but that will be your undoing. I knew a bully in Tennessee. He used to get a few things his way by being a bully, but he ended up by not having a friend in the world."

When Hull returned, the President and a huge congressional contingent greeted him at the airport with a hero's welcome. Gratified, a fatigued Hull (who had lost ten pounds on his excursion) took a few minutes to give Roosevelt his impressions of Stalin, then prepared to address a joint session of Congress the next day. Ever the idealistic Wilsonian, he expressed the hope that there would "no longer be need for spheres of influence, for alliances, for balance of power, or any of the other arrangements through which, in the unhappy past, the nations strove to safeguard their security or to promote their interests." Beginning in April 1944, he met periodically with a bipartisan group of eight Senators to answer their questions about the administration's plans. He opened talks with British and Soviet representatives in August at Dumbarton Oaks, a private Washington estate, and secured the agreement of Republican presidential nominee Thomas E. Dewey to keep the talks out of the fall campaign. By October, virtually all outstanding questions had been resolved except that of the voting procedure to be used in the General Assembly and the Security Council.

By this time, Hull's tuberculosis had spread to both lungs, and Hull was admitted to Bethesda Naval Hospital in late October. Two of his teeth had to be extracted, blood had been found in his urine, and his diabetes had reached an advanced stage. Hull had submitted his resignation earlier in the year. Roosevelt, knowing Hull's standing with the public, not only declined to accept it but offered him the vice presidency. It was FDR's intention to allow Hull to complete the arrangements for the United Nations; under no circumstances would he let Hull resign before the election. Only a week after being reelected did FDR visit Hull at the Bethesda Naval Hospital and realize the extent of his deterioration. It was with "very great regret" that he finally accepted Hull's resignation two weeks later.

Hull spent seven months in the hospital and only in March of 1945 did he walk again. He was indeed fortunate that doctors had only recently developed a medication to treat his illness. He could not attend the San Francisco meeting of the United Nations, at which FDR had hoped Hull would head the U.S. delegation, but he did speak nightly with successor Edward Stettinius about the day's events. Hull left the hospital in May, but was still too frail in December to sail to Sweden to accept the Nobel Peace Prize for his work in creating the United Nations. With a ghostwriter's help, Hull completed a massive set of memoirs in 1948. Rarely thereafter did he venture far from his apartment, though he did stay in touch with old friends from the State Department and the Congress. More and more, he was in and out of hospitals, and he became a virtual invalid after Frances Hull's death in 1954. He died from complications following a stroke on July 23, 1955.

Cordell Hull liked to summarize his accomplishments by citing his paternity of the income tax and the United Nations and his long efforts to lower trade barriers. This was a short but accurate and impressive resume. In the broad scheme of world history, Cordell Hull will be remembered as the pragmatist who brought the vision of Woodrow Wilson into reality.

Chapter 5

George L. Berry

1937–1938

Flamboyant Union Leader

(1882–1948)

No soul ever reached the Senate from a humbler station in life than George L. Berry. Sadly, no Senator ever left this earth in greater disrepute. But within the contradictions of his character lived a man whose worthier devotions, although by no means excusing his transgressions, also deserve to be remembered.

George Leonard Berry liked to describe his father as a Confederate captain, who, while serving as a deputy U.S. Marshal, was ambushed and killed by moonshiners. But chroniclers from the authoritative *Dictionary of American Biography* note the absence of any reference in either Confederate or Justice Department records to a Captain Thomas Jefferson Berry. What is known is that George L. Berry was born to Thomas and Cornelia Trent Berry on September 13, 1882, in Lee Valley in East Tennessee. Young Berry was orphaned at an early age, and he was sent first to live with an aunt in Des Moines, then to a Mississippi foster home. When he ran away at age nine, he slept in depots and lumberyards and earned enough to feed himself by mowing lawns. Luckily, he happened to encounter the mother of the publisher of the *Jackson* [Mississippi] *Evening News*, who arranged for him to work for her son for $1.50 a week. Young George had no formal schooling and he did not learn to read or write until he was sixteen. He developed a strong Baptist faith, never swore, and was always a patriot. When war with Spain broke out in 1898, George Berry enlisted as a private in the Third Mississippi Regiment. He saw no action, but that was natural, since he was only sixteen years old.

Berry returned to the states to take a position as a pressman with the *St. Louis Globe-Democrat*. St. Louis soon proved too confining for the restless, stocky, even then balding Berry. The six-foot, 185-pound youth ventured to Nebraska City, Nebraska, where he joined the Printing Pressmen and Assistants' Union (now known as the Graphic Communications International Union), the union that would consume the rest of his life. His stint near Omaha was brief, and like so many others in the nineteenth century, Berry heeded Horace Greeley's call to "Go west young man!" He headed to Nevada, working his way across the prairies and the mountains as a railroad section hand and a brakeman. Once in the Silver State, he found enough gold to buy into three mines.

In the West, Berry proved himself to be a tough competitor in body and mind. When some of his cohorts labeled him "sissy" because he would kneel to pray each night, Berry determined to prove them wrong with his fists. After handily taking care of one of his tormentors, he won a reputation in the gold fields and came to mediate disputes between local aggressive ruffians and more timid sorts. His success in dealing with bullies led him to entertain offers for a boxing career. A quick and muscular light-heavyweight, Berry won several bouts under the name of the Tennessee Kid. He even garnered the admiration of legendary heavyweight James J. Corbett.

Union business was never far from Berry's thoughts. He moved to San Francisco in search of more stable employment, where he met and married Marie Margaret Gerhes, the daughter of a local vintner, and took on four jobs to help make ends meet. Like all too many other union men of the time, George Berry was a nativist, and as director of the Japanese-Korean Exclusion League he strove to keep foreigners out to protect American workers. He also served as editor of *Sunset*, the in-house tract of the Union Pacific Railroad. He was superintendent of a commercial printing plant, secretary and business agent of the San Francisco branch of the Pressmen's Union, and president of the Central Labor Council. When a vacancy occurred in the national Pressmen's Union presidency in 1907, Bay Area locals boosted him and swung enough votes his way to carry him to a narrow majority on the second ballot. He was only twenty-five, but his position as Pressmen's Union president established his general outlook and *modus operandi* for the rest of his life.

Berry, it seems, was made to be an old-time union boss. A flamboyant man with a hearty grin and deep-set brown eyes, he always dressed nattily and frequently chewed on a cigar. He hailed friends as "Pardner" and "Old-Timer," and his informality sometimes led European acquaintances to misconstrue his meaning when he saluted them with "Hello there, old fellowe."

As union president, Berry fought long and hard for workers' rights. He secured an eight-hour day for those in his craft and saw to it that its practitioners were retrained immediately whenever technological advances rendered old machinery obsolete. Unlike many other union presidents of the time, he almost never allowed local subsidiaries to strike, believing that "it didn't pay." His preference for "industrial peace" was such that he insisted that all workers abide by their initial agreements. In at least two instances, he broke wildcat strikes by dissident members by vocally backing firms that hired scabs to replace his members who he believed had violated their contracts.

The Pressmen's Union had been headquartered in Cincinnati when Berry took its reins, but it was always his intention to move its operational center to Tennessee. In 1911, he ventured to Knoxville to try to organize workers there. In the course of this seemingly unsuccessful trip, he made a side trip to his father's grave in Hawkins County. Not far from there was Hale Springs, a location that Berry believed would be ideal for the hospital he planned to build to treat the large number of tuberculosis victims among the pressmen. Berry bought the site and thereon established the sanitarium, a trade school, and a residence for retired printers and their families. Pressmen's Home, as it was known by the 1920s, later became one of the showpieces of Tennessee.

During these years, George Berry became a power in the American Federation of Labor (AFL). In 1912, AFL founder Samuel Gompers chose him as his personal representative to the British Trade Unions Congress. A year later, Berry produced a book on his findings, entitled *Labor Conditions Abroad.*

A man with the ambition of George Berry could not be satisfied with union office alone. Just thirty-two years old in 1914 and only three years back in Tennessee, he sought the governorship but lost in the Democratic primary to Tom C. Rye. Wisely, he made his peace with Rye and secured a position on the Tennessee Tuberculosis Commission in 1915.

World War I saved George Berry from the ignominy of a reputation as a perennial candidate. After the United States entered the war in 1917, Berry was one of nine AFL members to attend the Inter-Allied Labor Conference in London. A Wilsonian internationalist at the time, he believed it the patriotic duty of all to support their president. Moreover, he considered the defeat of the Kaiser to be necessary for the spread of democracy, which he believed would elevate the socioeconomic standing of the European worker. Berry entered the service as a major in the Engineers Transportation Corps of the American Expeditionary Force. His duty on arriving in France in October 1918, a month before the war ended, was to supervise the building of roads and bridges at sites from Bordeaux to Verdun. Following the war, Berry served on the staff of President Wilson's closest advisor, Colonel Edward House, and as "liaison officer" to Samuel Gompers, one of the two American representatives on the Labor Commission at the Versailles Conference.

Although Berry never saw combat in WWI, his vanity henceforth led him to demand that he be addressed as Major. This credential prompted Samuel Gompers to send him in 1921 to the first organizational meeting of the American Legion as his personal representative, where he was elected as their First Vice National Commander.

Credible now as a champion of workers and veterans, Berry sought to secure the vice presidential nomination for himself at the seemingly interminable Democratic convention of 1924. Friends boasted that his selection might deter union members from swinging behind Progressive nominee Robert LaFollette and thereby strengthen labor solidarity behind Democratic standard-bearer John W. Davis. Memphis delegate C. M. Bryan placed Berry's name in nomination, but no one had had time to talk with a weary Davis, who had won his nod only after 103 ballots amidst two long weeks of conventioneering. Though Davis had a rare talent for swaying juries to accept his point of view, he could not persuade either of his first two choices to accept the second slot. As the first ballot's roll call concluded, Berry actually had a 263½ to 238 lead over his closest challenger. In those days, the Democrats had a rule requiring two-thirds of the delegates to back a candidate before his nomination would be secured, leaving Berry still 480 away. It was only at the end of the roll call that delegates learned that Davis had agreed in one of those proverbial smoke-filled rooms to run with Nebraska Governor Charles Bryan. Then, hordes of delegation chairmen from all but a handful of states rushed to microphones to announce that they were switching their votes from favorite sons to the governor, the brother of three-time Democratic presidential nominee William Jennings Bryan. Berry, alone among the initial entrants, continued to fight. Bryan, however, had scant difficulty winning the needed two-thirds. He got a slot on a ticket that ran two to one behind Republican Calvin Coolidge.

Now, our northwestern neighbors in Missouri are a bit blunter than we in Tennessee. Harry S. Truman, a Missouri native and one of our nation's most forthright men, once declared that "No man can get rich in politics unless he's a crook. It cannot be done." One can only admire President Truman's candor. What George Berry clearly began in the 1920s was a pattern of abusing his position as a union president for not always benevolent purposes. He apparently acquired a 30,000 acre cattle ranch, a quarry, and the *Rogersville Review* honestly. However, Elizabeth Faulkner Baker, a scholar hardly unsympathetic to the union, has concluded that he "undoubtedly . . . used Union funds too freely."

The evidence of impropriety is indeed clear. Berry created a pension fund for the Pressmen, but in 1921 he used $165,000 from that fund to buy a hydroelectric generator in his own name that would provide cheap power for Pressmen's Home. A court ordered him to reimburse the Pressmen, but the Pressmen forgave this debt, a habit that group never lost. They reimbursed him for a $5,000 loan he made to the soon-defunct *Nashville Times*. In 1927, he got the union to put up $700,000 to finance the creation of the International Playing Card and Label Company, a firm that specialized in printing five-color cigarette packages. Though ostensibly he aimed to give union printers an opportunity to compete with nonunion firms, he eventually left the company to his wife in his will. A Canadian hunting lodge that the union bought for $24,000, Elizabeth Baker tells us, was resold for $24,000, "which . . . President Berry pocketed." He used union funds to buy stock in three banks. Shares that came to pay 20 percent dividends were issued in his name. One of the banks he eventually came to manage and he served on the board of directors of the other two.

George Berry, clearly, could not have survived the scrutiny of today's media, but in his time, many of his transgressions went unnoticed. By the 1930s, the only hint of scandal that had reached any newspaper involved a bid by Berry and a syndicate to which he belonged to claim $5 million from TVA for marble deposits they said lay under land they had owned that had been inundated when TVA created Norris Lake. Unfortunately for Berry, it was found that the deposits were worthless, and there was no award. This earned him the nickname of "George Marble Berry" from Memphis Boss Ed Crump.

Democrats generally overlooked George Berry's financial shenanigans, as he seemed to be delivering the Pressmen's votes. Irving Bernstein, a leading historian of American workers, has found that Berry and Teamsters' Union President Dan Tobin were the only "consequential" union heads who were working hard to elect Franklin D. Roosevelt in 1932. Berry was disappointed when FDR tapped Tobin to head the Democratic Labor Committee, and he and Tobin were both annoyed when Roosevelt opted for Frances Perkins to be his Secretary of Labor. Even so, Berry dutifully attended a conference Perkins convened soon after Roosevelt's inauguration and he suggested that the federal government should provide money to the states to help the unemployed. This was the President's intention all along.

For his seeming compliance, FDR honored Berry with a series of positions as a voice for labor within the administration. In the early stages of the New Deal, Berry served on the Cotton Textile Board, the Allotment Board, the Social Security Board, and the National Labor Board. In 1935, Roosevelt named Berry as his Coordinator of Industrial Cooperation to oversee the Council for Industrial Progress, which he had formed after the Supreme Court had severely limited the powers of the National Recovery Administration to seek some form of cooperation between labor and management. In none of these positions was Berry's role of much consequence. Specialists in the New Deal era tend to echo the judgment of the eminent historian Alan Brinkley that Berry was a "flamboyant self-promoter." Berry did excel as a fund-raiser. With Sidney Hillman of the Congress of Industrial Organizations (CIO) and John L. Lewis of the United Mine Workers (UMW), he formed the Non-Partisan League for the alleged nonpartisan purpose of assisting in Roosevelt's reelection. Some believed that the troika intended to build a labor party along the lines of the European Social Democratic parties of Europe, but neither Berry nor anyone else was ever able to keep the sturdily independent and unpredictable Lewis on speaking terms with the others. What they did succeed in doing was uniting union members behind the Roosevelt-Garner ticket and providing $770,000 to his war chest, feats for which FDR was suitably grateful.

The course of the New Deal did not run smoothly. Several reforms of Roosevelt's "bold experiment" were ruled unconstitutional after the "First 100 Days" ended in May 1933. In the wake of the continuing depression, leftists wanted the program to be expanded considerably, but Roosevelt concluded after his mammoth reelection victory in 1936 (over Howard Baker's second father-in-law, Governor Alf Landon of Kansas) that only one threat remained—the Supreme Court. Aiming to ensure that New Deal programs survived, he introduced a plan to expand the Court's membership to fifteen, a move that was known as his "court-packing" plan. It was a highly controversial proposal that prompted considerable opposition, even from Democrats. Roosevelt needed every last congressional vote, and the death of Senator Nathan Bachman in April 1937 afforded him a chance to pick up one more from Tennessee. He convinced Governor Gordon Browning to choose someone who might be amenable to the court-packing scheme. Browning opted for Berry, and Berry immediately appointed F. L. Browning, the governor's brother, as his administrative assistant. Evidence that the Berry choice might not have been the wisest one for FDR or Browning came no later than July 22, the day the Senate voted on the court-packing plan. George Berry was one of six Senators to be absent.

George Berry was one of Tennessee's least effective Senators. He never spoke on the floor, and no significant legislation bears any trace of him. Unlike most other southern Democrats of the time, he allied with the isolationist Senators of the Midwest in opposition to the foreign policy wishes of Roosevelt and Secretary of State Cordell Hull, his fellow Tennessee Democrat. What seemed to dominate his tenure were feuds over patronage with senior colleague Kenneth McKellar. These were petty fights that no junior colleague could win with the crusty and venerable McKellar, and it was folly, not principle, that drove Berry to undertake them. Roosevelt had long before cast his patronage lot in Tennessee with McKellar, a New Deal loyalist, and he was not about to jeopardize an established relationship to appease someone such as Berry who had proven on several occasions to be less than supportive.

It was hardly surprising that Senator McKellar and ally Ed Crump would set out to find a challenger to Berry for 1938. McKellar readily agreed to Crump's choice of his friend Tom Stewart, who had vowed to vote the New Deal line. Berry stood little chance of being elected to a full term. He retained the support of the Pressmen, but Crump controlled the unions in Memphis and FDR had his loyalists among them, too. Virtually all Berry could do was to berate Stewart's allies for soliciting contributions from the employees of New Deal agencies in the state and liken the New Deal to "state socialism." Here were hardly compelling reasons to give Berry another six years in the Senate, and he went down to an overwhelming defeat.

The last years of George Berry's life were less than happy. By 1940, he was supporting Republican Wendell Willkie for president, citing his opposition to a third term for FDR or any other president. Inquiries into his financial activities intensified and he did not contest his conviction in early 1948 on a charge of income tax evasion. True to form, he convinced the union to pay the outstanding bill and his $10,000 fine. Even his death from a gastric hemorrhage on December 4, 1948, did not deter further investigations into his finances. Instead of bequeathing his printing firm to the Pressmen as he had promised, he willed it to his wife and a Mrs. Alva Berry of Mooresburg, variously described as a cousin, a niece, and a friend. Pressmen began writing Senators such as Wayne Morse of Oregon, then a Republican, requesting further inquiries. Almost all wrote anonymously or asked for the strictest confidence, fearing that their employment might be terminated or that their locals might be dechartered. Only in 1952 was a settlement finalized. Instead of the largest share of what had been a $750,000 estate, Berry's wife received a pittance of a pension, and the government and the Pressmen split the rest.

Finally, justice of some sort had been achieved. It would take a Shakespeare to explain appropriately the contradictions in George Berry's character. How could a man so gregarious and compassionate toward orphans, widows, and victims of tuberculosis squander so much money? Perhaps it is fortunate that Sinclair Lewis was too enmeshed in his native Midwest and its flaws to find time to scar the good name of Tennessee with a portrait of George Babbitt's seeming working-class soul mate George L. Berry.

Chapter 6

A. Thomas "Tom" Stewart

1939–1949

Scopes Trial Prosecutor

(1892–1972)

Tennessee has long been blessed with more than its share of honest and able small-town lawyers, not a few of whom have reached national prominence. Howard Baker likes to boast about one of his mentors, Ray Jenkins, "the terror of Tellico Plains," who he found "could hold his own with the best of them" while serving as chief counsel in 1954 to the committee investigating Joseph McCarthy's scurrilous allegations of Communist infiltration of the army. More recently, Baker (of Huntsville) and Fred Thompson (who grew up in Lawrenceburg) were thrust into the national spotlight during the Watergate investigation. That both were frequently described as presidential timber thereafter is no small indication of the dignity and capability they showed in the summer of 1973. But no other Tennessee lawyer ever found himself so deluged by uninvited scrutiny as did A. T. "Tom" Stewart of Winchester during the Scopes trial of 1925. The media, as Senator Stewart's sons Tom and Fricks suggest, made "a monkey out of a trial." Still, their father emerged with his local reputation enhanced, something that could not be said of his co-counsel in that case, three-time presidential nominee William Jennings Bryan.

Tom Stewart first saw the light of a Middle Tennessee day on January 11, 1892, in Dunlap. He was born to Thomas L. and Mary Fricks Stewart, sturdy Scotch-Irish Methodists who formed part of the gentry of this small valley hamlet. Young Tom took after his father, who served for many years as Trustee of Sequatchie County and capped his career with a thirty-year stint as Chancellor of the Twelfth Chancery District, a fifteen-county jurisdiction so vast that some journeys within it had to be made by train. A broad-shoul-dered but lanky lad, Tom Stewart was quite a sportsman who spent much of his youth hunting birds, riding Tennessee walking horses, and playing base-ball. As an adult, he was one of those rare ambidextrous souls who could challenge people to a tennis match and beat most either right- or left-handed.

Presbyterians would argue that Tom Stewart was predestined to be a lawyer. He followed much the same career path as his father, attending the public schools of rural Tennessee until age seventeen, when he enrolled in Pryor Institute, a Methodist junior college in Jasper. He moved on to the Uni-versity of Tennessee, but had to withdraw when he came down with malaria. He taught in the public schools of Marion County, then finished his under-graduate studies at Emory University in Atlanta. Having read law under the tutelage of a series of mentors, he completed his legal education at the Cum-berland University School of Law in Lebanon, Tennessee.

As a young attorney, Stewart married the former Helen Turner of Jasper. Theirs was a happy marriage and one that produced several distinguished progeny. Tom, Jr., his oldest of three sons, was an able attorney who served for a while as his administrative assistant. L. Fricks, his third son, followed in the footsteps of his grandfather as chancellor, a post his own son Jeffrey holds today. Another grandson, Mark Stewart, won the 1996 Democratic nod for the Fourth District seat in the U.S. House; still another, Shelby Coffey, was editor of the *U.S. News and World Report* for a while in the 1980s and until recently served as editor of the *Los Angeles Times.*

Stewart began his legal career in 1913, in Birmingham, Alabama, but it wasn't two years before he returned to Jasper. By 1917, he had taken a po-sition as assistant to Ben McKenzie, the attorney general for the Eighteenth District. Two years later, Stewart moved to Winchester. Upon McKenzie's res-ignation in 1923, Governor Austin Peay appointed Stewart to the vacancy, knowing him to be a shrewd attorney who insisted on the truth. One tool he mastered was that of turning with his eyes glaring, then repeating the ques-tion if he thought a witness was being less than candid. The frequency with which witnesses provided different replies the second time Stewart asked a question led McKenzie to warn him jokingly that he would one day "get a confession out of someone who's innocent." Stewart was never one to gloat. An unpretentious man, he almost always introduced himself by his name, not his title. Only once did he violate that rule, says his son Fricks, an occasion when he picked up a hitchhiker, who promptly pulled a bottle of wine out of his knapsack and offered his driver a swig. Stewart notified his passenger that Prohibition was still in effect and that it would be his duty to enforce that law unless the wine were recorked.

Although Stewart served four terms as district attorney general, he is remembered almost exclusively for the 1925 trial of John Scopes, although hardly to the degree of the two major protagonists—Clarence Darrow, the ever-rumpled but razor-sharp champion of civil liberties and modern science, and William Jennings Bryan, the aging, rotund symbol of agrarian economics and virtues. Were one to read the court record the same way one reads a box score to judge a pitcher's performance, the winning attorney would be Stewart. However, historical memory of this trial is rooted in its depiction in the play and movie *Inherit the Wind,* dramatizations that celebrate Darrow's humanism but take many liberties with the record that do not reflect accurately or charitably on the other participants in the case.

Little of what transpired in Dayton in July 1925 was of Tom Stewart's initiation. George Rappleyea, a transplanted New Yorker who worked as a mining engineer in the district, noticed an ad placed by the American Civil Liberties Union (ACLU) stating that it would like to challenge the recently enacted Butler Act, the state law that banned the teaching of evolution in any public school. A free-thinking Methodist, Rappleyea relished arguing the wisdom of the matter with virtually anyone. One frequent sparring partner was a man named Sue K. Hicks, an attorney and a close friend of Stewart's. Rappleyea could not convince Hicks that the law was foolish, but the two did agree that a test case would do wonders for the local economy. Rappleyea went to John Scopes, a teacher and football coach at Dayton High, and suggested that he had broken the Butler law. Scopes taught physics, and ordinarily had no opportunity to present Darwin's ideas, but then one day he filled in for an absent biology teacher. The text was Hunter's *Civic Biology,* a state-prescribed tome, and Scopes taught from its chapter on evolution. Once he was arrested, as he knew he would be, Dayton got the attention Rappleyea and Hicks wanted, the ACLU got a case, and satirists such as H. L. Mencken got a mine of material they could use to continue trashing the South as the "Sahara of the Bozarts."

Stewart saw the case as a simple misdemeanor and wanted to dispense with it quickly, but both the ACLU and fundamentalists intended to make it a showcase trial. Stewart convinced local elders not to build a new auditorium and thereby encourage crowds. Unfortunately for him, both sides found outside help. William Jennings Bryan declared his willingness to represent opponents of evolution everywhere as part of the prosecution team if he were so invited. Indeed, for several years he had shown his determination to challenge the evolutionist view, even traveling to Nashville in 1924 to give a speech entitled, "Is the Bible True?" Sue Hicks, by then assisting Stewart, welcomed Bryan, thinking his stature would add luster to the trial. It certainly raised the stakes, but it hardly reaped rewards for the prosecution. Bryan's talents were in politics, not in law; he had not tried a case in thirty years. His presence led Scopes's allies to move to bolster his defense. The first lawyer Scopes retained was John R. Neal, a brilliant but eccentric and unshaven law professor now better known for his twenty-seven unsuccessful bids for statewide office. The ACLU then honored its commitment to the defense by financing the services of a 1920s dream team composed of Clarence Darrow, Arthur Garfield Hays, Dudley Field Malone, and former Secretary of State Bainbridge Colby.

Stewart was awed by his counterparts, but not overly so. An instinctive student of people, he knew that local juries were likely to be biased against such outsiders. Even better, he was sufficiently experienced to sense how and when to exploit those prejudices. He took the carnival-like atmosphere that descended on Dayton with humility. He dined and joked with Darrow, Scopes, and their colleagues. Ben McKenzie, his predecessor, even warned him that he was getting "too cozy with their scientists." Yet Stewart never lost sight of his objective, that of convincing the jury that Scopes had violated the law. Scopes himself described Stewart in his memoirs as a "conscientious and studious" attorney and a shrewd courtroom strategist. Had Stewart succeeded in limiting testimony to the facts of the case, the trial would probably be long forgotten. However, he was blocked every step of the way, not just by Darrow, but especially counterproductively by William Jennings Bryan.

Darrow and his associates framed their defense around the premise that the Butler Act violated both the Tennessee Constitution and the due process clause of the Fourteenth Amendment to the U.S. Constitution. Stewart fought back, doing what he could to reinforce the commitment of the jury to what he perceived to be their way of life. He successfully objected to the admission of scientific evidence from all but one defense witness. He insisted that each session begin with a prayer and chided Darrow as the "agnostic counsel for the defense." Darrow was prepared, however. Aiming to demonstrate to this rural Protestant jury that the Bible and Darwin could be reconciled, he had four theologians ready to question whether Genesis really was undermined by the theory of evolution. When Judge John T. Raulston denied a defense motion to let them testify, Darrow and Hays unleashed a trap. Their next witness, Hays told a stunned court, would be a self-professed Bible scholar named William Jennings Bryan, an old friend Darrow knew to be a rarely outperformed orator but, more importantly to him, a trusting and reflexive defender of the literal view of the Good Book rather than an independent student of its teachings and its history.

The battle-royal between Darrow and Bryan occurred on Monday, July 20, not in the courtroom, but in the open air under the trees in front of the Rhea County Courthouse. The weight of the gallery watching the trial in the second-floor courtroom had so stressed the floor that plaster had begun falling from the first-floor ceiling below. Judge Raulston decided, therefore, to move the proceedings outside. The move also enabled the flood of spectators to witness history in the making. According to press reports, the throng laughed, applauded, and thoroughly enjoyed the experience.

Stewart objected vociferously almost as soon as Bryan took the stand, but the proceedings had passed from his control. Gone was his strategy of restricting the case to the facts. Now the Butler Act was on trial, not the defendant. Darrow's questioning was probing. Among other issues, he grilled Bryan about Jonah and the whale, Joshua's trumpet, Adam's rib, and Cain's wife. Bryan, often thrusting his fist into the air, offered mostly a stale, evasive defense of the calculations of Bishop Ussher, a seventeenth-century British clergyman who placed the date of Creation at 23 October 4004 B.C. Both Darrow and Bryan played to the crowds, but even the most ardent literalist had to admit that Darrow got the best of it after he got Bryan to concede that the six days of Creation may have lasted longer than 144 hours. Stewart objected repeatedly throughout the two-way harangue. He very nearly nol-prossed the proceedings, ending the trial. Only Judge Raulston's order adjourning the session for the day brought the spectacle to an end. Even then, Bryan wanted to continue his testimony when court reopened.

During the adjournment, Stewart regained control of the prosecution. Bryan wanted to put Darrow on the stand as a hostile rebuttal witness, but Stewart would not have it. He told Bryan in a heated tone that neither Bryan's continued testimony, nor his interrogation of Darrow would serve their case. Bryan relented, but only grudgingly. When the trial recommenced on the next day, Tuesday, order was momentarily reestablished. Judge Raulston ordered the Darrow-Bryan exchange expunged from the record, but then Darrow followed by asking the jury to find Scopes guilty. Knowing that Bryan wanted to sum up and had prepared a peroration he deemed superior to his "Cross of Gold" speech that had lit up the Democratic convention a generation earlier, Stewart saw a way to prevent the statement and took it. "What Mr. Darrow wanted to say," Stewart told the jury briefly, "was that he wanted you to find his client guilty but did not want to be in the position of pleading guilty because it would destroy his rights in the appellate court."

Stewart got his conviction, but lost on appeal to the Tennessee Supreme Court in 1927 on a technicality; the jury had not stipulated a financial award, which, as Stewart had tried to point out to Judge Raulston, was a requirement in any Tennessee case imposing a fine of $50 or more.

In the court of American public opinion, the real loser was Bryan, who had staked his reputation on the outcome and came out looking like a shopworn fanatic, no longer the champion of rural America. Such a feeling was not so prevalent in Tennessee, and Stewart gladly accompanied Bryan to a series of events in the four days following the verdict. Everywhere, the once-husky and now-obese Bryan displayed an appetite worthy of a National Football League training table. In the July Tennessee heat, such a course was dangerous. For Bryan it proved to be fatal. The former Secretary of State died in his sleep of "apoplexy" five days after the trial ended.

Reviewing *Inherit the Wind* for a moment, admittedly both the play and the movie had dramatic punch, but to achieve that power the authors had to play fast and loose with the facts. One cannot help, for example, being struck by the depiction of Bryan's death in the course of a rather pompous address begun right after the judge adjourned the court. In that memorable but fictional scene, Daytonites filed out of the courtroom, oblivious to Bryan's words. In reality, few rural Tennessee Protestants would ever show a man of Bryan's stature any discourtesy, much less embarrass him. Indeed, the opposite was true. During the first week of the trial, for example, one of the jurors went to Bryan's lodging with a bouquet of homegrown flowers to honor the three-time presidential nominee. Stewart, meanwhile, who is nearly absent from the play and movie, actually won a reputation for great compassion and legal knowledge for his role. W. B. Ragsdale, one of the reporters on the scene in 1925, wrote his remembrances of his "three weeks in Dayton" in the 1970s. He called Stewart "studious, conscientious, [and] well schooled in state legal procedures." He added that Stewart was "the real ball carrier for the prosecution," who had "worked hard to keep the trial moving and in the end [had] sought to save Bryan from his fatal mistake."

Stewart first ventured into the political arena in the 1910s and remained there for the next four decades. He was a most fervent Democrat. In later years, when like-minded Democrats kidded him about his continuing attachment to a party that was increasingly urban-dominated and liberal, he almost always chided them that he would rather be a "yellow dog" than a "stray dog" Democrat. In the early days as a Wilsonian, Stewart supported laws restricting child labor and granting suffrage to women.

Stewart contented himself with working at the local level until 1936, when he ventured into statewide politics by managing the gubernatorial campaign of Burgin Dossett. Although Dossett was trounced by Gordon Browning, the effort gave Stewart a chance to cement ties with an old friend, Kenneth McKellar, who guessed that Browning might try to unseat him. It was always McKellar's practice to try to keep geographical balance in Tennessee's senatorial delegation by finding candidates for the other seat from the Middle or East. Once Stewart announced in 1938, it was easy for McKellar to follow his ally, boss Ed Crump of Memphis, and throw his influence behind Stewart and against the man Crump called "George Marble Berry." Their support, coupled with a strong showing in the counties where he had served as attorney general, gave Stewart an overwhelming victory in the Democratic primary, which at the time was tantamount to victory in the general election.

Tom Stewart was a quiet but generally effective Senator. He was faithful to Franklin D. Roosevelt's ideas as the domestic phase of the New Deal waned and preparations for World War II began. He backed the repeal of the Neutrality Acts in 1939, the draft in 1940, and Lend-Lease and the arming of American merchant ships in 1941, all the while warning that Hitler was "bent on world conquest." In the eyes of the Washington press, Stewart was even more deferential to an aging Kenneth McKellar than he was to the President. Humble to the core, Stewart accepted this assessment, always maintaining that it was McKellar's support that had gotten him to the Senate. More than twenty years his senior in age and Senate service, "Old Mack" had long before snapped up most of the choicest committee assignments open to Tennessee. Stewart was content to focus his legislative attention on measures to help the Tennesseans he knew best, those in areas the size of his own Winchester—or smaller.

Although he rose to the chairmanships of both a special panel in 1940 investigating the wiretapping of several Rhode Island Democratic politicians and the Interoceanic Canals Committee, Stewart spent most of his time working on measures before the Agriculture and Interstate Commerce Committees. Throughout his ten years in the Senate, he pushed for additional funding for soil conservation and rural electrification programs. Noting that 42 percent of the roads in rural America were "still mud," he backed a vastly expanded federal highway program, particularly targeted toward helping farmers get their crops to market. Another Tennessean, Albert Gore, Sr., would eventually see to the enactment of the bill creating the interstate highway system in 1956, but it was Tom Stewart, after having seen the efficiency of the German Autobahn, who introduced the first such bill ten years earlier.

The issue Stewart pushed most ardently throughout his tenure was that of ending the freight-rate differential, a condition he thought had served to keep the South an effective colony of the North since Reconstruction. In 1939, he told a national radio audience that the cost for Southerners to ship commodities was nearly one-third higher than it was for Northerners. Actually, the rates were nearly equivalent on raw materials, but discriminated against small or new manufacturers who could not secure "exception" rates generally accorded bulk cargo. Stewart declared that these inequities limited prospects for industrial growth in a region Franklin D. Roosevelt had recently characterized as the "Nation's Number One Economic Problem."

"Place all sections on an equal basis and end territorial discriminations," Stewart said. "That is the American way." Not until 1947 would the Interstate Commerce Commission order the institution of uniform rates for all shippers throughout America. Thanks to the steady insistence of Tom Stewart, Texas Congressman Wright Patman, and a host of southern governors, all producers now had equal access on our railroads to all American markets.

As a good Wilsonian, Stewart identified with rural small-businessmen. During World War II, he chaired a subcommittee that heard grievances from these entrepreneurs. Instinctively, he distrusted the "$1-a-year men" who headed many wartime agencies, thinking their expenses were higher than those of most salaried federal employees and that they might steer contracts back to their own businesses. For the long-range future of Tennessee, he was especially fearful that the temporary substitution of rayon for cotton might eventually put thousands of textile workers out of work. Stewart also advanced the cause of public education in Tennessee. Some southern newspaper editors likened the idea of federal aid to education to the Blair Bill of the 1880s that would have apportioned funds equitably among white and black schools, but Stewart discounted such arguments in 1943. He noted that the average pay for all Tennessee public schoolteachers was a mere $16.58 per week and that such funds were sorely needed.

If history is unkind to Senator Stewart, it will stem from his approach to immigration. Throughout the 1940s, he favored severe restrictions on newcomers. In 1941, he introduced a bill to bar aliens from working in defense industries, noting reports of Nazi "Fifth Columns" which were trying to gain influence in Latin America. Later, he was quick to add his name to American Legion-drafted legislation that outlawed any new entrants in times when unemployment surpassed one million. He defended these views by insisting that they were necessary for the war effort or to protect American working people. What is not so easy to excuse is Stewart's position toward the Nisei, those native-born Americans of Japanese descent who were confined in camps in the West during World War II. Here, Stewart's position was intractable.

In early 1942, Stewart introduced the infamous bill calling for the internment of all Japanese-Americans. He justified the bill, declaring that Japanese law mandated that anyone whose father was Japanese was a subject of the Emperor. He noted that many of the Nisei lived near oil reserves or naval bases. A "Jap is a Jap everywhere," he alleged, and the Nisei's "dual citizenship" meant that every one was a "potential spy and enemy." Perhaps in the aftermath of Pearl Harbor, it was understandable that a man of that era would lambaste the "slant-eyed devils" who had reiterated their peaceful intentions to his friend Cordell Hull at the very moment their bombers were finishing their first run over Oahu. He was not alone. Military leaders and FBI Director J. Edgar Hoover tended to discount any possibility of sabotage by Japanese-Americans, but liberal Californians, such as Senator Hiram Johnson and state Attorney General Earl Warren (both Republicans) and Democratic Congressman Jerry Voorhis, all urged that the Nisei, along with the Japanese-born Issei, be evacuated and placed in camps. Franklin D. Roosevelt heeded their wishes and ordered the internment, producing the one dark stain on America's noble record during World War II. Democracy itself, the historian Page Smith wrote later, was "on trial."

In fact, the Nisei of Hawaii formed the 442nd Infantry Combat Team in Europe, one of the most decorated units in American history. Over 4,500 Japanese-Americans volunteered for the initial formation of the unit, with over 14,000 passing through its ranks in a single year. A little-known fact is that it was the artillery battalion of the 442nd that, on the way to meet General Patton, stumbled on and freed those interred at the Dachau concentration camp. How do I know this? One of their finest, an authentic American hero named Dan Inouye, sits across the aisle from me in the Senate, never bemoaning the kidney and right arm he lost in Italy while fighting for our freedom.

Stewart was not an inveterate racist, but a representative of his times. He was quick to insist that war internment be directed only against Americans of Japanese descent and would not stoop to the level of Mississippi Democratic Congressman John Rankin, who vitriolically likened World War II to a "race war." In 1942, Stewart applauded boxer Joe Louis for the gift of his purse from a heavyweight title defense to the Naval Relief Fund. On several occasions, he heralded the "colored people of the South" for their absolute loyalty to the war effort. He was active in efforts to save Meharry Medical School in Nashville, one of the two black southern medical schools, and he based his support for federal aid to education on his belief that both black and white southern schools needed additional funding. Still, Stewart was preeminently a man of the Old South, always maintaining that his land was making progress in solving its racial problems and resisting all federal efforts to accelerate that progress.

On foreign questions, Stewart was a Cold Warrior who believed that America was too generous to other countries with its resources, and he vigorously opposed President Truman's 1946 plan to extend a multimillion dollar loan to Britain. Still, if Stewart could see a valid use for such money, particularly if it were to be used to contain communism, he would support the programs. In 1947, he supported the Marshall Plan, which provided economic aid to Western Europe, and the Truman Doctrine, which led to $400 million in economic and foreign aid to Greece. On the question of aid to Turkey, he berated Armenian-Americans on the floor of the Senate for opposing that program, saying they had put their ancient Old World animosities ahead of the

U.S. national interest of limiting the expansion of the Soviet terror that was beginning to engulf Eastern Europe.

Despite what we may think today, Stewart's politics were not far out of step with those of his Tennessee constituents. What ultimately doomed him in his home state, however, was his support for Kenneth McKellar's bids to require Senate confirmation of all high-level TVA employees and to force TVA to get its funds from congressional appropriations rather than from the revenues it derived from its own customers. McKellar introduced the measures so he might rein in TVA Chairman David Lilienthal, who he thought had been less than candid with him about TVA projects in Tennessee. While alienating the well-placed Lilienthal, the maneuver was more significant in Tennessee politics because it caused Ed Crump to move to reassert his control over the state. Stewart sided with McKellar, a position made easier for him in 1942 when Lilienthal warned several groups "against the opening of a second front in the battle to make this region the spoils of a narrow and old-fashioned kind of politics." To him, these were none-too-thinly disguised attacks on McKellar. Yet it was Stewart, not McKellar, who faced the voters in 1942 and he read Lilienthal's remarks as subtle appeals to TVA employees to vote for Edward Ward "Ned" Carmack, Jr., his opponent, a feeling strengthened when Lilienthal allies at the *Chattanooga Times* and the *Nashville Tennessean* started referring to him as "Senator Me Too." That year, Stewart's margin in the primary was substantially reduced from 1938. Carmack actually carried fifty-seven of Tennessee's ninety-five counties. Only a huge majority in Memphis allowed Stewart to carry the state.

Stewart squeaked by in 1942, but he would not survive the growing rift with Ed Crump. Crump was furious because Stewart did not take Crump's advice on West Point appointments and had an editorial about world peace by *Memphis Press-Scimitar* editor Edward Meeman, one of Crump's sternest critics, reprinted in the *Congressional Record*. Meanwhile, Will Gerber, a Jewish confidant of Ed Crump, had long considered Stewart's nativistic positions a sign of latent anti-Semitism, and he told the Boss as much. The allegation seems ludicrous; indeed, Stewart was one of the first members of Congress to hail General Dwight D. Eisenhower in April 1945 for his request for a congressional delegation to travel to Germany to inspect the mass carnage left behind by the Holocaust. Nevertheless, Crump listened to Gerber's ill-founded complaints.

The final split came in 1948. Crump's increasingly rigid commitment to the old segregationist order had become an ever more dominant determinant of his behavior. It even led him to back the third-party Dixiecrat presidential ticket rather than incumbent Harry Truman. Stewart, meanwhile, remained loyal to the national Democratic Party and to his close friend, President Truman, even as he described Truman's civil rights program as "the worst insult to the South since the Civil War." With Kenneth McKellar, at seventy-nine, too weak to try to deter Crump, it could hardly have come as a surprise to Stewart that the Memphis boss would recruit Judge John Mitchell of Cookeville, a segregationist with the added qualification of having been a veteran of both world wars, to challenge him for the seat.

Neither Stewart nor Crump benefited from the rivalry. Stewart had provided effective constituent service throughout his tenure and so retained the support of most of Crump's usual allies in East Tennessee and in the press. Meanwhile, it seems that Mitchell's backing was solely among the state's veterans and in Shelby County and the environs of his native Cookeville. That Crump would drop the incumbent led a few who had long loathed the Boss's organization to reconsider and switch to Stewart, but the feud made the idea of a third candidate attractive.

Estes Kefauver walked through the opening created by Crump's split with Stewart. The principal anti-Crump organ was the *Nashville Tennessean* and its editor Silliman Evans, Sr., had pledged in early 1947 to back then-Congressman Kefauver if he would shake five hundred hands a day. Kefauver, although hardly a stirring orator, had an unmatched one-on-one appeal and he quickly surpassed Mitchell in the polls. On seeing the effect of his feud with Stewart, Crump panicked and tried to get Mitchell to drop out. He then let it be known that he might reconsider and back Stewart. Kefauver caught wind of this and publicized it, prompting Crump to reiterate his support of Mitchell to preserve his credibility. Fricks Stewart, meanwhile, tried to get his father to accept Kefauver's challenge to debate, knowing he was far superior to Kefauver at public speaking. Stewart declined at the behest of his managers, thinking that a debate might enhance Kefauver's stature, win or lose. This may have been a fatal decision, but many tides were running against Tom Stewart in 1948. East Tennessee Republicans who had crossed over to vote for him in 1938 and 1942 had hot congressional primaries in both the First and Second Districts and their defection allowed Kefauver to carry all of East Tennessee. Stewart's support for the Taft-Hartley Act had antagonized the American Federation of Labor (AFL), a group that found a friend in Kefauver. The ultimate blunder was Crump's dividing the state party organization. His hold over Shelby County, particularly its increasingly vocal black community, had weakened substantially at a time when he needed every advantage. The number of votes Mitchell polled was more than double Kefauver's 41,918 vote victory over Stewart. Whether all of Mitchell's votes would have gone to Stewart can only be conjectured. How many of Stewart's votes would have gone to Kefauver in such a circumstance is equally debatable. What is not open to question, however, is that Kefauver won with only 42 percent of the vote and his success stemmed in no small part from disarray in Crumpdom with the main victim being Tom Stewart.

Stewart took his defeat in stride. His ego was one of those rare ones in politics that led him to be grateful to Crump and McKellar for affording him the opportunity to run in the first place. He returned to Nashville and opened a general practice of law. He specialized in civil cases and handled the accounts of Tennessee Gas, Colonial Gas, and other large firms. He never got rich, but, as son Fricks Stewart recalls, Tom Stewart always found a way to help out someone who was down on his or her luck. He resisted overtures to challenge Kefauver in 1954, thinking "the people of Tennessee had made up their minds" on him in 1948. Still a stalwart Democrat, he lent his support from time to time to Democrats of agrarian origins and moderate-to-conservative politics whose convictions matched his own, particularly men like Frank Clement and Prentice Cooper who had supported him. Stewart's wife Helen died in 1965. He died on October 10, 1972, of a heart attack as he was working in his office.

Long before, Tom Stewart had recognized that his day in the political sun had passed. He was first and foremost a servant of the small farmer in a society that was becoming increasingly urbanized. He was a paternalistic man of the Old South at a time when Tennesseans were beginning to reexamine how our laws affected our African-American citizens. He was a workhorse attorney and a quiet, friendly, and generous person who was comfortable allowing others to hog the limelight. The role of Senator may not have been a terribly natural choice for a man of Stewart's temperament, but it was one this boy of Winchester, Tennessee, via Jasper and Dunlap, handled with grace and dignity. May small town virtues never die and may there always be a place in our system of government for conscientious, humble men like Tom Stewart.

Chapter 7

C. Estes Kefauver

1949–1963

*Voice Against
Organized Crime*

*Democratic
Vice Presidential Nominee*

(1903–1963)

That long tall guy Nashville singer Hank Fort warbled about in 1952 in "The Long, Tall Guy in the Coonskin Cap" was Estes Kefauver, the man journalist David Halberstam calls "the first political star of television." Kefauver won that characterization in his 1950 investigation of the role of organized crime in our society. His probe attracted so much attention in New York City that Consolidated Edison had to build an extra generator to service the customers who bought televisions to watch the hearings. Kefauver's probe exposed close relationships between leaders of organized crime and several big-city Democratic machines. The attention gave Kefauver viability as a presidential candidate, but it also created enough resentment among urban party bosses that it guaranteed that he would never be nominated. Kefauver expected to arouse the wrath of the bosses, but he insisted that those who acted in ways that he believed were harmful to the public must account for their mistakes. His reforming odyssey was that of one schooled in the Progressive ideology of Woodrow Wilson and Louis Brandeis. As a physician, I can appreciate that mindset. Indeed, the last of Kefauver's probes resulted in considerably stronger scrutiny of the safety of prescription drugs and limits on the ability of drug manufacturers to fix their prices, long overdue reforms vital to the public health and absolutely essential to the economic security of older Americans.

Carey Estes Kefauver seemed destined to live a political life. He was born on July 26, 1903, in the lower East Tennessee town of Madisonville, the second of four children of Robert Cooke Kefauver and the former Phredonia Bradford Estes. Cooke Kefauver was a public-spirited citizen who made his living first as the owner of a hardware and farm equipment store, then as a realtor and the manager of the Kefauver Hotel. His avocation, however, was politics. He served five terms as the Democratic mayor of that Republican town. Politics actually ran on both sides of Estes Kefauver's ancestry. Phredonia's first cousin was Missouri Governor Joseph Folk, a Democrat who had earned a reputation for rooting out graft in his days as district attorney for St. Louis. By the time he turned thirteen, young Estes was accompanying his father as he stumped Monroe County for Woodrow Wilson. A quiet, studious boy, he took the opportunity to listen to the speeches and political discussions of "Cousin Joe" and his father. Through their influence, he adopted a philosophy akin to that of Wilson's and clung to it throughout his life. Kefauver would always champion both the concept of collective security as a means of guaranteeing world peace and the cause of the small entrepreneur and the consumer any time he believed overly large aggregations of private wealth posed a threat to their interests or safety.

According to Charles Fontenay, a gifted biographer who was close to Kefauver, the death of Kefauver's older brother Robert was his most formative early experience. In the summer of 1914, Estes and Robert were swimming in the Tellico River with friends when Robert suddenly went under. Estes had already swum to the other bank and by the time he made it back across the river, his friends had pulled his brother, unconscious, from the waters. Estes and his friends tried desperately to revive Robert and rolled him on a barrel to get the water out of his stomach, but Robert did not regain consciousness until some time after they got him home. Robert seemed to have made it through the ordeal but then lapsed into a coma after supper and died in convulsions some days later on August 9. Estes was very much affected by the tragedy and, being a very good swimmer, may have even blamed himself for not staying closer to his brother that day. Robert was only two years older than Estes, but it was Robert, more than Estes, whom the elder Kefauvers had counted on to make a name for himself, and Estes determined to make his parents' dreams for Robert come true in his own life. Estes resolved in his early teens to become a lawyer and then set out meticulously to broaden his knowledge of matters that might be helpful in his craft. By the time he was in high school, Kefauver had begun to read voraciously in history and to scan the works in the extensive law library his mother had acquired from the estate of his late grandfather, Albert Carey Estes, who had been a prominent attorney in Brownsville, Tennessee.

Kefauver left Madisonville for the University of Tennessee in 1920. To a sophisticate, he must have seemed a naive rustic; for he carried little more than a straw suitcase and wore on his six-foot three-inch gangly frame a suit that seemed to change colors. Although he felt out of place at first, he soon excelled in a variety of fields. He served as editor-in-chief of the student newspaper, was president of his junior class, and won admission to several honor societies. By the end of his four years, he had already begun to take classes at UT's law school. Even so, his special forte was sports. Although he had been a star center on his high school basketball team, at UT he turned his attention to track and football. Over his four years, he added fifty pounds of muscle and became the school record holder in the discus and a starting guard in football, a sport he had never played before.

Kefauver's aim upon graduation was to continue at UT in the law school, but he felt compelled to take a break when his mother's rheumatism worsened. He went with her and his sisters to Hot Springs, Arkansas, and took a job as a high school math teacher and football coach. He stayed only a year, for the law was his true calling. In 1925, he left for Yale Law School and met his bills with the help of a scholarship, a loan, odd jobs, and poker winnings. He earned his L.L.B. *cum laude* in a class that included future Senator Brien McMahon, future Supreme Court Justice William O. Douglas, and future Attorney General Herbert Brownell. Unlike many of his colleagues, "Keef," as fellow Yalies called him, had no intention of joining a prominent New York law firm. His practice would be in Tennessee, a fact he signaled when he passed the Tennessee bar exam in 1926, a year before his graduation from Yale.

Kefauver went to work in Chattanooga in the firm of his cousin, Judge W. B. Swaney. He started slowly, supplementing his income by teaching night classes at the Chattanooga College of Law and a local vocational school. In his first year he earned only $800, but he developed a sizable and loyal group of clients in Chattanooga's black community, whose divorce and other civil cases he handled at rock-bottom fees. Kefauver spent much of his time doing legal research and published three articles in the *University of Tennessee Law Review* during the 1920s. One of the pieces so impressed a former Chattanooga mayor that he offered him a position in his own firm, which handled more lucrative cases. Kefauver accepted the promotion and began to prosper for the first time in his career. He joined several clubs, including the Jaycees and the Rotary. Then in 1935, he became chairman of the Hamilton County Planning Board; he spent the bulk of his time in that role lobbying for the construction of the Chickamauga Dam. This was where he first gained an intimate knowledge of the workings of TVA, one that would serve him and Tennessee well for the rest of his life.

Kefauver participated actively in Chattanooga's social life. He played squash and a lot of golf, although his partners were quick to note that he tended to slice on his drives. His strong, gracious personality made him a hit with women as well. It has become common in recent years for scholars to allude to his frequently roving eye, but Kefauver met his one true love in 1934. She was Nancy Paterson Pigott, a bright, red-haired Scotswoman who had graduated second in her class from the Glasgow School of Art. That summer Nancy and her sister Eleanor were visiting an aunt in Chattanooga when Kefauver was asked at the last minute if he would be Eleanor's blind date. Kefauver accepted reluctantly, but as the night progressed, he found himself drawn ever more toward Nancy. Before her visit was over, the two were engaged.

Estes and Nancy Kefauver were married in Scotland in August 1935. They honeymooned near Loch Ness, then returned to Chattanooga, where Kefauver resumed his law practice. Eventually, they had three daughters, Eleanor (who answered only to "Lynda"), Diane, and Gail, and adopted a son, David.

Kefauver entered the political arena for the first time in 1938 as a reform-minded candidate for the state senate. Like the Progressives of the early twentieth century, Kefauver wanted to make government more efficient and responsive to the average citizen. His main talking point was that a state constitutional convention should be called to consider reforms to open up the political process. He wanted to add an amendment allowing citizens to change their local governments through referenda. He also suggested changes that would allow for a state income tax to make the tax burden more equitable and would eliminate the poll tax, thus ending the disenfranchisement of the poor. These planks won him the support of the unions. His thoughtful demeanor and presentation won him the backing of Chattanooga's two major dailies, the *Times* and the *News*. Unfortunately for Kefauver, he was running against an entrenched machine. Indeed, many believed he made a good showing when he lost by a mere 307 votes. There were credible allegations of fraud and supporters urged Kefauver to contest the election, but he declined, thinking that the experience of running was itself invaluable. Kefauver's restraint proved prudent, for it limited any resistance to his appointment as Governor Prentice Cooper's commissioner of finance and taxation. Kefauver's stay in Nashville was short, however. The death of Congressman Sam McReynolds opened up his seat just a few months later and Kefauver was determined to fill it. This time, Kefauver had the support of virtually all Democrats and he won the general election by a margin of almost three-to-one.

Because he was elected in the middle of the session, Kefauver found himself stuck on four insignificant committees when he arrived in Washington in September 1939. With little to do, save attend sessions on the floor, he sought out men he had long admired and got their advice. From Speaker William

Bankhead, he learned to see that constituents got prompt, earnest, and personally signed replies to their inquiries. Cordell Hull echoed Bankhead and also suggested that Kefauver confine himself to mastering one issue. Given the state's interest in trade and commerce, it is not surprising that Kefauver used his maiden speech to urge that members extend Reciprocal Trade Agreements, a major achievement of Hull's. The paramount issue for Kefauver throughout his career was the problem of business monopolies and its effect on the common man. Early on, he struck up a relationship with Senator George W. Norris, the Nebraska maverick known to Tennesseans as the father of TVA and to a generation of Americans as a determined foe of the vested interests. Corporate lobbyists in time would find Kefauver so well versed in the doctrine of competition that they joked, "In Kefauver We Antitrust."

Kefauver's voting record in the House reflected his association with Franklin D. Roosevelt and the *Nashville Tennessean*-led opposition to the Crump organization. He proved a staunch ally of FDR on virtually all questions related to the war effort, declaring that the people wanted "action." His position was clear by January of 1941, when he took the floor to declare a need to shore up Great Britain and other foes of nazism with Lend-Lease assistance. He was as quick to hail GOP titular head Wendell Willkie for standing behind the President as he was to berate the President's isolationist critics for trying to limit his power in this time of emergency. After Germany invaded the Soviet Union in June, he urged that aid also be extended to the Soviets.

"We in this country have no use for Communism," he tried to reassure the House; "We can deal with the communistic challenge by our democratic processes." The real enemy, he insisted, was nazism and it was incumbent upon America to do whatever it took to stop Hitler. On domestic issues, he enlisted with Albert Gore, Sr., and the editors of the *Tennessean* in a twenty-year fight to eliminate the poll tax, a voting restriction that he believed struck "at the heart of democracy." "If the so-called qualifications become unreasonable," he declared in 1942, "the federal government has an abundance of power to remedy the situation."

Like all the other members of Tennessee's delegation, Kefauver took a deep interest in TVA. He counted TVA Chairman David Lilienthal as a friend and he even accompanied Lilienthal to hearings to testify against Kenneth McKellar's plans to curb TVA's independence. McKellar had proposed moving TVA's headquarters from Knoxville to Washington, requiring confirmation of all employees earning more than $4,500 a year, and returning TVA surpluses to the Treasury rather than using them for operations. Kefauver could not dissuade the Senate from siding with McKellar, but he was part of a Tennessee Valley bloc that stood tall each year between 1942 and 1944 to thwart Tennessee's senior Senator. In doing so, he made an implacable enemy in McKellar, a man to whom FDR had long since ceded effective control over Tennessee patronage. Kefauver could hardly have relished the wrath of such a powerful foe, but it took courage for him to fight in the interests of his constituents in full knowledge of the likely consequences.

Kefauver also took a keen interest in the processes of our democracy. As a Wilsonian, Kefauver was ever mindful of the tactics opponents had used to defeat the Versailles Treaty in 1919–20. He, therefore, sponsored a constitutional amendment in 1945 that the House approved, 288–88, that would have revised the treaty-making process to allow ratification by simple majorities of both chambers. The fact that few Senators would willingly surrender a long-held constitutionally mandated prerogative made it an unrealistic proposal, but it indicated the depth of Kefauver's devotion to ideas that he believed would make our government more responsive to national, rather than local, interests. Like Wilson, Kefauver found much to admire in the British parliamentary system, especially its requirement that Cabinet members submit themselves to questioning by the legislature. But he was every bit as quick to suggest less encompassing reforms that he thought would smooth the functioning of the wheels of our government. In 1947, he joined Dr. Jack Levin in publishing *A Twentieth-Century Congress,* a thoughtful tome that contained well-argued briefs on limiting the number of committees, installing an electronic voting system, easing the process of ending filibusters, and establishing a closer liaison between the Congress and the President.

Kefauver had long thought of moving up to the Senate. "Congressmen are a dime a dozen," he once said. In 1942 and 1946, he resisted seeking a berth as the anti-Crump organization candidate, thinking such a fight unwinnable for someone largely unknown outside of his own district. He estimated correctly; Edward W. "Ned" Carmack, Jr., ultimately wound up making the futile attempts to unseat Tom Stewart and then Kenneth McKellar. In light of the Crump machine's growing coolness toward Stewart, however, Kefauver guessed that 1948 might offer a better opportunity. Labor had distanced itself from Crump because of his support for right-to-work laws. Blacks had done the same for a variety of reasons. Kefauver, therefore, gained confidence that he might successfully challenge Stewart. His senatorial aspirations got another boost in the middle of 1947 when Silliman Evans, Sr., the editor of the *Nashville Tennessean,* pledged his support if Kefauver would shake five hundred hands a day until the election.

Kefauver possessed one of the more distinctive styles of campaigning in American history. He was too soft in tone and calm in manner to be much of a stump speaker, but he seemed to transfix his audiences with his command of complex issues and his slow, easy smile. Howard Baker likes to compare Kefauver's oratory to that of Senator John Sherman Cooper, the respected moderate Republican from Kentucky. Like Cooper's, Kefauver's sincerity was transparent and, according to Baker, "there was something to the quality of both of those speeches that made you want to help them out." Kefauver's greatest success came in areas where personal contacts were most important. The warmth of his handshake and the graciousness in his demeanor convinced people that they and their problems were the only things on his mind. His energy was boundless, and his ability to remember previous meetings with voters was legendary, although somewhat overstated. At one gathering, he worked the crowd and saw the son of an old acquaintance. "How's your dad?" he inquired. "He's dead," the young man responded. Kefauver expressed his regrets, then made another round and encountered the young man again. "How's your dad?" he asked. Kefauver had to be startled when the young man responded that he was "still dead."

Kefauver announced his Senate candidacy a full year before the election. He pledged that he would run a positive campaign that stressed the importance of world peace and TVA. There was little separating him from Tom Stewart on global issues, as both aligned behind Truman's program of Soviet containment, but, unlike Stewart, Kefauver had steadfastly opposed McKellar's efforts to curb TVA. Kefauver recognized that most of the political bile that would be directed at him would come not from Stewart, but from Memphis boss Ed Crump, who had abandoned Stewart in favor of Judge John A. Mitchell. Kefauver benefited from the fact that more conservative Democrats were split. He knew that the conservatives, particularly Crump, would try to define him as a leftist. Anticipating this, he declared there to be "a few who define 'Communist' as 'anyone who opposes their candidates'—in other words, anyone who opposes government by political dictation."

Kefauver was prepared for the onslaught that generally met anyone who challenged the Crump organization. For a while, he heeded the suggestion of *Memphis Press-Scimitar* Editor Edward Meeman, who advised him against baiting the "Old Red Snapper." But Meeman also counseled Kefauver to "fight back" if Crump, as was his pattern, struck first. The inevitable blast came on June 10, when Crump bought ads in every major Tennessee daily headed, "ESTES KEFAUVER ASSUMES THE ROLE OF A PET COON." Kefauver, wrote Crump, had been "a darling of the Communists and Communist sympathizers" throughout his stay in Congress, as shown by his criticism of the filibuster, his vote against continuing the House Un-American Activities Committee and his support of the Fair Employment Practices Commission (FEPC). In truth, Kefauver, like his two opponents, was critical of President Truman's civil rights program, especially the FEPC, and he would never embrace anything resembling a civil rights bill until after the 1954 *Brown* decision. His staff scanned Crump's record and got Kefauver to declare at most stops that Crump had branded each of his forty-five previous opponents "a Communist, a Fascist, a blackguard or a thief." It was Crump's "dictatorship," he would add, that "was as dark as Stalin's. The only thing red about me is my redheaded wife."

Kefauver fashioned the response that would become his trademark. "You wouldn't find a coon in Russia," he told a crowd on June 14. "It is one of the cleanest of all animals; it is one of the most courageous. . . . Mr. Crump defames me—but worse, . . . he defames the All American animal. We coons can take care of ourselves."

"I may be a pet coon," he admitted, "but I ain't Mr. Crump's pet coon." Kefauver took to displaying a caged raccoon, but carrying the coon sometimes proved troublesome. Then, a supporter sent Kefauver the coonskin hat that lifted him out of obscurity. At the Peabody Hotel in Memphis, he reached in a bag, pulled out the hat, and put it on, and it was a rare appearance after that when Kefauver did not don the cap. In fact, the cap sealed Kefauver's image as a frontier fighter in the Tennessee tradition, a posture vivified when his opponents declined to debate him. Had Crump stuck with Stewart, he very well might have prevailed again. Unfortunately for Crump, Kefauver developed a strong personal organization of his own, one which featured the first separate women's division in Tennessee history. With just 42 percent of the vote, Kefauver easily surmounted a divided opposition. While able Republicans nowadays can count on picking up some dissident Democrats, that was hardly possible in 1948. Even with such a strong GOP candidate as longtime First District Congressman B. Carroll Reece carrying the GOP standard, Kefauver prevailed by a two-to-one margin, picking up even Ed Crump's support.

Having embarrassed an entrenched machine, Kefauver entered the Senate in January 1949 with the reputation of a nonconformist, a tag he did nothing to discourage. He would never be part of what then was called the Senate's "inner club," largely because of the sniping of Kenneth McKellar, who privately derided him as "Cow-fever" and suggested that his crime investigation amounted to little more than his being "out chasing crap-shooters." Kefauver did try to work with McKellar, but angered him irreversibly when he objected to the senior Senator's recommendation of a Strom Thurmond Dixiecrat rather than a Harry Truman Democrat for another term as U.S. Marshal. We can only speculate on whether Kefauver would have wanted acceptance into McKellar's sanctum, but as an economic progressive and a supporter of home rule for the District of Columbia he found himself fairly isolated among Southern Democrats. A likely ally might have been fellow freshman Lyndon Johnson, but Johnson never got over Kefauver's support of federal control of tidelands oil, a position that was anathema to the oil industry that dominated Johnson's Texas.

Kefauver assumed seats on the Armed Services and the Interstate and Foreign Commerce Committees in 1949. Later in the year, he took a seat on the Judiciary Committee where he resumed work on an anti-monopoly bill that he had introduced in the House in 1945. The bill proposed to close a loophole that enabled companies to skirt the Clayton Antitrust Act by buying the assets of smaller companies rather than their stock. It was a loophole Wilson-era reformers had not foreseen and one that Kefauver knew big firms had used to drive smaller competitors out of business. It was 1950 before the Kefauver-Celler bill became law, but it remains one of the last pieces of legislation to limit monopoly in any way.

By his second year in the chamber, Kefauver was engrossed in his role as chairman of a Special Committee on Crime that will forever ingrain his memory in the American consciousness. The subject had interested Kefauver since his 1945 chairmanship of a House panel that investigated charges of malfeasance against a Pennsylvania judge. Early in 1950, he drafted a resolution calling for a much larger inquiry, but Democratic leaders feared such an investigation. They knew that Republicans aimed to use the probe to examine ties between criminals and several Democratic machines, particularly those in President Truman's native Missouri. But when two Democratic officials who reputedly had links with crime bosses were murdered in April, the leadership had no choice but to allow the probe to continue. Vice President Alben Barkley, the former Senate Democratic Majority Leader, appointed three Democrats and two Republicans to the Special Committee. At the initial meeting on May 11, they elected Kefauver as chairman.

It was always Kefauver's belief that gambling was the cornerstone of organized crime and he concentrated his inquiry on cities, most of which were dominated by Democrats at the time. He had little patience with Democrats who warned that their party might be hurt. In his view, a reinvigorating effect was likely to follow for a party that moved to clean up scandals within its midst. He took his probe to fourteen cities in 1950 and interviewed more than eight hundred witnesses. To be sure, his inquiry more often than not merely rehashed material long known to local authorities and the FBI. The role of special committees is often one of public enlightenment more than discovery of new material, and Kefauver succeeded remarkably in bringing knowledge of the pervasiveness of the problem to the people.

As many Democrats had feared, Kefauver learned of numerous nefarious activities by officials linked with his party. In Miami, the panel found that a sheriff appointed by Governor Fuller Warren had been bribed to raid only those gaming houses not affiliated with the mob of the late Al Capone, and to stop even those raids once those houses made a Capone associate a partner. When Warren reinstated that sheriff without an investigation, he became a target for ridicule and blamed Kefauver, calling him an "ambition-crazed Caesar." Findings in Miami and other cities dictated that Kefauver would have to take his inquiry to Chicago, Capone's home, but he planned to delay these hearings until after the election. That plan became untenable with the September slaying of a committee informant and his lawyer, both of whom had been gathering evidence against Dan Gilbert, a police captain and the

Democratic nominee for sheriff of Cook County. On November 1, Gilbert confessed that he had been extraordinarily lax in his enforcement of gambling laws. Unbeknownst to Kefauver, a reporter posing as a committee employee got a transcript of Gilbert's testimony and saw to its publication right before the election. Few were surprised when Gilbert was trounced, but many voters vented their anger at him on the entire Democratic ticket. One victim of the backlash was Senate Majority Leader Scott Lucas, who lost to Everett Dirksen by 290,000 votes. Not even Kefauver's move to prosecute the reporter could placate Lucas, who refused even to meet with him and stood at the head of the opposition to Kefauver throughout the 1950s.

Committee hearings continued through the spring of 1951. Proceedings in New York produced the best-remembered image of the hearings, that of the hands of Frank Costello, the reputed king of the New York mob. Kefauver and his panel had deferred to Costello's request that his face not be shown, both to protect his rights and to keep from giving him an excuse to walk out. As a witness, Costello proved evasive and his arrogance in ducking questions about his activities fueled public outrage. Even so, the committee did elicit some evidence from Costello tying him to many important New York politicos. One was former Mayor William O'Dwyer, who returned from Mexico, where he was serving as our ambassador, to answer questions about his failure to prosecute several top mob figures. O'Dwyer also admitted that he had accepted campaign contributions from Costello and in return had named several of Costello's friends to key city jobs. What he did not foresee was a committee finding that he had been inattentive as mayor to many kinds of racketeering.

The Kefauver Committee succeeded in the short run only in awakening the public to the extent of the operations of organized crime. Senate turf struggles consigned the panel's legislative recommendations, including Kefauver's proposed Federal Crime Commission, to temporary oblivion. In time, however, more than seventy cities independently set up crime commissions and the Treasury Department established a rackets unit to investigate income tax fraud. For Kefauver, the hearings provided a window for the public to observe his calm, judicious temperament. He had made some powerful enemies, but by the end of 1951, he placed second behind Harry Truman when Democrats declared their choice for the next president.

Kefauver had indeed caught the presidential fever. Neither he nor anyone else could be certain whether Truman would seek another term, but he did know that his appeal lay among the grass roots of his party and not its leadership. If he were to win, he had to take his case to the people and not concern himself with Truman's intentions. He announced his candidacy on January 23, then practically moved to New Hampshire for the next six weeks to campaign in the Democratic primary there. The Granite State was one of the few states small enough to allow the bespectacled Kefauver to use the meet-and-greet style of campaigning that he had employed so successfully in Tennessee. Truman, in contrast, stayed away, sending Scott Lucas as a replacement. New Hampshire is known for its surprises and Kefauver tallied a full 55 percent and all of its delegates.

Kefauver's win in New Hampshire made him the front-runner. His status bothered Truman, who had thought him insufficiently protective of Democrats during the Crime Committee hearings. Unable to fathom the source of Kefauver's homespun appeal, the President took the results realistically as a measure of his own unpopularity and announced his retirement. The lateness of his withdrawal effectively denied Democrats loyal to him the opportunity to wage effective campaigns. Kefauver went on to win in Nebraska, Illinois, Maryland, Pennsylvania, New Jersey, Massachusetts, California, Ohio, South Dakota, and Wisconsin. Only in the District of Columbia, which rallied behind Averell Harriman, and in Florida, where a coalition led by the ever-vengeful Fuller Warren rallied behind Richard Russell, the respected Georgia conservative, did Kefauver lose.

Had today's rules been in place, Estes Kefauver would have been the Democratic nominee, but not so in 1952. Although he amassed nearly 2.8 million votes more than his nearest challenger, his victories had come in what political analysts call beauty contests, those primaries in which delegates are not bound by the preferences of the people. Tennesseans proved loyal to Kefauver, but most other Southerners were hostile, thinking a Yankee liberal preferable to a Southerner who was moderate on racial issues. Although they knew that Russell would never win the nomination, the southern bloc stuck with the Georgian. Party insiders loyal to Harry Truman, meanwhile, continued to search for an alternative. They hoped that they had found one in Illinois Governor Adlai Stevenson, Truman's first choice.

With the factions aligning against him, Kefauver looked for a way to shore up his support, but the price was too high. Governor Gordon Browning suggested that Kefauver might win Texas and a southern bandwagon might follow if he could sway Texas Governor Allan Shivers. Tempted, Kefauver sought out Shivers and learned that he could reap Texas's fifty-two-vote bounty if he would promise to allow states to own the oil in their tidelands. Here was an issue that had long defined Kefauver, and he flatly and conscientiously declined. Then Kefauver made a critical blunder. He went along with a resolution forwarded by northern liberals to require southern delegates to swear allegiance to their national party. He had been told that most southern delegates had assented to the resolution, but in fact they had not agreed. Forces loyal to Stevenson, who as yet had not agreed to run, used Kefauver's vote to sway southern support. Accordingly, at the convention, Kefauver led on the first two ballots, reaching on the second ballot an apex of 362 and a half of the 616 needed. Only then did Stevenson let it be known that he would accept the nod. Delegates committed to liberal Averell Harriman and a few not-so-loyal Kefauverites scrambled to Stevenson, leaving the Midwesterner two and a half votes short of the nomination. Only then would Speaker Sam Rayburn, a determined Kefauver foe, recognize Kefauver to concede. In fact, it was Kefauver's Utah delegates who put Stevenson over, a stroke of irony matched only by the convention's macabre rendition of "Happy Birthday" to Kefauver as he and Nancy left the arena.

After the convention, Kefauver proved a model of sportsmanship. He not only campaigned hard for Stevenson, but he also developed a personal friendship. He returned thousands of his own supporters to the Democratic fold, but it was not enough. The Republican candidate, Dwight D. Eisenhower, was an extremely popular war hero, and the general, like Kefauver, represented change. Eisenhower's election to the White House meant to Kefauver a diminution of responsibility, for "Ike" brought with him to Washington just enough Republicans to take control of the Senate.

Kefauver's philosophical orientation remained constant. On foreign policy, he generally aligned with Eisenhower. He led the fight that defeated the Bricker Amendment, a measure that would have severely limited any president's role in foreign policy. On domestic questions, Kefauver remained a dyed-in-the-wool progressive. He spoke for more than six hours as part of a filibuster against Eisenhower's plan to return control of tidelands oil to the states.

Kefauver made it his special role to monitor the administration's treatment of TVA. More quickly than anyone else in the Tennessee Valley delegation, he responded whenever any opponent of public power spoke in tones that seemed to portend a threat to public control of TVA. At first his targets seemed to be obscure sub-Cabinet level appointees, but he was quick to follow Albert Gore's lead in opposing the half-billion-dollar Dixon-Yates proposal to allow two firms to sell their power to the Atomic Energy Commission and thereby end any need for additional TVA power in West Tennessee or Kentucky. Kefauver was fortunate that Antitrust and Monopoly Subcommittee Chairman William Langer, a North Dakota maverick, was an undaunted champion of public power who made his panel a forum for critics of the proposed deal. There was publicity but no action to stop the deal until November 1954, when Democrats voted to make opposition to the deal party policy. Kefauver continued his attack on Dixon-Yates for the first few months of 1955, always stressing the added costs and lack of competing bids. In June, he became chairman of a special committee looking into the contract. His inability to gain access to Budget Bureau files led him to take the floor on June 27 and charge the administration with trying to "hide the . . . facts." Apparently, Eisenhower began to see a potential embarrassment, for three days later he asked the Budget Bureau to reevaluate the plan. Dixon-Yates was dead, yet the Kefauver panel continued its hearings for another six months, effectively warning all in the administration of the folly of any further threats to TVA.

Kefauver was just as ardent in defending what he saw as elementary civil liberties. An early opponent of the smear tactics of Senator Joseph McCarthy, he was undeterred by McCarthy's vow to campaign against his reelection. He made plans well before McCarthy's abuses were discredited in the Army-McCarthy hearings to campaign against McCarthy in his native Wisconsin. "McCarthyism is bad for the country," he explained. "I reckon I'll have to say so." The same year, he was the only member of the Senate to oppose a bill put forward by Senator Hubert H. Humphrey of Minnesota, making membership in the Communist Party a crime. Attorney General Herbert Brownell and FBI Director J. Edgar Hoover also opposed the bill, contending that it would drive the Communist Party underground and render prosecutions more difficult. Kefauver agreed, but also saw the bill as likely to lump misguided idealists with a few active agents and thereby set a dangerous precedent for prosecuting people with unpopular beliefs.

As Kefauver suspected, the issue of Communists in government arose when he stood for reelection in 1954. His primary opponent was Congressman Pat Sutton, a conservative Democrat from Middle Tennessee. Although lightly regarded even by fellow conservatives, Sutton had a hefty bankroll provided by Texas oilman H. L. Hunt to buy what became known as talkathons to reach voters. Sutton often grew tired as he talked, which was sometimes for more than a day, and he became even more strident in his rhetoric, always quick to term Kefauver "soft on Communism." Kefauver responded by pointing out his down-the-line support for the Truman and Eisenhower containment policies. And he had another virtue. As Lyndon Johnson insisted later, Kefauver was "the greatest campaigner of them all" and his person-to-person approach still resonated throughout Tennessee. Sutton tried to counter with a helicopter tour of the state, a tactic that won him attention at first but embarrassment when Kefauver revealed that the chopper was owned in part by Frank Costello. If Tennesseans did not know what to make of Sutton, they knew they had an independent Senator of real stature who took care to attend to their concerns in Estes Kefauver. In a race that he feared would be close, Kefauver prevailed by nearly a quarter of a million votes, carrying all but four counties.

With his seat secure, Kefauver prepared another bid for the presidency. In truth, his prospects were probably weaker than they had been in 1952. Not only was President Eisenhower popular, but also many Democrats were convinced that Adlai Stevenson had earned another chance. Undeterred, Kefauver set out on a six-week tour of the world in late 1955 to add luster to his foreign policy credentials. When he returned, he announced his candidacy, literally throwing his coonskin hat into a ring four times. Again a decided underdog without the support of the bosses, he set out for New Hampshire for another round of grassroots campaigning and wound up defeating a weak write-in effort for Stevenson by an unheard-of margin of five-to-one. A week later, he took on Stevenson in Minnesota, where the Illinoisan had long ago sewn up the backing of the party hierarchy. Many close to Kefauver had advised him to duck the contest, but he plunged in, knowing that the race afforded him another chance to show off his "people against the bosses" appeal. He demanded higher agricultural price supports and confounded nearly everyone by capturing 57 percent of the vote.

Kefauver again was a contender, but he still lacked support among the party establishment, particularly in the South. Segregationists had long distrusted him, and their enmity grew after he refused to sign the Southern Manifesto. Many white Southerners actively supported Stevenson, even though his moderate approach to civil rights was not terribly dissimilar to Kefauver's. Prior to the Florida primary of May 29, Stevenson did his best to emulate Kefauver's personal brand of campaigning. He built a curious coalition that included both segregationists and urban blacks and managed to eke out a narrow victory. Kefauver maintained a pace every bit as furious as Stevenson's. His schedule drove him to near exhaustion. In California for the last primary, he went negative, blasting Stevenson for accepting the support of "old-guard politicians" and segregationists like the "Talmadges, the Ellenders and the Caldwells," referring to Georgia Senator Herman Talmadge, Louisiana Senator Allen Ellender, and former Florida Governor Millard Caldwell. Such attacks seemed out of character, even desperate. It is hard to gauge what would have been the effect of a more positive tone, as Stevenson's base in the state was strong, but many have since cited Kefauver's methods in California to explain his thorough 460,000 vote trouncing.

California was the end of Kefauver's line. While some of his backers encouraged him to cut a deal with New York Governor Averell Harriman that might block Stevenson's nomination and thus give him a chance to prevail at the national convention, Kefauver would have none of it. Gallup polls indicated a bandwagon building behind Stevenson, and Kefauver recognized that further campaigning would brand him as a spoiler. Two weeks before the national convention opened, he withdrew from the race and asked his delegates to vote for Stevenson. Their support virtually assured Stevenson the nomination and a grateful Stevenson began to consider favorably suggestions that he tap Kefauver as his running mate.

By the time the 1956 convention opened the only question remaining was who would get the party's nomination for Vice President. Stevenson opted to let the delegates decide. This gave Kefauver an advantage, for he alone retained a large following of delegates who had backed him for president and he had picked up the votes of some Stevenson backers who appreciated the graciousness of his departure. He was strongest west of the Mississippi River, but had pockets of strength in the Midwest, whose delegates United Auto Workers head Walter Reuther was lobbying assiduously on his behalf. He had virtually no southern support, where delegates were backing Albert Gore, a man they deemed less liberal. Only New Hampshire backed him in New England; that region's other delegates stood firmly behind Senator John F. Kennedy.

On the first ballot, Kefauver tallied 483½ of the 687 votes needed to win, a full 179 ahead of Kennedy. By the second ballot, the contest had shaped up as one pitting Kefauver against Kennedy. When New York City Mayor Robert Wagner withdrew from contention, his supporters in New Jersey and New York switched to Kennedy. Texas had supported Gore on the first ballot, but Lyndon Johnson and Sam Rayburn aimed to stop Kefauver and they saw this as the opportune time to move their state's fifty-six votes to Kennedy. Similar bolts from four smaller southern states put Kennedy just thirty-nine votes from victory. Kefauverites led by *Tennessean* publisher Silliman Evans, Jr., cornered Gore and warned him that they would see to his defeat in 1958 unless he withdrew immediately and threw his support to Kefauver. Gore stoically went to Governor Frank Clement, a staunch Kefauver rival, and told him that he would have to leave the race and enforce a delegation rule requiring members to support any Tennessean who stood a chance of being nominated. In other delegations, Kefauverites who knew of Rayburn's aim to block Kefauver rushed the podium yelling "Tennessee Is Going for Kennedy." Pro-Kennedy officials alerted Rayburn, and he recognized Gore. Gore withdrew, then yielded to Clement to switch Tennessee's votes to Kefauver. Hubert Humphrey sent his sixty-seven delegates Kefauver's way soon thereafter, swinging the pendulum toward Kefauver and allowing switchers from Oklahoma and California to put Kefauver over the top.

Kefauver's GOP counterpart was Richard Nixon and he used his acceptance speech to revivify a general Democratic image of Nixon as the man who provided "the smear under the protection of the president's smile." Actually, the two had no personal animus. The Nixons and Kefauvers were neighbors whose daughters and cocker spaniels played together. There were sharp political differences, however, and Kefauver stressed these when he took to the hustings. Kefauver proved particularly effective in the farm belt, where he advanced plans to improve the lot of the family farmer by creating full parity and a food stamp program. He was less successful elsewhere. Perhaps he, more than Stevenson, a self-styled highbrow, was constituted to employ class-laden rhetoric. But such appeals usually fall flat in times of prosperity, and the 1950s were prosperous indeed. In fact, Stevenson fared worse in 1956 than he had four years earlier in all parts of the country save the farm states where Kefauver had concentrated his campaigning. The distribution of the vote was not lost on the party faithful. Polls in 1957 showed that Kefauver led the Democratic field of presidential contenders with 29 percent, a full six points ahead of John F. Kennedy.

Kefauver's standing in the Senate was never as strong as it was in the country as a whole. Unlike Lyndon Johnson, he had never taken the time to cultivate southern elders. Many were hostile to him, a reaction that stemmed more from Kefauver's aloofness than from his ideology. On civil rights, his record scarcely differed from Johnson's. Both supported the Civil Rights Acts of 1957 and 1960. Both also voted more often than not with the southern bloc for legislative amendments that Republicans and northern Democrats deemed dilatory. Kefauver, in fact, got the Senate to approve one such appendage in 1957 that allowed those charged with criminal contempt in violating federal court injunctions the benefit of a jury trial. It was fortuitous for him that in the midst of this debate a Knoxville jury rendered guilty verdicts against John Kasper, a man Kefauver termed a "Yankee agitator," and six local defendants for their role in obstructing school integration in Clinton, Tennessee. This lent credence to arguments that southern jurors would punish lawbreakers in their midst, although white Southerners outside of Tennessee, sadly, rarely acted so responsibly. Northern arguments that most other southern states had no such requirements came to naught as the Senate sided with Kefauver, 51–42. Had the Senate acted differently, Lyndon Johnson had the votes to delay the bill indefinitely. This disturbed Kefauver little, for he saw the participation of white Southerners as essential if desegregation were to work. In the end, his move ensured the bill's final passage, though the bill conferred too little power on enforcement authorities to allow much relief to those deprived of their rights.

Defenders of a segregated South took Kefauver's actions less as a sign of moderation than as one of betrayal. In 1960, for Kefauver's second reelection campaign, they induced Andrew "Tip" Taylor, a jurist with statewide contacts, to stand against Kefauver as the champion of their way of life. Taylor was relentless, scoring Kefauver at every turn for his support of both civil rights acts; he even accepted endorsements from John Kasper, the Ku Klux Klan, and the White Citizens' Council. Kefauver was too wise to the ways of the Old South to portray either vote as one for integration. He cast the issue as one of defending the right to vote and asked crowds to speak up if they disagreed. Few volunteered. While continuing his people-oriented campaign, he was no longer the lone wolf he had once seemed. His presidential aspirations gone, he had mended fences with Lyndon Johnson, even supporting Johnson for president in 1960. While Johnson won the vice presidential nod rather than the top slot, he was glad to repay the favor. Identified much more than Kefauver as a man of the South, Johnson made plans to attend a Democratic rally in Nashville the Saturday before the primary. One can only imagine Tip Taylor's expression when he saw Johnson enter the Colemere Club and greet Kefauver with a Texas-sized bear hug. The display portended a movement toward Kefauver of moderate Democrats. A race billed as too close to call just two weeks earlier turned into an almost two-to-one rout of Taylor.

As he approached his third term, Kefauver had begun to win the plaudits of his colleagues for his attention to legislative details in a way never before possible. After 1957, he ceased campaigning for a place on the Foreign Relations Committee, a panel once believed to be a showcase for Senators with national ambitions. Probably as a consequence of his improved relations with Johnson, he was offered and accepted in 1959 a position on the internally more important Appropriations Committee. This was a perch that he could use to better advantage for the people of Tennessee; from it, he monitored funding for TVA and Oak Ridge and secured funding for the West Tennessee Drainage District, the Cordell Hull Dam on the Cumberland River, a bridge over the Fort Loudoun Dam, and the Gatlinburg bypass.

Kefauver's work on the Judiciary Committee gratified him most. From 1955 until his death in 1963, he chaired the Subcommittee on Constitutional Amendments. Under his leadership, that panel set in motion the processes that led to the Twenty-Third and Twenty-Fourth Amendments. Both measures were long overdue. The Twenty-Third Amendment granted residents of the District of Columbia the right to vote for president. The Twenty-Fourth outlawed the payment of a poll tax as a requirement for voting in federal elections. Kefauver was less successful in securing a revision of the electoral college, an anachronistic institution that he had been seeking to reform for years. In the early days of his Senate tenure, thinking Congress unlikely to eliminate that system altogether, he had joined Henry Cabot Lodge in crafting a proposal to divide the votes of the electors on a proportional basis. This way, he thought, the South would no longer be taken for granted by Democratic candidates for president or ignored by Republicans. However, Northern liberals saw any concessions to the South as likely to dilute their inherent advantage and opted to hold out for a direct election amendment that would probably never come to be. Later, with Everett Dirksen, Kefauver worked to craft a contingency plan to deal with the problem of potential presidential incapacity. In the wake of the stroke and two heart attacks suffered by President Eisenhower, both were willing to contemplate a variety of ideas in the event that any President was too incapacitated to serve. Kefauver and Dirksen developed a workable proposal by 1958, but Congress did not act until the assassination of John F. Kennedy left the vice presidency vacant. Only then was there a sense of urgency that would spur members to craft an amendment addressing the twin contingencies of presidential disability and succession. Although Kefauver died before the states ratified the remedy, he and Everett Dirksen should properly be hailed as the granddaddies of the Twenty-Fifth Amendment.

Still a Wilsonian, Kefauver immersed himself even more fully in the work of the Antitrust and Monopoly Subcommittee, a panel he chaired for the last six years of his life. "I am not opposed to profit-making," he liked to say, "but I am opposed to profit-gouging." Kefauver used the panel to probe possible monopolies in insurance, transportation, hearing aids, and food, but he kept his closest eye on the steel companies. He found in 1959 hearings that the largest firms maintained the same prices to the thousandth of a cent per pound. National Steel, one of the larger firms, was operating at only 80 percent of capacity, but still maintained the same price. To Kefauver, a wiser business strategy for National might have been to expand production and lower prices. He suspected price-fixing, the result of which was inflation; for so many firms depended on steel. In the long run, the probe served to acquaint the public with steel-pricing practices. In the short run, it gave Kefauver a rationale for proposing the creation of a Department of Consumer Affairs. The prospect of another probe gave John F. Kennedy a bargaining chip in 1962 to use to compel steel producers to roll back a recent price increase.

Kefauver's investigation of the prescription drug industry, his biographer Joseph Bruce Gorman has written, produced his "finest hour as a public servant." The inquiry started out in 1959 as just another exposé of price-fixing. Kefauver's staff soon learned that 90 percent of the prescription drugs sold in the United States were produced by just twenty firms and that those companies sold their products abroad at a mere 17 percent of their price here at home. His 1961 report accounted for the difference by blaming advertising that forced druggists to sell their products under brand names rather than generic ones and patents that gave the holder a seventeen-year monopoly on the product. Well before, Kefauver had introduced a bill limiting drug patents to three years and requiring that drug producers be licensed, display generic names, and demonstrate that their products were safe before selling them. Once Kefauver's panel reported his bill, longtime ally Emanuel Celler introduced it in the House. Contrary to normal practice, however, the Judiciary Committee returned the bill to the Patents Subcommittee, which eliminated its patent provisions. Even more confounding to Kefauver was a move by the Kennedy administration through Congressman Oren Harris of Arkansas to forward a bill devoid of any limit on prices. Not long thereafter, other Senators met with administration and drug industry representatives and watered down Kefauver's bill even further, stripping it of most safety provisions. Thinking he had been "shoddily treated" not even to have been invited to the meeting, Kefauver took the Senate floor to decry a "severe blow to the public interest." "Today they swung a haymaker," he declared, "and just about knocked this bill out of the ring." Although he stopped the drug industry bill, he could not mount enough pressure on Congress and the administration to reconsider until a month later. Then, his staff leaked accounts to the press of babies born without arms and legs to mothers in Europe who had used the insufficiently tested drug thalidomide as a treatment for morning sickness. The bill went back to the Judiciary Committee, where Kefauver reinstated all but the patent portions. In the eyes of an antimonopolist such as Kefauver, this was hardly an ideal solution, for it did not guarantee the kind of competition that would drastically reduce drug prices. Even so, he could take heart in the fact that it stiffened controls on manufacturers and druggists that served to protect the public's health. Although a final try to restore time limits for patents failed, 28–53, it had to be gratifying that the Senate approved the Kefauver-Harris Drug Act without dissent.

When one catalogues Kefauver's final year, one finds a striking reminder of the qualities that so ennobled his tenure in Congress. Fellow Chattanoogan Bill Brock remembers fondly that Kefauver, a friend of his father's, threw a party for him upon his election to Congress to introduce him to official Washington. A few months later, Kefauver defended Brock against allegations that he might join Barry Goldwater in selling TVA, reminding reporters that Brock's grandfather had been one of the architects of the Authority. Once Tennessee ratified the Twenty-Fourth Amendment, Kefauver took the floor to hail longtime Democratic arch-rival Frank Clement for his work in securing its approval. Yet always uppermost in his mind was the work of his subcommittee. Here, he worked uncommonly long hours probing, among other things, truth in packaging legislation, trafficking in black-market babies, and the insurance industry. Kefauver's aim, said GOP Leader Everett Dirksen, a friend and frequent debating foe, was always "to lift the hand of monopoly from little people, that they, too, might survive and prosper."

Shortly into his third term, Kefauver's prodigious energy began to flag due to high blood pressure exacerbated by many years of heavy smoking. In the spring of 1963, he was hospitalized twice, once for two weeks with the flu and then for another week with a pulled tendon. But he never let up. He was on the floor arguing for one of his amendments to a communications bill when he began to develop a stomach ache. He felt no relief when he got home. Aides called and got him to check into Bethesda Naval Hospital. His pains had actually come from a dissecting aneurysm of the wall of the aorta, a mild heart attack. From where she was vacationing in Colorado, Nancy tried to find the best doctor available. Before one could arrive, the wall of Kefauver's aorta burst and on August 10, 1963, he died in his sleep.

As a doctor, I can say that Estes Kefauver's death was hastened by a long history of overworking, smoking, and other behaviors harmful to his health.

As a citizen, I can say that we as a nation will die if we do not find people like Estes Kefauver with the zeal and energy to stand as tribunes of the welfare of the common man against criminal and corporate predators. As a conservative, I'm grateful that I had predecessors such as Everett Dirksen who could nudge Progressives like Kefauver away from concentrating resources and power too heavily in Washington. Our system thrives best when all sides are well-represented. Millions of Americans are better off because there was that long tall guy in the coonskin cap.

Chapter 8

Albert A. Gore, Sr.

1953–1971

Father of the Interstate Highway System

(1907–1998)

"The pace and direction a man sets for his life can tell you a lot about his inner spirit," a 1970 ad for Albert Gore began, "and the people of Tennessee have learned to gauge his measure by the battles he's fought for them along the way—for TVA, tax reform, Medicare, interstate highways, Social Security, and education." Albert Gore was unquestionably one of the ablest and most principled cogs in the southern New Deal tradition, one that left an enormous legacy to the people of Tennessee.

Albert Arnold Gore was born to Allen and Maggie Denney Gore on December 26, 1907, in Granville, a Jackson County hamlet. Allen and Maggie Gore both hailed from humble Middle Tennessee stock, and shortly after Albert's birth, the Gores moved to Possum Hollow in neighboring Smith County. Young Albert grew up like any other rural child of the time as he swam and fished in ponds or the nearby Caney Fork River and hunted raccoons and squirrels. He was adept enough as a pitcher to play some semi-pro baseball during the 1930s. He was even better at basketball, despite being only five feet eleven inches, and revelled in telling of how he outmaneuvered defenders with the "fake and go." Gore participated in many of the activities of the Missionary Baptist Church and always took the opportunity to observe visiting lawyers and preachers. His historical heroes were agrarian Democrats such as Thomas Jefferson and Andrew Jackson. Among living politicos, he most admired Congressman Cordell Hull and often took the opportunity to ride his mule by the Hull home in nearby Carthage, a comparatively large burg of nearly 2,000. Gore was a clean-living young man; even as an adult, he never drank more than an occasional beer. He has always described his independence as a by-product of his upbringing in the isolated confines of rural Smith County.

Gore graduated from Possum Hollow High School in 1925. Like all too many other rural Tennessee youths of his time, he did not have the financial means to start college right away, so he took a variety of jobs to support himself. He taught school for $75 a month, waited tables, fiddled at barn dances, pitched hay, milked cows, sold furniture, developed a tobacco crop that brought in all of $89 one year, and helped his father drive cattle to a corral to be shipped for slaughter. The tenor of the times is illuminated by the fact that the shipping bill cost Allen Gore more than the cattle brought in. Although the Gores lost all their savings when three local banks failed in 1929, they had fortunately already paid off their mortgage.

Gore had to pursue his collegiate career when he could. He never attended a fall semester of college, because he had to work and save during those months so he might have enough to pay for spring tuition. He started at the University of Tennessee, where his funds were so low that he mailed his dirty shirts home to a laundry because it was cheaper. Eventually, he graduated from Teachers' State College (now Middle Tennessee State University) and went on to study at the Nashville YMCA Law School.

In Nashville, he met Pauline LaFon, a bright, sensitive, and vivacious young woman from Palmersville in rural West Tennessee. A woman whom Howard Baker describes as a "treasure" and many others hail as the best politician among the Gores, Pauline was the second female student ever to be admitted to Vanderbilt Law School. Gore would come into the coffee shop at Nashville's Andrew Jackson Hotel where she worked three nights a week to pay her tuition because he needed enough coffee to keep him awake as he drove the fifty miles back to Carthage. They studied for the bar together and both passed with scores of eighty-eight. Pauline moved to Texarkana for a year to start a practice, but the two kept in touch. They were married in 1937. The union spanned more than sixty happy years and produced two accomplished children. The eldest was Nancy, born in 1938. Nancy Gore Hunger was a talented girl who liked to accompany her father on the piano while he practiced his fiddle. She went on to serve in the Peace Corps and manage her father's 1964 reelection campaign before dying at the all-too-young age of forty-six in 1984. Her brother was Al, Jr., who will, of course, be treated in another chapter.

Gore, Sr., had gotten his first taste of politics long before entering college. He was active in the Young Democrats and campaigned for the Democratic ticket before he was even old enough to vote. In 1932, while serving as principal of a rural Smith County school, he entered the race for superintendent of schools. On election night, he was ahead narrowly, but he had erred in not trying to reach those who voted absentee. Once those ballots were counted, Gore joked later, he had been "slaughtered." He had run a positive campaign, however, and impressed Superintendent Hofheinz, who, upon learning the next year that his cancer was terminal, spent parts of his last days phoning county court members and asking them to elect Gore to fill his unexpired term. They agreed, and Gore, at twenty-five, became one of Tennessee's youngest superintendents and the first in Smith County to buy buses.

In 1934, Gore managed the unsuccessful bid of then-Congressman Gordon Browning to replace Senator Nathan Bachman. A grateful Browning, upon being elected governor in 1936, reciprocated by appointing Gore his Commissioner of Labor. In this job, Gore administered state unemployment compensation. At the urging of Senator George Berry, he went through printers' apprentice training at Pressmen's Home. He also took it upon himself to investigate conditions in the mines, actually going into a few to inspect them.

Gore left state government in 1938 when he learned that Fourth District Congressman J. Ridley Mitchell would be seeking George Berry's Senate seat. He and Pauline borrowed $3,000 to pay for a campaign to vie for the Congressman's vacant seat and returned to his parents' farm. During their stay, Gore worked on his campaign skills. He took many walks, occasionally practicing his public speaking delivery by talking to trees or boulders. Friends gave him constructive criticism, telling him that he was too formal, and Gore heeded their advice. In Jamestown, when someone who had heard he could fiddle asked him to play a tune or two, Gore replied, "I'll play, if you'll vote for me." The fiddling caught on and soon won Gore a picture on the front page of the *Nashville Tennessean*. "Congress has done nothing but fiddle around," Gore would kid. "I'll do the same," he would add as he interspersed renditions of "Arkansas Traveller" or "Casey Jones" with homespun tales. Some credit his strumming with giving him a small edge in the five-man field. With no GOP opposition, Gore was on his way to Washington.

Curiously enough, Gore rarely brought his fiddle out in the future, as Pauline and some others thought it undignified. He did play privately with Roy Acuff and boast later that onlookers considered him the more accomplished musician. When producers of *The $64,000 Question* learned that he had once played, they offered him $1,000 to do a bit of "The Ballad of Davy Crockett." Gore declined, thereby upsetting Pauline, who saw the gig as an opportunity for the two to spend a night in New York and for Gore to buy her the mink coat she had always wanted. She contacted the producers herself, then informed Gore that they were going to make him a better offer. "If you don't accept it," she cautioned, "I'm going to leave you." Gore got $2,500, expenses, and a happy wife. Many close to Gore always seemed to regret that he left the fiddle at home in his later campaigns, for they were convinced that he had abandoned a tool that enabled him to bond with constituents.

Upon arriving in Washington, Gore paid a courtesy call to his hero Cordell Hull at the State Department. "Stay on the floor and learn the rules," Hull advised him. "They will come in handy some time." Gore took his counsel, but also put some of his own native wisdom to use. At the outset of the session, Gore asked a senior Congressman from New York to find a job for one of his constituents on the Capitol police force. His colleague, a fellow Democrat, replied that it would be impossible for him to accommodate any rookie legislator in that way. Gore told his fellow freshmen about the incident and was prepared when that member wanted Congress to provide $275,000 for the New York World's Fair. Gore drafted amendments steering $30,000 of that largesse to the Carthage Fair, Mule Day in Lebanon, and the Petersburg Colt Show. He then invited other junior members to do the same. They managed to clog up the schedule so badly that Majority Leader Sam Rayburn had to pull the matter from the floor. In the end, Gore got his man on the police force *and* a trip to the World's Fair.

In his early years in the House, Gore served on the Banking and Currency Committee and was fairly active for a freshman. Describing himself as a "critical New Dealer," Gore lived up to that designation when he gave his maiden speech opposing an administration plan for the U.S. Housing Agency to lend $800 million for new units with amortization to come only after sixty years, and later rallied a bipartisan coalition to defeat that proposal. On foreign policy questions, he supported the administration regularly in the dire days prior to World War II. "We cannot allow the character of unpreparedness which existed in 1917 [to recur]," he said in arguing for the repeal of the Neutrality Act. Gore voted to extend Lend-Lease aid to any opponent of the Nazis, even the Soviet Union, and relished in chiding left-wing New Yorker Vito Marcantonio about his opposition to any defense expenditures. In November 1941, as war seemed imminent, Gore actually went far beyond the administration in preparedness, calling for price controls on all commodities. Franklin D. Roosevelt counseled Gore that his plan was not necessarily unwise, but it was certainly premature.

It is perhaps most accurate to characterize Gore in the early years of his congressional career as one of "Mr. Sam's boys." Sam Rayburn, the future Speaker who spent many of his formative years in Rockwood, Tennessee, took a liking to Gore and got him a seat on the powerful Appropriations Committee in 1943. In Tennessee, meanwhile, Gore's ties to Gordon Browning sealed his identification early on as a stalwart in the anti-Crump (the powerful Memphis boss, Ed Crump) wing of the Democratic Party. Gore's was a faction spawned in the soil of rural Tennessee and championed by the *Tennessean*, one that was impressed when Gore won battles during the 1940s to maintain farm price support systems that seemed to be working. Furthermore, it was Gore, more than Estes Kefauver or Percy Priest, who took the lead in blocking Crump ally Senator Kenneth McKellar's many bids to take control of TVA patronage.

Gore was a loyal supporter of the administration's handling of World War II. He backed the G.I. Bill and legislation facilitating absentee votes by servicemen. He lashed out at United Mine Workers leader John L. Lewis for allowing his men to strike in a time of national sacrifice. Gore himself made quite a sacrifice when he enlisted in the Army as a private, resigning from Congress on December 4, 1944, to serve on active duty. The experience proved invaluable in the long run. For one thing, it allowed him to observe the German Autobahn and got him thinking about how a similar system might boost America's development. In the short run, Gore produced a thoroughly brilliant report in March 1945 that outlined a program for the peaceful occupation of Germany, combining calls for the punishment of Nazi leaders with others to restore health and sanitary facilities and instill a desire for self-government in the German people. Gore did not question President Truman's decision to drop the atomic bomb. Having fought alongside many of the men who would be shipped to the Pacific once the European war ended, and being the representative of thousands of others, he felt certain the use of the bomb saved hundreds of thousands of lives. He returned to the Seventy-ninth Congress in the spring of 1945.

When one scans the papers of Albert Gore, one finds a particular zest to his work during 1947 and 1948, the two years of his House tenure when Republicans were in control. He served on the House Democratic Campaign Committee and reveled in admonishing Republicans, both on the House floor and in weekly broadcasts on WSM Radio, for tax cut proposals that he believed were unfair. Gore would not go down the line for President Truman, however. He voted for the Taft-Hartley Act, giving states the right to enact right-to-work laws. Like many others in Middle Tennessee, he backed the president's plan to outlaw poll taxes, but did not go so far as to support making permanent the operations of the Fair Employment Practices Commission, the forerunner of the Equal Employment Opportunity Commission. Throughout the late 1940s, Gore proved a staunch advocate of Truman's efforts to contain Soviet expansionism, calling in 1947 for a "global Monroe Doctrine" to prevent Russia "from boring from within and pressuring from without." He voted for economic and military aid to Greece and Turkey and for the Marshall Plan, which rebuilt Western Europe. In 1948, he tried unsuccessfully to restore cuts Republicans had made in Truman's budget for the air force. When war broke out in Korea two years later, Gore aligned firmly with Truman. He, however, warned the President that the internal and external weakness of other American allies in Asia made them less than ideal partners.

Like many House members, Gore had long eyed a Senate seat. Preeminently committed to making the tax code more progressive, he was frustrated by House rules that prevented any tax bill from being considered save the one presented by the Ways and Means Committee and a minority party alternative. His impact, he thought, was sure to be greater in a body of 96 than one of 435. Kenneth McKellar's seat would be up in 1952, and it was Gore's understanding that McKellar was ready to retire. Inspired by Estes Kefauver's victory over a Crump-organization candidate in 1948, Gore began testing the waters statewide in 1949. It surprised Gore when McKellar let it be known that he would be seeking a seventh term, but he was prepared.

Gore played particularly on the age difference between himself and McKellar. Aiming to present his youth and energy in a way that would build an image of himself as an agent of change, Gore took his campaign to every corner of Tennessee, often speaking a dozen times a day. Voters who had not seen the incumbent in Tennessee in years now came to know a potential Senator who was a veteran of World War II and reflected their own family values. When McKellar returned to the state in July, he stressed the value of his seniority in the Senate. Gore met McKellar's appeal by asking voters if they thought it was "about time to give another young man a chance," and citing Estes Kefauver, Paul Douglas of Illinois, and, curiously, GOP vice presidential nominee Richard Nixon as examples of freshmen Senators who had made a difference in a short time. Still hoping, McKellar's managers put up signs across the state reading, "THINKING FELLER, VOTE FOR McKELLAR." Gore recognized that the adage called attention to McKellar's experience, but believing it risky to denigrate the value of McKellar's seniority too stridently, he rejected the suggestion of one aide to run negative ads featuring a song entitled "He's Too Old to Cut the Mustard." Instead, he opted for a more folksy retort Pauline had devised: in front of every McKellar placard went the sign "THINK SOME MORE: VOTE FOR GORE."

Gore carried seven of the state's nine congressional districts and defeated McKellar by nearly 90,000 votes. Nationally, Dwight Eisenhower won the presidency and his victory helped return both houses of Congress to Republican control. Gore was sworn in on January 3, 1953, by outgoing Vice President Alben Barkley. That day, four-year-old Al, Jr., could not understand why he had to be in the chambers of the Senate. "Why do I have to go see Daddy hold up his hand," he asked his mother. "I'd rather go to the ten-cent store."

Gore entered the Senate in the shadow of Estes Kefauver. The two were both free traders in the tradition of Cordell Hull and Populists who suspected large concentrations of wealth. Both were internationalists who stood with

Dwight D. Eisenhower on foreign policy questions, particularly in opposing the Bricker Amendment, which would have severely limited any president's ability to manage foreign affairs. Kefauver's orientation was preeminently national, however, while Gore's was more directed to taking care of Tennessee. Although the two got along well and Kefauver was glad that the ever-sniping McKellar was gone, Gore did nurse a bit of resentment that his work was less appreciated than it might have been under different circumstances.

As a freshman Senator, Gore found himself assigned to the committees on Banking and Currency, District of Columbia, and Public Works. He had wanted a seat on the powerful Finance Committee, but Democratic Leader Lyndon Johnson was against giving a seat on that panel to anyone who, like Gore, favored federal control of tidelands oil or limiting the oil depletion allowance. Not in a position to move matters preeminently important to him, Gore had time to follow other interests. Long a champion of expanding TVA beyond its hydroelectric base, Gore learned in 1954 that the Atomic Energy Commission was planning to buy power from private power interests who would build a plant near Memphis. Thinking the plan economically foolish (costing about a half a billion dollars), that administration officials were hiding information from Congress, and that the deal might be part of a larger scheme to limit the reign of TVA in the Tennessee Valley, Gore twice took the floor in the spring to air his concerns. When an atomic energy bill reached the Senate in late June, Gore introduced an amendment that would block what came to be known as Dixon-Yates and similar plans and marshaled his arguments in a seven-hour oration. His semi-filibuster did not sway the Senate leadership, most of whom were sensitive to a need to dispense with other matters, but it did bring the public power issue to the fore. Aaron Wildavsky, the principal academic student of Dixon-Yates, considers its use by Senate candidate Richard Neuberger in Oregon as the key factor enabling him to topple a GOP incumbent. Gore and Estes Kefauver flew to Oregon to campaign for Neuberger and his victory helped return Senate control to the Democrats by a two-seat majority in 1955.

Thereafter, the bulk of the work on Dixon-Yates was handled by the Judiciary Committee, and it was Gore who persuaded its chairman to name Kefauver the head of a subcommittee that would investigate the matter. This was a deft maneuver on Gore's part. It gave the spotlight to a man who had mastered the art of attracting publicity. Kefauver soon discovered that Adolphe Wenzell, a vice president of the Boston bank that was financing Dixon-Yates, was simultaneously acting as a consultant to the Bureau of the Budget on the technical aspects of the deal. Here was a clear conflict of interest that led Memphis officials to announce that they preferred to build their own generator and caused Eisenhower to cancel the contract. From a policy standpoint, Gore was elated. In true populist fashion, however, he continued to berate the President for the "secrecy" in which the "contract was conceived" and for accommodating private interests rather than those of the general public.

Gore was not always at odds with Eisenhower. When Democrats again became a majority, he became chairman of the Roads Subcommittee of the Public Works Committee. Like Eisenhower, Gore had wanted to build a new highway system since he saw the German Autobahn during World War II and sensed that it was the key piece of infrastructure that allowed the Nazis to fight a two-front war. In 1955, Eisenhower sent a bill to the Senate for Gore's subcommittee to consider, but Gore opted to present his own. Why? Partly as a matter of congressional prerogative, but also because he had been in West Virginia a few months earlier and witnessed traffic on a highway known as "Suicide Alley." He discerned that the forty-five-degree angle exit design then in use tempted motorists to keep their speed up as they exited past gas stations and honky-tonks. It was incumbent on him as a subcommittee chairman to slow them down. Gore insisted on the cloverleafed exit ramps now in use and thus is responsible for saving thousands of lives.

The year 1956 proved to be a monumental one on many fronts. It was the year when Frank Clement faced down northern-based agitators who tried to disrupt a heretofore peaceful desegregation process in Clinton, Tennessee. In Washington, Gore and Estes Kefauver joined Tennessee Congressmen Howard Baker, Sr., J. Percy Priest, and B. Carroll Reece in refusing to sign the Southern Manifesto, a document that pledged signatories to resist any outside attempt to alter the South's racial status quo. Pressure on Gore to sign the Manifesto was intense, but his only reaction when he perused that infamous paper in front of a bevy of reporters from the Deep South was a firm "Hell, no!" He explained that one of his grandfathers had fought for the Confederacy and he was not going to waste his time toiling for another lost cause. Later, he described the Manifesto to historians James Gardner and Dewey Grantham as "the most spurious, inane, insulting document of a political nature" that he had ever seen. Regardless, it had some appeal in some quarters of Tennessee. "I don't want to eat with them or sleep with them (blacks)," one voter told Gore. "Do you want to go to heaven with them?" Gore replied. "No," the man said. "I'll go to hell with you and Estes Kefauver."

Gore's decision puzzled some Southerners but it so impressed many Northern Democrats that they thought that he might fit well as their nominee for vice president. At the outset of the 1956 convention, presidential nominee Adlai Stevenson led Gore to believe that he very likely would be his man. Then, almost inexplicably, Stevenson threw the selection to the delegates. Confounded, Gore threw his hat into the ring knowing that House Speaker Sam Rayburn and Senators Lyndon Johnson and Mike Monroney had been talking his virtues up to Stevenson for weeks. When the votes were counted after the first ballot, Gore had 177 votes from the South and Oklahoma and one from Hawaii, placing him a distant third behind Estes Kefauver with 483½ and John F. Kennedy with 304. Had Gore gotten the votes of Kentucky, North Carolina, and Virginia, he would have been ahead of Kennedy and perhaps in a position to win. Kefauver was anathema to much of the South. Arkansas, Mississippi, and Texas all bolted to Kennedy on the second ballot. With Gore no longer a factor and Kennedy just thirty-nine votes from a majority, a group of Kefauver loyalists led by Democratic National Committeewoman Martha Ragland and *Tennessean* publisher Silliman Evans, Jr., went to Gore and told him they would hold him responsible if Kefauver lost and would perhaps oppose Gore's reelection in 1958. Gore relented. He waved the Tennessee standard, was recognized by Speaker Rayburn, and withdrew his name in favor of Kefauver. Moments thereafter, Frank Clement switched Tennessee's votes to Kefauver, thus starting the bandwagon that catapulted the Chattanoogan to the vice presidential nomination. It is highly unlikely that Gore's presence on the ticket rather than Kefauver's would have made much of a difference for Democrats in 1956, but in purely personal terms, a Gore nod and respectable showing might have raised his stock as a viable contender in 1960.

As he would have under merrier circumstances, Gore returned with his family to his farm in Carthage. By 1956, he had accumulated 255 acres and a herd of six hundred Black Angus cattle. There, Nancy and Al, Jr., spent their summers in the same rural setting as their parents had grown up in, though in a much grander style made possible by proceeds from two cattle sales each year. Their playmates were primarily cousins and tenants, and Albert and Pauline encouraged this. Nancy took an interest in the management of the farm at an early age. It never occurred to the Gores that their children would be anything other than loyal Democrats. They were products of our state's Democratic heartland, and in Washington, they met many of their party's best-known leaders. It was Pauline who was the guiding force in their lives; for Albert Gore spent autumns of every election year in the 1950s traversing the country to help other Democrats. Despite his disappointment, 1956 was no different. Gore did everything he could to elect the Stevenson-Kefauver ticket, even though it burned him that Kefauver stole many of his best jokes when they campaigned together.

In spite of "massive resistance" from many Southern states, the first civil rights bill since Reconstruction came to the floor in 1957. The House bill, supported by Eisenhower loyalists and some northern Democrats, went nearly as far as the monumental acts of the 1960s in allowing the Justice Department to seek relief for those African Americans whose rights had been violated. Gore sympathized with the objective. In the 1940s, he had often made the Carthage to Washington trek with Pauline, Nancy, and Mrs. Ocee Hunt, Nancy's black nurse. Discrimination against Mrs. Hunt forced Gore to order her food so she could eat in the car and to ask gas station attendants if she could use their rest rooms. If the answer was no, Gore refused to buy gas and moved on. Eventually, he found one motel operator who would allow them to stay if they called ahead and arrived after dark. Infuriated, Gore was one of a few white Southerners who agonized about the repercussions if they moved farther toward a biracial society than their people were prepared to go. Lyndon Johnson was in the same quandary, but he found an out by rallying Senate Democrats behind an amendment that stripped a provision from the bill that denied a jury trial to anyone charged with depriving someone else of the rights accorded to them under the Fourteenth or Fifteenth Amendments.

It is easy today to see that Johnson's move made the Civil Rights Act of 1957 a toothless tiger. Few, if any, juries in the Deep South at the time were likely to side with the plaintiffs in such cases. Political realities meant that a bill that did not guarantee a jury trial to those accused would not pass. Gore voted for the jury trial amendment and the bill. In the process, he helped move the agenda of the civil rights movement forward, as majorities in both Houses of Congress acknowledged that a problem existed for the first time in eighty-two years. It was a key first step. Only when the public realized a few years later that existing laws were insufficient did Congress move to mandate the equality of all before the law that exists today.

Although he lent strong support to civil rights, it was still equity in taxation that most interested Senator Gore. In 1959, Lyndon Johnson finally granted him a seat on the Finance Committee. Gore had only one regular ally on the committee, Paul Douglas of Illinois, but he still managed an occasional victory. In his first year on that panel, he learned that a tax court had opened up a depletion allowance on finished manufactured products that would cost the Treasury $600 million a year. Dwight D. Eisenhower was furious with the move, but only Gore would put his amendment before the committee. There, only Douglas sided with Gore, but Gore took the question to the floor and attracted enough sympathy from the public that the Senate approved it unanimously.

Gore acknowledged in a political postmortem that he did contemplate a presidential bid, but in 1959, he recognized that he was too little known outside Tennessee and too underfinanced to wage a viable campaign. One might guess that he would have favored Lyndon Johnson, a fellow southern moderate, but Gore was never part of what some used to call the Senate's inner club, and he recoiled at Johnson's rule as leader and his ties to the oil industry. However, he found it easy to respond to the call of his colleague from Massachusetts, John F. Kennedy. Pauline and Jacqueline Kennedy were close friends and Gore deemed Kennedy the most educable of the candidates on tax matters. Later, he would term Kennedy the "best, brightest hope" in his lifetime. Once Kennedy won the nomination, he seriously considered Gore as a potential running mate. It was pragmatism alone that led him to opt for Lyndon Johnson. "I'm confident you could bring Tennessee," he told Gore the day he made his choice, "but I think I must have Texas." As a consolation prize, he made Gore the head of a kitchen cabinet that met periodically for the duration of the campaign.

Kennedy never became the populist that Gore hoped he would become. Indeed, Gore never reconciled himself to Kennedy's belief that his slogan "Let's Get the Country Moving Again" meant keeping a promise to expand the economy by 5 percent a year. In Kennedy's view, this would be impossible without a Treasury Secretary whom the financial community trusted. Once it became known that Kennedy intended to offer the job to Undersecretary of State Douglas Dillon, a Republican whom Eisenhower had recruited from a respected Wall Street investment firm, Gore wrote Kennedy and suggested that he change his mind. Gore thought a Democrat committed to spending programs like those of the New Deal would be a better choice, but Kennedy nominated Dillon. In 1962, Gore joined Estes Kefauver and Wayne Morse of Oregon in a quixotic fight against Kennedy's bill to subsidize COMSAT, the communications satellite corporation, thinking it a "giveaway" to big business. Later that year, Kennedy saw Gore at Eleanor Roosevelt's funeral and asked if he should cut taxes. "Forget it," Gore advised, suggesting that successful reductions would fuel calls for cuts in domestic spending and limit the possibility that loopholes might be closed in the future. Kennedy listened, but went ahead the next year with a call for a 30 percent across the board reduction. Action was incomplete on the bill prior to Kennedy's assassination, but a similar bill that Lyndon Johnson pushed to enactment over Gore's objections is often credited for the phenomenal growth of the mid-1960s.

Gore found more to applaud in the expanded federal presence mandated by Johnson's Great Society. He backed the War on Poverty, federal aid to education, and the creation of a Department of Housing and Urban Development. Gore took particular pride in the creation of Medicare. Instituting a program of health care for the aged had been a goal of his since Harry Truman forwarded the idea in 1949. On his own, Gore tried on August 17, 1964, to insert such a program into that year's Social Security bill. Once the Finance Committee voted him down, 11–6, Gore announced that he would try again when the bill reached the floor. He then hurried to the Democratic convention in Atlantic City, where he learned that the platform contained the weakest endorsement of the idea in nearly a generation. Gore sought out Hubert Humphrey whom he assumed Johnson would choose as his running mate and threatened to bring the matter to a fight on the floor. Humphrey got the message to Johnson, who not only sharpened the platform's language but threw his weight behind Gore's amendment. Gore prevailed in the Senate in September, 49–44, but passage would not come until 1965, when House Ways and Means Chairman Wilbur Mills reversed field and brought the House around.

Gore was not as supportive of Johnson on civil rights, even if the Senator's heart was in the right place. Tennessee had a somewhat better record than many other southern states when it came to protecting the right to vote, and Gore was quick to align behind the Voting Rights Act of 1965. In 1966, he and Ross Bass were the two Southerners to vote to bring cloture on the fair housing bill then before Congress. But Gore's most difficult vote came in 1964 on the bill establishing an Equal Employment Opportunity Commission and opening public accommodations to all. In a vote he concedes "may have been wrong," he voted "no" on the Civil Rights Act of 1964, citing the power it gave to the federal government to deny funds to any district it deemed noncompliant as his objection.

On foreign policy matters, Gore proved a true iconoclast. His influence was greater with John Kennedy than either of his successors. From the seat he had held on the Foreign Relations Committee since 1959, he urged Kennedy in the wake of the Bay of Pigs fiasco to fire Joint Chiefs of Staff Chairman Lyman L. Lemnitzer and hailed his virtual exiling of him to Brussels as our NATO Ambassador. He also proved a valiant and key supporter of Kennedy's Nuclear Test-Ban Treaty, but there was one American commitment that had long troubled Gore, the one to South Vietnam.

Gore's concerns over U.S. involvement in Vietnam came early and stayed late. They stemmed from a two-week tour of Indochina he had taken in 1958. He and Gale McGee of Wyoming met with South Vietnamese President Ngo Dinh Diem and his beautiful and domineering sister-in-law, Madame Nhu. Even at this early date, Gore was alarmed by the "authoritarian" direction of the Diem regime. Especially disconcerting was the Diem policy of settling the Montagnards of northwest South Vietnam behind fences so low that tigers could jump them and steal calves. In years to come, CIA operative Richard Helms would feed Gore information that confirmed his suspicions about the tyranny and the weakness of the Diem regime. By 1963, Gore was convinced that the United States should remove all its military personnel. He sought and secured an appointment with John Kennedy to convey that advice and urged him to defend such a course by citing the Diem government's repression of its Buddhist minority. Like Gore, Kennedy was pessimistic, but he would not commit himself to any course of action. A day later, Gore learned from Kennedy's close friend Charles Bartlett that Kennedy feared that a pullout might provide ammunition to those who wanted to portray him as soft on communism.

Gore's wariness continued. As early as December 1964, he was calling publicly for a negotiated settlement. This got Gore a biting phone call from Lyndon Johnson, who suggested snidely that Gore was benefiting from the publicity. In August 1964, Gore had supported Johnson on the Gulf of

Tonkin Resolution, which let the United States retaliate against unprovoked attacks on its shipping. Later, he found that the evidence regarding the attacks was hazy and the resolution was being used to justify a full-scale escalation of the war. That most certainly had not been Gore's intention and he advised Johnson privately in early 1965 that he thought it unwise to introduce any combat troops. To Johnson, the conflict was a challenge to America's credibility and his own, but Gore disagreed. He believed that our intervention presented the United States to the rest of the world as a defender of an unstable regime at best and an aggressor at worst. Was there, in the phrase of the time, a light at the end of the tunnel? The estimates Gore got from CIA sources were not encouraging, and he came to discount administration projections that the war was winnable or that the South Vietnamese government would embrace anything resembling a democracy. "We were being lied to," he told interviewers later. And what was South Vietnam's strategic value to the United States? Gore saw none. In fact, he believed, the war had the counterproductive result of limiting America's chances to exploit the long-smoldering rift between the Soviet Union and China.

Gore's skepticism continued through the Nixon administration. He commended Nixon after his speech of May 14, 1969, in which Nixon ruled out a "purely military solution," but he was hardly so benign in his characterization of Nixon's means of withdrawal. Nixon called his program "Vietnamization" and aimed to buy time for the Thieu regime to get its political and military house in order. To Gore, this meant that Nixon would be further prolonging the war, and he continued to support measures to accelerate U.S. departure. He did not go so far as to back the McGovern-Hatfield amendment, requiring that America extricate itself within three months, but he did back the Cooper-Church amendment, limiting the President's ability to take steps to defend American troops from attacks launched from outside of Vietnam.

To many Tennesseans, Gore's actions smacked of partisanship. Former state GOP Chairman Tom Beasley was serving in Vietnam in the late 1960s when his division ended a fire-fight and found a dead North Vietnamese soldier. On his person, they found statements of Gore, Robert Kennedy, and George McGovern questioning America's role. "My God," Beasley declared when he saw that his Senator's words were being used to bolster the morale of men who were trying to kill him. When he returned home in 1970, this one-time Democrat from Frank Clement's native Dickson voted a straight GOP ticket and rarely deviated thereafter. Gore, when questioned by skeptics, would answer that his critics did not "have access to the information that I do." His response furthered perceptions that he was talking to voters but rarely listening to them, and that he was acting to bolster the interests of the increasingly liberal national Democratic Party while ignoring the wishes of his constituents. On this point, Gore lent plenty of ammunition to his critics.

In January 1969, he supported Ted Kennedy's successful bid to oust Russell Long of Louisiana as Senate Majority Whip. A few months later, he opposed a Nixon plan to deploy an antiballistic missile system. It was common for him to chide Vice President Spiro T. Agnew as "the greatest disaster since Vietnam" and to berate Nixon for his Southern Strategy. Such words were the kind of raw meat that northern Democrats ate up, but they indicated to many Tennesseans that Gore was not being fair to a president they supported and not concerned with their opinions, either.

If there was one vote that fixed permanently the impression that Gore had distanced himself from his constituents, it was his vote against the confirmation of Judge Clement Haynsworth of South Carolina to a seat on the Supreme Court. Recently, the eminent liberal newsman Tom Wicker conceded that Haynsworth "went on to long and reputable service on the Fourth Circuit and is widely regarded as having been worthy of confirmation." But in 1969, AFL-CIO chief George Meany mounted a campaign against Haynsworth in retaliation for a series of rulings he termed anti-labor. Northern Senators fell in line and played up spurious allegations of conflicts-of-interest and unfounded suspicions that Haynsworth was a foe of civil rights. Unfortunately, Gore sided with the accusers and helped deprive the Court of the services of a talented southern jurist. In later years, Gore defended his vote by citing the conflict-of-interest charges. At the time, he joined Howard Baker in recommending that Nixon select Judge William Miller, a distinguished Republican jurist from Knoxville, but Nixon ordered his people to find "a good federal judge further south and further to the right." They found G. Harrold Carswell of Florida, a jurist with credentials far too measly to justify a place on the Supreme Court. Gore found him "unfit" and voted against him. Gore did the right thing, but in doing so, exacerbated a sense that he was "anti-South," one that would not have been so pronounced had he steered away from the dubious campaign that defeated Clement Haynsworth.

Gore retained his credentials as a populist. In 1969, he won a fight that he had waged for nearly twenty years. He had always maintained that increasing each individual's personal tax exemption would restore some equity between those at the wealthiest end of the scale and those at the poorest end. A $600 exemption had been in place since 1948 and Gore found it high time for the tax code to catch up with inflation. He tried first with $1,250, then with $1,000. Although Senators did not budge, Gore got conservative Arkansas Democrat John McClellan to speak for an $800 exemption. Republicans scrambled to craft an alternative, an initial $600 exemption with a $50 a year hike over four years, but few Democrats went along with it. Although a conference committee limited the total increase to $750, its appeal led a political aide, Harry Dent, to write Nixon that it might be the only thing that could save Gore in his bid for reelection.

Gore knew he was in for a tough fight in 1970. Democratic fortunes had been receding in Tennessee. In 1958, he turned back a Democratic primary challenge from former Governor Prentice Cooper, who railed at his refusal to sign the Southern Manifesto and to join the mini-filibuster against the Civil Rights Act of 1957. Six years later, Republicans nominated Dan Kuykendall, an able former executive with Proctor and Gamble's Memphis branch, who blasted Gore for "vitriolic attacks" on business that he said discouraged industry from locating in Tennessee. In another year, Kuykendall might have succeeded, but 1964 was the year of Barry Goldwater and Goldwater's opposition to TVA saved Gore, who won by a 54–46 margin.

Well before 1970, Gore knew that his opponent in the general election would be Third District Congressman Bill Brock. By spring of 1970, Gore was deriding Brock as "Out of Step Billy," "a legislative oddball," a "negativist," and the "chosen weapon of the Southern Strategy." Gore, dubbed the "Old Gray Fox" by country singer Tex Ritter, Brock's opponent in the Republican primary, faced a much rougher challenge in the Democratic primary than he had anticipated from Hudley Crockett, Governor Buford Ellington's former press secretary. Crockett harped on the anti-South theme and held Gore to but 51 percent, a sure omen of trouble to come.

Brock picked up where Crockett left off, having his supporters place signs around the state reading "Bill Brock Believes." When Gore's people asked what it was that Bill Brock believed, Brock backers added "In What We Believe" to their placards. Gore took this as a challenge and tried to turn the race into a referendum on the New Deal and Great Society programs that he had supported and Brock had opposed. This allowed him to recapture some stray Democrats, especially among those who had supported George Wallace's 1968 presidential bid. Unfortunately for Gore, such programs were taken by many in the Tennessee of 1970 as symbols of extravagance. With Estes Kefauver dead, Gore was now Tennessee's most readily identifiable liberal and Brock pounced on this weakness. To Brock, the federal responsibility was one of "helping local government to meet its responsibilities, not to dominate." Like Howard Baker and even many liberal economists, Brock was pushing a revenue-sharing bill that would provide cash-starved states such as Tennessee with funds they could use as they saw best for their communities. Unlike many Democratic municipal officials in Tennessee, Gore opposed the idea, saying it somehow would benefit the richer states.

If there was one event that boosted Gore, it was his move to greet Vice President Agnew as he arrived in Memphis in late September for a Brock rally. Agnew had long been bashing Gore as "the Southern regional chairman of the Eastern liberal establishment." One could analyze the propriety of this tag for many pages. Suffice it to say that many Tennesseans recognized that they had benefited from some Gore-sponsored programs and that Gore's populism was rooted in the soil of Middle Tennessee. Appearances are everything in politics and Gore came off as a gracious host (and victim) while Agnew came across as a meddling outsider. A race in which Gore was once down fourteen points was soon rated a toss-up.

Any campaign contains some intangibles. Brock was a superb organizer and Gore lacked a strong personal following. If primary results are any indication, Democrats still held a majority. But they were deeply divided and even Gore's top aides were ruing privately the fact that some local Democratic chieftains were pointedly excluding the young. Gore did make some headway with ads ending with him telling Al, Jr., "Son, always love your country." The issues that better symbolized patriotism in 1970 were those Hudley Crockett raised in the primary—Vietnam, gun control, prayer in schools, Haynsworth and Carswell—and those Brock reiterated in the general election. Gore, to his credit, had taken what he viewed as a principled stand on each, but none of his positions meshed with the sentiments of the majority of the people of Tennessee and Gore had not taken the time to explain them to his constituents. In a hard-fought battle, a Gore aide told journalist Richard Harris, Gore "lost because he remembered that he was a senator and forgot that he was a politician." Though Gore polled 23,000 votes more than Democratic gubernatorial nominee John Jay Hooker, he still was caught in a Republican tide and finished 43,000 votes behind Bill Brock. Defeat was hard on all of the Gores, but they did find the silver lining the day after the election, when a lucrative deposit of zinc was discovered on their farm in Carthage.

Gore did not leave politics entirely when he left the Senate. He did some work for the presidential campaign of Edmund Muskie, gave freely of his advice to like-minded Democrats, and served for a time on President Carter's Foreign Intelligence Oversight Advisory Board. In 1972, he published *Let the Glory Out; My South and Its Politics*, a thoughtful semiautobiographical volume that called on the South to drop its preoccupation with race. In it, Gore displayed his uncommon integrity when he candidly confessed that he and fellow southern members of Congress had not acted as quickly as they might have to bring an end to the Jim Crow world our grandfathers left us. He also made a plea for a return to politics governed by Democrats with a populist-derived distrust of big business and banks. In the agrarian Tennessee where Albert Gore was born and bred, this may have been a sound approach, but voters by the 1970s recognized that such ideas were increasingly antithetical to growth and prosperity in an ever more urban Tennessee. Albert Gore's day had passed, but there will always be a place in government for people of his character, diligence, and honesty.

Gore made his living after leaving the Senate as vice president of Occidental Petroleum, the conglomerate owned by longtime-friend Armand

Hammer, and as president of the Lexington, Kentucky-based Island Creek Coal Company, an Occidental subsidiary that managed thirty-one mines. On occasion, Gore did some legal work for Occidental interests while Pauline took on a few clients of her own. If there was a project of which he was proudest, it was a 1982 deal he completed with China to have Occidental build the world's largest coal mine.

The Gores continued to maintain apartments in Lexington and Washington, but they also regularly returned to their farm in Carthage. Until his late seventies, Gore remained quite active as an executive. Only then did he take on semi-retired status. Even so, he attended Occidental board meetings religiously until his death.

It was Al, Jr.'s, national campaigns that rejuvenated the Gores. Prior to his decision in 1987 to seek the presidency, Al, Jr., met his parents at their Capitol Hill apartment in the Methodist Building and talked with them for nearly three hours about the prospects of such a race. Gore, Sr., tried to be as objective as possible, but told his son that he at thirty-nine offered the country the same kind of positive generational change after eight years of Ronald Reagan that he thought his friend John Kennedy provided after eight years of Dwight D. Eisenhower. It was Al, Jr., who touched on the negatives and the elder Gores thought that he had opted against a race when he left. They flew home to Tennessee and learned from their son the next day that "the word is go." Gore let out a yell that he later likened to that of "a Comanche." He and Pauline welcomed the opportunity to return to the hustings in their son's maiden venture into national politics. They repeated these excursions four years later once Bill Clinton named Al, Jr., as his running mate, and they ultimately campaigned for the ticket in fourteen states. The more consequential Gore in this race may have been Pauline. Her recounting of her experiences as a woman and as an attorney may well have tempered GOP criticisms of Hillary Rodham Clinton's perceived aggressiveness and focused attention on the many forms of discrimination that have long limited women. And who could be more elated by a son's victory than a man who had almost had the same opportunity nearly two generations earlier?

At the 1992 Democratic convention, Senator Gore told longtime aide Bill Allen that he intended to live at least until November 2000, and it is certainly clear why. To the sorrow of all Tennesseans, Senator Gore died on December 5, 1998. I joined the Vice President and his family and a delegation of U.S. Senators and Congressman at his memorial service in Nashville where the Vice President delivered a beautiful eulogy for his father. His words, which captured the essence of this great public servant, will serve over the years as an inspiration to future generations and as an enduring tribute of respect, admiration and love.

Chapter 9

Herbert S. "Mr. Hub" Walters

1963–1964

"Mr. Democrat"

(1891–1973)

Had Norman Rockwell hailed from Tennessee, he would have found no finer model of the sturdy small-town virtues he loved to portray than in Herbert Sanford Walters. A preacher's son, he practiced the Golden Rule and instinctively advocated it as his ideal. This unpretentious, selfless, innately intelligent gentleman from Morristown not only embodied the native shrewdness of the denizens of the East Tennessee hills, but he also gave proof of the notion that Horatio Alger-like rises from rags to riches are still possible to people of character anywhere in America.

Ironically, the apparently uncomplicated "Mr. Hub" Walters had quite a distinguished pedigree. In a commemorative tome of 1963, Howard L. Hill asserted that Benjamin Franklin was a distant ancestor. Hub Walters was the maternal great-grandson of Lawson D. Franklin, Tennessee's first millionaire. Hard times had fallen on the Reverend John Milo Walters and his bride Lula Franklin by November 17, 1891, the day Herbert, their third son, was born in a log cabin near Leadville. Devastation wrought by both armies during the Civil War had virtually wiped out the Franklin estate. All that was left to Lula Walters was Riverview, one of her grandfather's three mansions, located near White Pine, Tennessee. Upkeep costs were exorbitant and John Milo Walters found it hard to keep up with them on a Baptist minister's salary. Holding an A.B. and an M.A. from Bethel College in Russellville, Kentucky, the Reverend Walters tried his hardest to give his five children the same opportunities that he had enjoyed. He sent young Herbert to a two-room school near Leadvale, where playmates dubbed him "Hub." In his teens, Hub was sent to prep schools in Knoxville and Lebanon, but he soon learned that his parents were struggling and he dropped out so that they might have an easier time of it.

Hub Walters learned the value of hard work at an early age. At ten, he earned a quarter a day hauling water to crews harvesting wheat on an East Tennessee farm. By sixteen he had saved enough to pay for train fare to Milwaukee, where his brother landed him a job as an "axeman" for a railway survey crew in northern Michigan. Here, he won the nickname "He'p" for he had the habit of asking coworkers if he could "he'p" them out after he had finished his own chores. Though his pay was only $50 a month, he set aside at least $20 each month to send to his parents to pay for the education of his siblings. Over the next seven years, he worked on railroads from Michigan to Mississippi. By 1915, he thought he had accumulated enough money to complete his own schooling and so he enrolled at both Carson-Newman College and the University of Tennessee to study agriculture and engineering. These dreams came to naught. Within six months, both of his parents fell ill and he had to return home to help out. Times got even tougher when their medical bills rose so high that Hub had to increase his income substantially to avoid foreclosure on Riverview. In partnership with J. L. Harrison of White Pine, he purchased fifteen Angus heifers at $125 a head, fattened them up, then sold them at more than twice what he paid for them. Thus was Riverview saved and thus did the business career of Morristown's chief benefactor begin.

It was in the field of highway construction that Hub Walters made his fortune. In 1920, he joined brother-in-law Tracy W. Prater and Harrison in a subcontracting firm. Their first year, they completed a twelve-mile stretch from Coal Creek to Lake City. Their methods were somewhat primitive; they used mules as bulldozers, got their tools from war surplus sales, and bought all their machines on credit. But their work was of high quality and often it was completed well before schedule. Conscientious management and dedicated workmanship won them lucrative contracts in Tennessee (the Andrew Johnson Highway), Virginia (Skyline Drive), and the Carolinas.

Hub Walters was financially secure by 1928, the year he married the former Sarah Lockridge, a gracious, traditional, southern Presbyterian woman who loved to sew, garden, cook and work in her church. A wonderfully happy couple, they had no children of their own but would "adopt" able young people and nurture their development in business, or later, in politics.

Never ones who enjoyed the spotlight, they took pride in their protégés, chief of whom was that organ-tongued "boy wonder" of the Tennessee of the 1950s, Frank Goad Clement.

Hub Walters sought only one elective office, a seat in the Tennessee House of Delegates. That successful bid came in 1932, when he became the first Democrat since the Civil War to be elected to the seat encompassing Hamblen and Jefferson Counties. His work there won the attention of Governor Hill McAlister, who in 1934 named Hub state highway commissioner. Walters served just one year in this position, but was responsible for one major shift in policy that affected all forty-eight states. He had observed that the law creating the Works Progress Administration (WPA) had mandated that its entire budget be spent on wages for the unemployed, leaving no funds for materials and equipment. Hence, the only work possible was "make work," leading WPA critics on occasion to dub the program "We Poke Along." Certain that the only way to produce projects that would serve in the long run to expand the economy, and thereby create permanent jobs in the private sector, was to allow part of the funds to be used for materials and equipment, Walters went to Washington to present his case to WPA Administrator Harry Hopkins, Franklin D. Roosevelt's closest associate. Hopkins was persuaded. Had this tack not been taken, it is likely that Kenneth McKellar, from his perch on the Senate Appropriations Committee, would have killed the program. As it was, the funds thus appropriated put 25,000 Tennesseans to work and allowed the state to build dozens of roads and airports in the Tri-Cities—Knoxville, Nashville, and Memphis. The WPA adopted Walters's idea nationwide and some of FDR's "Brain Trust" even tried to get Walters to move to Washington to head their farm-to-market program. But in depression conditions, he rejected these overtures and others to stay as highway commissioner or run for governor, and instead returned to Morristown to tend to his own businesses.

By the 1930s, Hub Walters's entrepreneurial activities had begun to expand. In 1934, he was elected president of the Hamilton National Bank of Morristown. In later years, he served as a director of the Citizens Bank of White Pine, the Hamilton National Bank of Knoxville, the First National Bank of Rogersville, the American Educational Life Insurance Company, and the Tennessee Natural Gas Lines, Inc., of Nashville. In time, he became chairman of the boards of the Colonial Gas Company, where he employed Howard Baker, Jr., as its president, the Morristown Power and Water Commission, the East Tennessee Natural Gas Company, and the Cherokee Broadcasting Company. Hub Walters was no title collector, however; he was a working director. He led a campaign to raise $15 million to lay a gas line linking Springfield and East Tennessee, and he played the largest role in attracting the American Enka Corporation plant to Lowland, Tennessee, which eventually employed 1,800 Tennesseans.

Even more impressive was Hub Walters's work in the civic realm. For years, he served as Hamblen County fund-raising chairman for the American Cancer Society and the United Way Fund. Rare was a year when he did not exceed his goal. When heavy rains ravaged Louisville, Kentucky, in 1957, Hub Walters responded to a Red Cross appeal by shipping two large gas pumps for use in pumping water out of flooded buildings and streets. On Christmas and Easter mornings, he and Sarah customarily visited the poorer sections of Morristown to distribute gifts to nearly everyone they ran into. As was the case with Will Brock, the principal focus of the civic life of this underschooled but talented entrepreneur was the cause of higher education. The first beneficiary of this particular talent was the forty-student King College of Bristol. When the Presbyterian Synod of Appalachia named him as trustee and treasurer of its Endowment Fund in 1943, King College was unaccredited and had an operating budget of only $35,000 and an endowment of a mere $40,000, making it easily the weakest of the sixteen Presbyterian institutions in the South. Thirteen years later, the now-accredited school ranked sixth of sixteen and had an endowment of $1.2 million, and its graduates performed better in medical schools than those of any other Tennessee college. Walters was just as devoted to his two alma maters, Carson-Newman College and the University of Tennessee. He made five-figure donations to the library endowments of both schools.

Hub Walters was known to two generations of Tennesseans as "Mr. Democrat." He served twenty-five years as our state's Democratic National Committee representative and enjoyed two stints as chairman of the State Democratic Executive Committee. His own philosophy, he said in 1963, fell roughly halfway between the liberal view then best exemplified by Hubert Humphrey of Minnesota and the reactionary one then exemplified by Harry Byrd of Virginia. Here in Tennessee, that meant that in the factional wars of state Democrats he sided more often than not with the Democratic establishment, whose viewpoint tended to be echoed in the relatively conservative pages of the *Nashville Banner* and the *Memphis Commercial Appeal.* He generally, but not always, found himself allied with Boss Ed Crump of Memphis in the 1930s and 1940s. Walters, for example, stood solidly behind Tom Stewart in 1948 when Crump opted to abandon Stewart in favor of Judge John Mitchell. On occasions when *Nashville Tennessean*-backed candidates such as Albert Gore and Estes Kefauver defeated organization-backed rivals, Walters quickly moved to rebuild party unity immediately after the primary. Only in 1972 when George McGovern captured the Democratic nomination for president and Ray Blanton won his party's nod for Howard Baker's seat did Walters ever vote for a Republican for any office, and he cast that ballot quietly.

Organization Democrats were quick to acknowledge and recognize Hub Walters's talents. Governor Jim Nance McCord named him his 1944 campaign manager, his Coal Conservation director during the miners' strike of 1946, and a member of his tax revision committee. Governor Frank Clement placed him on his Highway Planning and Great Smoky Mountains Commissions. Of all of those he worked with, Clement was clearly his favorite. To Walters, Clement was the son he never had; and to Clement, Walters was not only a "second daddy," as Congressman Bob Clement put it, but an invaluable and even indispensable fund-raiser and ally both in East Tennessee and on the Democratic National Committee.

Older Tennesseans witnessing a presidential race in 2000 in which three of our best were at one time considered potential candidates—alphabetically Lamar Alexander, Albert Gore, Jr., and Fred Thompson—may well equate the circumstances at the dawn of the second millennium with those of 1956, when Wilma Dykeman (who since 1982 has served as Tennessee State Historian) opined that there might be "Too Much Talent in Tennessee." That year, three Tennesseans—Frank Clement, Albert Gore, Sr., and Estes Kefauver—all figured prominently in speculation regarding both slots on the national Democratic ticket. In the end, only Kefauver sought the top slot.

Walters, never enthusiastic about Estes Kefauver, preferred Frank Clement as a candidate. In January 1956, he announced that Tennessee's delegates would back Clement as their favorite son for president at the Democratic convention. Clement renounced the designation, knowing that at age thirty-six his chances for the top slot were remote at best. Once it was clear that the nominee would be Adlai Stevenson, Walters began lobbying DNC members feverishly and secured for Clement—a magnificent, old-time stump orator—the honor of keynoting the convention. Unfortunately for the young governor, the florid, biblically charged, prosecutorial rhetoric that he used so effectively on Tennessee courthouse lawns was inappropriate for the cool medium of television, and his robust, lengthy basting of the enormously popular Dwight D. Eisenhower seemed out of place and effectively ended Clement's chances at the second slot.

With Clement out of the race, Walters turned his focus to the nomination of Albert Gore. He had seen to it that delegates to the state Democratic convention had adopted a resolution requiring Tennesseans to back a Volunteer State candidate for either slot as long as he stood a reasonable shot at winning. When Stevenson opted to let the convention select his running mate, Walters led a united thirty-two-delegate contingent behind Gore. Later, Gore wrote Walters and told him that had three other southern delegations honored their commitments to him on the first ballot, he would have been second on that count. That would have been an ideal position to overtake Kefauver, who had the support of few Southerners but many from the Midwest and West. But when southern delegations left Gore for John F. Kennedy on the second ballot, Gore, having been firmly reminded of the Tennessee delegation resolution by Kefauver supporters led by *Tennessean* publisher Silliman Evans, Jr., grabbed the microphone, withdrew, and let Clement switch Tennessee's votes to Kefauver. Here began a bandwagon that allowed Kefauver to prevail narrowly over the future president.

Walters and Clement left the Chicago gathering disappointed. Trying in vain to hide any lingering discord, they worked as hard for the Stevenson-Kefauver ticket as they would for any other Democrats, certainly a Sisyphean task against Dwight D. Eisenhower.

Clement, meanwhile, never forgot his mentor's loyalty. When a heart attack felled Kefauver in August 1963, Clement and his son Bob were pressured everywhere, even at Kefauver's funeral, by people sponsoring various would-be candidates for the vacancy. Startled by the inappropriateness of their timing, Clement invited Walters to fill Kefauver's seat until November 1964, when voters would decide who would fill the remaining two years of Kefauver's term. It was understood but not stated publicly that Clement feared that voters would respond angrily if he appointed himself to Kefauver's seat. Because of his longtime rivalry with Kefauver, Clement knew that the Chattanoogan's backers would gasp, but he figured (inaccurately as it turned out) that their anger would subside if he waited for the special election before attempting to switch jobs. Hub Walters would make an ideal stand-in. Secure in his station, Morristown's most dedicated benefactor would gladly step aside as he always had when the ambitions of his protégé dictated that course.

Hub Walters was seventy-one when he entered the Senate. Surgery for throat cancer had rendered his voice barely more audible than a whisper. The few speeches that he gave were brief and to the point. Colleagues appreciated his characteristic graciousness and his willingness to preside over the Senate, a task that he spent 135 hours fulfilling in his fifteen-month stint and one that many of us find enormously tedious, but Hub Walters never seemed to mind. Vermont Republican George Aiken hailed his uncanny propensity "to see the sunny side," while Sam Ervin, our neighbor from the east side of the Smokies, praised his "understanding heart" as well as his "industry, intelligence, integrity, and courage." Walters compiled a voting record that one might expect from a moderately conservative Tennessee Democrat of the 1960s. He supported the Nuclear Test-Ban Treaty and the Kennedy-Johnson program to cut taxes by 30 percent.

Hub Walters dedicated much of his Senate time to the issue of race relations. He used his maiden address to lambaste the cowards who bombed a Birmingham church and killed four African-American girls, and he reprinted an editorial from the *Nashville Banner* in the *Congressional Record* that echoed his statement. He voted against the Civil Rights Act of 1964, but did not actively participate in the filibuster through exhaustive speeches. He did oppose the closing of debate and inserted *Banner* editorials calling for the protection of blacks by means no constitutional lawyer could question. Like the *Banner*, Walters called on whites to recognize and defend the legitimate rights of African Americans. He also appealed to white politicians to cease promising blacks more than they could deliver. To his mind, such unfulfilled expectations had led, particularly in the North, to the rise in the black community of leaders who rejected the nonviolent doctrine of Dr. Martin Luther King, Jr. Such a stand seems unenlightened today, yet only subtle nuances separated it from the positions of Albert Gore, Sr., Frank Clement, Howard Baker, Jr., and Bill Brock.

What distinguished Tennesseans inside and outside of Congress from denizens of nearly all other Southern states was our determination to see that the laws of our land were faithfully executed. Tennesseans as a whole did not condone the kinds of massive resistance that plagued our neighboring states. No one made this point better than Hub Walters. "A law-abiding people," he promised the Senate immediately after the bill's passage, "accepts the obligation of compliance."

Hub Walters never failed in his mission "to help the fellow who couldn't help himself." Upon leaving the Senate, he returned to Morristown, ever more generous with his time, his gifts, and his "he'p" to his party and his community. In 1972 ill health forced him to resign his position on the Democratic National Committee. A year later, he died, the grand old man of the Tennessee Democratic Party, albeit one largely forgotten in Washington. Still, no man could have a finer epitaph than the one Bill Brock gave him on his passing: "Hub Walters lived the golden rule every minute of his life."

Chapter 10

Ross Bass

1964–1967

Surgeon General's Warning on Cigarettes

(1918–1993)

Ten o'clock one night I was paged urgently to the bedside of a seventy-four-year-old man who was acutely short of breath. I'd been called out of the operating room at Vanderbilt Hospital where I was just finishing a heart operation. The man was Ross Bass. The date, April 6, 1992. I acted quickly, explained what I would have to do, anesthetized the chest wall, made an incision, and inserted a large tube to drain fluid from his chest. The surgical procedure was over in thirty minutes, but it was the three-hour exchange that followed that I will never forget. Much of what follows comes from that discussion between doctor and patient, between past Senator and, though completely unknown to me at the time, future Senator.

"It is a far greater distance to the United States Congress from Pulaski than it is from Hyannisport to the White House." So declared President John F. Kennedy in 1963 in honoring his friend Ross Bass, who then represented rural Middle Tennessee in the House of Representatives.

Ross Bass was born on a farm near Pulaski on St. Patrick's Day, March 17, 1918, the fourth of eight children of Reverend William Archibald and Helen Shook Bass. The elder Bass was a circuit rider in the Methodist church

125

whose ministry took him in time into thirty-six Middle and West Tennessee counties. Young Ross grew up among a wide array of rural Southerners and gained an almost instinctive feel for their hopes and aspirations. He graduated from high school in 1936 in Mt. Pleasant, but did not enter college immediately, as his family needed him to help make ends meet. He labored on several nearby farms and toiled in the phosphate mines before finally enrolling at Martin College in Pulaski. He completed the then two-year program on schedule and graduated in 1941.

Ross Bass was a flamboyant, perpetually tanned young man who dreamed of acting in films. He drove to California and found work briefly in a traveling troupe, but like many other aspiring thespians, he wound up making his living by other means. One lucrative stint had him chauffeuring the artist Salvador Dali around the country and serving as his valet and interpreter. In 1942, he enlisted as a private in the Army Air Corps. He served as a bombardier on dozens of B-17 raids over Nazi Germany, earning an Air Medal and an Oak Leaf Cluster. By the time of his discharge, he had risen to the rank of captain.

Like many other servicemen, Ross Bass fell in love during the war. He met Avanell Keith, a beautiful Powers model from Greenville, South Carolina, and married her in 1946. The couple returned to Pulaski, where Bass opened a nursery, a florist shop, and a bottling plant. He grew increasingly active in the Giles County community, joining the Elks, the Rotary, the American Legion and the VFW, as well as being elected vice chairman of the Board of Commissioners of the Pulaski Housing Authority. In 1946, he ran for clerk of the Giles County Court. He lost in the primary, but during the campaign came to know Joe L. Evins, the Democratic nominee for Congress. In 1947, then Congressman Evins got Bass named postmaster of Pulaski.

But Giles County was far too confining for a man of Ross Bass's ambitions. Over the next few years, he would serve as president of both the Tennessee Association of Public Housing Officials and the Tennessee Postmasters Association. The latter position soon put his talents to use as a lobbyist in Nashville and Washington. When incumbent Congressman Pat Sutton, a conservative, opted to leave his seat to wage a quixotic campaign against Estes Kefauver for the Democratic senatorial nod in 1954, Bass resigned as postmaster and threw his hat into the race to succeed him.

Bass entered the campaign as a heavy underdog, but he was, as Congressman Bob Clement called him, "a people person." He knew from his experience as postmaster what others seemed not to know—that more people were likely to be doing business or just visiting at post offices at any given point in the day than would be at courthouses or newspaper offices or banks. Before entering any other part of a town, he would check in with his postal brethren and say "hey" to any of their friends or neighbors who might be around. Unknown to many, he had lived as a boy in half of the largest towns in the district and had amassed a wide array of friends and contacts from his father's ministry.

The other candidates, Springfield Mayor John R. Long and State Senator Thomas E. Fox of Columbia, were better-known, but Bass made sufficient headway in his campaign to scare two of his critics. These two brothers, publisher John Seigenthaler likes to joke, had been visiting their "Old Granddad" for a few hours before arriving at a Bass rally at a country store and commencing to heckle him zestfully and mercilessly. When Bass responded by saying that his "momma would have taken [him] out and whipped [him] if he had acted like [them]," the brothers jumped him. One of them hit Bass with a soda bottle, injuring his back, cutting his wrist, and blackening his eye. Bass had the cuts treated just a tad. The next night, he drove to Nashville to tape a thirty-minute television spot. Upon seeing Bass, anchorman Judd Collins was startled enough to offer him a steak for his eye and some makeup to hide the cuts. Bass, ever mindful of the value of public sympathy, firmly retorted, "You touch that black eye and I'll kill you."

Bass liked to credit the attack for propelling him to his 3,067 vote victory in the Democratic primary, but, in truth, he was a dynamic campaigner. A talented public speaker, if not quite the equal of Frank Clement, he had a winning empathetic approach one-on-one, particularly with the many Tennesseans who had grown up in the rural areas. He also was a skilled organizer. In creating his campaign teams, he charged his staffs to fill every slot, even if they had to resort to filling them with "grease monkeys." In time, he found that his grease monkeys often delivered better for him than veteran pols, as his commitment to their hopes and aspirations inspired them. He had a rare political asset in Avanell, whom his brother, the Reverend Horace Bass, a former Tennessee welfare commissioner, describes as "one of the sweetest people you'd ever want to meet." Her warmth came across in her easy camaraderie with women's groups, in her appeals to voters in his campaign spots, and even more in her work in his office after the election.

Bass entered the House of Representatives in 1955 and became a member of the Agriculture Committee. He used this seat as a bully pulpit for the interests of small cotton and tobacco farmers, always trying to increase acreage allotments in USDA programs when prices were high and limit them in times of surpluses. He was a staunch advocate of maintaining parity at 90 percent, if not higher. Upon finding that imported Mexican braceros were earning more than local white and black laborers, he introduced amendments to pending agriculture bills that, had they been passed, would have denied federal benefits to any landowner who so discriminated.

Bass was indeed a populist, or, as Connecticut Democrat Thomas Dodd put it, a man with "an inherent dislike for the large, the impersonal, and the selfish." He tried unsuccessfully for years to raise the personal income tax exemption from $600 to $750 and to limit entertainment deductions for the affluent. Like so many other Tennesseans, he was a champion of free trade and loved to upbraid Republicans who were not. When a group of House Republicans tried in 1955 to limit the authority of GOP President Eisenhower to negotiate commercial agreements abroad, Bass took the floor to declare that the GOP was "making a political sucker out of the president. They take his first recommendation, and try not only to wreck it but the welfare of the country as a whole." Bass was even more vociferous when he thought a Republican was profiting improperly at the public till. When it was revealed in 1958 that White House Chief of Staff Sherman Adams had taken a vicuna coat from financier Bernard Goldfine, Bass described an oriental rug as a "cover-up job," mink as a "skin job" and vicuna as a "clip job." "But in either case," he added, "the American public is being fleeced by the top echelons of this administration."

Above all, Bass was a defender of TVA. He was instrumental in the creation of the Tims Ford Dam and in securing passage of the TVA Self-Financing Act of 1959. As befit a disciple of Estes Kefauver, which he was, he was a fierce critic of the Dixon-Yates proposal to supply private power at Memphis. By the terms of a 1954 agreement, firms headed by Edgar H. Dixon and Eugene A. Yates would sell their power to the Atomic Energy Commission, thereby eliminating any need for additional TVA power in West Tennessee and Kentucky. In making their argument in favor of the half-billion-dollar plan, supporters of Dixon-Yates had called the TVA "socialistic" and claimed that the whole concept of TVA was "un-American." With Eisenhower content to maintain TVA power facilities at their current level, Bass tried to link the cause of TVA with that of the Democratic Party. To charge that TVA was socialistic, he told the House in his maiden speech, was "to blaspheme the Constitution." TVA, he insisted, was a business proposition that had galvanized industrial development in a depressed region and had proven a significant "antidote" to socialism. His rhetoric here was restrained compared with that he produced in October 1963 when he learned that Barry Goldwater had suggested selling TVA. Dixon-Yates, he declared, had been "penny-ante poker" when compared to the Goldwater proposal. He warned that it would be "utterly stupid" for any Tennessean to contemplate a vote for Goldwater or anyone who agreed with him.

The issue on which Bass's position fluctuated was civil rights. This I say as a matter of record, not of criticism, for Ross Bass was truly one of the South's most enlightened representatives in the 1950s and 1960s on questions involving race. He first experienced discomfort with the existing order while stationed at Fort Knox during World War II. There, as he sat comfortably with a few white soldiers in one truck, he looked out the back and saw black soldiers, enlisted in the same cause and en route to fight the same enemy, sandwiched one up against another. This struck him as wrong and probably led to his initial refusal to sign the now infamous Southern Manifesto of 1956, which pledged signatories to resist all civil rights legislation, but matters were not so easy, not in the 1950s. Were an enlightened white Southerner to defy time-honored southern conventions, he might face retribution at the polls. A loss there would embolden the resistance to racial progress and give it another voice in Congress. Bass demurred for a few hours. When he recognized that Pat Sutton, his ultra-conservative predecessor, was contemplating a return to Congress, he took a step he truly regretted and signed the manifesto. As he surmised, Sutton entered the race and battered him throughout the campaign for his slowness in signing. Even so, Bass prevailed by a three-to-one margin, in what would be his last House reelection bid featuring a serious challenger. To a large degree, Bass had led the Sixth District to accept a reasoned approach to race relations. He resisted going any further during the Eisenhower administration, and voted quietly against the Civil Rights Acts of 1957 and 1960. As time passed, Bass felt increasingly uncomfortable with his record. In 1964, he cast his lot firmly in favor of that year's monumental Civil Rights Act. There are those today who would say that it was too little, too late, but I would remind them that only two others from any southern House delegation outside of Texas voted aye. Not one other House member from a rural southern district did so. Ross Bass's vote was an act of supreme political courage.

By 1963, Bass was contemplating new challenges. In August, he went to Hilton Head Island, South Carolina, to meet with Attorney General Robert Kennedy, the President's brother, who invited him to join the administration as Postmaster General. Here was an appropriate move in two respects. Bass had a postal background and the Kennedys wanted to show some signs of involving southern Democrats in their deliberations. Bass considered the offer seriously until he learned of Estes Kefauver's death. He kept his deliberations private, but let the Kennedys know well before President Kennedy's death in November 1963 that he would not be joining the administration.

As Kefauver's most visible ally, Bass stood to inherit much of the late Chattanoogan's following were he to enter the race in November 1964 to fill out the two remaining years of his term. From the beginning, it was clear that his principal opponent would be Governor Frank G. Clement, Kefauver's longtime rival. Clement's decision to run after having been elected to a third term as governor in 1962 perturbed many who had been close to Kefauver. Although some aligned with Newport businessman Milton M. Bullard, most sided with Bass. Nancy Kefauver endorsed him, as did the *Nashville Tennessean,* the *Chattanooga Times,* and the *Memphis Press-Scimitar,* papers that had long supported Kefauver. Even so, Bass recognized that he would have to build his own identification with the people if he were to win.

In the year between Kefauver's death and the August 1964 primary, Ross and Avanell took their campaign to all ninety-five counties, traveling a total of 80,000 miles. He stressed that he, unlike Clement, was sacrificing his job to make the race. Like Kefauver, he said, he believed in "government by the people—not by machine." Here was a clear allusion to the Clement organization, but Bass's focus in the primary was his support for programs that were the basis of Lyndon Johnson's Great Society. He backed the so-called War on Poverty, saying that an impoverished community was the "primary breeding ground for Communism." He spoke of "equal rights for all," firming up a recent alliance with African Americans in the state. He highlighted his desires to decrease the age of Social Security eligibility from 65 to 62, to increase the minimum wage, and to expand aid to education and the free school lunch program. He contrasted his support for the Kennedy-Johnson tax cut with Clement's imposition of a 3 percent sales tax in 1963. He professed his pride in "the miracle of TVA" while berating Clement for instituting fees on users of TVA recreation facilities. In the process, he forged a Kefauver-like coalition that shocked nearly everyone when it defeated Clement in the primary by almost 100,000 votes.

After such a hard-fought campaign, tensions inevitably lingered between the Democratic factions, leading many to speculate that Bass might be in jeopardy against a strong Republican challenge. That challenge came from Howard Baker, Jr., who had entered the primary late but was beginning to gain support from many who had backed Clement. Baker's closest friend, Bill Swain, suggests that the campaign started out as "little more than fun and games," but it quickly turned into a horse race. It remained so until September 16, 1964, the day Barry Goldwater flew to Knoxville and reiterated his support for privatizing TVA. Bass exploited this opening, linking his fortunes as tightly as possible with Lyndon Johnson's. In television ads and personal appearances, he never mentioned Baker by name. He took the time to hail the President as a man intent on continuing "peace and prosperity" and representing "all of our people." Then he would play his trump card—TVA. Old enough to remember thousands of homes being lit by kerosene lamps, Bass liked to recount the days when people in the Tennessee Valley had to pay a "ransom" for electricity. He suggested that GOP victories anywhere might mean a return to similar conditions. While voters liked Howard Baker and many knew that he and his father had long since disassociated themselves from Goldwater's approach, Bass's tack reinforced his identification with TVA and Lyndon Johnson and almost certainly accounted for his 51,575 vote victory.

Once in the Senate, Bass proved to be one of Lyndon Johnson's most ardent loyalists. Only two Senators went further down the line for LBJ than he did in 1965, arguably the year of the most encompassing liberal reform in American history. He voted for the Twenty-Fifth Amendment (which provided a process for filling a vacancy in the vice presidency), the Voting Rights Act, the war on poverty, Medicare, federal aid to education, funding for water pollution control, and Lady Bird Johnson's highway beautification program. He went to bat for the unions in their battle to repeal Section 14(B) of the Taft-Hartley Act and thereby end the power of states to maintain right-to-work laws, even engaging Senate Minority Leader Everett Dirksen, the leader of the filibuster against the measure, in a lengthy floor debate. He also tackled LBJ's critics on foreign policy questions. He cast his ballots faithfully against moves to limit foreign aid to authoritarian American allies, such as Pakistan and Iran. He even defended Johnson on Vietnam and chided as "completely asinine" those who protested the war. Bass was proud of his association with the "Sage of the Pedernales" and the Eighty-Ninth Congress, one, he said, that should be designated as a "commemorative stamp Congress" because it "cured some of the great ills of the country."

What Ross Bass will be remembered for by history is his work to require the health labeling of cigarettes. A statistical correlation between smoking and cancer had been established in the early 1950s, but several questions remained about the link until the Surgeon General's Advisory Committee on Smoking and Health issued its report in January 1964. "Cigarette smoking," it declared, "is a health hazard of sufficient importance to warrant appropriate remedial action." In the wake of that report, the Congress and several federal agencies tried to decide just what action to take. Working with Thruston Morton, a Republican from Kentucky, one of the few states that produces more tobacco than Tennessee, Bass elicited testimony from a variety of interested parties. Anti-cigarette advocates wanted strong warnings to be placed in advertising and on cigarette packages. Tobacco farmers expressed fears about their livelihood, and the tobacco industry discounted the medical evidence, evidence that we know today turned out to be overwhelmingly true. The cigarette industry opposed any government regulation. With such disparate fears prevalent, Bass and Morton devised a relative consensus behind a legislative package that would require manufacturers to place a warning label on every pack and carton of cigarettes, but would delay similar warnings in advertisements. The exact language for the warning came directly from Ross Bass: "Smoking May Be Hazardous to Your Health." These few words have since become the most recognized words in public health history in the world. The impact in terms of improved quality of lives and longer, healthier lives cannot be underestimated, and as a heart and lung surgeon, I appreciate this Bass public health legacy.

In 1966, Bass's interim term was due to expire and he faced another challenge from Frank Clement. This one was more serious than the 1964 contest. Clement had regained much of his earlier stature; gone was the immediacy of the furor over the 1963 tax increase and the intensity of the Clement-Kefauver rivalry. Clement indeed had to some extent made amends with African Americans by hiring black secretaries in his office and black officers in the highway patrol. He also had appointed future NAACP President Benjamin Hooks to a Shelby County judgeship, making him the first black judge in Tennessee since Reconstruction. In contrast, support for Lyndon Johnson was waning as voters grew increasingly wary about the mounting costs of Great Society programs and the seemingly endless Vietnam War. Bass's ardor in LBJ's defense was less of a virtue than it had been two years earlier, but he was hurt even more when he walked out of a Democratic women's fund-raiser after being introduced with "He's known in the Senate as Big Mouth Bass, The Senator from Tennessee, Ross Bass, Avanell's husband." He had worn the nickname since his days of joint service in the House with Perkins "Small Mouth" Bass of New Hampshire, and Bass's quick-tempered response soon made him a target of ridicule. Bass later managed to play down the taunting on the stump by telling friendly crowds that Clement wanted to go fishing and catch a Bass, but his tax increase "was the wrong can of worms."

Had there been a closed primary or had there been no other contests on the Democratic ballot, Bass very well may have defeated Clement again, but there was a gubernatorial contest that year and Republicans fielded no candidate. Happy with either Howard Baker or Ken Roberts as their potential senatorial nominee, many Republicans crossed over to have a voice in the gubernatorial race. Overwhelmingly, they opted for Buford Ellington, the conservative former governor, over John Jay Hooker, the flamboyant liberal businessman. Their votes had little effect on the gubernatorial election, which Ellington won easily, but they did affect the senatorial contest. Ellington Republicans generally cast their senatorial ballots for Clement, his seeming partner in our leap-frog governorship of the 1950s and 1960s. Their crossover votes provided well more than Clement's margin of victory of just 18,243 votes.

The primary battle had been rigorous but clean and Ross Bass took his defeat stoically. The day after the election, he drove to Clement's headquarters and presented him with a $1,000 campaign contribution. He scarcely worried about might-have-beens. He had narrowly beaten Howard Baker in 1964, the best Democratic year since the Great Depression, and Baker's polls showed him as early as July beating either Bass or Clement. Bass must have seen some of the same data and known that Baker's strength as a candidate and the general trend away from the Great Society would have sealed his fate just as it had Frank Clement's. In truth, Bass had done the job he told the people he was going to do. He boasted throughout the campaign that the Bass platform had become law. For his back-bench role, Bass could be and was rightly proud.

Ross Bass's life took many twists after he left the Senate. He went on to represent the country music industry and other interests as a lobbyist. He played golf frequently and, especially after Avanell divorced him in 1969, enjoyed the company of many women. "Both Ross and I," joked longtime friend John Jay Hooker at a posthumous commemoration, "married beautiful women. I can't understand why they left us." Bass remarried twice, finally to a wonderfully supportive woman named Jacqueline Coulter.

The political bug never completely left Ross Bass. In 1974, he saw that anger at the Watergate affair had opened opportunities to Democrats and he entered the gubernatorial primary. Had he moved more quickly, he might have won and spared our state the anguish of the trials and tribulations of the Governor Ray Blanton years. As he soon learned, however, he was but one of twelve Democrats (and one of eight considered serious candidates) to enter the race. His late entrance meant that even some of his closest associates had committed to others, most to Jake Butcher, the multimillionaire Knoxville banker, or to Franklin Haney, the wealthy Chattanooga developer. An astute politico, Bass recognized that he did not have the personal fortune to compete with Butcher or Haney for the same liberal constituency and ordered that no further money be raised for or spent on his campaign. Two years later, he sought the Democratic nomination for the Sixth District seat in the House then held by Republican Robin Beard. He defeated former Congressman Pat Sutton, Estes Kefauver's nemesis from 1954, in the primary. The district, however, had changed from one dominated by small, traditionally Democratic towns like Pulaski to one dominated by the increasingly Republican suburbs of Memphis and Nashville. The dedication of the youthfully exuberant Beard to serving his constituents in even the most Democratic areas of this greatly transformed part of Middle and West Tennessee meant that this comeback attempt, Bass's last, would be unsuccessful.

Bass continued lobbying for a while, but concluded after he reached his sixtieth birthday that the time had come for him to retire. He summered in Tennessee, but spent the better part of the year in Florida. Sundays he spent in church, Mondays taking care of business, and the rest of the week he spent on the golf course. He retained an interest in politics, frequently phoning his brother Horace in Nashville to get the latest news from Tennessee. He also gained insights sporadically from the family and old friends like John Jay Hooker and Howard Baker when they vacationed in Florida. But he recognized, as all too many others do not, that his time had passed and that it was appropriate for a new generation with new ideas to try its hand at governing.

Ross Bass died on New Year's Day 1993, about nine months after I had rushed to his bedside to insert a chest tube into his lung cavity to remove two quarts of malignant pleural fluid so he could breathe more comfortably. Did his smoking two to three packs a day until the age of 62 contribute to his lung cancer? Possibly, but his accomplishment in guaranteeing that the Surgeon General's warning would appear on every package of cigarettes has saved thousands and thousands of lives. That alone makes the long haul from Pulaski to Washington that John F. Kennedy described so eloquently seem eminently worthwhile.

Chapter 11

Howard H. Baker, Jr.

1967–1985

Majority and Minority Leader

*Watergate Committee
Vice Chairman*

*Chief of Staff to
President Reagan*

(1925–)

"There's Howard Baker," Dan Quayle liked to say in his Senate days, "Then there's the rest of us as far as Senators go." Between 1980 and 1984, each time Senators, Senate aides, or the press were polled on whom they found to be the best Senator, the most influential, the most effective or the most persuasive, Howard Baker finished first. Privately, many Democrats were among his strongest boosters. Connecticut Senator Abraham Ribicoff, John F. Kennedy's HEW Secretary, said that Howard Baker would be "the perfect president." Thomas Eagleton of Missouri went even further, labeling Senator Baker "one of the five ablest men by any standard" with whom he served over three terms and one who would have been "a great president."

It is my good fortune that Howard Baker is my political mentor. When I first considered entering politics, I systematically sought advice from everybody who could help shed light on the unknown journey that I was about to undertake. Through a friend in Nashville, John Van Mol, I was formally introduced to Howard Baker in Knoxville in March of 1990. In retrospect, I am sure that I was just one of hundreds who traipsed through his office seeking encouragement and guidance about a life in politics. I left that meeting with a clear picture of what my next steps should be. Over the next year and a half, I had three formal meetings with him, all initiated by me. Mostly, he listened intently but dispassionately, counseling me less about the possibility of losing than about the positive effect campaigning, if handled properly, could have on me and, more importantly, my family. In his mind, I needed to have very good reasons to take a recess from my medical career; he obviously had tremendous respect for the healing profession and all it represented as a form of public service.

By the end of our third conference, probably because of my persistence more than anything else, Senator Baker implied a victory in a statewide race was possible for me. Were I to make such a dramatic move, he suggested, I should aim high for a position where I would have the opportunity to influence society most broadly. This meant setting my sights on a federal office. Shoot for the position where I could have the greatest impact nationally and internationally, he told me; shoot for the U.S. Senate. But to forgo local and regional politics, to initiate my public service at the statewide level, he counseled, would take a total commitment. I would have to leave my medical practice altogether and spend a full year traveling to every county in Tennessee, shaking thousands of hands and listening to everyday concerns. Senator Baker's advice encouraged me, but it really was not until he sat down with my wife, Karyn, that he became convinced that I could really pull off the feat of winning. Karyn talked with him of her concerns about politics. She was not concerned about losing the race, or losing our privacy, or losing income. She was most concerned about the effect on raising a family. Karyn's demonstration of her priorities apparently convinced Senator Baker that public service would suit us well. "The two of you have what it takes to have a successful family here," he told us at the end of the meeting. In fact, he suggested that political life could bring our family even closer together.

These discussions scarcely ended all trepidation within my family. Dad knew that I wanted to seek office so that I might make a contribution to our society in a larger way, yet he, a family physician for fifty-five years, felt that there was simply no more blessed profession than medicine and was not so sure that I was making the best decision, even at age forty-one. As the personal physician to eight Tennessee governors, he had seen politics in a personal, intimate way that very few ever do. In July of 1993, knowing that I had gone to Senator Baker for advice and that I respected the counsel of a man who had traveled the road of public service, Dad called Senator Baker at his home one evening and told him "Senator Baker, don't talk my son into running for the United States Senate. He's spent nineteen years becoming a great heart transplant surgeon and is doing great service here." Senator Baker had been a counselor, not a prodder. To him, it was second nature to reply, "Dr. Frist, I'm not about to tell your son not to run . . . I'm not going to encourage him too much, but I'm not about to tell him not to run." This told Dad that the decision would be mine, not Senator Baker's. Yet the retelling of that tale from both sides suggested to me that Baker had come to see me, at the very least, as a viable candidate, thereby making my final decision easier.

Howard Baker, unlike me, hails from a political family. The Zeus in his pantheon of heroes is his maternal grandmother, "Mother" Lillie Ladd, who became sheriff of Roane County, Tennessee, in 1932—the first woman sheriff in Tennessee. She succeeded her husband, John Christopher Ladd, who had resigned when a fatal illness set in. Their daughter, Dora Ladd Baker, his mother, was president of the Scott County PTA when she died in 1934. Baker's father, Howard Baker, Sr., served as district attorney general, state representative, state Republican chairman, and, finally, Congressman for the Second District of Tennessee until his death in 1964. Upon his passing, Baker's stepmother, Irene Bailey Baker, was elected to fill his father's unexpired term, then was chosen as Knoxville's welfare commissioner. Baker's cousin John Sherman Cooper represented Kentucky in the Senate for twenty-two years. In 1959, he challenged Everett Dirksen of Illinois, Baker's father-in-law, for the position of Minority Leader. Dirksen, a gifted orator, bested Cooper narrowly. Cooper came to be known as a rock of integrity to Democrats and Republicans alike; Dirksen is regarded as one of the truly great Minority Leaders of this century. And there's another shrewd, aspiring politico with Dirksen-Baker blood in her veins. That's Baker's daughter Cissy, who at twenty-six ran a hard but unsuccessful race for Congress in 1982, a big Democratic year. Since then, she has been managing editor at CNN, and she currently serves as bureau chief at Tribune Publication Network, which is the *Chicago Tribune* office in Washington, D.C. Just maybe, she'll run again someday.

Howard Henry Baker, Jr., was born to Howard and Dora Baker in Huntsville on November 15, 1925. His parents were part of the upper strata of Scott County society, but they mixed comfortably with rich and poor alike. Baker was a friendly, bright youth who read much more outside of the classroom than most of his playmates did inside. It came as a real trauma when his mother died suddenly in 1934. Her recently widowed mother Lillie Ladd moved into the Baker household to fill the maternal void in his life. Two years later, Howard Baker, Sr., married Irene Bailey, a Sevier County native whom he had come to know in his legal travels. For Howard Henry, it was another trauma, for he had become devoted to his grandmother. Perhaps this is when he developed the introspective quality that leads him to closely guard the fullness of his thoughts from even his closest associates. It was about then that Baker acquired his lifelong hobby of photography, one that serves as his creative outlet. My Senate colleagues say he was rarely seen in public events in Washington without his camera around his neck. His talents have been obvious. Indeed his talents are many. Over the past quarter of a century, several exhibitions have featured his photographs, as have his books on Washington and the Big South Fork River and Recreation Area.

Baker fared well in Huntsville public schools with little effort. His parents, however, wanted more for him. They sent him to Chattanooga's McCallie School, where he found the academic program more rigorous and the military emphasis not at all to his liking. His performance there was not impressive, but its high standards prepared him for college. Upon graduation from McCallie in 1943, at five-foot-seven and still baby-faced, Baker had to opt between enlisting in the armed services or being drafted. He chose the navy's V-12 program, which required him to spend vacations on training maneuvers while allowing him to pursue degrees during the academic year. In two years at the University of the South and Tulane University, he picked up three years of academic credit and a commission in the Naval Reserve. He spent the 1945–1946 school year as a PT boat skipper charged with decommissioning PT boats returning from all points abroad. He had planned to complete his electrical engineering degree at the University of Tennessee the next year, but he had second thoughts after a summer as a mining engineer and a day waiting in line at UT. As he prepared to go home, he drove by the law school and saw the light still on and no line. Thus was born the legal career of a man fellow barristers came to know as "Ole Two to Ten."

By the time he graduated from law school in 1949, Baker was already a political veteran. He had gotten his first taste of politics in 1936, when his father took him on a tour of the state in support of the Landon-Knox presidential ticket. When Howard Baker, Sr., successfully campaigned for the Republican nominations for governor in 1938 and Senator in 1940, Baker often accompanied him. These were somewhat quixotic campaigns as Tennesseans still voted as their grandfathers had shot, a tendency only accentuated during the heyday of the New Deal. Still, East Tennessee remained GOP turf. When key Republicans became disillusioned with incumbent Second District Congressman John Jennings, Jr., in 1950, the elder Baker announced his candidacy and hired Baker as his campaign manager. The two made their rounds of middle East Tennessee and ousted Jennings by a remarkable two-to-one margin. Rifts from the primary were slow to heal, and Second District Democrats nominated a stronger candidate than usual, J. Frank Wilson, an able Oak Ridge attorney. Tired and frustrated, Baker, Sr., came home one night and asked Baker to promise him that he would never seek public office (a promise he flatly refused to make). But fences mended sufficiently by election day to allow Baker, Sr., a narrow victory. His margin grew substantially during each of his six bids for reelection.

When Baker, Sr., moved to Washington, Baker helped his father organize his office, then returned home to resume his law practice. His sister, Mary, stayed in the nation's capital and was chosen Tennessee's Cherry Blossom Princess for 1951. During the festivities, she befriended Illinois princess Joy Dirksen. The two met again at a September 1951 wedding. When Baker spied them lighting up a cigar in a car, he ran over, pulled Mary out, rebuked Joy for her "very corruptive" influence on his sister and pushed her into a rosebush. Baker realized he had overreacted and phoned Joy a few days later to ask if he could come by and explain the next time he was in Washington. She agreed and sparks flew when they met. Within twenty-five minutes after he arrived, he proposed, and she accepted.

Howard and Joy Baker had a successful marriage that produced two wonderful children: Darek and Cissy. Joy Baker was a woman of rare grace who always made a point to greet anyone who might be in Baker's office. She had a disarming wit and instincts about people, which were as astute as Howard's, and she was interested enough in politics to make political science her college major. Joy was fundamentally a shy woman, one who as a child had experienced long periods of separation from her father as events kept him traveling around the country. Her apprehensions led Baker to remain on the periphery of their father's campaigns until Baker, Sr., died. Friends thereafter noticed her physical frailty, which was far more pronounced after she won a lengthy battle with alcoholism in the 1970s. Her problem was an open secret in Washington, though unknown to the general public until an aide to Gerald Ford leaked it at the 1976 Republican convention. It took a lot of courage for Joy to acknowledge her illness, and her revelation encouraged many other afflicted people to seek treatment. Over the years, she battled an assortment of ailments, from a chronic back condition to the lung cancer that eventually took her life. All the while, she remained as constant and steady a source of comfort and counsel to Howard as he was to her.

Howard and Joy settled and prospered in Huntsville. In a seventeen-year legal career, he defended sixty-three clients on murder charges, and not one went to the electric chair. Baker had a folksy manner that endeared him to all in the courtroom. He also had a knack for framing questions that drew out more information than witnesses wanted to reveal and for making his points succinctly enough to convey his message powerfully. In the civil cases where he made his living, he developed an uncanny ability to bring suits to settlement by treating all sides with courtesy and respect, using his briefs to outline the points on which all agreed and then crafting solutions that satisfied all parties. If this approach failed, he was prepared to go to court, as the United Mine Workers found out in 1959 when they lost a $1 million judgment to a firm he represented.

Baker took an interest in his community. He was instrumental in forming the Highland Telephone Cooperative, the Huntsville Utility District, and the Scott County Hospital. He chaired the Scott County Airport Authority and served on the boards of several local businesses. Most profitable was his participation in a partnership that bought the controlling interest in the First National Bank of Oneida, which the former owners had been preparing to close. Baker became chairman of the board, lowered credit requirements, and brought the bank out of its lethargy.

It was always Baker's ambition to be president, yet he never developed a specific plan to reach that objective. Everything that came to him came by happenstance. When Baker, Sr., died in 1964, a delegation asked Baker to consider a race for the remainder of his term. He pointed to Irene Baker, who was standing nearby, and replied, "No, Mother, you run." She ran and won. Three months later, Dan Kuykendall, who had clinched the GOP nod to challenge Albert Gore, and Republican activist Johnny Waters called on Baker at his law office and asked him to become a candidate for the remaining two years of the term of the late Estes Kefauver. Bill Brock had already turned them down, they said, and they needed a more credible Republican candidate than any of the three who had already announced. Baker agreed to mull over the possibility with Joy. Having concluded that Darek and Cissy were old enough to move to Washington in a "healthy kind of way," Baker agreed to run if Waters would manage his campaign.

In truth, Baker expected his initial campaign to be "little more than fun and games." His challenge took off, however, as voters became acquainted with his rational, down-home demeanor and his youthfully exuberant brand of pragmatic conservatism. He carried 85 percent of the votes cast in the Republican primary. As Democrats experienced an even more divisive contest than usual, he grew ever more confident, knowing that many supporters of Governor Frank Clement, who lost the Democratic primary to Ross Bass, were moving into his camp. He remained optimistic until September 16, the day that presidential-nominee Barry Goldwater, during a campaign stop in Knoxville, affirmed his position that TVA would benefit more people if it were privatized. Baker's throat clutched. The idea would never fly in Tennessee and his opponent, Ross Bass, capitalized on it, linking his campaign ever more closely with Lyndon Johnson's. Even so, Baker won more than double the total polled by any previous Republican nominee for statewide office and ran three percentage points ahead of Goldwater. Not surprisingly, the *Knoxville Journal* touted him as the "new titular head of the Tennessee GOP."

Baker bided his time for the next few months. Joy, Everett Dirksen, and his closest personal friends were all opposed to his running for a full six-year term, thinking that Tennessee was not ready to elect a Republican. Baker thought differently, however, especially after a poll he commissioned revealed that 65 percent of Tennessee's voters would indeed back a Republican under the right circumstances. By the time he decided, however, Vanderbilt law professor Ken Roberts, a genial man who had coordinated

Tennessee Goldwater volunteers, had entered the race. Who should withdraw? The two met privately and concluded that a civil primary would attract more voters. They made and kept a gentleman's agreement to refrain from personal attacks and set out to organize the state. The edge inevitably went to Baker, for he had already laid the groundwork. In a race expected to be close, he prevailed with 76 percent. It would have been out of character for Howard Baker to gloat or Ken Roberts to whine. Less than an hour after the polls closed, Roberts conceded and predicted a big Baker win in November. Baker heaped praise on Roberts for a "fight in the American tradition" and named him as his chairman for the fall campaign. That should be the model for how primaries should be conducted, and it is the only way that kindles faith in either a party or the system as a whole.

With Republicans united, the November election was wide open. Democrats had had another rip-roaring primary, this time with Governor Frank Clement defeating incumbent Ross Bass, and given Tennessee's Democratic heritage, most pundits forecast an easy Clement victory. Baker, however, had polls even before the primary showing that he could beat either Bass or Clement. He traveled to every county, directing his campaign against the Great Society program of Lyndon Johnson, which he termed one of "guns and butter and a little fat," and painting Clement and his organization as "complacent guardians of the status quo." He made a pointed bid to reach out to minorities and farmers, attracting more than a Republican's usual share. And he sought to ease the conversion of traditional Democrats in the Middle and the West. "The Democrats of this state," he said often, "are no longer concerned with what their Democratic granddaddies may think if they vote Republican, but with what their grandchildren may think if they don't." The hardest thing for Baker was overcoming the sense that a Republican could not win, even as a mid-October poll indicated that 56 percent of those who had made up their minds favored him. Having been received warmly on Beale Street and the union halls of Memphis, however, he began to project a 100,000 vote victory. In what Bob Clement and Ken Roberts today call "one of the cleanest elections ever," he fell just 780 votes short of his guess and became the first Republican ever elected to the U.S. Senate by the people of Tennessee.

Baker entered the Senate most intent on securing the passage of a revenue sharing bill, a measure that he had made the centerpiece of his 1966 campaign. The program would give those officials most familiar with the needs of their communities more latitude in determining which programs to fund and provide money for those officials to carry out their programs. Only in 1971, after the Vietnam War began winding down, could he convince the Democrats who ran the congressional revenue committees that funds were available to start such programs and thus set in motion the process that enacted his bill. Baker then moved into the work of the committees to which he was assigned and soon found his niche on the Air and Water Pollution Subcommittee chaired by Edmund Muskie, the forceful Maine Democrat. Within months, Muskie came to rely on Baker, who he knew had studied engineering and fully understood the complexities of pollution control. Baker, Muskie said, was "a great believer in the potential of American technology" and in the need to establish "standards that would force industry to expand the potential of technology for dealing with environmental problems." Yet Baker was also a fiscal conservative. He and Muskie determined that regulating air and water quality standards would put exorbitant burdens on taxpayers, transfer considerable authority to the bureaucracy, and shift the burden of cleanup from polluters to the government. In markup sessions, Muskie would often get nervous and even angry. More often than not, he would look to Baker and ask him to see what he could do to effect a solution. Baker had a knack for building coalitions through a disarming brand of conciliation—a rare knack for any member, especially a freshman. His compromises addressed the concerns of those interested, limited the problems that might arise, and left all sides in good spirits. It is no small testament to Baker's skills that the Senate approved the monumental clean air and water bills of 1970 without dissent.

Baker's work in the ecological realm had only begun. In 1971, he saw to it that the Atomic Energy Commission had to comply with all environmental laws. Two years later, he and Muskie crafted a measure that allowed states to use part of their highway money to build mass transit systems. In 1977, he authored a compromise that revised the Clean Air Act by limiting delays in compliance schedules proposed in an auto-industry-backed House bill. More importantly for Tennessee, he fought hard to end the most ecologically disruptive aspects of strip mining by limiting federal licenses to those operators who practiced the most advanced techniques of reclamation. When he and John Sherman Cooper introduced the first such bill, strip-mining companies had their employees drive freighted trucks to Baker's Huntsville home and threaten to dump coal in his driveway. They feared that reclamation costs would put them out of business and claimed that such fees would lead to a hefty rise in consumer prices. Baker addressed these concerns on the Senate floor, pointing out that reclamation costs were but $2 a ton and declaring that the stripping policy had allowed some operators to dump whole sides of mountains into nearby roads and streams, forcing the people of Appalachia, the poorest in America, to unfairly subsidize low power rates everywhere. He could not convince Presidents Nixon or Ford, but was grateful when Jimmy Carter saw his idea to enactment soon after taking office in 1977.

It was clear early on that Baker had a broad streak of independence, yet he was a faithful Republican. His brand of partisanship was not the blind, glandular sort that often characterizes recent converts. Rather it was rooted in his East Tennessee heritage. Ideologically, he felt more akin to the Eisenhower-Nixon strain of Republicanism than the Reagan variety, and he did rejoice inwardly in later years when he discerned that Reagan was more of a pragmatist than some of his followers made him out to be. In his first term, he supported Nixon's plans to end the draft, provide for the direct election of the President, and expand the right of suffrage to those eighteen and older. He had qualms about America's involvement in Vietnam, yet he backed Nixon's handling of the conflict. He did question during the Pentagon Papers controversy why people were not forcing Kennedy-Johnson Defense Secretary Robert McNamara to "testify about why he was telling the president one thing and the Congress another." He opposed busing for purposes of racial balance, but he helped Everett Dirksen draft the compromise that banned realtors from discriminating against home buyers on the basis of race. He pushed legislation that would limit the power of states to evade the Supreme Court's "one man, one vote" dictum, knowing that the beneficiaries would be blacks and Republicans, groups long denied an equal voice by Bourbon Democratic state legislatures. He managed the enactment of Nixon's revenue sharing plan, the cardinal feature of his "New Federalism."

Given his performance in the Senate, it is not surprising that participants, in a predawn meeting following Nixon's 1968 nomination, thought Baker one of Nixon's two most likely choices for the vice presidency. Why Nixon opted for Spiro Agnew must still baffle those present as much as it does me. Nor is it surprising that Nixon had Attorney General John Mitchell offer Baker a seat on the Supreme Court in 1971. In recent years, Baker has likened the atmosphere he found in the high court to that in a funeral home and he was forever grateful when Mitchell rescinded the offer, knowing Baker preferred the more active life of a Senator.

That life took a dramatic turn in 1973 when Republican Leader Hugh Scott tapped him to act as senior Republican on Sam Ervin's committee investigating the Watergate affair. Baker had challenged Scott twice for the leadership and lost but narrowly, leading many around Washington to dub Baker's placement on the Watergate committee as "Scott's revenge."

Investigating allegations of chicanery is difficult under any circumstance, but especially so when the investigator and the accused are longtime associates. Nixon and Baker had campaigned for each other at their own expense, and the offer of the justiceship was of sufficiently recent vintage for it to be not far from the back of Baker's mind. Indeed, Baker believed at first that the probe was a bid by Democrats to put a better face on the overwhelming defeat they had suffered in 1972.

Despite his suspicions, Baker took his own investigation seriously and intended to nip any hint of scandal in the bud as quickly as possible. Letting evidence pile up over a long period of time might hurt the Republican Party and weaken the presidency. Two weeks after the panel was formed, he got a private audience with Nixon, whom he initially believed to be innocent, and pled with him to drop his claims of executive privilege with respect to the testimony of his top aides. Far more experienced as an attorney than the president was, he counseled Nixon that only the prompt appearance of those closest to him before the committee would remove growing doubts that they (and he) had nothing to hide. Nixon balked, leading Baker to suspect that there might be more to the case than met the eye and to reiterate his advice to his staff to "let the chips fall where they may."

By the time public hearings opened on May 17, 1973, participants had begun to blow the whistle on several top-ranking employees of the Committee to Reelect the President (CRP) and the Nixon White House. That day, Baker promised an "objective and evenhanded but thorough, complete and energetic" investigation that would develop the facts before the public and recommend appropriate statutory changes. As witnesses appeared, Baker let others rehash questions the staff had put to them in background interviews. He used his own queries to probe the motives of the participants, queries that evoked the fears of witnesses that they would be seen as somehow disloyal to those higher up in the CRP and the White House.

After a month of hearings, the scandal had still not made its way directly into the Oval Office. That changed on June 26 when former White House counsel John Dean came before the committee. Baker's turn to question Dean came three days later. At lunch that day, Baker told Ron McMahan, his press secretary, that the committee had been "chasing rabbits" and needed to find "the central animal." In a subdued Senate caucus room, he told Dean that his testimony had finally established the focus of the probe: "What did the president know and when did he know it?" After establishing that Dean did not know whether Nixon had prior knowledge of the break-in, he moved to the cover-up. Dean testified that the President seemed to know what was transpiring as early as September 15, 1972, six months earlier than Nixon himself had acknowledged.

To Baker, Dean's charges strongly suggested "presidential malfeasance," but the committee still needed corroborating evidence. The break came when Republican Deputy Counsel Donald Sanders elicited an admission from former White House aide Alexander Butterfield that a tape recording system existed and was still in use in several of the White House offices. As soon as Butterfield completed his public testimony, the committee asked Nixon to submit the tape recordings of five conversations with Dean. Nixon declined, saying that different people might construe them differently and that their release might violate the principle of executive privilege. Upon receiving Nixon's letter, Baker moved in open session to subpoena the tapes.

Like all but one motion that this panel considered, it passed unanimously. Yet the committee never got the tapes, for the courts awarded them in October to Special Prosecutor Archibald Cox.

The details of the Saturday Night Massacre are well-told elsewhere, particularly in Sam Ervin's *The Whole Truth*. Let it be said, however, that Baker and Ervin were earnestly seeking accommodation with Nixon when they agreed to recommend to the panel his proposal to let Mississippi Democrat John Stennis transcribe their Watergate-related contents for the panel's use. What neither they nor Stennis were told was that Nixon was trying to force Cox to accept only transcripts of tapes the courts had awarded him and virtually ordering him not to seek any further tapes or documents. As events unfolded and Cox was dismissed, it became clear, as maverick Republican Lowell Weicker put it, that Baker and Ervin had been "zonked." The agreement they forged was the only means they had to get any access to the tapes. Their intent was the same as it had been all along, to secure the evidence for the benefit of their committee. It hardly helped Richard Nixon or his defense when he reneged on his pledge; in fact, it exposed the fallacy of his argument that he intended to comply with the law.

Even so, Baker continued to urge Nixon to make a full disclosure. He focused his attention, however, on matters that the committee had de-emphasized. All along, he had suspected that the CIA had played a role in the Nixon scandals, if only because its leaders were less than cooperative with routine inquiries. Upon completing the probe, he published a report that cleared the CIA as an institution, but raised a bevy of troubling questions about the suspicious relationships some of the burglars had had with one-time agency colleagues. Especially relevant to the issues of today, Baker warned of an "orgy of reform without direction" as Congress prepared a bill designed to prevent future Watergates. With Sam Ervin, he offered an amendment to give individuals a full tax credit for the first $50 they gave candidates or parties each year. He called for raising the limit on individual contributions from $1,000 to $3,000 and introduced an addendum completely banning donations from groups. "Corporations cannot vote," he said. "Common Cause cannot vote. Chambers of Commerce cannot vote. Why should they contribute?" Had this measure passed, the power of special interests and their political action committees would have been severely curtailed. Yet in 1974, the Senate was dominated by members who depended on union money for their campaigns. What Baker could see but his colleagues could not was that corporations and ideologues would soon form their own PACs and the system would eventually be more engulfed with special interest money than ever.

Watergate made Howard Baker a household name for the first time. In a presidential preference poll conducted in the midst of the hearings, he was one of two Republicans to best Democratic front-runner Ted Kennedy. Later in 1973, he ran third when *Newsweek* asked Republicans whom Nixon should choose to succeed Spiro Agnew if Agnew resigned the vice presidency. Knowing how some Nixon sycophants resented his independence on the Ervin Committee, it hardly surprised him when Nixon opted for Gerald Ford. When Ford acceded to the presidency ten months later, Baker's name rose quite often in speculation about who should replace him as vice president, but Ford thought the circumstances warranted executive branch experience and that meant Nelson Rockefeller. When Ford moved to replace Rockefeller before the 1976 GOP convention in order to boost his nomination chances, Baker's name again figured prominently. Ford wrote in his memoirs that his choice eventually came down to Baker and Bob Dole. Ford was closer to Senator Dole. He had served with Dole in the House and even credited him with swaying the four deciding votes in his 1965 bid for the House Republican leadership. Dole's reputation then was more one of a fierce partisan than of the talented leader of the Senate he became. Baker, in contrast, had been known as an able lawmaker since he entered the Senate. In Ford's eyes, this image suggested compromise, a notion he feared might project weakness to the public at a time when he was running thirty-three points behind Jimmy Carter. He thought Dole might bring back to the GOP farmers who had been disenchanted with his Soviet grain embargo. Carter's lead in the South, meanwhile, was such that Ford heeded those who suggested that he face up to losing our region. As much as I respect Bob Dole, I am convinced that President Ford beat himself by not choosing Baker, and I have good southern company in that belief. Among Democrats, publisher John Seigenthaler and former Georgia Senator Herman Talmadge agree, as did Sam Ervin. As it turned out, the ten Confederate states Carter carried and our neighboring states of Kentucky and Missouri provided more than Carter's margin in the popular vote and 139 of his electoral votes. In five of those states, Ford lost by five or fewer percentage points. Would choosing Baker have made the difference? Definitely, as Walter Mondale, Carter's Vice President, has been telling people for years.

Strangely enough, the Ford loss proved a boon to Baker's career. Had Ford won, the vacancy in the Republican leadership left by Hugh Scott's retirement would surely have been filled by Bob Griffin, an able legislator from Michigan. But Baker was more vibrant than Griffin and a far superior communicator. Seeing a fresh, articulate face as a must for a Republican leader at a time when Democrats controlled the White House and both Houses of Congress, several members who had backed Hugh Scott in the past let Baker know that they wanted him to run. Baker was interested, but he had to be persuaded. The day before the vote, New Mexico Republican Pete Domenici called Baker at home and told him that he needed to rush over to the Capitol. He told Baker to address the eight Republican freshmen, suggesting that he speak substantively and not just say "if I run I want you to know what I'm like if you decide to vote for me." Five of the newcomers pledged their votes by nightfall, but Baker was still three shy of the nineteen needed to win. He got one at the door, but was still uncertain about even having his name put in nomination until he met Griffin at the door and sensed anguish in his eyes. He gestured to Charles "Mac" Mathias of Maryland to place his name in nomination, then remained oblivious to signs that he had won—even the friendly nod in his direction by Ed Brooke of Massachusetts, who was counting the ballots—until Brooke declared "Baker, nineteen, Griffin, eighteen."

Characteristically, Baker was as magnanimous in victory as Bob Griffin was in defeat, saying, "It could just as easily have gone the other way." He got down to business right away, creating GOP task forces to develop alternatives to Carter's economic and energy programs. He named to each an amenable group of members of all stripes of Republican opinion and thus forged a basis for future unity. The committees' reports generated blueprints for programs that Republican candidates would develop and articulate in 1978 and 1980. Baker maintained close contact with all of his colleagues and encouraged them to come to him with their concerns. Knowing where each Senator was likely to stand on any issue, he had no trouble determining which members could be persuaded and how to negotiate.

Baker's way was to compliment, to persuade, and to appeal to party loyalty. He kept pledges to campaign for each of his Republican colleagues and he attended to their concerns in discussions with Majority Leader Robert Byrd about the Senate schedule. If they felt Byrd had been less than fair, they would vote with Baker on procedure even if they agreed with Byrd on substance. Opponents of public financing of congressional campaigns and a 1978 bill that would have limited the rights of businesses in labor disputes found these concessions crucial to block these well-intentioned if unwise pieces of legislation. Indeed, with a united Republican front and a few Democratic defections, Baker could tie up any measure Democrats deemed important. Baker is not an obstructionist by nature and he used this option sparingly. Yet the degree of unity he forged within the Republican caucus gave him substantial leverage over any matter Democrats deemed crucial.

We in Congress cannot align with the majority of our party on every vote, nor do our consciences allow us to follow blindly what we think a majority of our constituents believe on every vote. Sometimes, we have access to more information than they do and it is up to us to educate them about our different conclusions and hope they understand. The toughest vote for me politically during the 104th Congress was the one I cast to break a filibuster over President Clinton's nomination of Dr. Henry Foster to be Surgeon General. I knew Hank Foster and knew that he had the potential to be an outstanding Surgeon General. I had read his medical writings, many of which were taken out of context in congressional hearings to make it seem like he was an uncaring person. Having read through all his publications, I realized that there was quite a bit of misinformation circulating about what he said. While Hank's critics suggested that he had some wild-eyed abortion program, the word abortion appears only once or twice in all of his writings and he was a strong advocate for abstinence. Still, nearly all of my field people in Tennessee recommended that I vote against Hank. For me, the right course was precisely the opposite. Even so, I called Senator Baker to get his perspective. I knew I was doing the right thing when he told me, "This just may be your Panama Canal."

The Panama Canal held a particularly important symbolic place in the growth and prosperity of our republic. Baker had always considered its construction to be the "moonshot" of the early twentieth century. In the 1970s, when perceptions were growing that our country no longer had the will to defend our principles or interests anywhere, the canal indeed provided a vivid symbol of American strength. The shifts in the Panamanian political landscape opened up the issue of whether our nearly eighty-year-old arrangement with the Central American nation needed reform.

Baker had crafted a pragmatic Republican consensus of foreign policy that focused on limiting Soviet Cold War expansionism. Sharing the belief of conservatives that America must be strong enough militarily to oppose the Soviets, he was quite critical of President Carter's abandonment of the B-1 bomber and neutron bomb, his cuts in naval construction, military manpower, and troop strength in South Korea, and his failure to link a Strategic Arms Limitation Talks (SALT) II Treaty to the curtailment of Soviet "adventurism" in other parts of the world. In instances where he felt Carter had acted in the national interest, as in his plans to resume military aid to Turkey and sell jets to Egypt and Saudi Arabia, Baker not only devised legislative packages that could win approval but helped swing undecided Senators behind them. It is clear that Baker kept in mind the main source of America's troubles. "If there's going to be a standoff with Russia," he contended, "it's not Panama where the real danger is."

The issue of Panama encapsulated the anxieties of many conservatives more powerfully than any other in recent memory. Senate Republican legislative counsel Howard Liebengood wrote Baker in 1977 that Panama was a symbol of American strength and beneficence, leading many to respond emotionally to prospective changes in the relationship rather than think rationally through the potential consequences of inaction. Surveys taken just prior to the signing of the treaties showed that 78 percent of the people polled did not want to "give up" the canal.

Baker hoped that the treaty issue would be resolved on the basis of reason. Schooled in the tradition of a bipartisan foreign policy, he aimed to give any president a fair hearing on any proposal that involved overseas questions. His pledge to decide the question on its merits and not emotion heartened Jimmy Carter. Baker also insisted that if the pacts were to be approved the public had to be "educated." Publicly, he vowed "not to decide" until "I know what I'm talking about."

A few things were clear to Baker. The canal, in reality, no longer handled much American shipping. To Panamanians and many other Latinos, it was a symbol of what one Tennessee Republican leader called "the nearest, purest, most colonialistic experience this country had had." Every American president since Eisenhower had concluded that America's national interest lay in the use of the canal, not its operation. In fact, by the 1970s, the canal was less susceptible to an attack from any external force than from sabotage by extremists from within Panama. With U.S. generals testifying that it would take a 100,000-man presence to prevent such an attack, it was not hard for Baker to conclude that the canal was "more effectively defended in partnership with Panama."

Baker understood that some new pact was needed, but he questioned whether *these* treaties were the right ones for America. There were two treaties. One treaty, a Neutrality Treaty, said that Panama would manage the canal and keep it safe and open to peaceful transit by all vessels. The United States could help Panama defend the canal, but Panama alone had the right to keep defense installations after the year 2000. Panama, however, would grant U.S. warships the right to cross the canal expeditiously in times of war. The other, the Panama Canal Treaty, said that the United States would be the primary operator and defender of the canal itself until 2000, but that the Canal Zone would be integrated into Panama within three years of the approval of the treaties and a new Panama Canal Commission would pay Panama $20 million a year for salaries and maintenance and 30 cents per ton of canal revenues.

The contents of the pacts seemed to fit Baker's criteria, and he charged each of his top aides with drafting advice. Most agreed that a new relationship was needed. Some feared that Carter had heightened expectations in Panama to a point where a rejection of the pacts might lead to violence, even war. All of Baker's aides agreed that an "aye" vote might mean that he could never be nominated for president. Approval of the pacts, Baker quipped privately, "might save the party and whip me."

Baker thus realized early on the possible effects of his decision on his political future, the outcome of the debate, and the future of U.S.-Latino relations. He urged Carter to create a public interest lobby to sell the treaties to the public. Then, he hired consultants to provide arguments for and against the pacts and made them available to every colleague. Their papers clarified his understanding of the issues involved. What confused the issue was the Panamanian negotiator's assertion that Panama did not have to keep the canal open if it ceased to be profitable, nor give the United States preferential passage in wartime or allow the United States to defend the canal against an attack from a third country. This had not been Baker's or Carter's perception and Carter tried to clarify the matter in a joint statement of understanding. To Baker, the statement merely bound Carter and Panamanian leader Omar Torrijos Herrara to its ruling and it could be easily renounced in the future. He needed assurances in the text of the treaties that what Carter and Torrijos had agreed upon would bind all future leaders of the United States and Panama. He commissioned a poll in Tennessee that showed wide support for his position, but not Carter's, then took the results to Carter and told him that neither he nor the Senate would back the pacts without the addenda.

Knowing that losing Baker's support would kill the treaties, Carter arranged for Baker to fly to Panama and meet with Torrijos. Today, what members of Baker's party remember most vividly about the trip is meeting an obviously hungover Torrijos, who seemed to calm down only after a rather long belt from his canteen, and being accosted in an obnoxious way by Manuel Noriega, who gave them a lengthy diatribe about the vulnerability of the canal to sabotage. Most pressing at the time, however, was the need for Baker to make his pitch to Torrijos, which he did in his kind but firm manner. "You're trying to negotiate new treaties," Torrijos said. "I have no intention of negotiating new treaties," Baker shot back, "but . . . the Senate will not ratify the treaties unless these amendments are attached." Only after Torrijos publicly assented to the amendments after Baker returned to Washington did Baker drive to the White House to tell Carter that he would support the accords if the Senate approved his addenda.

Baker stirred the ire of many Republicans by his support for the Panama Canal Treaties as amended. Some 64,000 letters arrived in his office, 98 percent of them from opponents of the treaty. Some disgruntled Republican activists in our state suggested that he had traded his vote for a promise from Carter that Democrats would not field a strong opponent against him. Twelve House Republicans demanded that he resign as leader, saying he had "no right" to use his office to advance the accords over the objections of the American people. In fact, February 1978 polls indicated that Americans *favored* the Carter pacts narrowly, and favored those as amended by Baker by a better than two-to-one margin. Yet the vehement statement of these conservatives reflected the anxieties of many Republicans who intended to seek retribution at the polls in 1978 and 1980. This sentiment Baker had to heed. "You can doubt their judgment," he said, "but you better never doubt their authority."

In Washington, Baker acted to ensure that Senate proceedings did not become riddled with the same passions. He secured access to relevant documents for treaty opponents and joined them in requests for drafts of bills implementing the pacts and for evidence of Torrijos's alleged involvement in a drug ring. To facilitate intraparty harmony even further, he swapped desks with anti-treaty manager Paul Laxalt for the debate's duration and kept him apprised of his latest headcounts. And he hailed critics of the accords—many of whom had co-sponsored his amendments—for making contributions to the debate that improved the accords and assured compliance by future leaders of the United States and Panama.

Baker's courtesies masked a fierce determination to see the treaties ratified. Knowing that failure would have dire geopolitical implications, he and Majority Leader Robert Byrd opted to lure votes by letting undecideds amend the resolution with reservations that Panama could accept and joined the recalcitrant in meetings with Panamanian and State Department officials to find language expressing their concerns that would not provoke Torrijos. One by one, they fell in line, quite often crediting Baker's addenda for making their votes possible. In the end, both pacts were ratified with 68 votes, one more than the number needed. Why? Perhaps the best answer comes from Paul Laxalt, who credited the outcome "solely . . . to the effectiveness of the Leadership." Our Western friends speak their minds, and he and Orrin Hatch still deem the pacts unwise. Yet gentlemen such as they recognize that voting one's conscience regardless of the consequences is always a sign of strength, and they are loud in hailing Baker for an act of "courage."

Some conservative activists like to say that it was Baker's votes on Panama that kept him from being elected president. I disagree. Polls taken in the early stages of the 1980 campaign indicated that Baker had the lowest negative ratings of any of the Republican candidates. This indicated that Republicans of all stripes had a great deal of respect for Baker, as did many Democrats. Henry "Scoop" Jackson said privately that the nation would be "safest" in his hands. Abraham Ribicoff met with Jim Cannon, Baker's longtime chief of staff, and advised him whom in Connecticut to recruit to assist his candidacy. But respect in politics is not devotion, and devotion rarely comes on the basis of a reputation. Particularly as Minority Leader but even before, Baker never subordinated his Senate or family duties to his campaigns. Unlike Ronald Reagan or George Bush or even Bob Dole or Lamar Alexander, he never systematically cultivated the campaign industry or the political activists who so dominate the nominating process. His daughter Cissy found him fully confident he could handle the job of president better than anyone else, but "it's just getting there he wasn't committed to." I suspect Baker's weakness in presidential campaigns stemmed from his most obvious strength. Because he was smarter and wiser than those around him, he had difficulty yielding total control to a large-scale campaign organization.

Until the last two weeks of 1979, Baker was a "weekend warrior" as a campaigner. He spent his weekdays attending to work in Washington. Foremost in his mind was the SALT II Treaty. Convinced that SALT II was not fair to the United States, he aimed to recommit the pact to Carter and instruct him to return to negotiations and produce an agreement that would remove some of the inequities. He hoped voters would hear of his scrutiny of the treaty and appreciate it. The debate he expected to dominate never ensued; for the Soviet invasion of Afghanistan rendered nonexistent the small chance that SALT II might be approved.

Since 1980, Baker has made clear his belief that "one has to be unemployed to be elected president." As Baker was focusing on SALT II, George Bush was attending cattle shows, county fairs, and coffees all over Iowa and New Hampshire, doing the kind of "retail campaigning" necessary to win endorsements and votes. Activists who preferred either Bush or Baker to Reagan, even some who thought Bush "light" compared to Baker, noted Bush's "fire in the belly" and the meticulousness of his workers. Curiously enough, Baker's staff had him traveling all over the country in 1979 rather than focusing on the states with early primaries or caucuses. By November 1979, when Baker workers got around to asking Iowa's five-term Governor Robert Ray for an endorsement, most of Iowa's key Republicans had signed on with other candidates. Ray preferred Baker and lent him a few of his ablest lieutenants, thus creating the potential for a three-man race. Only in December did Baker's effort start to gel, when the cameras of consultant Doug Bailey caught him shouting down an Iranian student who berated him vituperatively after his government had taken sixty-three Americans hostage at the U.S. embassy in Teheran. The powerful advertising spots that featured this one-sided exchange pushed Baker past Bush in the polls and close to Reagan. "In terms of popular opinion on the day of the caucus," guessed Bailey, "if it had been a primary, we would have had a three-way tie." Baker's rise came from a media boost rather than an organizationally generated boost, and in caucus states, organizational strength is often the key to victory.

As Phil Gramm put it in 1996, there are usually "two tickets out of Iowa." Everyone knew that in 1980 one would go to Reagan, the other to Baker or Bush. The strength of George Bush's organization gave him the other ticket out of Iowa, for he outpolled Baker two-to-one, and he even surpassed Reagan.

Baker remained in the race for a while, but resisted the classic prescription for a catch-up race, a negative campaign. Instead, he ran his earlier ads, new ones laying out an idea for a ten-year program to develop a nongasoline powered car, and an especially ironic but powerful five-minute film featuring his photographs. "I am not driven to be president," he said. "If you have . . . such a burning desire to be President, you'll probably fail on the job. If you have to be pathological about it, skip it." These ads certainly strengthened his image as a thoughtful issue-oriented candidate, but for moderate conservatives, the central question was who could beat Reagan. The only answer they had seen was Iowa's Bush. But many wondered whether Reagan, at sixty-nine, was too old to handle the job. The answer came at a Manchester, New Hampshire, debate featuring all seven candidates. Reagan seemed to hold his own and shot up to a twenty-point lead over Bush in New Hampshire. Bush's fate was sealed soon thereafter when he froze at a one-on-one encounter with Reagan when Reagan tried to include the field. Anger at Bush for this gaffe moved many to leave him, but they scattered in many directions. Persistent rumors had it that Bush's fade might lead Gerald Ford to enter the race. Were that to happen, Baker knew that much of his remaining support would dissipate. A healthy realism led him to acknowledge that his campaign was not "going anywhere." The "late start," he said, may have been his problem, but if it were, he had no regrets, for he did not believe America needed "two and three year campaigns for the presidency." While Doug Bailey was quick to hail the organizational efficiency that established Bush as the moderate alternative to Reagan, he regretted that Baker, "the one who could survive the long look, couldn't get there to get looked at." Just as certain was Reagan manager John Sears, who thought that if Baker "had been in Bush's shoes, he might have made more of his position."

When Baker withdrew, he pledged to spend that fall campaigning "as hard as time and . . . energy permit" to elect a Republican Senate. Two weeks later, it became clear that Reagan would be the nominee and Baker promised to endorse him at an opportune time in the not-too-distant future. No one worked harder than Baker for the Republican ticket that autumn. He campaigned in twenty-five states, assuring skeptics that Reagan recognized a duty to "represent all the people" and telling the faithful that his election would "create a new spirit of optimism." He was even more instrumental in legitimizing his party's nominees, many of whom were more conservative than he, in the eyes of Republican moderates. As early as June, he was predicting a Republican takeover of the Senate. Many scoffed, but the election turned out as he predicted. Republicans picked up twelve seats and took control for the first time in a generation. As the year ended, Baker helped negotiate the charter of the "Superfund" legislation to clean up toxic wastes. More importantly, he devoted considerable time to planning the transition of his caucus from minority to majority status. No longer did Republicans have the luxury of being dissidents. Now he warned them publicly and privately that they had to "perform."

By Inauguration Day 1981, Baker and Reagan's closest associates had fashioned a solid basis for cooperation between the White House and Congress, something altogether missing during the Carter years. He brought Reagan appointees together with the congressional leaders who had jurisdiction over their departments. Inside the Senate, he initiated weekly meetings of the leadership and his committee chairmen, always inviting one or two freshman

Senators. He took great care early on to let Reagan know that he intended to help him keep the commitments he had made during his campaign. There were things they would disagree upon, he said, "and . . . if I must take a separate position, I will try to let you know in advance. But you should also know that on every . . . close call, I'm going to resolve the issue in your favor."

With inflation at 13 percent and unemployment rising, Baker felt certain that Reagan's economic recovery program should receive first priority. Because discussions of social issues would divide his caucus, he vowed to keep them off the floor until 1982, a decision agreed to by Reagan's core of advisors. His decision met with the sneers of a few single-issue groups, but it allowed him to maintain the cohesiveness of his new, narrow 53–47 majority. Cohesiveness was important because lobbyists were swarming around the Capitol in search of the largesse to which they had become accustomed. The way Baker held his troops together for the Reagan tax and budget programs during dozens of tough votes led Democrat Senator Daniel Inouye of Hawaii to label him "the best of the Republican leaders." Never did more than two Republican members bolt from the Republican position on any vote. The success Reagan had, said Colorado conservative Bill Armstrong, was "sixty percent Ronald Reagan and forty percent Howard Baker."

On difficult foreign policy questions, it was Senator Baker to whom President Reagan turned to do his bidding. When Reagan revived a Carter plan to sell five AWACS jets to Saudi Arabia, he found only twelve Senators prepared to vote with him. "That's counting me," Baker said, "and I don't want to vote for it." As evidence of the instability of America's friends in the Arab world mounted, most notably with the assassination of Egyptian President Anwar Sadat, Senators began to reconsider. Only when Baker organized Reagan's lobbying effort and devised an instrument to address senatorial concerns about Israeli security did a 52–48 majority appear for the sale.

It was Baker as well who defused Reagan's only major faux pas of his first year. Reagan's aim was to restore solvency to the Social Security system, but the proposal he floated, penalizing early retirees and eliminating the minimum benefit, angered senior citizens. Reagan wanted to fight for his plan, but Baker and House Republican Leader Bob Michel advised him that his bill could not pass. Instead, Baker suggested, Reagan should create a body similar to the Water Quality Commission he had once served on to produce a solution. Reagan did and the panel devised a compromise that won lopsided majorities of both Houses of Congress and indeed kept the program alive.

As early as 1966, Baker was telling friends that no one should serve more than three terms in the Senate. Thereafter, he continually warned of the dangers of America being run by career Congressmen who adopted the mindsets of "elected bureaucrats" and "tourists in our own constituencies." Even so, the news in January 1983 that he might retire stunned many. SAY IT AIN'T

SO, HOWARD, wired Bob Dole. It was so, though. To be sure, there was a political dimension to Baker's calculations. If he opted for life after the Senate, he could replenish the finances he had sacrificed and have a chance to "experience . . . a perspective" more attuned to the country at large than that of Washington, one he figured he needed if he were to make another bid for the presidency.

Baker's position was weaker than it had been during his first two years as Majority Leader. He still had fifty-four members, but the House coalition of Republicans and Boll Weevil Democrats that had emerged for Reagan programs had been decimated. More than in the past, he had to couple his partisan duties with his institutional role to make the Senate work. Days and nights were longer and rifts were more difficult to bridge as the 1984 elections drew near. Still, the Ninty-eighth Congress produced some momentous legislation—the bills preserving the Social Security system, making a $140 billion down payment on the deficit, creating a holiday honoring Dr. Martin Luther King, Jr., and revising the criminal code to, among other things, transfer the burden of proof of insanity from the prosecution to the defense, all of which he played a role in shaping.

After his retirement, Baker intended to spend 1985 and 1986 practicing law and building a viable presidential campaign, but politics soon took a back seat to his new work advising clients all over the world. He was even more attentive to Joy, taking her to Mayo and other clinics to see her treated for a chronic abdominal condition. Never would he allow himself to be away from her for more than three days, and he would not give his closest associates the go-ahead to determine if he could raise the necessary campaign funds until doctors assured him that her pain was unrelated to the cancer that seemed in remission. He had built a strong organization in New Hampshire and seemed to be putting one on the ground in Iowa. Operations elsewhere were so limited that one associate was joking that the good news was that "our strategy hasn't killed us."

By February 1987, the Reagan White House was in even greater disarray. Public confidence in the Gipper was at an all-time low after it was learned that some of his aides were selling arms to Iran and diverting some of the profits to the Nicaraguan Contras. This happened on the watch of Chief of Staff Donald Regan, who had shown little respect over the years to Congress or the media. "Half of Washington wanted him out," Nancy Reagan wrote later, and Regan's discourtesies to the First Lady further hastened his demise. But who would replace him? Reagan's inner circle met to contemplate that question. "Whoever was selected," said Paul Laxalt, had to be "someone who knew the Hill, . . . [and] the agencies, had . . . credibility with the press and [would] be the kind of person to come into a turbulent White House and restore some peace." Baker's name "rang out." When Laxalt let the Reagans know, their eyes lit up. But would Baker abort his presidential campaign?

Minutes later, Reagan called Baker at his Florida condo. Baker was with his grandson, and Joy told Reagan, "Howard is at the zoo." "Well," replied the President, "Wait till he sees the zoo I've got in mind for him."

Baker had once seen Reagan as a "movie star who'd fall flat on his face," but he had come to "admire" and "like" the Gipper. The President was at the low point in his political career and was crying out for help. With the administration in what Bill Brock called a "blue funk," Baker took the job as an "obligation," knowing that it extinguished his ambition of becoming president.

How did he fare? "Sometimes people say one man can't make a difference," said Daniel Inouye; "That one man made a difference." It had been Baker's advice to Richard Nixon to come clean quickly, and thus repair rather than merely contain the damage to his administration. He gave the same advice to Reagan, who had the inner security and good sense to heed wise counsel. He got Reagan to admit in a nationally televised appearance that "what began as a strategic opening . . . deteriorated . . . into trading arms for hostages." Baker charged Counsel A. B. Culvahouse with determining what this President knew and when he knew it and making his findings, as well as such sensitive documents as Reagan's private diary, available to the congressional panels probing the matter. Democrats and Republicans alike became convinced that no smoking gun would point to Ronald Reagan. Reagan could then refocus his presidency on the timeless concerns of war and peace and bread and butter. That Reagan, leaning on Baker, succeeded is shown not only by George Bush's election in 1988 but also by the revival of Reagan's approval rating from a low of 36 percent to a more typical 61 percent when Baker left.

With Democrats having regained control of the Senate in 1986, there was little chance for Reagan to score any major legislative victories. Baker was certain that Reagan's military rearmament program had convinced Soviet leader Mikhail Gorbachev that there was no way to match America's might. This afforded a rare opportunity to "reduce the risk of nuclear annihilation" through a fair and equitable arms reduction treaty. In the wake of a series of resignations, Baker led Reagan to bring in a team, including a little-known National Security Advisor named Colin Powell, which was cooperative and comfortable with both his Strategic Defense Initiative and his aim of reducing nuclear arms. Many of Reagan's staunchest backers were wary of any deal with the Soviets, Reagan worried that he was alone in pushing the Intermediate Nuclear Forces Treaty. "Don't you worry," Baker replied. "There are millions who support you . . . and if you're ever in doubt about your official family, just remember this. I will back you up on whatever you decide tooth and claw."

When the summit came in December 1987, Baker noticed Reagan's envy of Gorbachev's mastery of details. As he headed for his living quarters, the President muttered that he "had better hit the books tonight." "I wouldn't do that," Baker counseled sympathetically. "Be Ronald Reagan. Remember who you are, what you believe and where you want to go. Let us take care of the facts." Colin Powell prepared the talking points that night and Reagan was Reagan the next morning. The results portended well for the pact's ratification, but Baker knew from experience that even the most popular treaties face serious Senate scrutiny. Only four days before another summit opened in Moscow in late May 1988 did Baker, Secretary of State George Shultz, and A. B. Culvahouse find language for reservations to the treaty that Senate leaders could accept, thus easing passage by a rare 93–5 vote.

Baker had struck "gold." The one policy goal he had set out to accomplish had been achieved and the Reagan White House was running on autopilot on a course Baker had charted a year earlier. Over the past few months, Baker had been spending his weekends flying to Knoxville to be with the ailing Joy and Irene Baker, his stepmother. His work at the White House, he thought, was "done," and Reagan could install his deputy Kenneth Duberstein in his place for the remaining six months of his administration with no decline in performance. It says a lot about Senator Baker that he would subordinate his ambitions to Reagan's and use his steadiness to defuse political minefields and win a few more for the Gipper. It says even more about the nonconsuming nature of his ambitions and his confidence in a team he had played a large role in building that he would voluntarily step down to attend to his wife and stepmother.

Senator Baker has remained active since 1988, advising a bevy of clients and giving untold hundreds of hours to guide aspiring Republican candidates like me on how to prepare to run for office, and even more importantly, to help us decide if that life is truly what we want. He joined former Vice President Walter Mondale and others in venturing to Eastern Europe to train legislators in those incipient democracies in the means of instituting workable political systems and in securing aid from American firms and institutions. However, his preoccupation was Joy, whose health continued to fade until April 24, 1993, when lung cancer finally took her life.

Throughout Joy's travails, Howard was a model of understanding. He held strong, never letting on that something might be troubling him. He seemed lonely for a while after her death, and I suppose I was one of the first to see that there might be a major change in his life forthcoming. A few months after I was elected, Senator Baker invited my family to spend three days with him in Huntsville. Karyn and I stayed in the cabin-like guesthouse he had built for Everett Dirksen's visits. My sons Jonathan, Bryan, and Harrison stayed in his home overlooking the New River. We'd planned to spend time canoeing and rafting on the streams of Scott County, but rain prevented that. Instead, Senator Baker took the opportunity to introduce my sons to photography. He showed them his darkroom, then ran a white piece of paper through the processor. Karyn and the boys were looking down at the paper as the image of a woman began to appear and sharpen. Then, it became clear that the picture was of my friend and Senate colleague Nancy Kassebaum, who served as my chairwoman on the Senate Labor and Human Resources Committee. He had told Karyn that he felt like a teenager the first time he had walked up to her apartment for a date. I suspected something more serious at our national convention when he invited Karyn and me to skip out on all the formal festivities to have a quiet dinner, with one caveat: "We're double-dating." We knew after spending four hours with Howard and Nancy and John and Virginia Chafee that something indeed was happening. It hardly surprised us when Bob Dole spilled the beans in Knoxville just before the election that Howard Baker and Nancy Kassebaum would be married in Washington by their former colleague Jack Danforth, an ordained Episcopal minister.

The legacy of Howard Baker continues in the Senate. It was beautifully articulated in a presentation he made to all current Senators on July 14, 1998, in the old Senate chamber as part of the Leader's Lecture Series initiated by Majority Leader Trent Lott. With more than a little pride, I listened alongside my colleagues to his reflections on his years as leader, reflecting all the while as I took notes on the back of the program, soaking up his wisdom and magnanimity. It was so interesting to me then in the process of writing this book to learn that his great aunt Mattie Keene was personal secretary to Senator Kenneth McKellar, and I loved hearing him reminisce about his first trip to Washington to visit her.

In his speech entitled "On Herding Cats," Baker listed his "Baker's Dozen" of rules for being a successful Majority Leader, each a fundamental lesson in integrity, fairness and common sense, together a reflection of the man. The dozen were the following:

1. Understand the limits of the position of Majority Leader.
2. Have a genuine and decent respect for differing points of view.
3. Consult as often as possible with as many Senators as possible, on as many issues as possible.
4. Remember that Senators are people with families.
5. Choose a good staff.
6. Listen more often than you speak.
7. Count carefully and often.
8. Work with the President, whoever he or she may be, whenever possible.
9. Work with the House Members.
10. Present no surprises (for the Minority Leader).
11. Tell the truth, whether you have to or not.
12. Be patient.
13. (the Baker's Dozen) Be civil and encourage others to do likewise.

So the remarkable Howard Baker story continues to unfold. He remains an informal trusted advisor to many of us in Congress today. He is the model to which all Tennessee politicians should aspire. He is the mentor to Lamar Alexander, Fred Thompson, myself, and so many others. A true believer in the citizen legislator philosophy, he is active today in recruiting business for the law firm that bears his name. He continues to campaign aggressively at each election cycle for candidates he believes in. He serves on the Board of Regents of the Smithsonian Institution, maintains strong ties to the University of Tennessee, and for years he was on the board of the Mayo Clinic. And the job he enjoys the most is being a grandfather.

Chapter 12

William Emerson "Bill" Brock, III

1971–1977

Republican National Committee Chairman

U.S. Trade Representative

U.S. Secretary of Labor

(1930–)

A lot of people credit Howard Baker for creating a statewide two-party system in Tennessee. Senator Baker is not among them. That honor, Baker says, belongs to Bill Brock. In 1962, Bill Brock captured a congressional seat outside the historically Republican base in upper and middle East Tennessee—the first time any Republican had done so since 1920—and thereby inspired others dissatisfied with the Democratic status quo throughout the state to run for office. Fifteen years later, he became chairman of the Republican National Committee and presided over the revival of the Republican Party from its lowest ebb since the Great Depression. He led so effectively that the late Democratic chairman Ron Brown used to kid that he himself had succeeded so well in reviving his own party during the Bush years because he copied Brock's strategies. Through four decades in public service, Bill Brock embodied what the French call *noblesse oblige*. Born to wealth, he developed a sense of civic responsibility at an early age that led him to organize a variety of groups to help the less fortunate. His idealism made him an activist, for he believed the federal government should guide states and localities rather than be their master. He was certain that America's engines of progress were its schools and its entrepreneurs, for they were the forces that would spur the enterprise that would lead to millions of others partaking of life's blessings as he had.

William Emerson Brock, III, was born in Chattanooga on November 23, 1930. He was the eldest of the four sons of Bill and Myra Kreusi Brock. Like several of the other Tennesseans who have preceded me in the Senate, he had a distinguished political pedigree. His paternal grandfather was Senator Will Brock. His maternal grandfather was Paul J. Kreusi, who was the son of Thomas Edison's top assistant and served as a delegate to two Republican conventions and as an Assistant Secretary of Commerce in the Hoover administration.

A shy but earnest young man, Bill Brock grew up in a civic-minded household. He developed a wide variety of interests while attending first the public schools of Chattanooga, then McCallie prep school. A fine athlete, young Brock was a starter on the McCallie soccer team that went undefeated, untied, and unscored-upon in 1947–1948. Upon entering Washington and Lee University, he intended to study chemical engineering, but opted ultimately to pursue a degree in commerce and business. The choice seemed appropriate for someone who thought that he probably would wind up running the family business, Brock Candy. His studies also reinforced his beliefs that free-market economics could generate prosperity and full employment, and that free trade benefited all involved parties.

Shortly after graduating, Brock was commissioned in the navy as an ensign. He spent nine months of each of his three years in the service stationed off the coast of Southeast Asia and three months stateside. He enjoyed the sea and has since adopted sailing as a hobby. A lieutenant j.g. in 1956, he was considering reenlisting when, at a friend's wedding, he was paired off with Laura "Muffett" Handly, a quiet but big-hearted girl five years younger than he whom friends remember fondly as a "saint" and a "delight." Almost immediately, he started dating Muffett, fell in love, and gave up any thought of reupping when they wed in January of 1957. Muffett Brock was a supportive woman, who was in many ways what an older generation might call the perfect political wife. A first cousin to Nancy Kefauver, she was a wonderful mother to their four children, Bill IV, Oscar, Laura (who answers to "Hutchie"), and John.

The newlyweds settled in Chattanooga and Brock took a job as vice president of marketing at Brock Candy. Like their parents, they became intimately involved in the life of their community. Brock taught Sunday school at the Lookout Mountain Presbyterian Church. He served on the Law Enforcement Committee, the Good Government Committee, and the Citizens for Better Schools organization, and he chaired the Chamber of Commerce's Public Affairs Committee. He helped his father desegregate Chattanooga, and he chaired a fund-raising drive for disabled children that produced

17,000 contributors. Of all his early accomplishments, however, Brock remains proudest of his venture to raise literacy standards in Chattanooga. Appalled by a survey that showed that a far smaller percentage of local adults could read and write than the national average, he, Muffett, and some friends organized programs to instruct the less fortunate in the rudiments of reading and writing. Often, they would rise well before dawn to work with their pupils, many of them African American, before they went to work. Brock remains particularly proud of his tutelage of a man, who, after eighty years of clean living, burst into tears because he could finally read his Bible.

Brock got his first taste of politics in the 1956 Eisenhower campaign. Still a nominal Democrat, he was enlisted to run a poll-watching operation. During that experience he witnessed many questionable electoral practices. Democrats, in what were known as control wards, were so alarmed that Republicans were actually overseeing their activities that they beat up several of Brock's associates and threatened his mother's life. He saw several Democratic officials go into voting booths and cast votes for others. Many of the voting machines had vote tallies higher than the total number recorded, and a number of them were unlocked. The experience angered him, but he was "excited by the process."

During the 1960 election, Brock reevaluated his politics. He and several others from the Jaycees observed that some local Democrats appeared not to be interested in letting young people participate. They also realized that their political views more closely resembled those of the national Republicans than the Democrats. He and his colleagues celebrated Nixon's statewide victory, even though Kennedy won nationally. Brock still had not contemplated running for office, but then a friend's wife remarked that he and his colleagues were "just blowin' smoke" about their supposed success because they had not even fielded candidates for Congress or sheriff in 1960. Determined to prove her wrong, Brock and some friends organized a Young Republican (YR) club in Hamilton County and moved to form others in Jackson, Memphis, Nashville, and the Tri-Cities. They attended YR leadership conferences and Dale Carnegie courses to hone their political and oratorical skills. They got their wives and other female friends to form Republican women's groups. Nowhere did they find help from the state Republican Party, which seemed steadfast in its support of a stagnant state YR organization headed by a forty-five-year-old state chairman and a fifty-four-year-old general counsel. It took a vote at a YR national convention in 1961 to rule their group the legitimate one and for Brock to be named the national committeeman from Tennessee.

Brock's success in the Young Republicans whetted his appetite for politics. He sought the presidency of the Jaycees but lost. Had he won, he now says, he may well have remained at home. His YR allies had another proposition, however. In 1962, they needed a young, aggressive candidate for the Third District seat in the House of Representatives and he had the best-known name among them and the best chance to tap the substantial financial resources of Chattanooga's Lookout Mountain suburb. Would he run? Brock accepted willingly.

Brock and his team began to form a campaign strategy. His family was quick to enlist and brother Pat became his campaign manager. "All we knew," Brock later admitted, "was how to go out and ask for help." Someone threw a dart at a precinct map and that precinct became his or her starting point. Soon, Brock's allies filled most of the gaps in the long-dormant Hamilton County organization. All in all, they recruited a diverse lot of 4,000 volunteers—everyone from Brockettes to black ministers to conservative businessmen—and most of them were on board before the primary. In many eyes, the Democrats provided help by ousting conservative incumbent James Frazier and nominating the much more liberal Wilkes Thrasher. Brock painted himself as the champion of Third District conservatives and alluded often to Thrasher's ties to organized labor and the liberal wing of the Democratic Party. He also displayed a pragmatic streak, commending John F. Kennedy for his "intelligent and wholesome" handling of the Cuban Missile Crisis and expressing his support for Kennedy's Trade Expansion Act of 1962. In the end, enough disgruntled Frazierites linked with the new Republican base to give him a 2,007 vote victory.

The young Congressman took his narrow victory as a challenge. He set out to consolidate his base. Every weekend, he returned home from Washington to mingle with voters and attend to their concerns. The effectiveness of his constituent service made it certain that the Third District seat was his for as long as he wanted to serve.

Back in the Capitol, Brock tried to look after Tennessee's interests just as effectively. He opposed the Civil Rights Act of 1964, as did most of Tennessee's legislators in both parties. His experience in Chattanooga led him to think that other southern localities would work out their racial problems without federal legislation readily and peacefully as Chattanooga had. (He later acknowledged he had been "wrong" about that.) After the enactment of the law, he, like Albert Gore and other Tennesseans who had opposed it, took to the House floor and to the airwaves to urge Tennesseans to comply. "If we fear the intolerable burden of federal domination and control," he said, "then let us join hands in reason and restraint to prove that ours is and shall remain a government of laws and not of men." In 1965, he voted against the House version of the Voting Rights Act, which did not cover a few West Tennessee counties with historic patterns of voting discrimination, but did join the progressive third of the southern members who voted for final passage. A few years later, Brock's African-American political alliances had developed enough to provoke Klan-types in Chattanooga to slur him by presenting him with a chitlins supper, their supreme insult.

Always the party builder, Brock set out with a few allies to replicate his success at the state level. An important development in constitutional law and Barry Goldwater's 1964 presidential bid gave them that chance. The "one man, one vote" dictum in the Supreme Court's ruling on the reapportionment case of *Baker v. Carr* had weakened the stranglehold that the Democrats had on the South. It reset the electoral balance by moving it from depopulated rural areas to more populous urban areas. Brock and his colleagues looked to take advantage of the ruling to win the support of middle-class voters in the cities and suburbs, the loci of the largest Republican growth since World War II. True believers in free markets and limited government, the Brock team made Goldwater's *The Conscience of a Conservative* their Bible and set out to convert Tennessee. As it turned out, Goldwater catalyzed the movement of many theretofore yellow-dog Democratic conservatives into the Republican Party, even if he lost the 1964 presidential election by a near-record majority. A generation later, Brock would reflect that Barry Goldwater "was the salvation of the Republican Party in the South," but quickly added that Goldwater was also "a disaster," as his campaign cost the Republican Party "fifty years" in its relationship with the black community.

In 1965, Brock had his longtime associate, Bill Carter, installed as executive director of the Tennessee Republican Party. Together with a few allies, the two produced a ten-year plan for party development that they hoped would lead to Republican control of the governorship, both Senate seats, a majority of the state's seats in the House of Representatives, and a majority of Tennessee's sheriff's offices. They sought precinct chairpeople across the state and made even more vigorous bids to recruit energetic fiscal conservatives to vie for all offices. Interested less in partisan demographics than in the presence of aggressive individuals with teams of youthful volunteers, they set out to train candidates to campaign effectively. They emphasized local constituencies, particularly in finding candidates for sheriff, with the goal of gaining legitimacy for the Republican Party in rural Middle and West Tennessee. They hoped to create an image of energy in what was often the most visible position of authority and to develop a volunteer base for the future. It is no small testament to their success that they were ahead of schedule by 1970.

In the House, Brock voted a reliably conservative line. He was assigned to the Banking and Currency Committee, and over time, he developed into the principal Republican spokesman on banking and housing issues. He found that he often disagreed with Chairman Wright Patman, an anti-bank populist of the old school. He opposed and eventually defeated Patman's long-standing plan to politicize the Federal Reserve System. Here was a major victory in a negative sense, but victories like these were about the only ones available as the House was overwhelmingly dominated by Democrats throughout his tenure. Brock did not just block Democratic initiatives, however. He suggested putting the seignorage on coins in a trust fund to be used to reduce the deficit and proposed lowering congressional salaries by the same percentage the deficit exceeded the budget. Although he resisted federal aid to education, thinking it might lead to federal control, he did introduce bills to allow teachers to deduct expenses for educational purposes and to institute revenue sharing to support education only. Unfortunately, all of these bills were either defeated or ignored during the Johnson administration. Brock found readier company in the first two years of the Nixon administration. A Nixon surrogate in both 1968 and 1972, he cosponsored the revolutionary Family Assistance Plan, which would have streamlined the welfare bureaucracy and increased payments had it passed. He also argued in favor of Nixon's plans to cut domestic spending and subsidize a supersonic transport plane.

Perhaps more than any other conservative Republican of his time, Brock had an instinctive feel for the problems facing America's youth: drugs, education, the Vietnam War, and the right to vote. In the spring of 1969, he learned that a bill had been introduced that would deny federal funds to any university where a student disruption had occurred. Deeming the idea "insanity" and aware that it would "alienate every decent young person," Brock called Wisconsin Republican Bill Steiger, his best friend in the House, and asked him to have breakfast with him the next morning. Over the next six weeks, the two organized a team of twenty-two relatively young Republican Congressmen to tour fifty campuses, to meet with student leaders on college quads and in pubs, and to produce a report for President Nixon. At times during the tour, members smelled both marijuana and tear gas and one even felt a bayonet in his stomach, but all came back convinced that it was wrong to send those who could not vote to die for their country and that 99 percent of those they encountered were moderate souls, even though most desired an immediate, unconditional end to the war. The group eventually recommended lowering the voting age, an end to the draft, and an increase in funding to colleges and universities. Brock declared that the impression he got from the students was the same he had gotten from Chicago blacks and blue-collar Wallace supporters, an ever present fear that "nobody's listening" to them.

As 1970 approached, Brock began to consider moving up the political ladder. He had resisted overtures to run for the Senate in 1964 and the governorship in 1966. Brock, however, sensed that the time was right to challenge Senator Albert Gore. The day of Democratic hegemony in Tennessee had ended, and a strong field of Republican candidates and an expanding industrial sector had broadened the political landscape.

Gore's grip on his Senate seat was slipping. His was the age of the stump speech, and that era had passed. Gore seemed to spend his time in Tennessee visiting country editors more frequently than rank-and-file Democrats. Some voters sensed that he and Democrats at lower levels of government were taking their support for granted. Unlike Estes Kefauver, Gore had never developed a strong personal organization, and he had never won the same degree of loyalty from the state Democratic Party as had Governor Frank Clement. One close Gore associate later told journalist Neil R. Peirce that the Senator "rubbed people the wrong way even when they knew he was right."

Congressman Dan Kuykendall of Memphis was also interested in a race for the Republican nomination. To stave off an intra-party battle, Brock commissioned a poll that both men agreed to abide by to determine which would stand the best chance against Gore. The results favored Brock and Kuykendall bowed out. A few Old Guard Republicans not reconciled to Brock prevailed on country singer Tex Ritter to run. Brock, knowing he had the support of Richard Nixon and even some of the Old Guard, ignored Ritter except to say something nice about him at their joint appearances. Astute observers were hardly surprised when Republican voters cast three-quarters of their ballots for Brock.

Division reigned among Democrats. Sensing that state Democrats might prefer a more conservative nominee, Governor Buford Ellington's press secretary, Hudley Crockett, challenged Gore in the primary. Crockett pilloried Gore throughout the primary for his opposition to the Vietnam War, the antiballistic missile (ABM) system, and the nominations of southern federal Judges Clement Haynsworth and G. Harrold Carswell to seats on the Supreme Court. Crockett came within six points of defeating Gore. Had the vote been confined to traditionally Democratic Middle and West Tennessee, Crockett would have won. Not surprisingly, polls taken just after the primary showed Brock ahead by fourteen points. Neither Brock nor Gore could feel confident of victory, however, because the swing voters of 1970 were the 34 percent of Tennesseans who had backed George Wallace in 1968.

Early on, Brock and Gore both telegraphed their strategies to tap this bloc. Gore told audiences that he had grown up "with Tennessee dirt" on his hands, "not Chattanooga chocolate." He used Brock's general opposition to Great Society domestic programs to deride him as "Mr. No-No." Brock accepted the designation, saying he would be thrifty with other people's money. He appealed to those voters' sense of patriotism. A president whom the state had supported, he said, should have someone in the Senate who would vote with him rather than against him. When reporters raised the issue of defense, Brock mentioned Gore's opposition to the Vietnam War and the ABM, as well as his 1941 vote against the fortification of Guam. Brock echoed Crockett's derision of Gore for his votes against Judges Haynsworth and Carswell. He also pointed out that Gore had been absent for the votes on Nixon appointees Warren Burger and Harry Blackmun.

Both candidates went after the Wallace-ite vote. Gore focused on the populist concerns of the Wallace bloc. He loudly proclaimed his support for Medicare, tax reform, aid to education, and increased Social Security and veterans benefits, but Gore addressed only the economic portion of Wallace-ism. Many Wallace-ites were even more worried about an assault they saw on traditional virtues, a concern Brock addressed by trumpeting his support for voluntary school prayer and stiffer sentences for drug dealers and his opposition to gun control and busing.

As the election neared, Gore was making headway. Brock responded by trying to paint Gore as the "third senator from Massachusetts." Spiro Agnew chimed in by deriding Gore as the "Southern regional chairman of the Eastern liberal establishment." But Gore, recognizing that his party had been hurt earlier in the year when demonstrators disrupted a Billy Graham crusade at the University of Tennessee with Nixon and Brock present, defused any potential repercussions when he cagily opted to greet Agnew as he disembarked from Air Force Two in Memphis to attend a Brock rally designed to call attention to the plight of American POWs in Vietnam. Not even Brock's protests that Gore had skipped a hearing on POWs could hide an overwhelmingly favorable impression that Gore had made at Brock's expense.

The race tightened. Brock moved to shore up his support with campaign ads stressing Gore's opposition to Nixon's justices and a nondenominational prayer amendment. He also noted Gore's support for busing and gun registration. The tide turned. Brock swayed majorities in West Tennessee, but Gore captured the Wallace vote in Middle Tennessee with his New Deal-like appeals to their wallets. But even though Gore ended with 60 percent of the Wallace vote, Brock won a 51 percent majority statewide. Gore maintained that Brock prevailed because of the unexpectedly high turnout in the governor's race for Winfield Dunn in his hometown of Memphis. That explanation does not hold water, however, for Brock also ran ahead of traditional Republican showings in rural Middle and West Tennessee. Here was a classic, hard-fought race that matched a thoughtful New Deal liberal against a thoughtful modern conservative. Brock was quick to commend Gore for his long and conscientious dedication to what he believed was right.

After eight years in the House, Brock felt confident he "had something to say." He emerged as one of the more active Senate freshmen of the past half-century. In his first year in the Senate, he authored a constitutional amendment mandating that no student be assigned to any school on the basis of race. He signed on as a cosponsor of amendments guaranteeing equal rights to women and the vote to eighteen-year-olds. Over time, he maintained a generally conservative record, voting with the Nixon administration on most foreign policy questions. He also supported the revenue sharing and Cabinet reorganization portions of the administration's "New Federalism." He fiercely opposed the creation of the Legal Services Corporation, a Democratic proposal that on its face intended to provide legal counsel to those too poor to hire private lawyers, because he believed that the funding would more likely benefit left-wing organizations than litigants with individual complaints. The conservative Senator also opposed the Consumer Protection Agency, deeming it certain to add to unwise regulation. Fearing the expense of permanently funding new programs, he was a solid proponent of adding "sunset" language that would terminate a program's funding after a set time unless Congress voted specifically for a new authorization.

Brock's conservatism seemed to temper a bit during the 1970s. He saw a place for government aid to those in crisis. When he argued for bailing out Lockheed Aircraft, he spoke of the effect of a business bankruptcy upon 30,000 families. He took a broad view on one of the era's most pressing issues—crime. "It was time," he suggested, that "conservatives admitted that we have got to deal with the roots of the crime problem if we are going to stop it." He was also quick to point out that it was also "time the liberals admitted that you cannot put the rights of criminals above the rights of others." He described his outlook in 1974 to journalists Jack Bass and Walter DeVries. "Conservatism," he explained, "means an extension of personal freedom, less infringement on the part of government over a human life." "That is something that sells very well in the South." But he suggested that the new "law-and-order" campaign to end the upheaval in the nation's cities, especially in the black community, was too repressive. "That philosophy," he insisted, was "not only going to lose the black vote, which we don't have much of anyway, but it [would] also drive off whites who simply can't accept it."

Brock focused on fiscal policy while in the Senate. In 1972, while serving on the National Commission on Consumer Finance, he learned from aide Emily Card that many women could not get credit cards or even credit in their own names. Mayor Kathryn Kirschbaum of Davenport, Iowa, testified in public hearings that even she could not get a BankAmeriCard without her husband's signature. Finding the same was true for professional women throughout America, Brock suggested to Democrats William Proxmire and Harrison Williams, each the chairman of a key banking subcommittee, that they write amendments into the Truth in Lending Act that would outlaw such discrimination. Both agreed. Brock then went to women's groups and asked them to write him in support of his position. Ten thousand women responded within three weeks. Brock went to his colleagues in the Senate and asked them if they would like to receive a similar flood of mail in their offices. Then, he went to banking lobbyists and asked them to accede. They refused even when he promised to buy them "the biggest steak in Washington" if they could block his amendments. Brock got every Senator's vote and kept his steak money.

Like many other Republicans, Brock on several occasions introduced constitutional amendments requiring a balanced budget. Recognizing that such an amendment would not pass, he authored a bill providing for a larger congressional role in the budget-making process. There were several such bills before Sam Ervin's Government Operations Committee in 1973. After an especially raucous meeting, Brock approached Edmund Muskie, the highly respected Maine Democrat. "If you're serious," Muskie responded, "let's do it." For weeks, they would use every break in Senate proceedings to go to Muskie's hideaway office with Brock aide Harrison Fox and a Muskie counterpart to draft a bill. The two presented a measure that the committee passed without changing a comma and got it through the Senate with little dissent. The partnership paid off later, for the two put together a public works package in the dire economic days of 1975 that had the virtue in Brock's eyes of being countercyclical, that is, it was guaranteed to expire once the ongoing economic crunch subsided.

Brock, like Estes Kefauver and Howard Baker, also developed a deep interest in the process by which the Congress operated. As a young member, he saw power concentrated in a relatively small number of Senators. Frustrated, he went to Majority Leader Mike Mansfield with a bipartisan group of Senators and suggested that he create a special committee to study reforms. Mansfield acquiesced and named Adlai Stevenson, III, as chairman and Brock as co-chairman. The two produced a report that the Senate accepted which reduced the number of committees, limited members to one subcommittee chairmanship per committee, and entitled each member to have at least one staff member on every panel on which he or she sat. It's because of these reforms that junior members like myself can have an impact.

Brock came up for reelection in the dark days for Republicans after Watergate. He had publicly and privately encouraged Richard Nixon to "disclose, disclose, disclose." Once he learned that Nixon had gone along with a plan to have the CIA block the FBI investigation of Watergate, Brock wrote Nixon a letter he regarded as the "most painful" he had ever written. In it he told the President that it was time to resign. Brock realized that Nixon's misbehavior would hurt his own popularity when he ran into one of his veteran precinct chairmen in Chattanooga. "I don't think I'm even gonna vote," he told Brock, who knew instinctively that many less committed voters would follow suit.

The public's disillusionment with all Republicans after Watergate ultimately led to Brock's defeat. When the campaign started Brock was personally in a solid position in the polls. "The good news," Brock's pollster told him, "is that you're forty points ahead. The bad news," he went on, "is that you cannot win." The rationale was that Jimmy Carter's southern-fried appeal would bring every Democrat to the polls, and many would vote Democratic down the line. Had the Democrats nominated a known commodity, this may not have been true. They opted for Jim Sasser, a lawyer who was largely unknown to the public but who as state party chairman had reinvigorated Tennessee Democrats largely by copying the strategies Brock had devised in the 1960s to build the Republican Party.

Sasser was too new to have many enemies and had the enthusiastic support of most elements of the Democratic coalition. While Brock was away in Washington working to reform Senate procedures, Sasser ran a populist campaign. He tied himself, as he said, not only to Jimmy Carter's coattails but to his coat. He used Brock's generally pro-business voting record to paint him as a tool of the special interests. Sasser contrasted his humble background with Brock's wealthier one by releasing a statement disclosing his own modest wealth. Brock resisted doing the same, not because he had anything to hide, but because he thought Muffett's holdings, which were considerable, should remain private. When he released his tax returns for 1975, a bad year for him financially, Democrats noticed that he had paid $2,026 on an income of $51,670. Only Governor Ray Blanton charged impropriety, but Sasser's people did take to wearing buttons reading, "I paid more taxes than Bill Brock." Brock ran well ahead of Gerald Ford, but he ran 78,000 votes behind Jim Sasser.

The night after the election, Brock dined with friends and discussed what might be next for him. He decided to pursue the soon to be vacant chairmanship of the Republican National Committee (RNC). He was acceptable to both Ronald Reagan and Gerald Ford, the rivals in the most recent presidential primaries, but both had their own candidate. With a small but dedicated core of loyalists, Brock was perfectly situated to emerge as a compromise choice. He did so when James Baker, Ford's choice, dropped out of the running.

Brock's initial goal was to change the popular perception of the Republican Party "so we can identify with the majority of the American people." He succeeded to such a large degree that political commentator Morton Kondracke wrote in July 1980 that Brock was "widely considered among Washington political reporters to be the best Republican chairman in their memory, possibly the best of either party." Having learned the hard way, Brock deemed his principal mission to be to broaden the base of the Republican Party and welcome people who had long felt excluded from our party's ranks. He set in motion a series of efforts to recruit union members, blacks, women, and ethnic minorities as candidates. He computerized RNC operations and produced a direct mail program that doubled annual revenues with an average donation of $26, as compared with $500 for the Democrats. Thinking that the Republican Party had to build its "root-stock" if it were ever to recapture the White House, he channeled money to local races and held "Concord conferences" around the country to train candidates. He formed issue councils to inform the public and began publishing *Common Sense*, a Republican journal of ideas. Within two years, a party that had only recently been at its lowest depths since the Great Depression had captured three new Senate seats, six governorships, fifteen House seats, and thirteen state legislative chambers nationwide.

It was Brock's intention to redirect Republican candidates to problems affecting real people. "Work, Neighborhood, Family" was the slogan he prepared well before the 1980 convention for use by anyone who won the nomination. He counseled candidates to concentrate on economic issues. He organized a Tax Cut Blitz of Republican luminaries in 1978 to call attention to the Kemp-Roth 30 percent reduction that Republican candidates were promoting. He shunned single issues, thus antagonizing some of the ideological purists, and tried to be even-handed, hiring talented operatives from all segments of the party. Some critics bemoaned his refusal to let the RNC finance the travels of a bipartisan group fighting the Panama Canal Treaties, but he told them that he was not about to give money to any group that highlighted Democrats. A more raucous fight occurred when he wanted to hold the 1980 convention in Detroit. Knowing that the media would focus on the diamonds and minks of female delegates if the party met in a white-collar city like Dallas, Brock deemed this fight essential. Brock aimed to present the GOP as a blue-collar party to the country at large. A few Reagan staffers, however, suspected, incorrectly, that Brock's plan was to tilt the convention to Michigander Gerald Ford. A few Reagan loyalists went to Brock and threatened to oust him. "Try," Brock responded. He got the convention in Detroit but with just one vote to spare. Only after the 1980 election did Reagan backers relent. "You beat me every time," said Reagan aide Lyn Nofziger, who added in his memoirs that Brock had been "one of the best chairmen in my time."

Brock indeed had restored the Republican Party to a position where not only Reagan, but also George Bush, Howard Baker, or Gerald Ford could have defeated Jimmy Carter had they been nominated. The convention went off memorably, even if Reagan could not convince Ford to be his running mate. Brock appointed Nancy Kassebaum, then the Senate's only woman, as the convention temporary chairperson, and Dr. Aris Allen, an African-American former state House minority leader from Maryland, as its secretary. He began running generic ads featuring a Tip O'Neill look-alike that criticized the long Democratic control of Congress and the declining state of the economy. Playing on Carter's claims of an energy crisis, the ad ended with the line, "The Democrats are out of gas." In 1980, Republicans picked up the presidency, twelve seats in the Senate, thirty-two in the House, and over 5,000 in state and local races across America.

After Brock's success with the campaign, many believed that he would have his choice of position in the new administration. Jim Sasser was heard telling reporters as much and it seemed that Reagan agreed. The Gipper made a special trip to the RNC after the election to thank Brock. Although some Reagan aides thought Brock's personal commitment to Reagan was of insufficient duration to justify an appointment, the President-elect was of another mind. What Cabinet-level positions might you be interested in, Reagan asked. Brock responded that he preferred something like the U.S. Trade Representative. "That's not Cabinet level," Reagan replied. "It has been since 1979," Brock corrected him, noting that Jimmy Carter had made it such to accommodate Robert Strauss. "Why USTR?" Reagan asked. Brock pointed out that for someone with a background in business, Brock said, there could be no more exciting job in government. His appointment would be delayed until the middle of January while members of Congress blocked a bid to transfer its functions to the Commerce Department, but within two weeks after Reagan made his nomination public, the Senate confirmed Brock without dissent.

When one talks to Brock today, he describes his proudest achievement as USTR as "changing the way we think" about trade. Within a few months of his appointment, he observed that fewer of the new jobs being created in America were in the manufacturing and agricultural sectors and more and more were in intellectual property, service industries, and international investment. Recognizing that foreign governments and businesses would not let America sell them our goods unless we bought some of theirs, he moved on a variety of fronts to expand our trade. He initiated free trade agreements with Canada and Israel that created hundreds of thousands of American jobs in service industries. He did enough preliminary work with the European Economic Community that in March 1985 it agreed to a new round of negotiations on the General Agreement on Trade and Tariffs (GATT), a pact which came to fruition in 1994.

Unfortunately, all was not well for American trade in the early 1980s. Many Americans blamed unfair trading practices by foreign countries, particularly Japan, for the low state of our economy. They called for Protectionist restrictions denying the Japanese access to American markets, and to a degree, Brock found Protectionist sentiment, particularly in Congress, helpful as it increased his leverage when he negotiated abroad. He worked out limits on imports of Japanese cars and machine tools and European steel into the United States, which bought time for American producers. He also worked out an agreement with Japan whereby the United States would clamp high tariffs on motorcycles for three years, thus giving the Harley-Davidson Company time to improve its product or face bankruptcy.

Brock's experience as USTR led him to question if Americans were truly prepared to function in the global marketplace. He privately counseled leaders in business, labor, and education that they needed to "get off their duff if they want to compete." He blasted corporate executives who paid themselves extraordinarily high salaries without sharing much of the windfall with their employees. By 1985, AFL-CIO head Lane Kirkland was telling people that Brock had "earned our respect" because he was one of a handful of Reagan administration officials, with George Bush and George Shultz being among the others, who made time to carry on a dialogue and listen to labor's concerns. He made it clear to Americans that preparing to function in the new world economy would have to begin early in life. "We have to radically reshape our school system," he said.

Brock enjoyed his tenure as USTR and wanted to remain for the full eight years of Reagan's tenure. He resisted a series of overtures from White House Chief of Staff Donald Regan beginning in December 1984 to take over the Department of Labor, an agency long torn by investigations into the affairs of Secretary Ray Donovan. On March 20, 1985, Brock was tending his rose garden, a favorite hobby, when Regan called and asked him to meet with the President later in the day. Brock thought of declining as he rode to the White House. Once the President told him he needed him, Brock assented reluctantly, asking Reagan only for a veto on any appointments to his staff and for time to call Lane Kirkland. Reagan agreed. Brock won Senate confirmation by a rare voice vote.

The department Brock entered was in disarray, long demoralized by budget cuts and a predecessor who had distanced himself even from senior managers. Brock's first acts upon entering office were to dismantle the locks and take the doors off the hinges of his office and those of his senior assistants, thus signaling employees that he was willing to listen to them. He put up a banner in the department hailing "A New Pride." He frequently toured offices in Washington and around the country. He talked to workers, thanked them for their contributions, and asked if they were having fun. He kept in close touch with former congressional colleagues of both parties and ordered his staff to respond to any of their inquiries within a week. After a 1985 GAO report pronounced the department's performance unsatisfactory, he called for an unheard-of follow-up the next year. The second audit revealed quite a transformation. Brock also worked out a rescue plan for the Pension Benefit Guarantee Corporation. He got the states to require agri-businesses to furnish sanitary facilities for the migrant workers they employed. He hired the highest-ranking African-American woman in the Reagan administration and successfully fought efforts to scrap affirmative action goals for federal contractors. And he let the unions know that they had an ear when he hired Stephen Schlossberg, the former general counsel of the United Auto Workers, as his deputy secretary for Labor-Management Relations.

Brock's new sensitivity to labor did not make him a pawn of the unions. On occasion, he could be very blunt in his criticism of them. "It isn't easy to hear about mobbed-up locals or pension fund abuse," he told Teamsters at their convention in 1986. "It's impossible for me to ignore that. It is necessary for you to address it." Brock also kept his fiscal conservatism and his rational pro-business stance. He supported cuts in the Job Corps, saying they were necessary under the deficit reduction guidelines in the Gramm-Rudman-Hollings Act. Disturbed by a 43 percent unemployment rate among African-American teenagers, Brock declared that it might be impossible for those youths to acquire necessary skills for employment and argued for allowing employers to pay teenagers a sub-minimum wage. He also called for industry and all levels of government to create new training programs. "It is an insane tragedy," he told a Senate subcommittee in January 1987, "that 700,000 young people are coming out of schools who can't read their diplomas."

Over time, Brock came to advise labor and management that they would have to change their ways if they were going to be able to compete globally. He told businessmen that they would have to increase worker involvement in their decision-making processes if they were to retain their edge. He also commissioned a series of studies to analyze the traits of the employees of the future and to counsel employers on how to deal with them. *Workforce 2000*, one study he commissioned the Hudson Institute to undertake, showed that workers would have to be more flexible and creative and better trained if they were to thrive in the ever more rapidly changing economy of the future. He called on Americans to dignify alternatives to college for their children and, by February 1987, he could boast of preserving nearly $1 billion for an enhanced job retraining program. After testifying before the National Conference on Work and the Family that "employees should not have to choose between being good parents and being good workers," he went on to encourage businesses to expand programs of day care, parental leave, portable pensions, and flex time.

Brock's personal life during his tenure at the Labor Department went through difficult changes. His beloved Muffett died on December 30, 1985, after a short bout with pancreatic cancer. Not long thereafter, he underwent surgery to have two detached retinas repaired. His staff seemed to be guarding his privacy a bit until he got on a plane to fly to Nashville for a state Republican fund-raising dinner and sat down next to Sandy Schubert, a talented Maryland businesswoman. Brock and Sandy tried to meet for a few weeks, finally did, and they were married before the end of the year.

How did he fare at work? Perhaps the best possible evaluation might come from the career employees at Labor, 80 percent of whom identify themselves as Democrats. William Buhl, the author of the only thorough academic study of Brock's secretaryship, asked a large sample of senior managers how he compared with his predecessors. Eighty percent described him as "above average" or better, with a full 28 percent terming him "one of the best ever."

Brock would have been content to stay at Labor, but he thought he might have a greater impact on America if he took over Bob Dole's presidential campaign. Knowing of Dole's commitment to reducing the deficit and taking seriously his vows to consider new directions for human development and job retraining, Brock concluded that Dole was the best equipped candidate to make those changes, and he signed on as his campaign manager on November 1, 1987.

Brock's experience with the Dole campaign was uniformly disheartening. When he arrived, the campaign had already spent one-third of the funds allowed by law. The staff was engaged in fierce internecine warfare between loyalists long in his camp and outsiders from what some called the conservative movement. Only in the Midwest and the Northeast was there a semblance of organization. That, however, caused friction as many resisted the entrance of a new group of organizers loyal to Brock. Many on board from the beginning circumvented Brock's authority at every opportunity. There were days when Brock did not know where Dole was. Dole did carry initial caucuses in Iowa, Minnesota, and South Dakota, but in New Hampshire, the state of the first primary, Dole's staff could not agree on which tax ad should be run, and no one had bothered to buy airtime anyway. Brock counseled Dole to make sure to get some rest, advice he knew Dole had not taken when Dole flippantly refused to sign a pledge not to increase taxes handed him by rival Pete DuPont with the words, "I have to read it first." Given the momentum George Bush developed after his come-from-behind victory in New Hampshire, Brock knew that the primitive state of Dole organizations in the South would guarantee a Bush sweep on "Super Tuesday," even with the long-expected endorsement from Senator Strom Thurmond.

When the 1988 Dole campaign ended, Brock created the Brock Group, a consulting firm for businesses interested in selling abroad. The Brock Group's primary function was to advise American clients on how to enter markets in Brazil, Japan, and Korea, but Brock also counseled officials of Taiwan, Mexico, and Panama on trade issues. Before undertaking any new business, he checked with U.S. government officials to see if his work conflicted in any way with standing American policy and interests. If they demurred, he declined to take on those clients.

By 1986, Brock had bought a home in Maryland, but he continued to help Tennessee Republicans whenever he could. As I first began contemplating public service, I sought him out through a mutual friend, Jim Frierson, a politically savvy Chattanoogan who graduated a year ahead of me at Princeton. I remember quite vividly Brock's advice to seek out ways to appeal to those who were not part of the traditional Republican coalition. He listened to those who asked him to make another bid for office in Tennessee, but he had registered to vote in Annapolis, Maryland, in 1988.

Brock's activities in Maryland kept him plenty busy. He had become a senior counselor at the Center for Strategic and International Studies and by 1992 was chairing the University of Maryland's Center for Learning and Competitiveness. He was most interested in the success of the National Academy Foundation (NAF), a nonprofit group created to spur academic development in inner-city schools. This was a program designed by an old friend, Jim Robinson, who was the chief executive officer of American Express. Robinson had established pilot programs in a few schools and invited Brock to take a look the next time he was in New York. A bit skeptical, Brock toured a NAF school in the South Bronx and was astonished to hear sixteen-year-olds from lower income backgrounds discussing some of the intricacies of high finance. He investigated further and found that the NAF program had literally no dropouts and that its graduates were uniformly free of teen pregnancy and crime. He soon signed on as chairman of the NAF and took its "school within a school" approach to embattled schools in Washington, D.C., and Maryland.

Politics never completely left Bill Brock's blood. In early 1993, he resisted overtures from well-placed Maryland Republicans to seek the governorship, thinking himself too new to Maryland to be as familiar as he would have to be with that state's internal needs and legislators he would need to know to make his program work. But when Maryland's two popular GOP Congresswomen declined to seek the Senate seat, Brock found himself besieged by Maryland Republicans who wanted a candidate of some stature to challenge liberal incumbent Paul Sarbanes. A Senate race for Brock was a different question. He knew Washington well enough to have confidence that he could help change it and he knew trade issues well enough to think he could have a positive impact on those employed by the port of Baltimore. He was certain the battle would be uphill. Sarbanes held a commanding lead among registered voters, but Brock knew Sarbanes well and believed that his own accomplishments and experience in and out of the Senate surpassed Sarbanes's legislative output. He could win, he thought, but everything would have to fall his way.

Brock entered the race thinking he could unite the Maryland Republican party's long-warring factions, an assumption he now describes as his "first mistake." He took his message of jobs and opportunity to all corners of Maryland, carefully following Ronald Reagan's injunction against speaking ill of other Republicans. What he had not reckoned on was what he called the "meanness" of an unknown, but wealthy and well-financed opponent. She pummeled him with innumerable personal and often cheap attacks, focusing on his inherited wealth, his Tennessee origins, and his work as a "foreign agent." Her attacks did little to improve her own standing. Several of her early supporters switched to Brock. Some in her campaign left her, while several others told Brock-backers that they remained with her only because they felt bound by their word. What she did was create such anger toward Brock and herself among the general populace that she effectively ended any chance that a Republican could have prevailed. For five months, Brock stoically endured her unrelenting attacks. "It is not his nature to kick rear ends," explained lifelong friend Bill Timmons. Near the end of the campaign, when her father was murdered, Brock sent her flowers. To this characteristic show of gentility she responded by airing a radio ad featuring two phony Tennessee hillbillies bragging about how they had gotten rid of Bill Brock and a TV spot that portrayed him, of all things, as a liberal. Only in the last week of the campaign did Brock and other Maryland Republican dignitaries officially respond to her misstatements and question a less than pure business record that less viable Republican candidates had been pounding on for months. I could continue at length, but further discussion would dignify conduct that not only became even more bizarre but even dangerous to our system and our society after the election.

Brock prevailed by just twelve points in the primary. Had he advertised early and defined himself for the people of his new state or had he called attention earlier to his opponent's erratic and often errant barbs or her lack of moral authority to make them, things may have been different. As things stood, Brock was the wounded candidate of a divided minority party facing a fairly uncontroversial incumbent. Sarbanes could and did fix the terms of the debate. Both candidates ran tough, issue-oriented ads, but Sarbanes's ads seemed quite tame compared to those Brock had been barraged by during the primary. In the end, Maryland lost a chance to bring a good man back to the Senate and we in the Senate lost a chance to put Bill Brock's expertise on questions of trade and education to maximum use.

Brock today heads Intellectual Development Systems, Inc., a company he created to help schools identify children with learning disabilities at an early age, and to devise modes of instruction that might allow those students to function and then thrive in school and in life. "Finding the problem early and fixing it," he wrote in his mission statement, "is far preferable to waiting months or years to deal with something which has left a lot of emotional scars." At present, IDS operates in thirty schools, but Brock has many plans to expand. He has even taken his program to a few prisons and was especially touched when he saw some of the participating inmates hug the warden.

As his ads said in 1994, Bill Brock is making a difference for Maryland. I know he'll bring some of his findings back to Tennessee.

Chapter 13

James R. "Jim" Sasser

1977–1995

Chairman, Senate Budget Committee

U.S. Ambassador to China

(1936–)

Because I was the soul who brought Jim Sasser's legislative career to an end in 1994, some may say that I should not be the one to treat him in a work such as this. Perhaps that is true, but I maintain that one can learn as much about a rival in competition as in any other situation in life. If one is honest, one is as quick to concede a competitor's strengths as he or she is to note the points of contention. I salute Jim Sasser as a devoted public servant and a strong family man who raised two outstanding children and fought hard for the Populist principles he learned as a youth. In times when people wanted their government to take more of a role in their daily lives and were not so concerned about the level of spending, Jim Sasser was the ideal servant of his constituents. Those times have passed, however, and I was able to prevail in 1994 because voters sensed that this philosophy was no longer the solution to their problems, but had in fact become part of the problem itself.

Everything in James Ralph Sasser's background points to his development into probably the last of a long and honorable line of Populist-oriented Senators from Tennessee. He was born in Memphis on September 30, 1936, to J. Ralph and Mary Nell Gray Sasser. Upon graduating from the University of

Tennessee, Ralph Sasser started work as a county agent, then enlisted in the Marines during World War II. While Ralph Sasser was away in the South Pacific, Jim Sasser and his mother went to live with her parents in rural West Tennessee. There, he learned how to fix cars from his grandfather, a crackerjack mechanic. And he never forgot that he grew up among rural kids who went barefoot as a matter of course and had little to look forward to at Christmas except possibly an orange. Soon after Ralph Sasser returned from the war, he became head of the Soil Conservation Service for Tennessee. His business often took him to Fort Worth for southern regional meetings and to Washington, where he met with USDA officials and helpful Tennessee pols such as his friend Albert Gore, Sr. More commonly, he spent long hours driving the back roads of rural Tennessee and advising any farmer who seemed interested on how he might better use his land. Often, his son rode along. From these tours, Jim Sasser concluded at a very early age that "government ought to be an instrument to assist people in elevating the quality of their lives."

Sasser left home for the University of Tennessee in 1954, then transferred after a year to Vanderbilt. In Nashville, he began dating Mary Gorman, a gracious, attractive young woman from Louisville who was studying history. Like Sasser, Mary was civic-minded, eventually becoming active in the Children's Theater, the Nashville Symphony Society, the Historic Nashville Foundation, the Tennessee Bicentennial Commission, the League of Women Voters, and the Federation of Democratic Women. She is also a talented cook, as evidenced by the many recipes she has published in newspapers across Tennessee. At Vanderbilt, Mary roomed with Nancy Gore, and she and Sasser would frequently drive the fifty miles to Carthage to dine with the Gores. Their courtship continued after their graduation in 1958. Mary began teaching school and Sasser continued his education at Vanderbilt Law School, helping to pay his way by doing a six-year stint in the Marine Corps Reserve.

Only after Sasser completed his legal education did they wed. They remained in Nashville, where he opened a law practice that eventually attracted such clients as the Everly Brothers and Colonel Tom Parker, Elvis Presley's manager. In time, they had two fine children, Gray and Elizabeth. For relaxation, Sasser began jogging two or three miles a day, but his consuming hobby was restoring old cars. By 1980, he had bought and rebuilt three classic Jaguars. All of us have our peculiar honors, but it fits that Jim Sasser's favorite was being named grand marshal of the Daytona 500.

Sasser got his start in politics in 1960 when a law school classmate landed him a job as the driver for Estes Kefauver in his last reelection campaign. He still describes Kefauver as his hero, but his marriage to Mary dictated that he would develop even closer ties with Albert Gore, Sr. He joined Gore in the unsuccessful presidential campaign of Edmund Muskie in 1972, but was even more active in Gore's own races. In 1970, he directed operations for the

"Old Gray Fox" in Middle Tennessee, the one of the three Grand Divisions where Gore prevailed over Bill Brock in the U.S. Senate race.

Sasser was concerned enough about the state of his party in 1973 to take on the chairmanship of the state Democratic Executive Committee. He took office at the lowest ebb in the fortunes of Tennessee Democrats since Reconstruction; the organization was $65,000 in debt, and they had lost both Senate seats, their majority on the state House delegation, and the governorship. With the Democratic ticket headed by the unlikely and unelectable tandem of presidential candidate George McGovern and senatorial candidate Ray Blanton in 1972, it was easy for Sasser to sense "lethargy" in Democratic ranks, but he knew that the one cause that united many Democratic activists was a desire to avenge Albert Gore's loss. This would be a long-range goal; for Bill Brock's seat would not be up until 1976. Sasser set out on what at first must have seemed a lonely mission to revitalize Tennessee Democrats. He succeeded largely by copying many of the same procedures that Brock had developed informally for Tennessee Republicans. He opened a headquarters in Nashville; hired a staff of three; began sending out a newsletter, the *Tennessee Democrat*; compiled a mailing list; began a direct mail program; and worked with State House Speaker Ned Ray McWherter to recruit able men and women to seek all offices as Democrats. Certainly, Sasser was helped by the antipathy Tennesseans felt toward most Republicans, with the exception of Howard Baker, brought on by Watergate. Still, it would be impossible to overstate the credit Jim Sasser deserves for reinvigorating his party. He refused an expense account and even infused Democratic coffers with $3,000 out of his own pocket. In 1974, he helped put together a talented slate of candidates for the state Supreme Court and took the lead in raising funds to elect them. The campaign brought long-warring factions of Tennessee Democrats together and forged the unity that allowed Democrats to elect Ray Blanton governor in 1974. In spite of the extraordinary inflation in campaign costs and the additional overhead, he raised enough money by 1975 to retire his party's debts.

Always in the forefront of Jim Sasser's mind was recapturing what he had seen as Albert Gore's seat. Some little-known Democrats were interested, as was Tennessee businessman John Jay Hooker, but Sasser thought the others of too little stature. Hooker's image as a liberal and the failure of his firm Performance Systems, Inc., a highly oversold start-up company in which thousands of Tennessee investors lost money, made him too tarnished to wage a successful campaign against Bill Brock. With better-known Democrats opting against running, Sasser began contemplating a bid himself in early 1976. He had forged solid working ties with all wings of his party in the course of Jimmy Carter's enormously popular primary campaign. As a man of middle-class origins and bearing, Sasser would present a vivid contrast with Brock, who was portrayed by political opponents as a patrician. Seeing the fight as uphill but winnable, Sasser resigned as state Democratic chairman and entered the race.

Sasser worked tirelessly throughout his first campaign, touring the state in a Winnebago. Traditionally Democratic constituencies were looking for a winner and many of their leaders quickly lined up behind him. Unlike Hooker, he was a fresh face with few enemies. His gravelly voiced, thick-drawled intonations gave more conservative rural Tennessee Democrats a sense that he could relate to their hopes and aspirations. He also benefited because his father had worked with thousands of Tennessee farmers. "If you're Ralph's boy," they told him, "we're gonna be with you." Sasser made virtues of his newness and his lack of money. His 73,000 vote victory in the primary sealed his image of a David ready to take on another Goliath.

Sasser flavored his fall campaign with a biting populist idiom. "How," he would ask, "can a millionaire know the plight of the poor, the uneducated, the jobless, the sick?" He painted Brock as a servant of the special interests, claiming that Brock's brand of fiscal conservatism "ignored the needs of Tennesseans" and that his votes were "compatible with the profit motives of the oil companies." Noting the popularity of Jimmy Carter in Tennessee, Sasser liked to joke that he was attaching himself not only to the former Georgia governor's coattails but to his coat, even reminiscing that he had helped his own grandfather grow peanuts. He was careful, however, to adopt a more conservative posture on social issues than Carter. He distanced himself from the plank of the national Democratic platform calling for liberalized abortion laws, saying he was "personally opposed," and he flatly rejected Carter's blanket amnesty for Vietnam-era draft dodgers and deserters. Rare was it, however, when Sasser did not follow these comments with a long ringing endorsement of the Carter-Mondale ticket. His bonding with Carter paid dividends and by late September, he led Brock in the polls 41 to 39 percent.

Sasser would ride the horse of class envy for the rest of the campaign. Early on, he released a statement showing financial holdings so modest that Larry Daughtrey of the *Tennessean* likened him to a Boy Scout. Aiming to contrast his middle-class standing with Brock's wealth, he challenged Brock to follow suit. Brock declined because he thought that his wife's holdings should not be subjected to public scrutiny. Sasser then released a copy of Brock's 1975 income tax returns that showed he had paid but $2,026 on an income of $51,670. It was well known that business had not been good for Brock in 1975 and no one except Ray Blanton questioned the legitimacy of his deductions. Still, Sasser supporters began to sport buttons that read, "I Paid More Taxes than Brock."

For his part, Brock spent too much time in Washington to wage an effective campaign. In the eyes of Don Sundquist, Brock's chances of being reelected were next to nothing once Gerald Ford opted for Bob Dole as his vice-presidential running mate rather than Howard Baker. Brock had known since spring that polling data revealed that Jimmy Carter's appeal and Watergate would have a negative impact on his chances for reelection. Sasser indeed sought to further this connection by running newspaper ads that featured himself with Carter and Brock with Richard Nixon and Spiro Agnew.

As the campaign progressed, it grew increasingly negative. In Sasser's corner was Governor Ray Blanton. Blanton described Brock as "dirt" who had "ripped off the people of Tennessee." He lent Sasser the resources of his state organization and, in one instance when he was asked if state employees were contributing to Sasser's campaign, Blanton replied "they'd better." Brock countered with an ad depicting the tribulations of a Democratic voter who entered the booth and contemplated another vote for the "Sasser-Blanton" machine. It drew attention to the indictment of Blanton's transportation commissioner on charges of selling surplus state cars for personal profit and a newly launched probe of Blanton's possible sale of pardons. The timing of the investigations was sheer coincidence, but their closeness to the election allowed Blanton to defuse the issue by characterizing it as a "political conspiracy." What Tennesseans did not know at the time was that every charge against Blanton would later be proven to be true. Had they been aware of this, Bill Brock may have survived, for Sasser had been instrumental in Blanton's election. What voters were certain about, however, were the sins of Richard Nixon—sins that dampened Republican turnout across the state—and the virtues of fellow Southerner Jimmy Carter, which maximized Democratic participation. While Brock ran 40,000 votes ahead of Gerald Ford in Tennessee, that was still 78,000 votes behind Jim Sasser.

Sasser quite naturally entered the Senate as a staunch Carter loyalist. Being what he called "the new bull in the pasture," he recognized that Howard Baker would have a larger role in national issues. Wisely, he forged a strong working relationship with Baker on Tennessee issues. Sasser used his position on the Appropriations Committee to secure funding for the renovation of Nashville's Union Station, a clinical support facility for veterans at Mountain Home, and the U.S. pavilion at the Knoxville World's Fair. He helped Baker block President Carter's attempt to end construction of the Tellico Dam and supported Baker's ultimately unsuccessful bid to save the funding of the Clinch River breeder reactor.

While attending conscientiously to Tennessee interests, Sasser cultivated and managed to convey throughout his first term an image as a fiscal conservative. He used his perch on the Government Operations Committee to prompt the General Accounting Office to set up a toll-free hotline to enable ordinary citizens to report cases of government fraud and abuse. On the Senate floor, he secured passage of an amendment barring federal agencies from contracting for high-priced goods and services or paying firms to water office plants. Another Sasser amendment required agencies to estimate the cost to state and local governments of any new regulations before imposing them. Although he was not so successful in a fight to attach "sunset" provisions to federal programs, he established impeccable credentials as an opponent of government waste. His accomplishments limited the viability of any Republican challenger in the Democratic year of 1982. Even with some of the most creative ads Tennessee has ever seen, Robin Beard, the hard-charging conservative Congressman from Franklin, could muster only 38 percent against him.

Sasser continued as Tennessee's more parochially inclined Senator throughout the 1980s. Even after Howard Baker's retirement in 1985, the ability of Al Gore, Jr., to bring national attention to significant issues such as organ transplantation tended to obscure Sasser's presence in Washington. In these times, it was Sasser who attended to Tennessee interests more than either Baker or Gore. He continued a practice of frequently visiting the state each year and he took care in Washington to see that there were sufficient funds for TVA and the Appalachian Regional Commission. Sasser supported the creation of Vanderbilt's Kennedy Center for research on mental retardation. He also secured funding to clean up Kentucky Lake and negotiated the deal to ensure that Oak Ridge would not become a site for nuclear waste deposits.

In Washington, Sasser aligned firmly with Democratic leader Robert Byrd. That relationship tightened, interestingly enough, when Sasser secured a spot for Byrd on the Grand Ole Opry to fiddle his rendition of "Turkey in the Straw." In time, Senator Byrd made him his whip for the South and sent him to trouble spots abroad to scout conditions. The first such mission came in 1979, when Byrd sent Sasser with Max Baucus (D-MT) and Jack Danforth (R-MO) to investigate means of getting relief to genocide-torn Cambodia. Later, Sasser journeyed to Afghanistan to investigate the progress of the *Mujaheedin* who were resisting the Soviet invasion of their homeland. In 1987, when an inadvertent Iraqi attack on the *USS Stark* killed thirty-seven American sailors, Byrd again sent Sasser to investigate. There, Sasser helped forge a Democratic consensus that the United States should limit its involvement in the region or get our European and Japanese allies to share more of the costs.

During the 1980s, Sasser spent much of his time helping to formulate a Democratic alternative to President Reagan's Central America policy. As ranking Democrat on the Military Construction Appropriations Subcommittee, he toured Honduras in 1984, found U.S. airfields that Congress had not authorized, and warned that the Reagan administration might be trying to establish a permanent base from which to invade neighboring Nicaragua. It was, in fact, Reagan's intention to funnel aid to the Contras who were resisting the Communist Sandinista government, but Sasser so overstated his case that the Senate tabled an amendment he had drafted that would have limited Reagan's ability to respond to an emergency in the region.

In 1986, Senator Byrd tapped Sasser to give the official Democratic response to a televised Reagan plea for Congress to aid the Contras. In his clipped but reasoned tones, Sasser tried to assure viewers that Democrats, like Reagan, wanted peace and stability in Central America and would not allow Cuba or the Soviet Union to establish a permanent base in Nicaragua that would allow the Sandinistas to export their revolution. He suggested that Reagan had exaggerated the imminence of the threat and called on the President to work with the Sandinistas toward a negotiated settlement. But Sasser had overestimated the peaceful predisposition of the Sandinistas. Soon after the House voted down a bill authorizing aid to the Contras, Sandinista troops ventured into Honduras. This led the House to reverse course and approve a $100 million aid package to the Contras. Not so moved, Sasser first offered an amendment extending aid only if the Sandinistas refused to resume negotiations. This satisfied neither Reagan's supporters nor opponents of any aid, and it was rejected, 33–67. Sasser came back with another addendum barring any assistance, warning that the United States was moving "precisely down the path" that it had "traveled in Vietnam." This bid failed, too, but by a much narrower margin of 54–46. Only in 1988, the year he stood for reelection, would Sasser hint that he might reconsider his position against funding the Contras if the Sandinistas did not move to open their government and end the human rights abuses that had so riddled their tenure.

We can discern now from Nicaraguan election results that the Nicaraguan people were never enthralled with either the Sandinistas or the Contras. To Ronald Reagan, aiding the Contras was merely the best means of deterring the export of the Sandinista revolution and compelling the Sandinistas to create the Democratic system they had promised when they came to power in 1979.

One can understand Jim Sasser's aversion to risking the lives of American soldiers in anything that resembled the "quagmire" of Vietnam. But one finds in Jim Sasser's work an almost reflexive opposition to anything initiated by either Presidents Reagan or Bush. Indices compiled by liberal and labor groups throughout the 1980s and early 1990s reveal Sasser's steadily increasing identification with their agendas. Although Sasser did vote for the initial Reagan tax and budget cut proposals of 1981, he supported several amendments limiting the scope of the cuts.

Except for the Gramm-Rudman-Hollings budget reform bill of 1985, the Tax Reform Act of 1986, and a balanced budget amendment, one struggles to find any area where Sasser agreed with either Ronald Reagan or George Bush. In a vote that negated Al Gore's and antagonized many veterans, Sasser cast his lot in 1991 against authorizing President Bush to use military force to enforce a UN directive to Iraq to withdraw from Kuwait. He opposed the nominations of Robert Bork and Clarence Thomas to the Supreme Court, as well as the elevation of William Rehnquist to Chief Justice. He was one of the handful of Senators to vote against a second term as Federal Reserve Board Chairman for Paul Volcker, a fellow Democrat who was originally appointed by Jimmy Carter. Little concerned that Volcker had the confidence of the financial community, Sasser reasserted his Populist credentials with Tennessee Democrats, contending that Volcker's tight credit policies effectively raised interest rates.

During election years, Sasser focused on noneconomic issues. He was always quick to spotlight his highly effective service to constituents and his support for voluntary school prayer. Standing in 1988 against Bill Andersen, an affable and capable but little-known and underfinanced attorney from Kingsport, Sasser prevailed with 65 percent of the vote, carrying every county but one.

In 1989 Jim Sasser assumed his first Senate committee chairmanship, taking over the Budget Committee, on which he had served for six years. It was not a task Sasser savored and he kidded that he never particularly liked math. He even tried to persuade Fritz Hollings and Bennett Johnston, two southern Democrats senior to him, to take the post, which had been left vacant with the retirement of Florida's Lawton Chiles. When neither would leave chairmanships of committees holding jurisdiction over matters vital to their states, Sasser reluctantly agreed to take on the new responsibilities and became the first Tennessean to chair a major committee since Kenneth McKellar.

Sasser moved cautiously his first year. In committee meetings, he tried to allow every member a voice in the process. He did his best to restrain fellow Democrats, for he knew that the public would not take kindly to any immediate attempt to force President George Bush to violate his pledge of "no new taxes." In negotiating sessions with Bush's team in 1989, he took a back seat to House counterpart Leon Panetta. The next year, Sasser took a more calculated, partisan approach, declaring of the first Bush proposal that "simply putting a new suit on that old corpse isn't going to revive it." He resisted the calls of Panetta and other deficit hawks, who he believed wanted to rush into a budget summit without agreeing on a Democratic position. Instead, he counseled the kind of patience that would prod Bush into breaking his pledge. His shrewdness paid off, and Bush relented by June. Although House Republicans resisted, there were enough votes by October in both houses to approve a package capping discretionary spending and increasing several taxes. It was easy for Sasser to sell the package to fellow Democrats as one that promoted equity, for those well-off would pay much more. What was not so clear at the time was that his group of negotiators had produced the chink in George Bush's armor that first weakened his credibility within his own party and ultimately led to his defeat in 1992.

Sasser solidified his hold over the Budget Committee after 1990. He got the Senate to approve a move to limit the number of members, in part for the purpose of ousting Chuck Robb (D-VA), a more conservative Democrat. Two years later, he restored the size of the panel and recruited members who shared his predilections toward defense cuts and domestic spending hikes. In 1991 and 1992, he led an unsuccessful fight to tear down walls erected in the 1990 deal that limited the ability to secure a "peace dividend" by siphoning off defense funds. He did succeed in limiting funds for the Strategic Defense Initiative and a plan to build an airbase in Sicily, and he was part of ultimately successful coalitions that scuttled the Stealth bomber and the superconducting supercollider.

Once President Clinton took office in 1993, Sasser took a lead role in pushing the President's domestic agenda through Congress. He was quick to back a Clinton package to funnel $16.3 billion into the economy, a plan ultimately killed by a Republican filibuster. His particular responsibility was to manage Clinton's first budget, which contained one of the largest tax hikes in American history. Sasser persuaded Democrats on his committee to go along, telling them that Clinton needed an early win and that he would give them cover by going along with any number of "sense of the Senate" amendments. His strategy succeeded on the floor. Although seven Democrats bolted and Vice President Al Gore, Jr., had to be in the chair to cast a tie-breaking vote, not even a comma was changed in Clinton's proposal, much less a number, a rare accomplishment for any chairman at any time.

Several of Sasser's Democratic colleagues appreciated his dedication enough to suggest he run to succeed George Mitchell as Majority Leader once Mitchell let it be known that he planned to leave the Senate in 1994. Ever cautious, Sasser demurred until a senior colleague told him flatly that he ought to make the race or leave the Senate. Only then did Sasser agree to run. He spent considerable time touring offices and lining up commitments. He won the support of most of his colleagues on the Budget Committee as well as most senior Democrats, while Tom Daschle of South Dakota was the pick of most junior members. In October of 1994, Barbara Boxer of California, a staunch Sasser ally, revealed that her count had twenty-five votes for Sasser and twenty-two for Daschle among the fifty Democrats she thought would be returning in 1995. Had Jim Sasser been reelected, it is almost certain that he would have been elected Democrat leader of the Senate.

But Sasser's likely ascension to the leadership may have crippled his own reelection bid. His focus remained in Washington, and the energies of himself and his staff were spent there rather than in Tennessee. To voters back home, and reinforced by the Tennessee newspapers which were covering his run for Senate leader in Washington, he appeared more interested in the national Democratic Party than he was in the people of Tennessee. Already, his chairmanship of the Budget Committee had indelibly linked him in the public mind with national deficits, and his management of the 1993 proposal identified him as an advocate of higher taxes. And, unlike in years past, he would be seeking reelection at a time when a Democratic affiliation and a three-term resume would be liabilities rather than assets.

I was fortunate enough to win the Republican primary in August 1994 and thus the opportunity to run against Jim Sasser. A survey I commissioned in July 1993 revealed that Sasser had a respectable 63 percent job approval rating. But I knew, too, that the people of Tennessee had not rewarded any Senator with a fourth term since Kenneth McKellar and that 48 percent of those surveyed said that it was time to give someone else a chance. That told me that Sasser would be a tough mark, but that with the right opponent he could be beaten.

Although physicians as a group were not wildly popular, I knew that people do trust their own doctors. And that trust associated with being a doctor, if it could be communicated to Tennesseans personally and effectively, would benefit my campaign, especially in the anti-Washington atmosphere of 1994. I did everything my staff could think of to emphasize my status as an outsider and to highlight Sasser's Washington prominence. Since my goal in life was to be a successful physician, not a career Senator, it was natural for me to pledge to serve no more than two terms in the Senate and to adopt as a rallying cry, "term limits for career politicians and the death penalty for career criminals." In doing so, I highlighted a disagreement with Jim Sasser over a Clinton crime bill that was long on funding but short on sentencing reform. I did my best to show Senator Sasser's strong ties with the national Democratic Party by running an ad showing a pseudo-replica of Mount Rushmore emblazoned with his face flanked by the three other major Democrat Party leaders of the time—President Clinton, Senator Ted Kennedy, and Congressman Dan Rostenkowski—who were not so popular in Tennessee at the time.

The Sasser campaign, using Washington-based media consultants, fought back aggressively in the same Populist idiom that he used to defeat Bill Brock. His campaign ran ads showing pictures of my home in Nashville, tried to link me to the corporate affairs of the hospital company my brother and dad founded (though I had never worked there), produced commercials implying that I, a heart and lung surgeon, wanted children to smoke, and suggested that I would have a hard time understanding people working at minimum wage (even though well over a third of my transplant patients and families, with whom I worked day-in and day-out, fell below the poverty line). In other commercials, often run during the Rush Limbaugh radio program, he touted his support for voluntary prayer, a balanced budget amendment, and deportation of illegal immigrants. These were the few issues on which Jim Sasser's record squared with the generally more conservative philosophies of most Tennesseans. The general tenor of the rest of his record as measured by several liberal and nonpartisan groups was well to the left of Al Gore's.

If anything, the Sasser camp played into my hands when they began running commercials toward the end of the campaign touting his potential rise to the majority leadership, heralding the benefits that had accrued when Howard Baker held that office, and saying that his reelection would guarantee that Democrats retained control of the Senate. Indeed Sasser's pleas lent credence to my suggestions that he was closer to the Clinton administration than he was to the people of Tennessee. Two weeks before the election, I came to see victory as imminent when an enthusiastic crowd of 250 people greeted me at a seated dinner in Union City, a town in what had been the heart of Jim Sasser country of rural West Tennessee.

What I did not count on was the size of victory. Contrary to even my most optimistic projections, I prevailed by more than 200,000 votes, defeating Senator Sasser by a 56 to 42 percent margin. I won because voters wanted a change, not because they had any deep animosity toward Jim Sasser. If there was a message that should linger, it was what I said over and over, "Eighteen years is long enough." This certainly was the credo that I used every day across the state for political purposes, but I have the most fervent hope that my successor, be he or she Republican or Democrat, will come to Washington aiming to make a contribution within a few years, then, as Harry Truman put it, be prepared to accept a promotion to the role of private citizen. Our republic functions best with regular infusions of new ideas. Systems dominated by people who look on politics as a career itself rather than an interim of public service often seem immune to the transplantation of such vital new blood.

Defeat is hard on anyone. Jim Sasser, I am told, took his loss particularly hard, probably because neither he nor his staff nor much of the press gave an upstart newcomer like me much of a chance.

Like Al Simpson (R-WY) and some other recent departees, Jim Sasser moved to Harvard to spend a semester as a visiting professor at the John F. Kennedy School of Government. Once he completed that tour, President Clinton appropriately rewarded him for his long service to his party and to our country by naming him as our ambassador to Beijing. Managing our often tenuous relationship with the world's most populous nation would be difficult under any circumstances, but it is especially so in the post-Deng era. Our producers want to maintain access to Chinese markets, but all of us want to see progress on human rights from a Communist regime known for such barbarities as the Cultural Revolution and the Tiananmen Square massacre. It has been Jim Sasser's challenge to nudge the Chinese into more humane practices and pursuits.

Relationships with China have been strained during Sasser's tenure. The unlawful Chinese contributions to President Clinton's 1996 campaign coffers, the suspected Chinese espionage at Los Alamos National Laboratory, congressional investigations into inappropriate technology transfers, the war in Yugoslavia so openly opposed by China—all have proved a challenging backdrop to Ambassador Sasser's period of service.

Sasser, in true Tennessee volunteer spirit, remained in his post for a full year longer than he had anticipated at the request of President Clinton, in part because of the administration's inability to find a replacement. In May 1999, after the Chinese Embassy in Belgrade was mistakenly attacked by NATO forces, thousands of chinese besieged the U.S. Embassy in Beijing, trapping Sasser and thirteen other staff members inside for four days. Tens of thousands of Chinese students wielded stones and anti-American posters, flooding the streets in Beijing, in protest of the deadly accidental attack. Sasser, essentially held hostage by the threatening crowds and separated from his wife Mary and son Gray, confidently spoke by telephone and reassured the world that the was safe.

As this frightening experience demonstrates, public service has called upon those who have served Tennessee in the Senate over the years in trying ways. Jim Sasser has risen unselfishly to the occasion each time his state and country have called. Soon to return home from China, he will almost certainly continue to make substantial contributions to our community and country.

Chapter 14

Albert A. "Al" Gore, Jr.

1985–1993

Vice President

(1948–)

Over the course of the twentieth century, Tennessee has had more than its share of contenders for national office. Both Estes Kefauver and Howard Baker ran for the presidency and both had ample credentials. Had the national emergency brought on by World War II not prodded Franklin D. Roosevelt to seek a third term, Democrats very likely would have given their nomination to Cordell Hull in 1940. In 1956, Estes Kefauver captured the Democratic nod for the vice presidency. Over time, Albert Gore, Sr., Frank Clement, Howard Baker, and Bill Brock have been seriously considered for the same office. It is thus surprising that the only Tennessean to actually rise to one of the nation's two highest offices this century is Vice President Al Gore, Jr.

It would be possible to characterize Al Gore as a transplanted Tennessean. He was born in Washington, D.C., on March 31, 1948. Like many a congressional child, he spent the better part of most years of his youth in Washington, but he always seemed to love to spend his summers on the Gore farm in Carthage. One world was that of official Washington; where in his preschool years, he found himself being bounced on the knee of Vice President Richard Nixon. In Washington, his guides were his mother, Pauline, who always made time to sit with him for supper, even on the many nights she and the elder Gore went out, and his sister Nancy, who always seemed to know what was on his mind. His other world was that of Carthage, where his closest playmates were the sons of the tenant farmers who managed the Gore spread when they were away and where he could swim in the nearby Caney Fork River and hunt raccoons. Albert Gore was a stern taskmaster, however, and he saw to it that young Al chopped tobacco, baled hay, and cleaned even the filthiest stables. Gore would also charge his son with one tedious, demanding assignment that would occupy each summer. One such chore was to clear a large field of trees and shrubs with nothing but a hand-axe. If he did not finish, he was not paid. Perhaps this is where Al Gore developed the disciplined work ethic that is so readily apparent today.

Gore went to high school in Washington at St. Alban's. "Gorf," as classmates knew him, was an well-rounded student. He joined the Government, Religious, and Glee Clubs, served as class treasurer, and won an award for his artistic talents. He lettered in track and captained the football team. His best sport, however, was basketball. Gore led St. Alban's in scoring, though he is quick to note that his real strengths were his aggressiveness and team orientation. During his 1992 campaign for vice president, he exhibited an honesty rare among frustrated jocks when he admitted that opponent Dan Quayle had a better jump shot than he.

It was at a St. Alban's dance where Gore met Mary Elizabeth Aitcheson. Then as now, Mary Elizabeth, as Gore calls her at home, was better known as Tipper, a nickname she had worn since childhood. Both had dates the night they met, but Gore was so taken by her that he called her the next day to invite her to a movie. Within weeks, the two were talking of marriage and children. Gore left for Harvard that fall but continued to correspond with Tipper. He suggested that she find a college near Cambridge and she enrolled in Garland College in Boston. A bright woman known in high school for her talents as a drummer and a photographer, she earned her A.A. *cum laude*, then moved on to Boston University to earn her B.A. in child psychology and later to Peabody in Nashville for her master's in psychology. Within days of her graduation, the two were married in Washington's National Cathedral. And in the midst of the most intense media scrutiny imaginable, they have produced four remarkably well-adjusted children. Karenna was born in 1974, then Kristin in 1977, Sarah in 1979, and Al, III, in 1982.

At college, Gore seemed to be grooming himself for a political career. He was elected president of his freshman class and he majored in government. He took the time privately to tap the minds of Harvard's finest political scientists. He produced a psychohistory of his father and a senior thesis on "The Impact of Television on the Conduct of the Presidency, 1947–1969." His preparation continued even into the summers. One vacation he spent studying in Mexico City and he became sufficiently fluent in Spanish to translate for his father as he toured a Hispanic neighborhood. Another summer he took a course in Tennessee history at Memphis State University (now the University of Memphis). Dr. Charles Crawford, his professor, remembers him as an "extremely intelligent, hard-working" student who read far more than what was required, particularly about Tennessee's political past. His classmates at Harvard and elsewhere recognized his aptitude. The only thing one finds in his college record to suggest that he was not preparing for a run for office was his fondness for racing his motorcycle through the campus and the Massachusetts countryside.

Perhaps the overriding political issue for the young Gore was the Vietnam War. His college classmates, who opposed the war in Vietnam, saw Gore's father as one of their most eminent spokesmen. They knew that Al and Tipper shared their opposition, and they valued his insights. Gore would gladly engage them in discussion, if he thought them as rational as they were sincere. Interested in strengthening the system, not tearing it down, he channeled his antiwar feelings into the 1968 presidential campaign of Senator Eugene McCarthy and hoped the war would be ended by the time he graduated. When an uncle asked him what irked him so much about Vietnam, he replied, "I guess it's my Baptist religion," and cited the commandment, "Thou shalt not kill." While Albert Gore, Sr., had long been a vigorous critic of America's intervention, the real hard line among the Gores was taken by Pauline, who offered to join her son in Canada if he thought it right to avoid the draft. For Gore this represented a bit of a dilemma. He believed the war to be immoral, but he did not know how he could hold his head high in Carthage if his working-class neighbors went to fight, and he, a child of privilege, did not. Gore had studied enough of our state's history to know that Tennesseans pride themselves on a tradition of volunteering for wars and Tennesseans often have elected veterans. He was even more aware that a flight to Canada would likely bring an end to his father's political career. Gore agonized, but a variety of factors led him to enlist, each the mark of a man of character.

Gore was sent to Fort Rucker, Alabama, the training center for army helicopter crews. He was assigned to the base information office and his work primarily entailed writing stories for the base newspaper and drafting press releases describing the accomplishments of his comrades-at-arms for the benefit of the folks at home. A trailer nearby was Al and Tipper Gore's first home. The dearth of accommodations in the area made Gore feel blessed that there were a few basketball courts, and he also found some solace in painting. On ordinary weekends, the Gores would drive the countryside of southern Alabama. When they could get away, they returned to Tennessee to appear with his father on the campaign trail. Those who chronicle Tennessee politics remember fondly two TV advertisements featuring both Albert Gores. One showed the two riding their horses at a brisk pace on the Gore farm; a second ended with the Senator counseling, "Son, always love your country." The understated, positive tone of these ads paid dividends, as they put Gore, Sr., within striking distance of the once heavily favored Bill Brock. Families of public servants are aware of the achievements of their beloved members and even more familiar with their sacrifices, and naturally Gore was a bit disillusioned when his father lost. But there are many who wonder just what Al was thinking when the elder Gore declared in his concession speech that "someday soon . . . the truth . . . shall rise again . . . in Tennessee."

Gore left soon thereafter for a six-month stint in Vietnam where he continued as a journalist for his unit's newsletter and for *Stars and Stripes*. This time, however, his work took him to a combat zone. He saw horrors committed by both sides and continued to contemplate why his country had not taken his father's advice to resolve matters through negotiation. He wrote friends that he would enter divinity school if he survived to find out how "to atone for my sins."

Gore returned to Carthage more serious than ever. He spent some time on the Gore farm, and he later became a partner in a firm that was developing property on the outskirts of Carthage. Then, as he had planned, he began attending courses at the Vanderbilt School of Divinity, as he said, to "explore the most important questions" in his life. He went for a while, but then left.

"Did you find the answers you were looking for?" Gore, Sr., asked.

"I've learned to ask more intelligent questions," he responded. But what, he wondered, could he do to make enough money to support Tipper and remain independent?

Gore enjoyed writing and he thought about a career in journalism. One of his role models was the journalist Fred Graham, a friend of sister Nancy's. Tipper had taken a part-time job as a photographer at the *Nashville Tennessean*. She showed some of her husband's work from *Stars and Stripes* to editor John Seigenthaler and others. Gore interviewed for a spot as a reporter on the night beat and was hired almost immediately. At first, he covered merely routine stories, but he showed imagination. He covered one Christmas parade allegedly through the eyes of "Ebenezer Scrooge, as told to Albert Gore, Jr." My favorite of Gore's early reports is his account of an eating contest held by a small town Burger King. "Hopes of record-breaking performances," he wrote, "were dashed . . . when one of the contestants regurgitated his first three Whoppers on the table and dampened the morale of his competitors."

Gore soon moved up to the metro Nashville beat and honed his skills. He worked conscientiously and often late into the night, always digging to learn all he could about the subject he was covering. His reputation as a reporter flourished after he helped break two stories involving alleged bribes to members of the Davidson County Metro Council. The first came to Gore from a businessman who told him that a councilman would not sponsor an alley-closing ordinance unless he was given $1,000 up front. Gore called in the district attorney, then watched as the informant was wired for sound and drove with photographers to capture the payoff on film. The second involved a councilman who allegedly had taken $2,500 from a developer who wanted his help on a shopping center project. The mistrial-induced acquittal of one councilman and the suspended sentence given the other soured Gore on the state of our legal system.

Gore's experience as a journalist catalyzed in him a sense that he was an onlooker rather than a participant. He guessed that studying law might afford him a better chance to make a contribution to our society, so he enrolled in Vanderbilt Law School in 1974. He attended classes for two years, even as he worked nights at the *Tennessean* as an editorial writer. *Tennessean* publisher John Seigenthaler knew from experience that talented reporters had a habit of moving on to larger papers in larger cities, and sensing that Gore might be one of these, Seigenthaler told him that he wanted him to stay with the *Tennessean,* but if he opted to move on, "the sky's the limit."

In late February of 1976, Seigenthaler passed on a different kind of tip to Gore. Longtime Fourth District Congressman Joe L. Evins would be announcing his retirement later that day. Gore went home to talk with Tipper about a possible political race. She was up for his running, but she convinced him that he needed to establish his own identity and that his parents should restrict their participation to their votes. Gore announced his candidacy three days later at the Smith County Courthouse. He was a stiff campaigner at first, but he was earnest. His ideology was tinged with populism, if to a lesser degree than his father's. In 1976, he called most commonly for tax reform, sunset legislation, strip mining regulation, and the preservation of TVA. He did not have a clear field. Eight other Democrats, many of whom had been waiting for years for Evins to retire, entered the race. Best-known among them was State House Majority Leader Stanley Rogers, a six-year veteran of the legislature. Fortunately for Gore, all but one of them hailed from the district's southern end, leaving him a virtual free ride in the northern half. In the end, he won the primary by 3,559 votes. With no Republican opposition, he was on his way to his father's old seat in the House.

Gore always has told friends that his philosophy is "Early to bed, early to rise, work like hell and organize." He was keenly sensitive to the oft-stated criticism that his father had lost touch with Tennessee. It became his practice to hold scores of town meetings each year, first in his district, then elsewhere in the state, where he could measure the pulse of the public on matters of national and international interest as well as on those that were mundane or personal. When he finished, he made a point of shaking hands not only with everyone in the crowd, but also anyone who might be working in the kitchens or on the cleaning crews.

During his four terms in the House, Gore served on the Science and Technology Committee and the Interstate and Foreign Commerce Committee. These were hardly the most visible perches for a Congressman from Tennessee, but Gore made the most of them. He immersed himself particularly in the science panel's Investigations and Oversight Subcommittee. He studied issues intensively but rarely spoke out on them until he felt certain that he had mastered all their nuances. Within a term of his arrival in Congress, he was presiding over hearings in the chairman's absence, and by 1981 he chaired the subcommittee.

The Gore style developed in part during his days as a reporter. He would hold hearings that would arouse attention to problems that had been neglected too long, then call witnesses with enough public appeal to capture the attention of the news media. Because of this technique some likened him to the muckraking journalists of the early twentieth century, but that was not an apt characterization. History shows that muckrakers were notoriously long on outrage and short on solutions. Not Al Gore, who usually had a remedy in mind. Once hearings concluded, he would use the congressional Clearinghouse on the Future, which he chaired, to publicize his ideas and other options. He limited his own probes to two or three per year, in the hope of gaining action on those matters he deemed of utmost consequence.

If Gore were to choose any one of his probes as being particularly productive, it would almost certainly be his venture into the problems posed by toxic wastes. After he toured Toone, Tennessee, where chemical stockpiles had been dumped and rates of serious illness were high, he declared that the land should no longer be considered an "awesome sponge . . . that could absorb any . . . concoction that man could brew." He opened a series of eighteen hearings into the question and concluded that federal action should be taken to clear up those sites. This was the genesis of the "Superfund" program that initiated the process of eradicating those wastes from our environment. Gore is properly credited for using his oversight duties to push and secure passage of legislation requiring infant formulas to meet minimum nutrition and safety standards, protecting the elderly from unscrupulous insurance marketers, and increasing the availability of generic drugs. He also acted as an intermediary between the tobacco and health care industries in 1984 negotiations that led to the strengthening of warnings on cigarette packs and ads.

Al Gore was instrumental in passage of the National Organ Transplant Act of 1984. A year earlier, Gore had been disgusted when he learned that a Virginia doctor had concocted a profitable scheme to buy and sell organs from people in the Third World. "We must not allow technology to dehumanize people," he said, "so . . . they are regarded as things to be bought and sold like parts of an automobile." He became angrier upon learning that wealthy foreigners had received organs in U.S. hospitals before needy Americans. While arguing for the transplant bill, one story in particular, involving a young girl from Texas, caught the nation's attention. President Reagan appealed for a kidney for her. Gore hailed the President's call, but noted that the child had died before a donor could be found. Gore believed that her life might have been spared had there been a system in place to match donors and recipients. It was he who spurred the enactment of this extraordinarily vital piece of legislation authorizing a database linking the 110 hospitals where transplants were performed and providing $40 million to support reputable organ-procurement agencies. Curiously enough, there were some Democratic elders who chided him as a "publicity hound" for his attention to an issue with such "mom and apple pie" appeal.

Gore's major venture outside the scope of his committees followed a troubling experience at one of his town meetings in 1980. He asked a group of high school girls how many of them thought that America would wage a nuclear war in their lifetimes. Virtually every hand went up. "How many believe that we can change that if we really try?" he asked. Only five registered that hope. Gore then determined to learn everything he could about the intricacies of nuclear policy. He set aside eight hours each week to peruse available literature and consult with experts. It is a tribute to his homework that Reagan aides were calling him more knowledgeable than even acknowledged congressional experts such as Senators John Tower and Sam Nunn. He alone among members of Congress was responsible for a major shift in American arms policy. Unlike most, he had thoroughly scanned our negotiating stance with the Soviet Union. He determined that like us the Soviets were interested in a stable relationship and were quite fearful that the U.S. might develop a first strike capability. During the early 1980s, the most salient arms issue was our MX missile. Ronald Reagan had charged a commission headed by General Brent Scowcroft with recommending a basing mode. Gore counseled against a mobile system, thinking it might present the Soviets with a legitimate issue of verification. He recommended that the MX be installed in existing silos while America developed a new missile, the Midgetman, with but one warhead. This was precisely the stance the Scowcroft Commission took, and Gore, in tandem with congressional moderates such as Sam Nunn, Bill Cohen, Les Aspin, and Charles Percy, produced narrow majorities in both houses for a reduced number of these heavy missiles.

Regarding Gore's views on foreign and defense issues, those looking for a pattern other than one of thoughtful independence will come up empty-handed. He supported President Reagan's decisions to free Grenada and to provide military aid to El Salvador. He backed Reagan's ill-fated intervention in Lebanon. He voted against arming the Nicaraguan Contras. Gore heartened the post-Vietnam left with his endorsement of a nuclear freeze, but warned that "a proposal that ignores Soviet counterforce weapons and continued testing of those weapons is not in our . . . interest and not in the interests . . . of world peace." He had grave doubts about the efficacy of Reagan's Strategic Defense Initiative (SDI). At first, he thought that SDI represented a "lunatic fantasy" and that Reagan strained "credulity" to develop the system and then turn the findings over to the Soviets. As time passed, however, he monitored our negotiations in Geneva and came to see some SDI spending as a bargaining chip. Unlike many other Democrats, he was as quick to note a habit of the Soviets to "sulk in their tents about arms control" as he was to paint Reagan as the culprit for the failure of arms control negotiations. Throughout his years in the House, Gore constantly suggested a rethinking of our defense posture in ways that pleased neither peaceniks nor hard-liners. For example, he warned against an overreliance on the cruise missile because a Soviet decision to deploy the same submarine-based weapon would leave the heavily populated American seaboards in infinitely more danger than any part of the Soviet Union.

Gore got his chance to move to the Senate when Howard Baker announced his retirement in 1983. He moved quickly to organize and raised $1 million, which convinced other Democrats to avoid the contest. He could run on his record, which was moderately liberal. In those days, Gore generally voted against funding for abortions and spoke often in Tennessee for constitutional amendments to allow religious groups equal access to school facilities and a moment of silent prayer each morning. His town meetings highlighted a strong record of constituent service and he attended conscientiously to Tennessee's interests. Some of his views were controversial nationally, like his stands in favor of the Clinch River breeder reactor and the Columbia and Tellico Dams. Others had a purely local appeal, such as his move to preserve an AMTRAK railroad route that served Tennessee and a bill he spurred to enactment that subsidized high-cost rural phone companies.

With Lamar Alexander opting to remain in the governorship, Gore's Republican opponent in 1984 was state Senator Victor Ashe, now the outstanding mayor of Knoxville. At the time, Ashe was relatively unknown. He tried to increase his identification by familiarizing voters with his long-held nickname of "Bulldog." Gore said the election should revolve around the question of who was the more effective. Ashe countered in the year of President Reagan's greatest popularity by lambasting Gore's opposition to the Reagan tax cuts, a balanced budget amendment, and the B-1 bomber, and his support for a nuclear freeze. As the election neared, Gore responded that

Reagan had just signed into law Gore's bills strengthening warnings on cigarette packs, creating a national organ donor program, and stiffening sentences of career criminals. If there were a decisive blow, it came at a debate where Ashe pulled out a $10 bill and promised to give it to Gore if he would only mention his party's presidential nominee by name. "Walter Mondale," Gore replied, as he took the money and gave it to charity in Mondale's and Ashe's names. Gore won the race with 61 percent, carrying all but fourteen counties. Ashe was quick to recognize what hit him; he predicted within the decade, Gore would be on the national Democratic ticket.

Even faster than most House members who move up, Gore made his mark on the Senate. His assignment to the Commerce, Science and Transportation Committee afforded him a seat on a panel that covered issues similar to those he had concentrated on in the House. There, he resumed work on what became the High Performance Computing Act, a measure that supported the concept of the information superhighway. After the explosion of the space shuttle *Challenger* in 1986, he opposed the return of James Fletcher as administrator of NASA, saying that many of the troubles with safety control and cost overruns dated back to Fletcher's previous service in the 1970s. He knew he could not block Fletcher, but saw a need to impress on him a need to institute the strictest of administrative procedures. Gore continued to play a role in negotiations over the MX missile, helping produce a compromise that limited deployment to fifty. He also made a distinct contribution in the fight to bring gavel-to-gavel television coverage of Senate sessions, a fight that Howard Baker had waged unsuccessfully for nearly a decade. Gore, however, had a clear advantage over Baker, in that he had experienced television coverage in the House. Indeed, he had given the first televised House speech in 1979. To members, generally on the Democratic side, who feared that introducing cameras might increase the grandstanding, Gore replied that television had had precisely the opposite effect in the House. It had forced members to refine and focus their arguments. "The only thing we have to fear," he pointed out, "is the dark."

For much of Gore's first two years in the Senate, Tipper was the more visible Gore in the public eye. Unbeknownst to many, Tipper Gore has a long history of social activism. While in Tennessee, she worked with several mental health programs, and once in Washington, she began volunteering at a homeless shelter. There, she befriended Susan Baker, the wife of then White House Chief of Staff James Baker. In early 1985, the two found that they were both disturbed about the growing number of pornographic and violent words and images their children were being subjected to in records and music videos. Tipper Gore's awakening came after she bought the *Purple Rain* album by Prince for Karenna, then eleven. Mother and daughter enjoyed the title cut and a couple of others but were shocked when they heard the lyrics of "Darling Nikki." Tipper watched a few videos with her younger daughters. Having felt helpless to explain when six-year-old Sarah asked her why the teacher was undressing in the video of "Hot for Teacher" by Van Halen, she joined Susan Baker in forming the Parents' Music Resource Center (PMRC) to alert parents to the twisted messages that their children might be receiving. They hoped that they would get some cooperation from the recording industry in the form of labels that would advise buyers of the degree of violent or sexual content. Anticipating one potential criticism, Tipper Gore was quick to remind people of her own high school career as a drummer for the Wildcats, an all-girl band. "I'm not anti-rock and roll," she would say. "I grew up with it and I love it."

The Gores did not begin to gauge the degree of antipathy that Tipper and Susan Baker had aroused until Jack Danforth convened the Commerce Committee for a fact-finding hearing in September 1985. Al Gore watched from his perch on that panel as the late Frank Zappa described the PMRC as a group of the "wives of Big Brother" and their crusade as an "ill-conceived housewife hobby program." The lyrics offended parents, he said, "not kids." His words were fairly tame compared with some that followed. *SPIN* magazine published a fictional entry from "Tipper Gore's Diary," in which she planned to ban such innocuous songs as "Leader of the Pack" and "Teen Angel" before noon because they alluded to death. Mrs. Gore remained serene in the face of such attacks and declared that the issue was one of corporate responsibility and that her proposal amounted to nothing more than "truth in packaging." As Bob Dole would find when she welcomed his similar critique of the movie industry ten years later, her words bore the integrity of principle, and they paid off. Not long after the 1987 publication of *Raising PG Kids in an X-Rated Society*, a distinctly R-rated volume in part recounting her work, she was proud to report that twenty record companies had agreed to warn consumers of any potentially objectionable material.

Gore himself was contemplating a more visible role. At Christmas in 1986, Albert Gore, Sr., suggested that Al run for the presidency, telling him that he offered the country the starkest generational change since John F. Kennedy replaced Dwight D. Eisenhower. As the Iran-Contra scandal unfolded, he continued, voters would be looking for someone with an entirely different appeal than Reagan. Gore took his father's words to heart, but did not decide until after a nearly three-hour talk with his parents on April 9, 1987. He heard Sarah asking when "Social Security" would begin guarding her and little Al wondering if he could wait until he turned five. He also listened to Tipper's concerns, but both knew that their marriage was more than strong enough to withstand the rigors of a national campaign. Once she agreed to support whatever course he chose, he called his father and let him know that he was in the race, producing a yell that Gore, Sr., likened to a Comanche's for years.

Had Democrats thought long and hard about which of their candidates was most likely to recapture the White House in 1988, they would have chosen Al Gore. He had the attractive qualities of youth and intelligence. Unfortunately for Democrats, Gore's campaign suffered from the same fatal flaw that had rendered Howard Baker's 1980 effort a disaster; he opened operations far too late. Even before the withdrawal of front-runner Senator Gary Hart of Colorado in the aftermath of a scandal, most key Democrats had thrown their support behind other contenders. Dick Gephardt of Missouri had a base in the unions and among his House colleagues. Governor Michael Dukakis of Massachusetts drew support from feminists, fellow governors, academics, and northeastern liberals. Reverend Jesse Jackson had a solid base among African Americans, Arab Americans, and leftists. Senator Paul Simon of Illinois could tap Midwesterners and fellow New Deal liberals. Former Governor Bruce Babbitt of Arizona, while the least-known of the pack, could still count on support from fellow Westerners and some environmentalists. It would seem that Gore might have a base among fellow baby-boomers, but that was not to be. It is a sad fact of American life that the young vote in far fewer numbers than their elders. Some younger people who did vote somehow found compelling those spurious arguments that Tipper Gore's record labeling crusade smacked of censorship. Thus, all that was left to Gore was a strong base in Tennessee and neighboring states among white Democrats and a hope that he could arouse the Democratic center and right, never an easy task.

Gore opened his campaign at the Smith County Courthouse on June 29 with standard Democratic appeals, but he soon began to set himself apart from the rest of the field. "The politics of retreat, complacency and doubt may appeal to others," he told the National Press Club, "but it will not do for me or my country." "The American people," he added before an arms control group, "have been given the impression over the last several presidential elections that the Democratic Party is against every weapons system . . . and is prepared to go into negotiations with the Soviet Union on the basis that we get something for nothing." He alone among the six Democrats had backed a modicum of defense during the Reagan era. Although Gore aligned with the general Democratic positions in favor of a nuclear freeze and against the Strategic Defense Initiative and military aid to the Nicaraguan Contras, he did not shy away from proclaiming his support for Reagan's re-flagging of vessels in the Persian Gulf, his liberation of Grenada, or his bombing of Libya after a hit team hired by strongman Muammar Qaddafi killed an American serviceman in Germany. He lectured his rivals about their willingness to accept a Soviet client state in Central America, saying that the Nicaraguan Sandinistas could "not be totally trusted." He would not join in the Democratic choir of barbs at Reagan's rearming of America; in fact, he credited the toughened posture for bringing the Soviets to the bargaining table. Gore's stance solidified his support in the South, but brought him sharp attacks from his party's left. Reagan had taken Gore to the cleaners on the MX missile, said Michael Dukakis. "You sound more like Al Haig than Al Gore," added Dick Gephardt.

Given the traditionally liberal clientele who formed the electorate in Iowa, the state of the first caucuses, Gore faced a tough uphill climb to the nomination. He showed a prize bull from his farm at the Iowa State Fair, but soon decided that others had concentrated too much time there for him to try to draw Democrats from their long tradition of prairie isolationism. He overcame one potential obstacle by his candid confession that he had smoked marijuana in the late 1960s and early 1970s. And he managed to convince some Democrats of his commitment to their economic doctrines with pointed barbs aimed at Dick Gephardt for backing the Reagan tax cuts. In debates, Gore fared well. "He has won virtually every debate," said Tennessee Congressman Jim Cooper. "Unfortunately most Americans don't watch the debates."

Gore focused his attention on the twenty primaries that comprised that year's "Super Tuesday." He hoped that victories in several southern primaries would propel him into contention. His strategy was sound, but he was hurt by the intangible press coverage which in the week prior to Super Tuesday was focused on the GOP contest in which George Bush overtook frontrunner Bob Dole in New Hampshire. Still, Gore prevailed in Wyoming the next Saturday. When the big day arrived, he won in Tennessee, Arkansas, North Carolina, Kentucky, Nevada, and Oklahoma; and he ran second behind Jesse Jackson in Georgia, Alabama, Louisiana, Mississippi, and Virginia.

Gore's emergence as the southern regional candidate did not translate into popular support elsewhere. Even on Super Tuesday, he collected fewer delegates than either Michael Dukakis or Jesse Jackson. Although he secured the endorsements of the *Chicago Tribune* and both Milwaukee dailies, his initial wins came far too late to give his organization the boost it needed. He ran third behind Dukakis and Jackson in a number of northern states, then decided to go for broke in New York. In a debate there, he asked Dukakis about a Massachusetts program of granting "weekend passes for career criminals." The issue amounted to little in the Democratic contest, although it did give George Bush a major lift in the fall. The real thrust of Gore's New York campaign was a bold appeal to Jewish voters, one initiated when he blasted thirty Senators for condemning Israel's rejection of a U.S. appeal to open peace negotiations. He drew some support here, but much of it dissipated when he allowed Mayor Ed Koch to act as his spokesman in what seemed a vitriolic campaign against Jesse Jackson. Jackson had denigrated New York City and offended Jewish Americans when he called it "Hymie Town." Few Jews had to be reminded of Jackson statements they found offensive, but those intent on voting against Jackson could look at a delegate count and see that Dukakis stood a better chance of taking the nomination than Gore. "I was doing great until I turned forty," Gore quipped. In the end, he won just 10 percent of the vote in New York, leading him to suspend his campaign.

It took a few weeks for Gore to realize that Ed Koch had hurt him more with African Americans than he had helped himself with the Jewish community. He made Dukakis's list of six finalists for a vice-presidential nod, but Jackson's campaign manager was heard saying that African Americans would find his selection an "outrage." Dukakis discounted such talk. He knew that Jackson not only wanted the second spot, but also that he felt somewhat anointed, having finished right behind Dukakis in the popular vote. Wanting neither to insult Jackson nor put him on the ticket, Dukakis opted for Lloyd Bentsen of Texas. In a way, Gore was lucky. If the presence of a respected southern Senate veteran such as Bentsen could not steer one southern state into the Dukakis camp, it is hard to see how a Gore choice would have changed things. Going down to defeat would have branded him, perhaps irreparably, as a liberal and a loser. Instead, he used the fall of 1988 to campaign for the national ticket and mend fences with those he had offended in the spring. His stock soared within Democratic circles. When it seemed after the Persian Gulf War that no Democrat of stature was willing to take on George Bush, the respected *Congressional Quarterly* was describing Gore as one of the "heavyweights" his party hoped would enter the race.

By 1991, Gore was less governed by politics than he was by family considerations. Two years earlier, he and Tipper were leaving a Baltimore Orioles game with six-year-old Al when the youngster let go of his hand and walked into the path of a moving vehicle. The collision threw little Al thirty feet into the air before he landed and slid for another twenty feet. Gore raced over to where his son lay limp. It was fortunate that a hospital was nearby and ambulances arrived quickly. Little Al's injuries were so serious that he remained in a cast for five weeks. Once he was taken off the respirator, his lungs had to be suctioned hourly. One of his parents was at his side virtually every moment. Only once that month, when Democrats needed his vote on a minimum wage bill, did Al Gore enter the Senate chambers. Little Al kept in remarkably good spirits, however, and in one of the rare moments when neither parent was around, he suggested to sister Kristin that they "party." For his parents, the ordeal was an eye-opener. Gore at forty-one was young enough that he might have several more chances to seek the presidency. Time with his children was limited as it was, and it would be next to nonexistent if he ran in 1992. Had he run, it would have limited the rationale for a Clinton candidacy, and he very well may have been elected. Political foresight is never so certain, but Gore's other concerns were more compelling. With Al III not yet fully mended and Karenna entering her senior year in high school, he wanted to spend what time he could with his family. He opted to forgo the 1992 presidential race.

Gore's legislative attention by this time was focused on the environment. It was hardly a new interest. In his presidential campaign, he had tried to raise the "greenhouse effect" to the status of a major issue, but found the media and the public ignoring him. He began to travel around the world to investigate the impact of ecologically disruptive practices. He trekked to Uzbekistan to study desertification and to Brazil to inspect the effects of deforestation. A trip to Antarctica to gather facts on the hole in the ozone layer prompted him to move to limit any further growth in the hole. While many nations had agreed to end the use of the chlorofluorocarbons (CFCs) that had produced the greenhouse effect and he himself would see to it that the United States outlawed CFCs in 1992, Gore came to believe that the hydrochlorofluorocarbons (HCFCs) that had replaced the CFCs in aerosol sprays and refrigerators were nearly as dangerous. As early as 1990, he got the Senate to agree to an amendment calling on industry to phase out the use of HCFCs by the year 2000. Believing that public education was even more vital, he used his perch as chairman of the Science, Technology and Space Subcommittee to lay out his findings and push his resolution creating the Earth Day of 1990. Even more notably, he published the best-selling *Earth in the Balance: Ecology and the Human Spirit* in 1992, his vision of man's relationship with the environment.

As measured by several interest groups, Gore's voting record retained a moderately liberal character throughout the Bush administration, one well to the right of his fellow Tennessee Senator, Jim Sasser. Yet few could fail to notice a few departures from previous positions. Abortion rights advocates found him a much more frequent ally than in the past. Gun groups noticed a first deviation from their preferred course when he voted for a ban on assault weapons. Gore's rhetoric seemed to grow ever more partisan. Upon finding in 1989 that officials in the Office of Management and Budget had ordered government scientists to soften a conclusion that global warming would lead to unprecedented climatic change, he charged that "James Watt clones" in the administration had conducted "an exercise in science fraud," a reference to Ronald Reagan's ill-fated Secretary of the Interior who became a negative poster-boy for environmental groups. Gore joined in Democratic calls for Congress to investigate scurrilous "October Surprise" allegations that the 1980 Reagan-Bush campaign had sabotaged negotiations with Iran for the release of the fifty American hostages. After hailing Defense Secretary-designate John Tower's conduct as START (Strategic Arms Reduction Treaty) negotiator as "exemplary in every respect," he turned around as Tower was hit by charges of infidelity and alcohol abuse and joined a near-solid Democratic bloc to scuttle Tower's nomination.

Even when Gore aligned with President George Bush against a majority of his own party, he took special steps to remain in the good graces of his fellow Democrats. A case in point came in January 1991 when he voted to authorize Bush to take all steps necessary to enforce a UN resolution demanding that Iraq withdraw from Kuwait. In announcing his decision, he opened by blasting Bush and Ronald Reagan for thinking that they could "do business" with Saddam Hussein and for not calling for a UN investigation of Iraq's use of poison gas during its long war with Iran. Only then did he dismiss the suggestion of the Democratic leadership that economic sanctions might bring Iraq to leave Kuwait. The idea that sanctions could produce an Iraqi withdrawal without additional pressure, he maintained, "did not feel plausible." More likely, he said, the continuance of sanctions would merely infuriate the Iraqis enough to goad them into further aggression, possibly against our Saudi Arabian allies. A delay, he continued, might involve a far "larger, greater and more costly" effort than the one then being considered.

The spectacular success of Operation Desert Storm makes it easy to see the wisdom of George Bush and Al Gore and the sheer wrong-headedness of their adversaries. Today, we often forget that the Senate vote supporting Bush was a mere 52–47, with just ten Democrats joining Gore. One could hardly expect Bush's Republican allies not to try to exploit their support of one of our most successful military missions. Many sported buttons reading "I Voted With the President" and took pokes at those who had not. In Gore's view, Republicans seemed "determined to load their big guns with cheap shots." His ardor in defense of those who had been so wrong did more to shape his credibility with Democratic activists than any piece of public policy he had ever pushed.

Gore did not know Bill Clinton well before the summer of 1992. Even with their philosophic and geographic proximity, neither had supported the other's presidential bid. Their meeting after Clinton narrowed his list of vice presidential possibilities to six was only their second of any length. It was a productive one, however. The two talked for nearly three hours and hit it off. Although their areas of preeminent interest were dissimilar, Clinton liked Gore's commitment to public service, his energy, and his determination to find solutions to the problems he saw. Another Gore plus was the close-knittedness of his family, which Clinton had to figure might distract attention from his own well-publicized marital difficulties. To Clinton's credit, his utmost concern seems to have been which of the finalists was best-prepared to serve as president. "I may die," Clinton joked to one aide. A choice of a man from a state neighboring Arkansas would signal voters that he had made his decision for better reasons than those of political balance. The selection of a fellow babyboomer would symbolize change, the single message he wanted to convey most. Gore, in fact, was his first and only choice. With little Al's recovery complete and Tipper once again willing to hit the campaign trail, Gore accepted Clinton's offer without hesitation.

Gore opened his acceptance speech at the Democratic convention by joking that he was fulfilling a lifelong dream of being the "warm-up act for Elvis," but like many other vice-presidential nominees, he would deliver the harsher rhetoric of his ticket's campaign. It would be out of character for a Gore to abstain from the populist tactic of lambasting a Republican administration for taxing "the many to benefit the few" and Gore did not disappoint. After leading delegates in a mantra of "It is time for them to go," he lauded his running mate and followed the speech with an impromptu waltz with Tipper to the beat of the other Paul Simon's "You Can Call Me Al."

On the nine bus tours that came to be known as "Bill and Al's Excellent Adventure," Clinton and Gore adopted a tag-team approach to campaigning. Gore would again warm up the crowds. Yet when they allowed for questions, Clinton would adopt the unheard-of practice of deferring to his running mate on matters in which Gore's expertise surpassed his own. There were differences in the two approaches. Visitors knew that they were more likely to get a fresh quote from Clinton than from Gore, and that they could get a soda and junk food from the Clinton bus rather than the Gore staples of bottled water and fruit. The two men bonded into a solid partnership that served Clinton well before and after his election. It was Gore whom Clinton used to bash George Bush and Dan Quayle for their opposition to a family leave bill and a tax cut targeted to the middle class and to suggest that the GOP ticket was not pro-family. It was Gore who delivered his campaign's sharper one-liners. The day after Quayle suggested in their one debate that Gore's inaccuracy was such that he was "pulling a Clinton," Gore reminded voters of Bush's slowness to object to Saddam Hussein's military buildup. "To present George Bush as a truth-teller," he said, "is like trying to sell a Porky Pig diet book." This episode reflected a Gore family preference for ridicule rather than invective. By the end of the campaign, Bush could not resist retaliating by describing his opponents as "bozos" and Gore as "Ozone Man." Had George Bush found a way to keep the personal aspect of the campaign focused more seriously on the issues of character, as he tried to do, at the same time defining and defending his own agenda, he might have retained the presidency.

A vice president's responsibilities vary with the needs of the President he serves. Gore expected to have significant duties in shaping national security, technology, and environmental policy. Ironically, Clinton's first suggestion was that he chair his task force on health care, an area where Gore's experience was scant. Gore declined because it would have limited the time he could devote to those areas where he felt he could make a strong contribution, such as making law. He knew Washington better than Clinton and felt that he could guide Clinton through the legislative labyrinth. From his soundings on the Hill, he determined that Clinton would have to rely on Democrats alone to pass the 1993 deficit reduction package, one that contained one of the largest tax hikes in our history. Gore counseled Clinton as to the best approach to take with each wavering Democrat, but even that was barely enough. Seven of his former colleagues left the Clinton camp when the bill reached the Senate, meaning that his vote, as president of the Senate, broke the tie.

Gore's major assignment within the administration was chairing Clinton's task force on "Reinventing Government." Past presidents such as Richard Nixon and Jimmy Carter had announced similar intentions to streamline the federal government and thus cut costs, only to see their efforts fall apart in the face of fierce opposition from the bureaucracy and its allies in Congress. Though Clinton and Gore did not go as far as some of us would have liked, they had more success than any of their predecessors. Their images as fiscal liberals gave them a credibility with a like-minded bureaucracy, limiting potential resistance from that quarter. Even more important were the many town meetings that Gore held with federal employees. He went to each Cabinet agency and asked workers what he could do to make it easier for them to serve our people and how costs could be cut in their departments. He dramatized his findings on the improbable setting of the *David Letterman Show*, donning safety glasses before he broke a glass ashtray with a hammer to demonstrate the folly of a requirement that federal agencies procure only those receptacles that broke into fewer than thirty-five pieces. "It's crazy," he said, and he instituted an ongoing review process to scrutinize the performance of each agency. To be sure, some of the task force's accomplishments have been overstated, but its recommendations have produced savings and the lowest number of federal workers since the Kennedy administration.

If there was an issue of the early Clinton years that blurred party allegiances, it was the extension of a U.S.-Canadian trade deal, the North American Free Trade Agreement (NAFTA), to include Mexico. NAFTA had been negotiated by the Bush administration, but Clinton adopted it once he secured separate agreements with Mexico protecting American workers and requiring Mexican firms to institute environmentally sound practices. With workers blaming mounting competition from overseas for jeopardizing their jobs, the unions, who as always were an important cog in the Democratic coalition, were hardly mollified. Fanning their fears was an anti-NAFTA lobby funded by Texas billionaire Ross Perot, a one-time salesman (and successful businessman) who had demonstrated a remarkable capacity for reaching average Americans in his efforts to establish a national third party during his 1992 presidential campaign. Perot contended that NAFTA would make it easier for American businesses to move to Mexico and replace American workers with cheap Mexican labor at a fraction of the cost. Thankfully, the "giant sucking sound" he warned of has never roared, but his words did reverberate through the American consciousness. Polls taken in early fall of 1993 showed more Americans against NAFTA than for it, even while it enjoyed the backing of every living former president, Nobel Prize winning economist, and secretary of state, treasury, and defense.

Gore's contribution came in a debate with Perot on the *Larry King Show* on November 9, 1993. Expectations at the White House were not high, for Gore had seemed wooden and plodding the year before in his face-off with Dan Quayle, but Gore came prepared and, unlike Perot, focused. His selling point was the simple contention that an "even-Steven lowering of taxes at the border would expand trade and create jobs in both countries." When Perot pulled out pictures of an impoverished Mexican community, Gore reached for his own of Mr. Smoot and Mr. Hawley, the men whose protectionist tariffs he held responsible for the Great Depression. The point was a stretch, for the Smoot-Hawley tariffs merely made bad conditions worse, but this was his only miscue. He responded to Perot's litany of complaints about lobbyists by alluding to the many Perot had employed and pointing out that the pro-NAFTA lobby, unlike Perot's, had disclosed all of its contributors and expenditures. While Perot said frequently that NAFTA proponents were those who believed "in the tooth fairy," Gore cited a preponderance of studies that showed NAFTA created jobs and thus eliminated the prime reason for Mexicans to migrate north. He conceded that Perot had many valid criticisms of the Mexican government, but pointed out that the United States would have no leverage with which to effect change in Mexico if it rejected NAFTA. When Perot threatened a campaign against pro-NAFTA legislators, Gore called on Americans to opt for the "politics of hope" rather than the "politics of fear." Polls showed that viewers saw Gore as the winner by a 59–32 margin and that public opinion had swung from 34–38 against NAFTA to 57–34 in its favor. Even Dan Quayle found himself rooting for Gore, and it is clear that President Clinton had Gore to thank for his first major victory in the international arena.

Gore would rarely be as visible thereafter, but his influence within the administration remained. Privately, his demeanor is never as stiff as it often seems on television. He has a quick wit that is often self-deprecatory, leading those who know him to conclude that he takes his duties more seriously than he takes himself. Gore's political antennae were sharp enough that Bill Clinton turned to him and let him know that he would do everything he could to help him secure the Democratic nomination in 2000.

Once Republicans captured control of Congress in 1994, Gore joined in advocating consultant Dick Morris's strategy of triangulation. During the campaign, he labeled the GOP "Contract With America" a "contract on Social Security," but later he suggested that the President refrain from the blindly negative course that congressional Democrats were employing to thwart the momentum of Republican moves to limit spending and taxes. If Clinton were to be reelected, the White House surmised, he would have to set his own course. He would need to go along with Republicans on noncontroversial initiatives such as restricting unfunded mandates and requiring Congress to live by the same rules it sets for others. Clinton and Gore would also work with Congress to find consensus on welfare reform. They also agreed that they would draw the line on cuts in spending for education and the environment, and on reducing planned levels of spending for Medicare and Social Security. They would support the idea of a balanced budget, but not a balanced budget amendment to the Constitution, on their terms and their terms alone. It was Gore who often played the tough cop in negotiations with the congressional leadership. At one September 1995 meeting, for example, he responded to House GOP Whip Tom DeLay's assertion of the seriousness of Republican aims to balance the budget by pointing out matter-of-factly that "Our polls show that you guys lose if the government shuts down."

Once again, Gore's instincts proved sound. The December 1995 closing of the government dimmed the luster of the Republican Contract With America, even if many of its provisions had already become law. Clinton and Gore succeeded in setting the agenda for 1996. Their concession to the Republican demands for a balanced budget lifted the one obstacle to their reelection. With the economy robust, they could look for a values issue of their own. They found one in polls that showed that the public wanted tobacco companies to cease advertisements targeting teens. Originally, Clinton feared that such a campaign might lose him the tobacco-growing states, but Gore reminded him that he had been reelected handily in 1984 just weeks after he had helped devise the compromise that strengthened the health warnings on cigarette packs. There had been no negative fallout, he added, because he met the issue head on in tobacco country. Clinton limited his initial actions to endorsing proposed FDA regulations designed to limit ads targeted toward children. Once Bob Dole misspoke that smoking might not be addictive, Clinton seized this issue, allowing him to stand as a defender of values and an opponent of powerful special interests. Gore was his principal attack dog. "Kick the habit, Senator Dole," Gore admonished, adding "It's not worth stinking up your reputation with the smoky stench of special interest politics and the dangerous din of dishonesty." In his convention acceptance speech, he brought to life the hazards of smoking by recounting the last days of his beloved sister Nancy, who died of lung cancer at 46 after starting smoking at 13. Gore was devoted to his sister, and Frank Hunger, her husband, remains his closest friend. He pledged to pour his "heart and soul into trying to protect young people from the dangers of smoking."

Gore's role in the fairly tame fall campaign was to paint the presidency of Bill Clinton as a "bridge to the future." He adopted a respectful tone toward GOP standard-bearer Bob Dole. He saluted Dole's heroics in World War II and his lifetime of service to America, but always in the past tense. His barbs at Dole and running mate Jack Kemp were tough but confined to differences that separated the two tickets on policy. In his debate with Kemp, he concentrated his critique on Dole's and Kemp's votes against popular Democratic programs. Curiously, Kemp did not fight back as hard as Dan Quayle had four years before. Gore was ready to meet each of his points. When Kemp likened Dole's tax cut plan to "Niagara Falls," saying that it would produce hundreds of thousands of jobs and spawn additional growth for our economy, Gore responded that "the problem with this . . . Niagara Falls is that Senator Dole and Mr. Kemp would put the American economy in a barrel and send it over the falls." While the two reaired their differences on the abortion question, Gore actually got the best of the values debate when, referring to the latest *cause celebre*, he declared that the baseball player Roberto Alomar should be "severely disciplined" for spitting in an umpire's face. Polls thereafter showed Gore striking the closest to a knockout blow of any of the four debaters. In doing so, he raised the comfort level of the public with an administration presiding over a sound economy. What more can a president ask?

Gore is a candidate for the presidency in 2000. He has allies strategically placed all over Washington and is making the rounds of Democratic constituencies across our country. Time will tell if his fund-raising efforts for Bill Clinton or his close association with a man whose impeachment paralyzed the nation for almost a year will prove a hindrance. Those who say that a president needs a touch of gray to be taken seriously may be encouraged by his new status as a grandfather and the recession of his hair line; he can no longer be mistaken for country singer George Strait's twin brother.

Chapter 15

Harlan Mathews

1993–1994

Finance Commissioner,
State Treasurer

Deputy Governor

(1927–)

Governor Frank Clement always said that he wanted all of his department heads to be smarter than he. My father was Governor Clement's personal physician and he would be the first to say that Ole Frank was no slouch. But I can say that in promoting Harlan Mathews from the Tennessee civil service first to his budget staff, and then to Commissioner of Finance and Administration, Frank Clement found a gem of a public servant.

Harlan Mathews came from humble rural stock. His father, John William Mathews, grew up on a farm near Wedowee, a hamlet in central Alabama just west of the Georgia border. It was always his father's dream to buy a farm of his own. In his twenties, he wandered over to Sumiton, a coal-mining town of 2,000 just west of Birmingham, where he went to work sawing timbers to shore up the tongues of local mines. Soon afterward, he met and married Lillia Mae, the owner's daughter. There in Sumiton, Harlan Mathews was born on January 17, 1927. He would never live on the farm his father dreamed of buying. Instead, John William Mathews ran a plant that rented machinery, such as cotton gins and gristmills, to local farmers. In this atmosphere, Harlan Mathews developed an acumen for numbers and business procedures, talents he would put to good use in over four decades of government service.

Like so many other American youths, Mathews enlisted in the navy right after graduating from high school in 1944. His stint came at the end of World War II, and he worked mainly as a communications officer on a baby aircraft carrier charged primarily with ferrying training crews between the West Coast and Hawaii. He left the service in 1946, returned to Alabama and entered Jacksonville State College. The first of his immediate family to enter college, he graduated in 1949 with a B.A. in business.

It was always Mathews's dream to become a lawyer. On a professor's recommendation he set out for Washington, D.C., to seek employment at the FBI and to gain admission to George Washington University Law School. Once he arrived in Washington, his plans changed when he met a Vanderbilt University professor who offered him an internship, paying $1,000 a year. Mathews took it without hesitation.

Except for two years in Memphis and his two years in the U.S. Senate, Nashville would be Mathews's home for the rest of his life. He married Patsy Jones, a bright Memphis native who in time became an able Deputy Commissioner of the Tennessee Department of Human Services in charge of rehabilitation services under Governor Ned Ray McWherter.

Professionally, Mathews started out on the staff of the state Planning Commission in 1950. A kindly, courteous man with a booming bass voice, a thick rural drawl, and the endearing habit of crediting those around him for all of his successes, his talents soon caught the notice of Governors Gordon Browning and Frank Clement. In 1954, Clement designated him his Deputy Commissioner of Finance and Administration. In 1961 Governor Buford Ellington named him Tennessee Finance Commissioner, a job he held for the nine remaining years of the alternating Ellington-Clement "leapfrog" governorship. While working as Finance Commissioner, Mathews fulfilled his dream of becoming a lawyer by attending the Nashville School of Law at night and earning his J.D. in 1962.

Mathews cherished his early years in state government. He especially appreciated the opportunity to work with Governor Frank Clement, whom he regarded as a man with a genuine vision for the betterment of the people of Tennessee.

Mathews worked closely with talented young associates such as Edward Boling and Joseph Johnson, both of whom were recruited by Robert Clement, the governor's father, and who both later served as president of the University of Tennessee. Mathews served on Clement's Commission on Human Relations with able young men such as Boling and Benjamin Hooks and helped produce a code of fair employment practices for state government. He worked at the state level with a bevy of Kennedy and Johnson administration officials on New Frontier and Great Society initiatives such as the Appalachian Regional Development program.

Mathews moved into the private sector upon Governor Ellington's retirement in 1971. That year, he became senior vice president for Institutional Finance and Development with AMCON, an international firm that specialized in building multifamily housing units. Mathews's absence from state government lasted only until 1973, the year longtime state Comptroller William Snodgrass appointed him his legislative assistant. A year later, the General Assembly elected Mathews state Treasurer, a position he held for the next thirteen years.

It is his years as state Treasurer that Mathews found most enjoyable and satisfying. During this time, he helped the state maintain a balanced budget and maximize the interest earnings on its idle cash. He improved the financial state of Tennessee's government, which he believes to be his greatest contribution to public service.

Over the years, Harlan Mathews remained an active and loyal Democrat and earned a reputation as a talented fund-raiser. In 1993, Governor Ned Ray McWherter said of Mathews, "He's got friends everywhere. You can walk through a plowed field, and they'll pop up."

In 1986, Mathews managed McWherters's gubernatorial campaign. Mathews raised $5 million and, to the surprise of many, McWherter defeated the respected former Governor Winfield Dunn by a healthy 8 percent margin. A few months later, Governor McWherter appointed Mathews his Cabinet Secretary, a position many said effectively made him the Deputy Governor. McWherter's successful reelection campaign, again run by Mathews, concluded with a surplus of money, and in 1992, Mathews was a key fund-raiser for the Clinton-Gore campaign in Tennessee.

Al Gore's election as vice president in 1992 left a vacancy in the Senate. The choice to fill the seat for the two-year period prior to a November 1994 special election belonged to Governor McWherter. There was no dearth of prominent Democrats from whom to select. Reports had it that his initial choice was fellow West Tennessean John Tanner. Congressman Tanner, however, after considering the effects that moving to higher office might have on his family and possibly believing himself too conservative to win the 1994 Democratic primary, took himself out of the running. McWherter opted against choosing a younger or more ambitious Democrat, such as Bob Clement, Jim Cooper, Jane Eskind, or Bart Gordon. He feared that the choice of any of them, each of whom was chomping at the bit for the appointment, might alienate the others, and give him or her an unfair leg up in the 1994 elections. McWherter further worried that a person with strong political aspirations might succumb to political pressures that could work to the disadvantage of the new Democratic administration. McWherter therefore chose a "caretaker," someone who would be free of any political motivation except to secure enactment of the Clinton-Gore program and who was experienced and knowledgeable enough about the issues to make a positive contribution to Senate debates with Tennessee's interest at heart.

Who better to fill the vacancy than Harlan Mathews, a man devoted to McWherter, his party, his state and his country? Mathews had hoped that President-elect Clinton might choose to use his talents as a director of TVA. Yet when McWherter invited him to take the Senate seat, Mathews accepted on the spot, believing it his duty to the governor and knowing that the selection of virtually anyone else might infuriate an influential bloc in the Democratic Party.

In response to Mathews's appointment, Howard Baker said, "I am certain that his service in the United States Senate will be carried out with the same dignity and grace which have marked his long tenure in Tennessee state government."

In his long role in state government, Mathews had participated in structuring Tennessee's transition from a primarily agricultural, to a manufacturing and then to a service economy. During his state years, the existence of a right-to-work law and the absence of a state Chamber of Commerce were elements which Mathews believed helped create a climate that kept Tennessee borders open to new business, nurtured the freedom of workers to compete for jobs, and kept Tennessee consistently ahead of its neighbors. Mathews brought to the Senate deep and valuable experience accumulated over forty years of working with seven governors in developing Tennessee's economic and financial environment, and his appreciation for fiscal responsibility and open economic competition are evident throughout his career.

McWherter described his deputy as a government penny-pincher who would support President-elect Bill Clinton and Vice President-elect Al Gore as they worked to reduce the federal budget deficit and develop a more efficient health care system. Mathews described himself as a fiscal conservative as he entered the Senate. He was determined to work to cut the deficit and end the ongoing recession. Mathews proved himself a thoughtful advocate of most Clinton programs, though he resisted Clinton's move to allow gays in the military. He opposed the nomination of lesbian activist Roberta Achtenberg to be deputy secretary of Housing and Urban Development and fought a ploy by liberal Senator Howard Metzenbaum to require that half of any air traffic controllers hired be selected from those whom President Reagan had fired for leaving work in violation of an existing contract.

In response to those who challenged Mathews's loyalty to President Clinton when he opposed the nomination of Tara O'Toole for Assistant Energy Secretary, Mathews said, "While I am prepared to listen and participate in the debate about this nomination, I will certainly find it difficult to cast my vote in favor of bringing people into the government if their views are inimical to the ideas to which we aspire as a nation."

As the authoritative *Congressional Quarterly* found, Mathews aligned with the Clinton administration on 90 percent of the recorded votes in 1993 and 1994. He voted with Clinton on the tax-hiking deficit reduction package, the motor voter initiative, the crime bill, the "Brady bill" to regulate access to guns, and the elevation of the Environmental Protection Agency to departmental level and Cabinet status. He voted against the Striker Replacement bill and a constitutional amendment proposed by Illinois Democrat Paul Simon to require a balanced budget even though he had cosponsored it, opting for a substitute by Nevada Democrat Harry Reid that exempted Social Security from the calculations.

While Mathews generally followed the Clinton line, his work indicates that his ultimate loyalties were to the people of Tennessee and to the Senate as an institution. He endeared himself to most colleagues by graciously presiding over the Senate more than any other member. This is a task many find tedious and bothersome. He participated frequently in debate, and though not a trained orator, his words carried the authority of common sense. In one-on-one meetings with colleagues, he was eminently persuasive.

Mathews's work on the Commerce Committee helped secure a nonstop air route from Nashville to London for American Airlines and the civilian use of the Millington Naval Air Base. Through his work on the Foreign Relations Committee, Mathews was particularly active in developing the Asia Pacific Economic Cooperation Organization, a partnership that he knew would benefit all Americans by lowering tariffs and expanding trade.

Senator Mathews was a strong advocate of international commerce and free trade. He called on the United States to renew China's "most favored nation" status. Acting as a "lone sheriff," he argued, would harm the United States more than it would address the human rights abuses so common in China. In debating the North American Free Trade Agreement (NAFTA), a controversial trade initiative at the time, he declared that "the borders dividing nations must never divide their people from opportunity." He likened opposition to the pact to burying "our heads in the drifting sand," further noting that "when an ostrich stuffs its head in the sand, its rump is standing in the air." Here was the kind of Tennessee country wisdom that had served us well from Cordell Hull through Al Gore, Jr., from Will Brock through Bill Brock. Mathews perpetuated this wisdom in his last Senate address on December 1, 1994. This time, the question was ratifying the Uruguay Accords of the General Agreement on Trade and Tariffs (GATT). Mathews again sided with what very many Tennesseans described as the future and very many economists knew would create 300,000 to 700,000 American jobs within the decade. Alluding to claims that Al Gore, Jr., had discredited in the memorable debate of 1993, he declared that the "giant sucking sound" that Ross Perot claimed would be heard if NAFTA passed "is nowhere to be found."

My own contacts with Senator Mathews have been limited, but each has been extraordinarily enlightening. Having worked with every Democratic governor since Gordon Browning, Mathews knew my father well, as Dad had been the physician to each of them. Through Dad and a mutual friend, Jack Dalton, Mathews learned in 1988 that I, though a physician whose life in medicine centered on caring for the health of people, had an interest in public policy. Mathews, Dalton, and I had lunch at Houston's restaurant in Nashville. There, Mathews spoke passionately about the importance of public service to one's state and country. I recall thinking that his life commitment to state government, not fully appreciated by me until we had a chance to have lunch together, exemplifies the lives of so many other thousands of state employees who dutifully and unselfishly serve our state. This admiration for public service, voiced by people such as Mathews, affected my ultimate commitment to a period of public service outside of medicine.

My contacts with Harlan Mathews thereafter were sporadic until my election in 1994. My campaign had been hard fought, and my victory had stung my predecessor and his staff. It meant very much to me to receive a wonderful note from Senator Mathews soon after my election. He wrote, "Congratulations! Jack Dalton would be as proud as your father. Bill, if I can assist in any way in your transition to Washington, please let me know."

What I will forever treasure is the innate decency and institutional loyalty of Harlan Mathews that led him to sit down with me several times and patiently explain what was important for a newcomer Senator from Tennessee to know at both the state and federal levels.

Harlan Mathews truly loved being a Senator. What he enjoyed most was "getting to know the Senate as an institution and its role in shaping the lives of American people." He appreciated his association with his colleagues and their staffs, a group he called the "workingest group of people on earth," and greatly admired their "hard work and dedication to the people they represent." Had he not committed to serving only two years and had Democrats not rallied behind Jim Cooper, Mathews might have been a formidable rival for Fred Thompson for the remaining two years of Al Gore's term.

Mathews did not fret about leaving Washington. He returned to Nashville as a partner in the law firm headed by longtime Democratic activist Bill Farris. The firm concentrates on lobbying for some health care providers and State Industries, a major producer of water heaters. I see Senator Mathews every now and then. His word is as good as gold and his ethics a model of integrity, something I can't say about every lobbyist whom I encounter. He remains and will always be a personal inspiration to me.

As we move into the twenty-first century, I'm confident that we'll see a more diverse group of Senators than we have in the body today. There certainly will be more women than the current nine we have today. There will be Asian Americans representing states other than Hawaii. Although Senator Carol Moseley-Braun was not reelected in 1998, there will be more African Americans elected in the not too distant future. Ben Nighthorse Campbell may not be the only Native American, and there will certainly be Hispanic Americans. I hope the more diverse Senate will include more nonlawyers and nonbusiness people. I'd certainly like to see more of my brother and sister scientists seated alongside me in this body. It would be nice to see more people who have risen from the lower rungs of the civil service to the top of their fields. Can such people make a successful transition from the executive to the legislative branch? I present Senator Harlan Mathews as Exhibit A for the affirmative.

Chapter 16

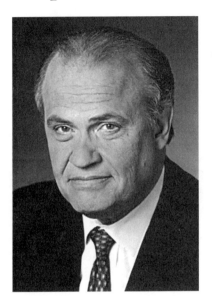

Fred Dalton Thompson

1994–

Watergate Committee Minority Counsel

Defense Attorney for Marie Ragghianti

(1942–)

Fred Thompson is my partner for Tennessee. We decided to run for the Senate at exactly the same time, we campaigned together across the state for almost a year, we were indoctrinated into the ways of the Senate together, and we have lunch together almost daily and discuss issues as we serve the people of Tennessee.

Although Fred is often tagged as an actor-turned-politician, what many forget is that his first Hollywood role was as himself in a film chronicling the case that led to the exposure of the most egregious group of scandals in Tennessee over the past three-quarters of a century. To some extent, his background resembles that of Ronald Reagan, whom some remember as a movie star who never got the girl while they forget that he served a momentous twelve-year stint as president of the Screen Actors Guild. Thompson has a shrewd lawyer's sense for the bottom line and, like Reagan, a special gift for framing questions in terms the common man can understand even though he has worked and played with the elite in Nashville, Washington, and Hollywood. Another similarity Thompson shares with Reagan is his very real empathy with people like those he grew up with in Lawrenceburg.

Fred Dalton Thompson was born in Sheffield, Alabama, on August 19, 1942, the elder of Fletch and Ruth Thompson's two sons. A few months later, the Thompsons moved just north of the border to Lawrenceburg, Tennessee, where Fletch opened a used-car dealership. Fletch Thompson was a warm-hearted, jocular salesman who tried without success to win the Democratic nominations for Lawrence County sheriff and finance commissioner. Ruth was and is a genuinely sweet woman. The Thompsons were devout members of the local Church of Christ and Freddie, as he was known as a child, and brother Kenny, eight years his junior, participated in many of its activities. Like other small-town kids, the Thompson boys learned how to shoot both guns and basketballs. Fred developed into quite an athlete, lettering in basketball and football in high school. With his study habits somewhat underdeveloped at this stage, the information he found most important was what he picked up while hanging out at his grandfather's café, located on the town square. There Thompson not only caught the juiciest of gossip, but he could also follow the goings-on at the Lawrence County Courthouse across the street.

Most important to Fred Thompson, six-foot five-inches tall by the time he reached sixteen, was Sarah Lindsey. A man whose grades were not the best and who jokes that he will always be able to use the slogan "not just another pretty face" was smitten with an attractive honor student a year older and more than a foot shorter than he. His attention was reciprocated. By his junior year, he was spending so much time with her that he nearly missed an important basketball game. Sarah's grandfather saw something in Fred, too. It was he who got Thompson interested in the law, then hooked him on it when he lent Thompson his copy of Clarence Darrow's autobiography. From that time on, there was no question as to what Fred wanted to do with his life.

Sarah and Fred Thompson were married at the start of his senior year in high school. They lived with his parents until son Tony was born, then moved in with hers. That September, they enrolled at Florence State College in Alabama and moved into a government-run housing project. Thompson went out for basketball and made the team as a walk-on. He soon left the team, because his real aim had simply been to prove that his high school coach was wrong when he said Fred was not good enough to play at the college level. It would have been tough if he had continued as a student-athlete anyway. Even with loans, the Thompsons had trouble making ends meet, especially after daughter Betsy was born. One semester Thompson had to drop out and work days at the Lindsey church pew plant, nights at the Murray Ohio bicycle factory, Saturday mornings at the post office, and weekend evenings at the drive-in theater.

Only after he became a father did Thompson concentrate on his studies. At Florence State and then Memphis State, where he and Sarah transferred after two years, he majored in political science and philosophy. The academic debate that engaged him then, as now, was the one waged in the eighteenth century between Edmund Burke and Jean-Jacques Rousseau over the moral nature of man. In classes, he almost always opted for Burke's more conservative line. "People are prone to error," Thompson explained. "More often than not, it's a helluva lot harder to do the right thing than the wrong thing." It was easy for Thompson to equate Burkean philosophy with Barry Goldwater's message of individual responsibility and he soon abandoned his ancestral Democratic roots. Making it through college was not so easy, however. The Thompsons had to juggle their schedules so that one could take care of their babies while the other was in class, but a then-focused Thompson did well enough to win a scholarship to Vanderbilt Law School.

Not long after Thompson enrolled at Vanderbilt, his third child, Daniel, was born. He was fortunate to find a night job as a motel desk clerk, which allowed him time to study when business was off, and he excelled academically. He made Vanderbilt's national moot court team, a forum that allowed him to develop ways of using his slow baritone in cadences that would allow juries to see the point he was trying to make and in words they could understand. In later years, he would try his best to be as "scrupulously fair to witnesses" as he knew how. "If the average citizen thinks you're being unfair," he told Tennessee trial lawyers in 1973, "you've completely lost your effectiveness."

Upon graduating, Thompson returned to Lawrenceburg to become a partner in Sarah's uncle's law firm. In his spare time, he coached a youth baseball team. He founded the first Young Republican club in Lawrence County and won a seat on the Lawrence County Republican Executive Committee. This gave him a chance to become acquainted with Howard Baker, Bill Brock, and other state Republican leaders, and he soon earned their confidence. At a time when a Republican label was still seen as a ticket to obscurity in Middle Tennessee, Thompson fell into some luck. Richard Nixon's election gave Tennessee Republicans some patronage and Thompson was appointed as an assistant U.S. attorney, a plum position for a man of twenty-six. Thompson today likes to joke that he may have benefited from a dearth of Republican lawyers in Middle Tennessee at the time. Yet he established a solid record, generally handling cases involving bootleggers, bank robbers, and crooked sheriffs. During his three-year stint, juries convicted fourteen of the fifteen defendants he prosecuted.

Thompson returned to private practice in Nashville on the very day that five would-be burglars were arrested in the Democratic National Committee headquarters in the Watergate Hotel. He served during the fall of 1972 as the Middle Tennessee director of Howard Baker's reelection Senate campaign. Thompson jokes that his duties amounted to little more than driving Senator Baker. Ordinarily, Baker's response to this kind of modesty is to place his hand on his wallet. But Baker knew Thompson, and he knew that Fred had been instrumental in helping him carry Middle Tennessee and accomplish an overwhelming triumph statewide, a feat that no Tennessee Republican Senator had accomplished since Reconstruction. When Senator Baker was appointed vice chairman of the Senate Watergate Committee, he sought a counsel whom he knew well enough to trust implicitly. When Lamar Alexander declined the offer, thinking he would feel uncomfortable investigating people with whom he had worked in the White House, Senator Baker turned to Thompson.

Thompson arrived in Washington in February 1973 expecting, as is often the case with young people coming to Washington, to stay just a few months. Just as Baker originally thought that the investigation was the Democrats' "best effort to put a different face on a bad defeat," Thompson thought the burglary was the work of a few "crackpots." All he knew about Watergate at the time was what he had taken in the night before he left at the Vanderbilt Library. All the evidence the committee had in its possession was a file of newspaper clippings that Baker's staff had collected. Thompson sifted through them, then set out to assemble a staff. He turned away applicants who would not be able to shun the spotlight or work long hours. At each interview, he reiterated Senator Baker's admonition to "let the chips fall where they may," but told applicants that he never wanted to have to "worry about who is 'us' and who is 'them'" if it came down to that. His choices included a talented but then obscure group of attorneys who, like him, became accustomed to eating their first meal of the day after dark. His deputy was Donald Sanders, a quiet but tough former FBI agent who made the single most important discovery of the hearings. Just beneath him were Howard Liebengood, a brilliant law school classmate of Thompson's who later became the Senate sergeant at arms, and Mike Madigan, whom Thompson tapped in 1997 to serve as chief counsel to the Special Investigation of the Senate Governmental Affairs Committee. Although provided with only one-half of the funding accorded to the Democratic majority, the minority staff made important, material contributions throughout the investigation.

Once the hearings opened, Thompson's turn in the questioning generally followed that of Majority Counsel Sam Dash. He did his best to avoid being repetitive and tried to open new lines of inquiry. Viewers became familiar with his soft but forceful voice, his sideburns, and his habit of smoking his pipe while listening to testimony. Once when he took Sarah out to a restaurant when she visited Washington, they received applause upon entering. It must have been heady stuff for a thirty-year-old from Lawrenceburg, but Thompson kept his perspective. His down-to-earth nature and generous sense of humor served him well when he was mistaken by an autograph seeker for fellow six-foot-sixer Senator Lowell Weicker, a Connecticut Republican committee member frequently at odds with the Nixon administration.

Ordinarily, Thompson's day had just begun when the hearings recessed for the afternoon. He would then do what he could to find the sources of frequent leaks, meet with aides who had spent their day interviewing prospective witnesses, perhaps negotiate with White House lawyers, and prepare a packet for Senator Baker for the next day's hearings. Having so little time, it scarcely bothered him that his quarters were a small, one-room apartment with a five-foot bed. What did bother him was his time away from his family. His initial plan to be a "weekend daddy" over a four-month period fell by the wayside as continuing revelations extended the committee's life by more than a year. Although Sarah and the kids did visit him in Washington, Thompson found himself fortunate if he could fly home to Nashville twice a month. Placing things in perspective was his call to give Sarah the news of the critical testimony of Alexander Butterfield about the existence of a White House taping system. "Never mind that," she said. "I've just run over one of the kids' bicycles in the driveway."

The indelible moment that defined Thompson during the hearings came on July 16, 1973. Like John Dean, Richard Nixon's former counsel and subsequent principal accuser, many on the committee suspected that White House conversations had been recorded. That a recording system existed became known to the committee the day deputy Republican counsel Donald Sanders got former White House aide Alexander Butterfield to acknowledge that it had secretly been in place for two years. Three days later Butterfield testified. Howard Baker had one request of Chief Counsel Sam Dash: because it had been a Republican staffer who elicited the information, he asked that the Republican counsel be the one to bring it to public light. Dash found the request reasonable and turned the floor over to Thompson.

"Mr. Butterfield," he opened, "are you aware of the installation of any listening devices in the Oval Office of the president?" He was, he said, and there were other bugs in the Cabinet Room and Nixon's office in the Executive Office Building, as well as on the phones in the Executive Office Building and the Aspen Cabin at Camp David. Thus an answer could be found to Baker's oft-repeated query, "What did the president know and when did he know it?" In Thompson's view, the tapes would either demonstrate Nixon's innocence or lead to his impeachment. At first, Thompson felt certain that Nixon was far too shrewd ever to say anything on tape that would incriminate him. If his hunch were correct, the way for Nixon to clear himself and regain public trust would be to make the full and complete disclosure Senator Baker had been recommending, publicly and privately, since February. This now meant releasing the tapes. Thompson joined his Democratic counterparts in doing everything possible to convince White House lawyers to persuade Nixon to release the tapes.

As counsel for the Republican members, Thompson never lost sight of the fact that the thousands of Republican candidates who had no involvement with Watergate would be among the principal victims of its fallout. He continued to question witnesses aggressively but fairly; he worried, however, that the hearings were losing any sense of decorum. A case in point came during the questioning of former top White House aide John Ehrlichman. Thompson used his time to probe contradictions between Nixon's public confession that he had instructed White House Chief of Staff H. R. Haldeman and Ehrlichman to keep prosecutors from looking into tangential operations and Ehrlichman's denial that Nixon had so ordered him. Ehrlichman's exchanges with Chairman Sam Ervin were far more rancorous and the audience began to cheer Ervin and boo his nemesis. Ervin and Howard Baker both asked the crowd to remain quiet, but Thompson was certain enough of more outbursts that he used his closing time with Ehrlichman to admonish the audience indirectly. "It's not that you, Mr. Ehrlichman, are to be treated any better than any other witness," he said, "but you shouldn't be treated any worse."

Thompson was even more alarmed when he saw reports attributed to committee sources describing Nixon speech-writer Pat Buchanan as an "architect of the 1972 dirty tricks strategy." Instinctively, he knew that the majority staff had leaked some of Buchanan's memos to the press. Only the night before Buchanan was scheduled to testify did Thompson see the memos and all he saw was standard political advice. Knowing that whoever leaked the memos had blown Buchanan's role out of proportion, Thompson suspected that Democrats might not have allowed Buchanan to review all of his writings. Thompson traced Buchanan through the White House switchboard and discovered that the majority staff had indeed withheld most of the documents from Buchanan. After the two rehashed what was in a thick pile, Buchanan was primed the next day to lash into the majority for "an apparent campaign . . . to malign" him and for not providing him with copies of his writings as they had promised. When Sam Dash replied that such a course might produce rehearsed testimony, Thompson heatedly responded that the staff was denying Buchanan even those rights accorded a criminal defendant. Sam Ervin sided with Thompson. Buchanan's response to Dash's query about the extent of his loyalty to Nixon took the wind out of many Democratic sails. "What tactics would I be willing to use?" he asked rhetorically. "Anything that is not immoral, unethical, illegal, or unprecedented in previous Democratic campaigns."

Once network coverage of the hearings concluded after Buchanan's testimony, Thompson worked hard behind the scenes to tie up loose ends. He and his staff secured nearly forty affidavits showing that demonstrators had vandalized, taken over, and, in one instance, even fired shots into various headquarters of the Nixon campaign. He headed a task force that probed the involvement of CIA agents in Watergate, one that Baker concluded was necessary after learning not only that considerable evidence had been destroyed but also finding that several CIA employees had been less than forthcoming in response to routine inquiries. The task force members produced a report that they were quick to concede raised more questions than it answered. Only after Nixon resigned did journalists follow up on those leads, thus prompting further investigations of agency misdeeds and calls for strict and permanent congressional oversight.

Thompson was the principal negotiator for the Republicans in compiling the committee's final report. Like Baker and Ervin, he believed that the report should refrain from making conclusions about the guilt or innocence of anyone. He fought strenuously to see that the committee's mandate was followed and often found himself frustrated. "We've come too far to let this happen," Senator Baker told him. The final report contained no startling revelations, but Thompson took particular pride in making certain that it did not contain a false claim by a majority aide that he had discovered the tapes.

Once the investigation ended, Thompson opened a law office in Nashville with Watergate Committee associate Howard Liebengood. He spurned entreaties to accept a post on the Federal Elections Commission and even rejected Howard Baker's appeals to seek the Fifth District seat in the House of Representatives. Although Baker thinks Thompson could have won even at a time when public memory of Watergate was still high, Thompson knew that a race in heavily Democratic Nashville would have been an uphill fight under any circumstance. At the time, Thompson was not terribly well-off financially and he believed his responsibility to his family was to resume what was just beginning to become a reasonably lucrative career in private practice. He did publish his candid, but light-hearted memoirs of the investigation, *At That Point in Time,* in which he attributed the sins of Watergate to the "corrupting nature of power."

Tennessee had a constitutional crisis of its own in the 1970s. Although the State Transportation Commissioner had been indicted for selling surplus state cars for personal profit and a U.S. attorney was investigating the alleged sale of pardons, Thompson guessed that these scandals would not touch Governor Ray Blanton. Out of curiosity, he met with Marie Ragghianti, the embattled chairman of the Board of Pardons and Paroles, who was known to believe that the Blanton administration had become overly generous in extending clemency to violent criminals. At first, Thompson assumed her troubles were strictly political and advised her to make peace with Blanton. He reconsidered after a talk with acting Nashville FBI office head Hank Hillin, who had been looking into reports that pardons were being sold in the governor's office. When, as the journalist Peter Maas infers, the Blanton administration set Ragghianti up on spurious charges of drunk and reckless driving, Thompson got her cleared. Blanton, however, had much more in mind. Although he had announced that he would not fire any aide under indictment, he ordered Corrections Commissioner C. Murray Henderson to demand that Ragghianti resign as chairman. In return, Henderson said, she could have any job in state government outside the paroles and pardons board at the same salary. Ragghianti refused. Blanton fired her and accused her of a variety of transgressions while in office. The contents of the letter of dismissal were out before Ragghianti had even read her own copy of it in Thompson's office. She was livid as she scanned allegations that made her out to be an embezzler.

"What did you want to do?" Thompson asked. Ragghianti wanted her job back. Thompson understood, but pointed out that the governor had a right to staff his administration. Her chances were slim, he told her bluntly, and she should think it over. Ragghianti returned to the Capitol and secured all of her papers. The next morning, she and Thompson met the press and declared most of the allegations against her to be false or exaggerated. She had not "played the game," she said, and she was not done fighting.

Thompson examined the documents at length and found that they supported Ragghianti's view. For her to prevail, he had to put Blanton on trial. The letter of dismissal gave him an opening because it facilitated a trial by jury rather than by a judge perhaps beholden to Blanton or other powerful Democrats. Instead of focusing on whether Blanton had the right to fire Ragghianti, he could establish her fitness to remain in office and call into question Blanton's charges against her.

Thompson used his opening statement to tell the jury that the governor needed "good cause" to fire appointees to certain offices, and "good cause" had to involve some form of malfeasance in office. Had Marie Ragghianti abused her office? Hardly. While Governor Blanton purported to fire her because she had misused her office, his rationale was contained in a letter that Thompson characterized as equating "her conduct with that of the criminal element she was supposed to be supervising." Blanton's motives had been strictly political, he averred, and not at all related to the reasons he cited in the letter.

Thompson strove to establish Ragghianti's reputation as an honest and committed public servant. He opened by calling district attorneys and judges who had worked with Ragghianti, all of whom described her as the only pardons and paroles board member who had ever solicited their opinions. He further established that she had been chairman of the Southern Paroling Authority, a position that had enabled her to observe and study the programs of other states. He then called Ragghianti and led her through a recounting of her increasing concerns about well-founded reports of clemency bribe offers and pressures from high within the administration to ignore those reports. At one point, she disclosed that Sherry Lomax, a secretary whom Blanton had assigned to her, had rewritten a clemency order and forged Ragghianti's signature. She had fired Lomax, then found herself called to

Blanton's office and told that she had been put on "probation" herself. Even more astonishing to Ragghianti, her colleagues on the board voted against national accreditation for Tennessee's board. After establishing that Ragghianti had been offered another job in government if she would resign, Thompson closed by getting her to refute Blanton's charges that she had missed several board meetings and bilked the taxpayers for $7,500. In the process, he got Ragghianti to concede that she had overlooked errors in travel vouchers prepared for her by Ms. Lomax.

The state's witnesses were Blanton loyalists, who reported complaints about Ragghianti but often seemed forgetful or evasive on other matters. Who had been critical of Ragghianti? Thompson asked. The two generally cited were Lomax and Kevin McCormack, a friend of Ragghianti's who had written a letter complaining about her after he was pressured from above. When Murray Henderson cited McCormack, Thompson saw a Mack truck-sized opening. Noting that Henderson had not mentioned him once in his pretrial deposition, he asked if McCormack was "the young man who was found murdered a couple of weeks ago." The state objected that the police had not yet ruled McCormack's death a murder. So Thompson asked Henderson if he was "aware Mr. McCormack was found with his own belt wrapped around his neck, found dead." Henderson admitted being aware of the fact and Thompson followed by prompting Henderson also to admit that Blanton's letter of dismissal had been composed in the office of a Nashville Democratic activist and that he had offered Ragghianti another job at the same pay, thereby demonstrating that Blanton could not have been too concerned that Ragghianti was guilty of malfeasance. The last Blanton witness was Charles Traughber, Ragghianti's successor, whose term had just expired. Traughber seemed forgetful under cross-examination until Thompson brought out that he could be reappointed or left hanging, just like Ragghianti.

Thompson's closing arguments were short and poignant. "Do you think that she lost her job for the reasons they gave," he asked the jury, "or do you think it was because she just didn't play ball?" He suggested that the "governor and his boys thought if they hit her hard enough, she'd collapse like a house of cards." "But a remarkable thing happened," he exclaimed; "she didn't collapse. She fought back. Not for a job, but because she had to. . . . I hope I never see the day when I stop believing that people still do that." He impressed on the jury members the importance of their decision, for the precedent they would be creating might tell other people that "if they have to take a stand, they don't have to stand alone."

Thompson grew a bit wary when the judge charged the jury with determining the answers to seven questions, not just that of "good cause." Ragghianti gained some hope when the court stenographer told her that she was "praying for you to win." Although the jury returned within the hour,

Thompson was not certain he had won until the foreman answered "yes" to the judge's last question, whether Ragghianti had been fired "arbitrarily and capriciously."

Thompson was not finished with the Blanton gang. In December 1978, three of Blanton's top aides were arrested for accepting bribes to influence commutations. On January 16, 1979, four days before he was scheduled to leave office, Blanton pardoned fifty-two inmates, among them twenty-four convicted murderers. With reports that Blanton was preparing further clemencies, Democratic state officials asked Governor-elect Lamar Alexander to take the oath of office early to prevent them. That night, Thompson was called home from Washington to act as temporary counsel for the new administration. There was much work to do. When Finance Commissioner Lewis Donelson entered the Capitol, he found Robert Lillard, Blanton's counsel, drafting more commutations. Donelson immediately barred Blanton and Lillard from the Capitol. It became Thompson's job over the next three months to sort out the papers and act as Alexander's liaison with federal and state prosecutors.

Thompson continued to handle sensitive assignments for Howard Baker from time to time. When a few Democrats foolishly tried to disqualify Baker as a candidate for reelection in 1978 by declaring his signature on his qualifying petition to be a forgery, Baker's people called Thompson, who practically sprinted the few blocks over to the state election commission office. Thompson got an explanation, then called Baker from a pay phone. They discussed all options, but Baker instructed Thompson to "keep [his] eye on the ball and . . . get it straightened out . . . and the easiest way the better." Thompson strode back to the election commission and found the principal perpetrator. "If it were me," he said, peering down from his six-five frame, "I would play this for all it was worth and sue you guys and . . . get you thrown out of office. Fortunately for you, it's him and he's going to let you get out of this . . . gracefully if you're smart enough to do it." Whether it was Thompson's common sense that led Democrats to consider reason or his size that just plain scared them, they opted to certify Baker if he would affirm that the signature on his petition was indeed his.

Even more appropriate was Senator Baker's designation of Thompson as counsel to the Foreign Relations Committee while Alexander Haig's nomination to be Secretary of State was being considered. This one-time Watergate Committee counsel's faith in Haig's innocence in the crimes of Watergate neutralized a plan by some Senate Democrats to reopen the wounds from that nearly decade-old scandal. A few months later, Baker enlisted Thompson as special counsel to the Senate Intelligence Committee to quell a dispute between Chairman Barry Goldwater and CIA Director William Casey. Goldwater and two colleagues had called for Casey's resignation once they learned that Max Hugel, a Casey aide with no experience in intelligence, had embarked on a harebrained scheme to overthrow the government of Libya. Thompson allowed time for tensions to calm, then worked out a solution whereby Casey would apologize for appointing Hugel and the Intelligence panel would approve a Goldwater motion declaring Casey "not unfit."

As time passed, Thompson worked more and more away from Tennessee. It had to have put a strain on his marriage; he and Sarah separated in 1979 and divorced six years later. They remain friends, however. Thompson declined Howard Baker's request in 1983 to run to succeed him. Instead, he began to accumulate corporate accounts as a lawyer and a lobbyist. By the end of the 1980s, he had taken on the legal business of the Teamsters Union pension fund, Westinghouse, General Electric, and the Toyota Motor Corporation, to name a few.

Thompson also picked up an interesting new hobby. In 1984, film mogul Dino De Laurentiis came to him to discuss a movie he would be making about the Marie Ragghianti case and suggested that he might want to use some of the participants in the cast. While Thompson jokes today that some of the producers wanted him to play the disgraced Governor Blanton, they eventually decided to cast him as himself. Thompson had many ideas about the best way to shoot several of the scenes. Director Roger Donaldson allowed him to revise some of his dialogue, but he drew the line elsewhere. "You know, Fred," he quipped, "it must be tough acting and directing your first film at the same time." Thompson pulled back and won favorable reviews for his role supporting Sissy Spacek as the heroine in *Marie*. What viewers of this movie saw was the Fred Thompson I know: a shrewd, wisecracking lawyer with a commanding presence and a keen sense of how to convince juries that his client's interest served the cause of justice.

Thompson's performance won him scores of calls from Hollywood over the next decade. He did not abandon the law; in fact, he accepted only those parts that he thought he might enjoy and only those he could work into his legal schedule. He has now appeared in eighteen films, six made-for-TV movies, and four TV series, with no formal acting training at all. Thompson liked to kid that he was waiting for "whatever role John Wayne would have played next." Directors, said Roger Donaldson, typecast him in small but visible roles that Lee J. Cobb might have been offered a generation earlier. Some of his characters were good guys, such as the CIA director in *No Way Out*, the lawyers in *Cape Fear* and *Curly Sue,* and the FBI agent in *Feds.* Others were heavies, such as the factory manager who fired *Roseanne*, the hypocritical White House chief of staff in *In the Line of Fire*, and the NASCAR official in *Days of Thunder.* Almost all were authority figures. Although there were years when his Hollywood earnings exceeded those from his law practice, Thompson rarely had more than a few days to stay on sets and gallivant with other actors. Often, he ran up huge phone bills from Hollywood hotels keeping abreast of developments in his true vocation. It is understandable when he says that his favorite big-name star with whom he worked was John Goodman, for both embody the same good-old-boy appeal.

Howard Baker and Lamar Alexander always believed that Thompson's persona would translate into success at the polls. With Al Gore's rise to the vice presidency, they sought to recruit Thompson to run for Gore's seat in the special election in 1994. It was understood that Harlan Mathews, who was appointed to fill the office until an election would be held, would not run for reelection, and that the seat would be open and by definition, winnable. The conditions that led Thompson to decline such offers in the past were no longer controlling. He was financially secure. No longer just a father, he was a grandfather five times over, and one disturbed about the direction our country was heading. He decided to give it a shot.

I had not met Fred Thompson until the fall of 1993, when we quietly met on two separate occasions at the University Club on Vanderbilt's campus to discuss our futures in politics. The location was convenient for both of us, but proximity to the operating room and intensive care units—important for me at the time—ultimately dictated the spot. During our first meeting, we talked about the pros and cons of running for the U.S. Senate, each taking a turn explaining why we might run and discussing which seat would be more appropriate. I had not yet made a final decision to run, so it was useful for me to talk to someone who had thought long and hard about the process and about what could be accomplished in public service. Thompson recognized the advantages of running for the open seat, whereas I saw advantages in being the challenger in a race that would focus on the clear choice between an unconventional, fresh candidate—the physician with no political experience—and an eighteen-year entrenched incumbent.

Our next meeting several weeks later, again private and at the University Club, focused on how to build a campaign organization. I had still not publicly committed to run, though I was further along than Thompson realized at the time. Thompson told me that he would want me to be his campaign chairman if I ultimately decided not to run. His confidence in me at that early stage led me to believe correctly that we would be close and strong friends over time. The confidence we have in each other, which can be traced back to that early meeting, has continued to grow.

In the early days of the campaign, Thompson journeyed to Republican gatherings across Tennessee and echoed Howard Baker's longstanding calls for a citizen-legislature. Although Thompson and I were campaigning at the same time on almost exactly the same issues, we were careful not to appear to be campaigning hand-in-hand across the state. We were defining our own separate identities and styles. With Don Sundquist's campaign for governor, the three Republicans campaigning for statewide office had loud and consistent voices in all three of Tennessee's Grand Divisions. We all crossed paths regularly at the Republican Lincoln Day dinners, which during the campaign cycle extend throughout the winter. There were five others running in my primary, and the six of us would line up at the podium at these dinners like a train of freight cars, each limited to two minutes because there were so many of us. Then Thompson, who had no serious primary opponent, would stand up and deliver a thoughtful, powerful address that would speak directly to and capture the crowd. I remember thinking then, someday this fellow could be president. I watched him very closely. I knew I could learn from him.

Thompson had no difficulty raising money. He was able to saturate the airwaves with a biographical spot extolling his work as a prosecutor and his investigations of the Watergate and Blanton scandals. Even though he won his primary by a nearly two-to-one margin over unknown conservative John Baker, he clearly was not having fun and those around him began to sense it. He felt cooped up traveling around the state in a customized van loaded with fax machines, cellular phones, and even a television he saw no use for. Thompson recalled the television ads that he had done for Chevrolet trucks and he knew the response they had generated for both Chevrolet and more importantly for him. "What I'd really like to do," he told street-smart, trusted advisor Tom Ingram, "is just get in a truck and get in my work clothes and hit the road." "Why don't you?" came the response. Thus was born the only campaign motif in modern Tennessee history as familiar as Lamar Alexander's flannel shirts or Estes Kefauver's coonskin cap.

Within days, Thompson hit the road in a rented red Chevrolet pickup, always wearing blue jeans and cowboy boots, leaving home the tie. This tactic crystallized his image as a down-home outsider in an anti-Washington year and provided a sharp contrast to opponent Jim Cooper, a well respected, mild-mannered, conservative six-term Democrat Congressman from Shelbyville. Although Cooper's campaign tried to portray Thompson as a "Gucci-wearing, Lincoln-driving, Perrier-drinking, Grey Poupon-spreading millionaire Washington special interest lobbyist," Cooper was the one who always seemed to dress in white shirts and traditional ties. Cooper tried to make a virtue out of his refusal to accept contributions from political action committees. Yet when he went negative on Thompson, he exposed himself to the charge that much of his financing had come from the health insurance industry. To Thompson, this was the "old congressional two-step."

Cooper, in fact, had authored a popular, industry-supported bill mandating managed competition in health care. From a conservative's perspective, the Cooper bill was an innovative, market-based approach and far better than the Washington-based, one-size-fits-all approach proposed by President Clinton and the First Lady. Had the President been wise enough to embrace

Cooper's plan, I believe there would have been a major health care bill passed in 1994. Unfortunately for Cooper, key Democratic constituencies made such a course politically untenable for Clinton in 1994, and they, like the more liberal Democrats in Tennessee, proved less than enthusiastic about Cooper's candidacy. Many who found merit in the Cooper-managed competition plan saw its failure as a symbol of a failed presidency and party, an image reinforced by one of Thompson's ads showing Cooper jogging with Clinton with the voice-over, "He's running with the wrong crowd." So Cooper earned the enmity of two camps in Tennessee—the pro-Clinton crowd who resented Cooper's popular challenge to the Clinton health care plan and the anti-Clinton crowd who saw Clinton and Cooper as too friendly.

When Thompson and Cooper met during the campaign, the contrast was even more pronounced. Thompson's size commanded attention and his earthy speaking style, fortified by years of practice in courtrooms and movie sets, proved tailor-made to convince Tennesseans that their concerns were his. Although Cooper derided Thompson's pickup as the "rented stage prop" of a "Hollywood actor," Tennesseans found it easier to identify with a one-time worker in a bicycle factory than a Harvard- and Oxford-trained attorney and politician. It helped that the issues of 1994 were Republican issues and that Thompson framed them beautifully as those of "common sense" that was "not common in Washington right now." "You can't spend more than you got coming in," he declared. "We can't tax ourselves into prosperity. . . . You can't pay people more not to work than to work. And criminals can't hurt anybody if they're behind bars." Thompson not only caught up with Cooper in the polls by early October, but trounced him by twenty-two points.

Elected to fill the remainder of an unexpired term, Thompson took his oath of office in December and got a leg up on the rest of the class of 1994 in seniority—seniority that catapulted him two years later into the chairmanship of the Governmental Affairs Committee. Less than a week after he was sworn in, Majority Leader Bob Dole astutely tapped him to give the Republican response to President Clinton's first major post-election address. "We welcome the President to help us lead America in a new direction," Thompson declared. "But if he will not, we will welcome the President to follow, because we're moving ahead." His presence, his experience on the screen, and his effectiveness as a communicator were made apparent to the whole country that night. Favorable comparisons to Ronald Reagan were made and whispers of a presidential campaign began.

Once the new Congress convened, Thompson was quick to cosponsor a constitutional amendment mandating term limits for members of Congress. Our freshman class called for a balanced budget amendment, and we successfully pushed through the Senate measures limiting unfunded mandates and requiring members of Congress to live by the same rules we impose on everyone else. Within the Republican caucus, Thompson served on a task force that successfully recommended limiting the tenure of all committee chairs to six years.

As much as any other Republican freshman, Thompson positioned himself on the side of those measures designed to shake up Washington. "The people must be able to trust their messenger," he said often. He scorned legislation that would allow a more assertive federal presence in the marketplace, but he saw no justification for subsidizing individual businesses with tax benefits or spending programs that might give them an advantage over their competitors. In 1995, he joined in sponsoring a measure that would outlaw the "corporate welfare" provided by those subsidies.

Thompson also had a few ideas about how we might restore confidence in our electoral process. One of the few reforms from Watergate that he thought had served the public well was the law that created a fund to finance the presidential campaigns through a voluntary checkoff box on each income tax return. When the initial 1996 budget bill eliminated that option, Thompson took the floor and got it reinstated. His sense was that the fund alone preserved a semblance of public faith that the outcomes of presidential campaigns were not solely determined by wealthy special interests.

Like most of the rest of us in Congress, Thompson thinks our time would be better spent if we could devote more of it to ordinary constituents and less of it to raising money. Accordingly, he joined Republican Senator John McCain from Arizona and Democrat Senator Russ Feingold from Wisconsin in sponsoring a campaign reform bill that would outlaw "soft" money, limit political action committee contributions to candidates and parties, curb the practice of bundling as well as the percentage of out-of-state money a candidate could use, and grant free television time to those federal candidates who agreed to limit their expenditures. The bill was an idealistic effort that neither party truly embraced. Both parties rely to some degree on funding from various so-called special interests to get their messages out. The Democrats rely heavily on union contributions collected from members' dues, and Republicans rely on business groups and financially strong conservative groups. The McCain-Feingold bill fizzled. Senator Mitch McConnell from Kentucky, an outspoken defender of free speech, including campaign spending on free speech, successfully led the opposition to see that McCain-Feingold never saw the light of day on the Senate floor. Still, the bill was the starting point for more incremental reforms that we will likely see in the future.

Thompson's independence and his willingness to buck the leadership in the Senate sometimes gives him the aura of a moderate, but in truth his voting record is quite conservative. On the issues raised in the House Republicans' Contract With America, he broke ranks just once, on the issue of product liability. He sympathizes with those who point out that the litigation explosion of recent years has forced doctors to pass on growing insurance costs to their patients. However, as a lawyer, he is familiar with the occasional meritorious malpractice case and thinks any reforms are properly handled at the state level. Thompson is resolute in his desire to preserve the prerogatives of state and local governments, which led him to oppose a measure to make it a federal crime to bring guns to school. For him, the issue wasn't a question of crime, but whether the federal or state governments were best equipped to handle such cases. He came down on the side of the states.

Thompson and I differed on President Clinton's nomination of fellow Tennessean Henry Foster to be Surgeon General. Thompson like me knew Hank Foster to be a responsible doctor and he expressed distaste for the irrelevance of some of the attacks on Foster and the ardor with which they were made. For him, the question was not whether Foster was a good and decent man or whether he was qualified to serve in a high administration post. Both answers he knew to be yes. In the wake of the disastrous tenure of former Surgeon General Joycelyn Elders, however, he thought circumstances called for someone thoroughly unconnected to the abortion question. He held his counsel until the last minute, but concluded that Clinton had given us an "in your face" choice. He told the Senate that he would vote for Foster for virtually any other job, but that he had to vote against giving a "symbolic victory to one side" in this instance.

Because he was filling the unexpired term of Gore, Thompson had to start running for reelection immediately after his first victory. Thompson had connected with the voters and the Democrats knew it. Democrats were hard-pressed to find a presentable challenger in 1996 until a little known but respected Covington lawyer, Houston Gordon, agreed to take on the task. Gordon mocked Thompson's ads, chiding him for not wearing the seat belt in his pickup in one of them. More often, he tried to paint Thompson as a close ally of then Speaker Newt Gingrich, the Republican whom Democrats most loved to demonize. For the better part of 1995 and 1996, Democrats had been doing their best to paint Republicans as hard-hearted demagogues who would strip away Social Security and Medicare benefits. Thompson got word that Gordon would be using the same tactic against him and he was prepared. He cut a down-home commercial showing him bringing his mother a bag of groceries. After saying hello, he turned to face the cameras and introduced Tennesseans to his "number one adviser on Social Security and Medicare." He told voters he had the "best reason in the world" to protect those programs. "You sure do, son," she said. "I sure do," he replied. "I'm glad his momma loves him," a flustered Gordon told reporters. Most other Tennesseans do too, apparently, for Thompson amassed nearly 1.1 million votes, more than any other candidate in Tennessee history and a full 200,000 more than Clinton and Gore that year.

Thompson opened his first full term with an entirely new set of responsibilities. A series of Republican retirements coupled with his seniority in our freshman class allowed him to leapfrog to the top of the seniority ladder of the Governmental Affairs Committee, a rare occurrence for a Senator in his third year. It was the intent of Majority Leader Trent Lott that this panel would devote its entire operations during 1997 to investigating the illegal and improper fund-raising abuses that had plagued the previous year's presidential campaign.

I call Senator Thompson my partner and he is in many ways. Our mutual respect is illustrated by the outcome of a call he made to me in December of 1996. Thompson knew that the committee's mission would be difficult, and to be fair, he would need senior staff he could trust, and who had the maturity to gain the trust and respect of both Republicans and Democrats on the committee. His call was to ask me whom I would trust more than anybody else in the world in this position.

I immediately thought of my chief of staff, Mark Tipps. Mark had come to Washington with me in late 1994 and had served as my chief of staff for two years. He was preparing to return to his Nashville law firm, Bass, Berry and Sims, having exhausted his two-year leave from the firm. In fact, his wife, Joi, and three children had already moved back to Nashville in preparation for his return. I told Thompson that there was no one whom I trusted more, who displayed more integrity, who worked harder than Mark Tipps. Thompson trusted my assessment and hired Mark, who jumped in to oversee the hiring of nearly seventy people for the special investigation staff. He became Thompson's right-hand man for the next nine months.

Thompson's experience with the Watergate inquiry governed his planning for the probe. He told the Senate in late January that he desired a "fair and evenhanded" investigation that would look into the activities of both parties, but one with a "sense of priorities." He hoped to enjoy some cooperation from the minority party, much as Howard Baker had provided during the Watergate hearings. He pledged to respect barriers between the executive and legislative branches and noted that he, like many Democrats, had been for campaign finance reform "when it wasn't cool." Having seen staff members leak information that harmed thoroughly innocent people during Watergate, he announced that he would not allow it to happen this time. Although he said that he preferred building things up rather then tearing them down, he declared that the American people had a right to know if our national security had been breached or our foreign policy damaged and that a responsible inquiry generally resulted in a strengthening of our system.

Thompson's plans did not materialize as he had hoped. In his original budget, Thompson called for a $6.5 million outlay. The Democrats, who were terrified of press reports linking the President to illegal fund-raising activities, saw the budget request as an issue they could use for leverage, and they immediately objected. They offered a resolution for $1.8 million. But while publicly the battle was over dollars, I don't believe that was the Democrats' real concern. What they really wanted more than anything else, and what they eventually got, was a time deadline for the investigation of December 31, 1997, thus ensuring that the probe would end before the next election year. Thompson objected strenuously to this, knowing that the surest way to cripple any congressional investigation is to place a time limit on it, because it invites witnesses and other parties with information to engage in stalling tactics.

The other thing the Democrats wanted was a guarantee that the language in the resolution would be broad enough to allow them to probe GOP fundraising practices. Some of our Republican members in turn wanted to restrict the inquiry to those matters that were clearly illegal, which would have resulted in Thompson looking at only Democratic activities. To Thompson, this approach was far too limited in scope. After all, the scope in the Watergate investigation called for a probe of "illegal, improper and unethical" activities. He held tight until Joe Lieberman, a thoughtful and independent-minded Connecticut Democrat, drafted an amendment to let the panel examine both "illegal and improper activities." While the addendum was in line with Thompson's thinking, it did not mesh with Majority Leader Lott's desires. Thompson let the Majority Leader know that he would not support limiting the probe. Thompson believed that any attempt to limit the scope such that only Democrats were targeted would immediately destroy the committee's credibility and integrity and taint any findings it might make, no matter how serious or far reaching. At one of our weekly Tuesday Republican caucus luncheons, a handful of Senators totally surprised Lott by siding with Thompson and Lieberman. In effect, Lott embarrassingly had to accede to Thompson's position. His acquiescence to what seemed to be a Democratic demand led a united Senate to approve a $4.35 million budget.

Thompson's committee paid a huge price for the scuffle over the budget. In the end, while he got most of the money he sought and the scope he wanted, the Democrats got the December 31 cutoff date. Moreover, because of the delay over the budget, the investigation did not really begin until late March. Thompson was faced with the daunting task of conducting an enormously complex investigation, holding public hearings, and preparing a final report, all within nine months, something unheard of in previous investigations of this magnitude. Additionally, the press immediately began asking when the televised public hearings would begin. Thompson was between a rock and a hard place. To delay the public hearings too long risked having the investigation labeled a failure before it ever got started. To start too early risked doing a poor job and overlooking the key facts. Thompson had a tightrope to walk, and he worked meticulously and at a feverish pace throughout the spring to prepare for the hearings. He kept behind the scenes, avoiding interviews in the hope that he could defuse charges that the hearings would be a partisan witch-hunt. Although he tried to spur some bipartisanship by citing Ronald Reagan's waiver of executive privilege during the Iran-Contra hearings, he got little cooperation from Democrats at the Democratic National Committee and the White House. From the beginning, the Democrats derided the inquiry as partisan, insisting that its budget was well over that provided to probe other scandals in the past. Actually, when figures were adjusted for inflation, the costs were far lower than those of Watergate, and Thompson was quick to note that "charges of partisanship can be a partisan tool." In truth, Justice Department officials proved slow in granting immunity to witnesses whose testimony the committee desired. Periodically, the Democratic minority blocked subpoenas and Republican requests for immunity for several other witnesses. Ten witnesses fled the country altogether. Thirty-five others, including close associates of the President, avoided testifying by invoking their Fifth Amendment privilege. Because the White House and most committee Democrats seemed to be balking at any suggestion he might propose, Thompson finally got squash partners Arlen Specter (R-PA) and Carl Levin (D-MI) to negotiate a resolution to many of the disputes, thus injecting a new spirit of bipartisanship into the investigation as the public hearing phase rapidly approached.

Thompson opened the hearings on July 8, 1997, by dramatically calling attention to a plan by "high level Chinese government officials . . . to increase their influence over the U.S. political process." As we would later learn, the content and wording of his statement were approved, and in part prepared, by the appropriate federal intelligence agencies, but because the information was classified, he was prevented at that time from disclosing the specific sources. In essence, all Thompson was doing was making information public that he had received from, and that had been cleared by, the federal intelligence community. He did not intend his statement to be an "allegation that would serve as the road map for the testimony to follow," but that was how the media took it. Also, the Democrats, sensitive to any attempt to strike at the White House, took what was not intended to be a partisan issue and turned it into one, denying at first that they had seen any information to support Thompson's statement. Democrats, however, again thanks to Joe Lieberman, did confirm over the next few days that the Chinese had covertly tried to assist some congressional campaigns, but they refused to acknowledge that the presidential campaign was targeted. Unfortunately, this opening salvo, as Thompson said later, "set the bar too high." It created expectations that could never be met because so many witnesses took the Fifth Amendment and left the country and because of the one-year limit on the Senate investigation.

It soon became apparent from the hearings that John Huang, along with his former employer the Lippo Group (run by the Indonesian-based Riady family) would be central figures in the investigation. The evidence showed that beginning as early as 1992, Huang brought thousands of dollars, much of it from Lippo, into state Democratic parties and the DNC. Huang and James T. Riady both had ties to Little Rock and had been close friends of President Clinton since the late 1970s.

Following Clinton's election in 1992 Huang was appointed, with White House support, as a Deputy Assistant Secretary of Commerce, despite objections from senior Commerce officials who deemed him unqualified. His ties became even more suspicious when the committee established that despite his being "walled off by his superiors at Commerce from any matters involving China," Huang had frequent contact with Chinese officials, particularly at the Chinese Embassy, at a time when he was receiving regular classified intelligence briefings at Commerce regarding Southeast Asian economic affairs. This was particularly disturbing once it was determined that from 1992 through 1997, the Lippo Group, Huang's former employer, had undergone a significant organizational shift and was now partially owned by the Chinese government through a government-run entity known as China Resources.

The committee also established that the DNC hired Huang in late 1995 as Vice Chairman of Finance solely because of requests from the White House, including a specific request from President Clinton to a senior DNC official. Huang's hiring took place just a few weeks after he and James T. Riady had met with the President in the Oval Office, apparently to discuss Huang's going to the DNC. Further details of this conversation are lacking because Riady fled the country, Huang took the Fifth Amendment, and the President declined the committee's invitation to testify.

A few weeks later, the committee heard from several Buddhist nuns who had given $5,000 each to the DNC in conjunction with an April 1996 fundraiser at the Hsi Lai Temple in Hacienda Heights, California, featuring Vice President Gore. Initially the nuns took the Fifth Amendment and refused to testify. The Department of Justice and the Democrats at first resisted granting immunity to the nuns, but eventually agreed after several weeks of delay. Because the nuns had taken a vow of poverty and received only a $40 per week stipend, the committee focused on the true source of the money, eventually determining that the nuns had been reimbursed by the Temple. The committee showed that this laundering scheme was organized and carried out by John Huang, as Vice Chairman of Finance for the DNC, and Maria Hsia, who had been a Gore friend and fund-raiser since 1989. These findings raised questions about the original source of the funds and whether Gore and his staff knew of the laundering scheme. Along with millions of dollars from other questionable sources, the DNC eventually returned the laundered donations from the Hsi Lai Temple.

The panel also looked at the role of Yah Lin "Charlie" Trie, a Democrat fund-raiser and former Little Rock restauranteur who first became friends with President Clinton in 1977. Trie never appeared before the committee because he had taken the Fifth Amendment and fled the country to his native China. Trie had given hundreds of thousands of dollars to the DNC in the 1996 election cycle, despite his limited personal means. He was also credited with raising almost a million more for the DNC from various other sources. FBI investigator Jerry Campane testified that based on bank records and wire transfer documents, much of it from the Bank of China, it appeared that almost all of Trie's money originated from his Chinese associate, Ng Lap Seng (also known as Mr. Wu), a Macau businessman who served as an economic advisor to the Chinese government. In what was one of the most frustrating events for Thompson, within hours after agent Campane's testimony about the mysterious Mr. Wu, the White House turned over to the committee Secret Service records that had been requested months earlier showing that the same Mr. Wu had visited the White House over ten times in 1995 and 1996 as a guest of Trie. The White House said it had merely "overlooked" these records. This same scenario of producing documents after the subject had been uncovered in public testimony was repeated throughout the hearings by the White House.

The committee also looked into Trie's attempt in the spring of 1996 to donate to the President's Legal Expense Trust ("PLET") over $600,000 that he had raised through a Buddhist sect known as Suma Ching Hai. The investigators were able to show that the money was coerced from many members of the sect and that after they donated, the members were reimbursed with money wired from Taiwan and Cambodia. The PLET eventually returned all the money donated by Trie, but the White House did not disclose this connection with Trie until after the 1996 election. In short, the evidence was undeniable that Democratic fund-raisers such as Huang and Trie had raised hundreds of thousands of dollars for the DNC from overseas sources.

Perhaps the most memorable testimony came from Roger Tamraz, a Lebanese-American oil man wanted by Interpol for allegedly defrauding a bank in Lebanon. Tamraz was trying to put together a deal for an oil pipeline through the Caspian Sea and needed U.S. support. When his attempts to meet with the President and vice president were denied by the National Security Council (NSC), Tamraz gave $400,000 to the DNC and various state Democratic parties and made it known he wanted to meet with the President. The DNC intervened on his behalf and he eventually attended four White House functions with the President, despite the NSC's attempt to bar him. Tamraz testified unapologetically at the public hearing that he intended to buy his way into the White House and that he was successful. In his words, "If they won't let me in the front door, I'll climb in the window." The Tamraz story was representative of many other stories told to the committee as they investigated the 1996 election.

Thompson did his best to keep his panel's deliberations on a bipartisan plane. In late July, he provided Democrats a week to present evidence of unseemly Republican Party activity. Their principal target was former Republican National Committee (RNC) Chairman Haley Barbour, who proved more than willing to engage Democrats in some good-natured partisan combat. When Democrats tried to chide Barbour for accepting $50,000 from Panda Industries, a firm run by an Indonesian family, he was quick to point to the $250,000 the DNC had taken from the same firm. Responding to charges that the GOP's National Policy Forum (NPF) was a "sham" organization, Barbour noted its similarities in purpose to the Democratic Leadership Council, a group that unlike the NPF enjoyed tax-free status. Yet the NPF had received a $2.2 million loan from businessman Ambrous Tung Young, a Taiwanese citizen, and $1.6 million of that had been passed on to the RNC. Barbour testified that he thought that the loan had come from Young's U.S. subsidiary. Unfortunately, Young lost $750,000 when the NPF closed and defaulted on the loan. In Thompson's view, our national committee had a "moral obligation" to repay the loan. "When you step back from it," he lectured Barbour, "it looks to me like we [the RNC] owe him some money."

Despite all the barriers placed in his way by both parties, Thompson and his committee told a revealing albeit sometimes distasteful, story of the 1996 elections. Notwithstanding the time deadline placed on them, and despite the fact that the key witnesses fled the country or took the Fifth Amendment, the committee was still able to interview more than three hundred witnesses, review more than 1.5 million documents, and conduct thirty-two days of televised public hearings with seventy-two witnesses testifying. As Thompson predicted from the outset, the investigation was not "another Watergate." He had cautioned early on that congressional hearings should not be a game of "gotcha," in which success or failure is judged by whether a president or other high ranking official is chased from office or by how many indictments are handed down. Rather, the committee's job was to "pull back the covers" and "shed light" on the problems in such a way that the American people could judge for themselves what had happened. The Thompson committee did just that, and history will likely judge that they did it in a thorough and professional manner.

The final chapter to the campaign finance investigation has not yet been written. In March 1998, Johnny Chung entered into a plea bargain with federal prosecutors. By May, the press was reporting that Chung's cooperation with the Justice Department had confirmed Senator Thompson's allegation of a "China Plan." Chung was claiming that much of the money he donated to the DNC had come from Chinese military intelligence accounts via Liu Chaoying, the daughter of a top Chinese military official. Though Senator Thompson was too modest to claim vindication, it was clear that the stories proved his central claim at the hearings.

In addition to Chung, other events refocused much attention on the campaign finance investigation. Charles LaBella, who had been handpicked by Attorney General Janet Reno to lead the Department of Justice's campaign finance task force, delivered a lengthy memorandum to her in July 1998, in which he urged the appointment of an independent counsel to investigate the scandal. His memorandum concurred with the assessment of FBI Director Louis Freeh, who also urged Reno to appoint an independent counsel in November 1997. An independent counsel was never appointed by Reno.

In the 106th Congress, Thompson serves on the Finance Committee and he continues to call for campaign finance reform and regulatory simplification.

How far will Thompson go? It is probably healthy for his psyche that he does not have the single-minded dedication to seeking the presidency that motivates so many in high office. The Senate has been an incubator for presidential candidacies, but a mortuary for presidential campaigns. In this century, only two Senators, Warren G. Harding and John F. Kennedy, have ascended directly to the White House and neither was known as a senatorial workhorse. Thompson now has a national following. He's earned it and he deserves it. His past illustrates a keen sense of appropriate timing for making major commitments. He would be a formidable competitor for either slot on the ticket, now or in the future. In the meantime, Tennesseans can enjoy the leadership, vision, and good common sense of Fred Thompson in the U.S. Senate.

Chapter 17

William H. "Bill" Frist, M.D.

1995–

Transplant Surgeon, Citizen Legislator

(1952–)

by J. LEE ANNIS, JR.

First impressions aren't everything. While I knew Bill Frist had performed hundreds of heart and lung transplants, my initial instinct after watching him debate Jim Sasser was to discount him as another Jefferson Smith, the idealistic but hopelessly naive movie character that Jimmy Stewart brought to life so movingly in *Mr. Smith Goes to Washington*. To my surprise, the good doctor wound up being the only challenger to defeat a full-term incumbent Senator in 1994. What's more, he knocked out Jim Sasser by more than fourteen percentage points, a rare margin for any nonincumbent. So much for my powers of prognosis. What I did not know was that Frist had called upon Howard Baker, about whom I'd just completed a biography, nearly five years earlier to discuss the possibility of his entering politics. At that first meeting, Baker determined that Frist was a "well-organized" man of "substance" with "a pretty clear view of what this job was," something he did not find in every prospective candidate who sought his advice.

As usual, Baker was right. The exuberance I originally saw in Frist was hardly naivete, it was a touch of nervousness tucked within the bedside manner of a skilled surgeon and scientist in the first stages of a new chal-

243

lenge. While Frist is not a traditional Senator, his medical background provides the diversity that the Founding Fathers envisioned in a body that at its best forms a reasonable cross section of the American people.

William Harrison Frist was born in Nashville on February 22, 1952, and hails from a family of physicians. Both of his older brothers, Tommy, Jr., and Bobby, have medical degrees, as does his cousin John. A maternal uncle was a physician and, through him, Bill's father Thomas Fearn Frist met his mother Dorothy Harrison Cate. But the origin of Bill Frist's love of medicine and commitment to service goes back to his father.

The story of Thomas Frist is a success story so quintessentially American that Horatio Alger himself could have drafted it. Although his Tennessee roots were strong (he was a direct descendant of Isaac Baldwin, one of the original fifty-three founders of Chattanooga), he was born in 1910 in Meridian, Mississippi. At eight, he was left fatherless after Jacob ("Jake") Chester Frist, the town's railroad stationmaster, died from injuries sustained five years earlier in a heroic and successful bid to save a woman and her grandson from the path of an oncoming locomotive in which he took the blow himself. In 1915, Jake Frist was awarded a Medal of Honor by President Woodrow Wilson through the Interstate Commerce Commission (ICC).

The character which motivated his heroism and the esteem in which he was held is evidenced in a friend's letter to Jake Frist following the accident. His friend wrote, "The act is nothing more to you than you had to do; and you can't see how it's possible for any one to have ever thought of doing anything else, and that's natural too, for you are built that way; but it requires only a little meditation for one to realize that if only every one was built that way what a different world this would be." In a March 26, 1915, letter of gratitude to the ICC upon receiving the honor, Jacob Frist wrote, "I shall hand them down to my children and hope my boys may do the same thing when they grow to be men. . . . I think it the duty of every man, when women and children are in danger of being killed, to try to save them."

After his father's death in 1919, Thomas Frist's mother, Jennie Jones Frist, was left to fend for herself and soon opened her home to boarders to support herself and her four children. One of the boarders was Dr. S. H. Hairston, a surgeon who hired young Tommy once he turned twelve as an orderly at the town hospital. Hairston's influence inspired the young Frist to contemplate a medical career. At sixteen Frist went to Southwestern (now Rhodes College) at Memphis, then to the University of Mississippi, with just that intention. Funds were short, and he had to work his way through both those schools and later Vanderbilt Medical School. At Ole Miss, he carted students and their trunks from the train station in Oxford to their dorms in a mule-driven wagon. There and at Vanderbilt, he published football schedules on desk blotters, making a few dollars with the sale of advertising for local shops. He further supplemented his income during his medical training by laundering hospital uniforms, installing and filling vending machines, and running a boarding house, affectionately known as Paupers' Paradise, near campus. It was his habit to send $30 a month home to his mother, even during the depression when every penny came hard. After his general medical residency training at the University of Iowa and unable to afford advanced surgical training, he accepted an offer to return to Nashville to go into practice with a prominent internist, Dr. William Robert Cate. Frist met Cate through Cate's younger sister Dorothy, a schoolteacher and graduate of Ward Belmont College and Peabody College (1932). Dorothy and Tommy were married on June 11, 1936.

The early days of medical practice were a financial struggle for Frist. He supplemented his income by running the medical clinic at the state penitentiary, where he started a hospital to treat inmates suffering from tuberculosis. To build his practice and earn enough to marry Dorothy, he would do physical exams after hours for an insurance company in Nashville.

Thomas Frist was the old-fashioned kind of general practitioner who worked day and night treating patients in his office and at their homes. Except for his service as major and chief of medical services at Maxwell Field Air Force Base in Montgomery, Alabama, during World War II, his practice was headquartered in Nashville. There, over fifty-five years, he established a solid and loyal clientele, ranging from Minnie Pearl to eight governors of Tennessee and a multitude of Middle Tennesseans.

Tommy Frist's three sons would later follow in his footsteps. The Frists' first child was Tommy, Jr., born in 1938. Like his father, he earned a medical degree, but his real genius lay in the realm of business. It was he who devised the concept of using market capital and public funding to build state-of-the-art hospitals that would join in bulk purchasing and service-sharing programs and thus create economies of scale theretofore unknown in the hospital sector. The elder Frist was skeptical of his son's vision for quite a while, and he initially strongly advised his son not to leave the clinical practice of medicine. Tommy, Jr., went to his mother and enlisted her support, and Frist, Sr., eventually was swayed by his son's determined argument that he could ultimately help more people by making care more accessible, especially in rural communities. This was in 1968. Bill Frist was sixteen years old. He often thinks back to those discussions over the dinner table in those days—the debate over how to best serve people, his father's commitment to patient care, the power of a visionary idea, the role of private enterprise, the American dream. Frist, Sr., and Frist, Jr., hooked up with local financier and fried chicken magnate, Jack C. Massey, and founded Hospital Corporation of America (HCA). HCA grew to 342 hospitals and became the first company in the history of the New York Stock Exchange to reach $1 billion in sales within its first decade of operation.

Young Bill Frist grew up with a father who gave not to just his patients and family, but also to his community. Frist, Sr., joined in founding the Cumberland Heights Foundation for the rehabilitation of alcoholics, the Medical Benevolent Association to help medical missionaries deliver health care throughout the world, and the Park Manor Presbyterian Apartments for the Elderly in Nashville. The elder Frist continued to be active in the community until his death at eighty-seven years in 1998.

For Bill Frist, eldest brother Tommy served as a "guiding light," though Bill actually spent more time as a youth with his three other siblings, sister Dottie born in 1941, Bobby in 1942 and Mary in 1946. Bill was the baby of the family by six years. In *Transplant*, his insightful book about organ donation and life as a transplant surgeon, he describes himself as a strong-willed youth with tremendously supportive parents. Dorothy Frist was an ever-optimistic, ever-present, nurturing woman from a family of fourteen children in Hopkinsville, Kentucky. Her mother raised her children with a deep sense of individual responsibility, love of family, and concern for the well-being of others. During his childhood, Bill Frist remembers his mother serving as surrogate mother for most of the kids in the neighborhood, always welcoming them to their home for a meal, a sleepover, or just to chat. Dorothy Frist sought to instill inquisitive habits that would lead the children to examine all facets of problems that beset them in life, at school, or at work. Her influence upon Bill was so deep that he acknowledged it soon after his graduation from college by establishing a book fund in perpetuity in her name at Princeton University. It was to his mother's side of the family that Bill Frist attributed his own interest and commitment to education.

Today, Bill Frist likes to joke that he treated his first patient when he was seven. A neighbor boy asked him to look at an ugly laceration on his dog's neck, thinking he might have some magical cure because he was the doctor's kid. Frist found his dad's black bag, then pulled out some brown powder and sprinkled it on the wound. What the substance was he did not know. In fact, he felt confident only that the dog's pain would probably lessen on its own. Still, the look on his friend's face the next day when the cut began to mend told him that someone thought he had made a difference. It gave him an inner glow, and the notion of becoming a healer like his father began to take shape.

As a youth, Frist strove to achieve, just as his brothers had. Teachers at Montgomery Bell Academy saw him as a "bright, good-hearted kid with a touch of the devil in him." Like his brothers, both of whom were athletes in high school, he played quarterback on the football team. Encouraged by his brother Tommy, he learned to fly, soloing when he was sixteen years old. He edited the yearbook and was elected president of the student council.

A signal event in his life was a severe accident after his freshman year in high school that occurred as he was riding his brother Bobby's motorcycle: it nearly cost him his life. A shattered kneecap which was surgically removed meant he could no longer be the athlete that he had so badly wanted to be. His energies would be directed elsewhere. A concussion, multiple facial and extremity fractures, and a fourteen-inch leg laceration left him contemplating his own mortality at an age when others were thinking themselves immortal. He began to realize that he would have to leave Nashville, at least for a time, to determine whether his success was due to his family name or his own accomplishments. After a long discussion with brother Tommy, he decided that he would go away to college to some place where his name might as well have been Smith.

Frist's siblings had all gone to college in Nashville. But, not wholly in tune with the wishes of his parents who felt there was no better place to be educated than right in Tennessee, Frist left Nashville to go to Princeton. He was as active in college as he had been in high school. He enrolled in Princeton's pre-med program, but found greatest comfort in a broad-based curriculum that included economics, history, and art. He still found time to serve as the head of the Big Brother program, a resident advisor in the dorms, president of the flying club, a student government representative, and vice president of his senior class.

The summer of 1972 would prove to be prophetic for Frist, who spent that two months in Washington, D.C., as a legislative intern for Tennessee Congressman Joe L. Evins. Frist recalls Evins telling him on the last day of his internship that if he ever wanted to serve in Congress that he should excel in some other career first, then come back to Washington. That concept of the citizen-legislator was planted.

Frist spent his junior and senior years at Princeton in the Woodrow Wilson School of Public and International Affairs, where he continued his multidisciplinary approach to education, specializing in health care policy. He used this opportunity to write his junior paper on the civil rights of mental patients, a project he researched by going so far as checking into a large, state-run psychiatric hospital as if he were a patient (with the consent and knowledge of its administrators). During his senior year he was selected as a Wilson School Scholar, which allowed him to pursue independent scholarship. His performance at Princeton was impressive enough to win him the Harold Willis Dodds Achievement Award for outstanding leadership and at graduation to be elected by his peers to serve as a trustee on the Board at Princeton.

Frist left for Harvard Medical School in the fall of 1974, and he soon found his stamina challenged by a pace exhausting even for him. The needs for food, sleep, and exercise were eclipsed by his determination to assimilate the mountains of facts in his textbooks. He found that nothing in his previous training had prepared him for the rigors of medical school, designed to train prospective doctors to think clearly on their feet under circumstances of extreme duress.

Frist worked meticulously to develop his scientific research skills. Frist's first published article appeared during his second year in medical school, and it was based on research that he had done at Princeton. Working with several more experienced researchers, he evaluated the efficiency of a VD hotline in one New Jersey county. While the costs per call seemed a bit high, he and his colleagues found that the hotline's presence had succeeded in shifting the principal source of VD treatment from emergency rooms to clinics. This marked the work of a mature public policy scientist at a young age, one focused upon the needs of patients and one willing to examine all potential costs and benefits to society of any piece of public policy.

The same year, in his physiology class, he cradled the still-beating heart of a dog in his hands for the first time, and thus began an all-consuming fascination with the human heart. It would become the predominant focus of the next fifteen years of his life. Here was the organ mankind regarded as "the sanctuary of our emotions," but in function he knew to be "just a little pump." Once he cut through the muscular wall and looked at the delicate valves, he was fascinated by the intricacies of its structure. He was hooked. He spent much of his third medical school year in a cardiac physiology laboratory dissecting hearts, designing investigations to determine what happens to the pumping power of heart muscle when adequate oxygen is not available. The scientific method of hypothesis and testing, the compilation of accurate and complete data, the formulation of specific questions to ask—these skills, he said in later years, he learned in these months of laboratory experimentation and discovery.

Little else would be so simple for Frist. Though he graduated from Harvard Medical School with honors, he had to adjust to the cruelest realities of medicine not long after he entered his surgical training at Massachusetts General Hospital when he could not save the life of a little girl who had severe burns covering 65 percent of her body. Could he withstand the physical and emotional rigors of the training? Could he accept the limits of technology and science which dictated that not every life could be saved?

Then, during his residency training at Massachusetts General Hospital (MGH), he met Karyn McLaughlin. For Frist, it was love at first sight. The similarities between Karyn's native Texas and Frist's Tennessee, especially against the backdrop of Boston, Massachusetts, sparked conversation. The two talked again, then met for dinner. Frist was mesmerized by her West Texas charm, her southern manners, her conservative bent, and her big, wide eyes. The rest of his life would be with Karyn. She was born into a Lubbock, Texas, banking family in 1954. A graduate of Texas Christian University with a degree in special education, she was teaching part time in Boston as well as working as a flight attendant when she met Frist. The two were married in 1981, and she worked until she became pregnant with their first son, Harrison. In time, the Frists had two other boys, Jonathan and Bryan.

After four years at Massachusetts General as a surgical house officer, Bill and Karyn left for England, where he spent almost a year in Southampton General Hospital as a senior registrar in thoracic surgery. Employed directly by Britain's socialistic National Health Service, he grew disillusioned by the government's rationing of health services, the age limits placed on kidney dialysis, and the long waiting lists for routine heart surgery. Frist then returned to Boston to assume the chief residency position in cardiothoracic surgery at the MGH.

However, it was not until his next stop at Stanford that he found true fulfillment. There, in 1985, he came under the tutelage of Dr. Norman Shumway, the pioneering father of heart transplantation. It was Shumway, more than any other surgeon in the world, who made transplantation of the human heart possible by defining and developing techniques to monitor the transplanted heart and to detect the earliest signs of rejection. A new field in medicine was opening up, and Frist wanted to be there. The MGH in Boston made a policy decision not to begin heart transplantation, so Frist packed his family up and went to the frontier of thoracic transplantation.

Frist found Shumway an inspiring teacher. While holding his team to the high standards required for survival and success on the cutting edge of medicine and science, Shumway was patient and even playful, and he made assistants want to do their best solely out of respect for him. "Cardiac surgery is not hard to do," he would say. "It's just hard to get to do." He encouraged residents to keep their operations simple, as complexity increased the chance for error. His lightheartedness brought out the creativity in a rare group of talented surgeons who eventually came to staff many of the most prestigious medical centers in the United States. In Frist, he reinforced many of the same lessons Frist's father had long before instilled in him about the joy of medicine, the importance of teamwork, the power of humility, and the pleasure of helping others. Like Shumway, it was rare for the surgeon Frist to begin any procedure without asking nurses and assistants about their insights into his patients and their special needs. He listened with an optimistic and perceptive intensity that let associates know their participation and opinions were appreciated, even if the final decision were his alone.

Shumway's influence led Frist to seek to establish a similar program. Boston, in its sometimes too traditional manner, was still lagging behind in heart transplantation endeavors, the West had Stanford, but the South was fertile territory for such innovation. Frist returned to Nashville in 1986 as director of heart and lung transplantation at Vanderbilt. The new program demanded that he be on call seven days a week, twenty-four hours a day for heart and lung transplant surgery. In addition to his surgical responsibilities at Vanderbilt, he operated one to two days a week at the adjacent Veterans Administration Hospital. Frist taught medical students and surgical residents not only the technical skills of surgery, but also the methods of scientific research, taking them on transplant runs and facilitating for some their first published peer-reviewed articles.

How good a surgeon was he? "If you need cutting," one satisfied bypass patient from rural Tennessee declared, "get Bill Frist to cut you."

During 1987 and 1988, Frist, drawing on his belief in bringing groups together to solve problems and building on a successful, established kidney transplantation program at Vanderbilt, began laying the groundwork for his concept of a multi-organ transplant center at Vanderbilt. He envisioned bringing together under a single roof multidisciplinary teams of surgeons, physicians, infectious disease specialists, psychiatrists, and ethicists to approach the challenges of the new and rapidly evolving field of organ and tissue transplantation. Frist became founding director of the new center, which soon gained national acclaim for the innovative approach to address the clinical, ethical, and scientific issues surrounding the new field. Frist performed Tennessee's first single lung transplant and first pediatric heart transplant, as well as the first successful combined heart-lung transplant in the Southeast. He performed approximately two hundred heart and lung transplants, flying through the night almost weekly to other hospitals across the country to surgically remove organs for his prospective patients. An active researcher and investigator, he published more than one hundred articles, chapters, and abstracts on heart and lung disease. While operating and teaching by day and spending a night or two a week operating until 4 or 5 A.M., he remained active in his community (taking after his father), finding time to serve on the boards of several civic organizations, a local bank, and Princeton University.

Watching patients needlessly die as they waited for a donor organ to become available, Frist recognized the power and necessity of public education to encourage organ donation. It was not unusual for him to devote several nights a month to educating his peers and the public about how they could save lives by donating their own tissues and organs. Frist worked with celebrities like Barbara Mandrell to raise public awareness of the need for more donors. He traversed Tennessee and other states, speaking about the history of transplantation and describing an exciting future for that lifesaving procedure if only more organs were available. He wrote the book *Transplant,* published in 1989, to help educate others about the field and to demystify transplantation; on the inside jacket cover of every copy was an organ donor card. Frist's first experience with the power of grassroots organization was the statewide campaign he put together to return the organ donor statement to the back of the Tennessee driver's license.

As the surgeon to thousands of patients, director of an innovative transplant center, and a civic activist, Frist was living the life of public service that his father had instilled in his children. His hands could replace worn out hearts and lungs, his team could literally save individuals from the grasp of death, but he saw that appropriate public policy and broad public awareness were absolutely necessary to bring to realization the full potential of the therapy. Perhaps there was a role for him to play in this larger field of public policy.

By 1990, confident that the Vanderbilt Transplant Center was firmly established, Frist began to consider other professional challenges. The motivation for his search was similar to what had moved his brother to start HCA: how could he best serve other people?

Frist's curiosity and disciplined approach led him to systematically meet with a number of Tennessee's preeminent leaders in academia and in both political parties. He found ready access to most of them, for through the practice of medicine, his father had long before befriended them. He listened intently to Al Gore, Jr., who shared his interest in scientific policy, and former Governor Winfield Dunn, who stressed the intangible rewards of public service. Philosophically, Frist was fiscally conservative and market-oriented in his approach to economics, and his personal experiences with rationed care in England led him to distrust a government-run approach to most problems. Over a third of his transplant patients were poor and on Medicaid, and they told him time and time again how the welfare system had taken away their incentive to work, and even encouraged them not to live with their families. As a doctor, he felt increasingly confined by what he called the "suffocating hand" of excessive managed care and government bureaucracies. More and more, he saw an abandonment of what he had once seen as a sacrosanct doctor-patient relationship. Health care, he worried, was moving toward a "cookie-cutter, one-size-fits-all, Washington-knows-best" approach, one hardly conducive to the best possible care for his patients. Even more glaring was the absence of any doctor at most tables where decisions were made about health care, a growing trend he found threatening to the quality of care delivered to individual patients. Frist's concern that the federal government was playing an increasingly meddlesome role in what should be decisions made between doctors and their patients was consistent with a lifelong conservative philosophy. It was his fundamental belief in individual responsibility, that individuals and families, not government bureaucracies, should make personal life decisions, that led to his own decision to commit to the Republican Party.

It was natural for Frist to call on Howard Baker. The two met for lunch on March 6, 1990, in Knoxville, and Baker was quick to apprise Frist of both the psychological rewards and the pitfalls of elective service. He opened by stressing the "demeaning" side of politics and the need to develop and maintain a thick hide, for abuse would come. Defeat was always a possibility, and one had to be prepared to return to a meaningful role in private life at any time. This is excellent advice for any prospective candidate, and Frist understood fully.

Baker was just as emphatic about the positive side of politics. "As you travel across the state, you will fall in love with the people of Tennessee," he told Frist. Were Frist to run for office, he should shoot for a post that would justify leaving the rewarding field of heart surgery. "Washington is where the action is," he counseled, adding that service in the Senate would afford him the chance to make the kinds of contributions that would improve the lives of people nationwide. And were he to run, Baker counseled, he should focus at least initially on health care, for he would naturally be seen as an expert. After listening to Frist, Baker thought that Frist had a good concept of the nature of congressional service, and he told Frist that such a race was "doable." He was not overly encouraging, nor was he about to make a commitment of support four years before a primary to someone who had not yet fully decided whether he would leave medicine. Still, Frist found it positive that Baker had not tried to discourage him and had promised to forward his name to some friends in Washington.

Frist exhibited his expertise on health care policy in four op-ed articles he wrote for the *Tennessean* just prior to the 1992 election. His tone was analytical rather than partisan. Indeed, he gently chastised both President Bush and then-Governor Clinton for misrepresenting the health care plans the other was forwarding to the American people. Frist was diagnostic rather than prescriptive, and he carefully laid out the complexities of various suggested reforms and the competing pressures that fell upon legislators in considering them. With even the definition of basic medical care in dispute among various forces in our society, he suggested that meaningful reform could ensue if our leaders recognized their common objectives of universal access to health care (including portability of insurance from one job to another), cost containment, and streamlined bureaucratic structures. Only at the very end of the last piece did he indicate his own preference for the direction he hoped that plan would take by adding pleas for promoting primary, preventive, and long-term care and preserving as much as possible the freedom of patients to choose their own physician.

Meanwhile, Frist continued to explore his political options. His respect for Baker's counsel led him to request another meeting with the former Senator, and they met again in March 1992. This time, Baker saw a seriousness of purpose and encouraged him to start attending GOP functions around the state. Meet people and find out what was on their minds, he advised; don't argue with them, and get involved in the state Bush-Quayle campaign. Frist listened, took notes and did exactly as Baker had counseled. He returned to Washington in June 1992, with Karyn to meet again with Baker and also with Jim Cannon, Baker's chief of staff during his tenure as Republican leader, whom Baker had asked to come as well. The appropriateness of Karyn's questions about the effects of political careers upon families and about the quality of life for their sons in Washington, particularly schools, convinced Baker that the two had what it took to have a successful marriage and career under the rigors of public life.

Frist's only political appointment prior to his election to the Senate came in November 1992, from a Democrat, Governor Ned Ray McWherter, who tapped him to chair his task force on Medicaid reform. Evaluating a program budgeted at $2.8 billion a year, about a fourth of the entire Tennessee state budget, gave Frist additional perspective on the influence of health care policy. He held hearings and listened to doctors, nurses, and advocates for the disabled, the elderly, and the infirm, and made sure that often underrepresented groups like the pharmacists had a chance to speak their piece as well. The governor's Medicaid task force helped pave the way for Tennessee to obtain a waiver to opt out of the traditional Medicaid program, only the third such state to do so. Frist saw how public policy could directly impact the care individuals receive. He saw firsthand the direct link between an individual's health and the policy of government. He witnessed how a few politicians could overnight transform the health care of one million people. Serving a patient and serving the nation's people suddenly did not seem too different.

Frist, after long discussions with his wife Karyn about the risks in leaving behind a medical career and the security such station provides, made a final decision to seek the seat then held by Jim Sasser in the late spring of 1993, and he took a leave of absence from Vanderbilt in December to organize and launch his campaign. Although his motivation to serve did not rest principally with health care issues, he took Jim Cannon's advice to make the central theme of his campaign the notion that "I want to be in the room when the major health care decisions affecting our children are made." He emphasized his life as a doctor in his announcement on March 1, 1994, where his family and many of his transplant patients stood at his side. He gave the event a nonpartisan dimension by handing out organ donor cards and asking those present to distribute them. His choice of symbols emphasized the healing image of his profession. In the wake of the legislative failure of the Clinton health care plan, the biggest surprise for Frist was the degree to which health care did not become an issue either in the primary or in the general election.

Frist had five opponents in the GOP primary, most of whom were nearly as new to politics as he. His principal competition came from Bob Corker, a successful businessman from Chattanooga. Frist and Corker met several times privately before either had announced, discussing at length each other's motivation to run. "It's going to be like a tough tennis match," Frist told Corker on a plane late one night, "tough, competitive, with only one of us winning." Corker lambasted Frist for his failure to vote during his surgical training. Frist took the attacks in stride, reminding Karyn that they would toughen him and prepare him for the general election. Rather than returning fire, he directed his campaign solely at Sasser, whom he branded as the personification of "this unresponsive, out-of-touch, imperial Congress" and a "career politician who is addicted to the perks and privileges of this office." Since polls tended to show that people liked Sasser personally but were prepared for a change, Frist knew his task was to educate Tennesseans about a voting record that had grown too liberal for most Tennesseans. Frist scored particularly heavily with an ad that showed a picture of Mount Rushmore being transformed into busts of Sasser next to President Clinton, Senator Ted Kennedy, and Congressman Dan Rostenkowski, three Democrats who were out of favor in Tennessee at the time. Heeding Baker's advice, he traversed Tennessee, finding contributors in all ninety-five counties, and built solid organizations in eighty of them. By the day of the primary, he was certain enough of victory that he spent the day calling his opponents' supporters and asking for their future help. His confidence was not overplaced. Large pluralities in Middle and West Tennessee propelled him to a twelve percentage point victory statewide.

Frist hit the ground running in the campaign against Sasser. He spoke of his desire to make the "American dream a real possibility for every Tennessean and every American." Even more often, he declared his wish "to give communities and individuals the freedom to solve problems and return to our basic conservative values." His agenda was similar to that forwarded by most Republicans in 1994. He ran ads promising to back "term limits for career politicians and the death penalty for career criminals" and was quick in most Tennessee venues to endorse welfare reform, voluntary school prayer, and spending and tax cuts.

That Frist's brand of conservatism was in vogue in Tennessee in 1994 was best evidenced by Sasser's decision to stress support for school prayer, deporting illegal immigrants, and "getting pornography off of television." These were the few conservative stands in Sasser's increasingly liberal record, and Frist was quick to blast the chairman of the Senate Budget Committee for backing "the largest tax hike in history." Even Sasser's attempt to point out the value to Tennessee of his likely ascension to the Democratic leadership backfired, as it made it easy for Frist to chide him as "the official water boy to Bill Clinton." In effect, Sasser had been stressing the value of politics in a decidedly antipolitical year, and undecided voters were quickly reminded of Frist's slogan of "Eighteen years is long enough." By late October, poll numbers showed leaners tilting rapidly toward Frist, and he felt confident of victory; only the size of it surprised him. Against an incumbent who had lost only one county six years earlier, Frist prevailed in all of Tennessee's urban centers and seventy of its counties and won by a full 211,000 votes. Frist was the only challenger to defeat a full-term incumbent Senator in the 1994 elections.

Since he had committed to serve no more than two terms, Frist intended to make an immediate contribution. He was one of the majority of the eleven freshman Senators to support Trent Lott's successful ascent to become Majority Whip. Frist thought the 1994 conservative "revolution" demanded that the GOP include new leadership to present a fresher, more vibrant vision for the future. That energetic impression would have emerged regardless of whom Republicans installed in their hierarchy, for Frist and other freshmen were soon placing the agenda they had promised in 1994 before the Congress. Frist joined in sponsoring a constitutional amendment requiring a balanced budget and bills limiting unfunded mandates and extending a line-item veto to the president. Comfortable only in the role as a citizen-legislator, a concept he deems central to our form of government, he especially reveled in preaching about the desirability of term limits. Limiting terms, he liked to quote Harry Truman, could "cure both senility and seniority, both terrible legislative diseases." Indeed, Bill Frist's first legislative proposal before the Senate was a term limits bill.

Frist took on as heavy a workload as any of his freshman colleagues. His first committee assignments were to Banking, Budget, Small Business, and Labor and Human Resources. On the latter, he immediately assumed the chairmanship of the Disability Subcommittee, where he drafted the first substantial changes to the Individuals with Disabilities Education Act since that law was enacted in 1975. Except for the effort to secure approval of his amendment to block the commingling of bank and thrift funds before the charters of such organizations were merged, Frist found his work on the Banking Committee to be the least stimulating. Preferring not to spend hundreds of hours wallowing in the Whitewater investigation, which had become the focus of the Banking Committee activities for the year, he took the opportunity occasioned by Bob Packwood's resignation to move to the Commerce, Science and Transportation Committee. There, he focused on issues to promote technology development as a means to encourage economic development in Tennessee. As one of the few trained scientists in the Senate, he put his scientific background and experience to optimum use. By 1997, he had both formed the Senate's first bipartisan Science and Technology Caucus and ascended to chair the Subcommittee on Science, Technology and Space, a perch from which he could make a strong case to attract the multibillion dollar Spallation Neutron Source to Oak Ridge.

The first political test of Frist's character came in the spring of 1995. At issue was President Clinton's controversial nomination of Dr. Henry W. Foster, Jr., the chairman of Obstetrics and Gynecology at Nashville's Meharry Medical School, to be Surgeon General. It was to Foster's extreme disadvantage that he was chosen in the wake of the dismissal of Dr. Joycelyn Elders, a woman whose rhetoric had often embarrassed the Clinton administration and angered conservative groups.

The conservative pro-life groups lobbied early for Foster's defeat, arguing that he was an abortionist. Frist knew he was not. As the Senate's first clinical physician since Henry Hatfield and Royal Copeland served West Virginia and New York, respectively, in the 1930s, Frist's stance on medical issues carried much weight with wavering members. It did not help that the Clinton administration had not compiled an accurate fact sheet on Foster before the President introduced him as his nominee, nor had anyone prepared the nonpolitical Foster for the intense scrutiny that he would face. Frist, having just gone through his first political campaign and experienced firsthand the scrutiny that frightens so many good people away from public service, was determined to focus on Foster's credentials, record, and aims as a possible Surgeon General.

For Frist, the incompetence of the White House's handling of the nomination was not the issue. As a private citizen, he had been appalled by the scorn he saw Democrats hurl upon Robert Bork, John Tower, and Clarence Thomas. Was it right for Republicans to heap the same kind of abuse on a nominee of a Democratic president? For Frist, the answer was clearly no, especially for a fellow Tennessean whose ethical standards he knew to be impeccable. While his staff suggested nine-to-one that he oppose Foster's confirmation because of the controversy and the widespread opposition by Republicans being fed information by others, his conscience guided him to reserve judgment until he completed his own thorough review of Foster's record.

Frist was legitimately concerned that Foster might echo the sharp-tongued, blustering extremism of Dr. Elders, but having known Foster in the medical community in Tennessee, he sensed that this would not be the case. Not relying on staff reports, Frist personally scrutinized Foster's writings and found nothing to suggest advocacy for abortion. He then invited Foster to his office and asked him to explain his concept of the Surgeon General's role. Foster replied that his priorities would be full-scale attacks on teen pregnancy and youth smoking, screening for breast and prostatic cancer, and AIDS research, answers hardly unacceptable to mainstream Americans. Frist reasoned that when the Senate confirmed C. Everett Koop as Surgeon General, a staunch opponent of abortion, that confirmation did not outlaw abortion. Therefore he concluded that confirming Foster would not mean voting to condone abortion.

For Frist, the sole question was whether Foster was qualified to serve as Surgeon General. He reserved a final judgment until the Labor and Human Resources Committee completed its hearings, skillfully asking questions to allow Foster to make his case. Frist spoke of standard medical practice and dismissed as misinformation the statement that a hysterectomy Foster had performed was an abortion. His support propelled Foster's nomination out of the committee, but he had too few GOP allies to break a filibuster on the Senate floor. Even so, Frist's stature rose within the institution. He had proved himself, even as a freshman legislator, as one who was thoughtful, independent and willing to swim upstream to do what he believed was right. Democrats began to approach him privately with queries about the reality of various medical practices and the effects of health care policies on providers and patients, even if they did not always go along with his proposed remedies.

Frist's initial foray into health care policy came during the debate over the fiscal 1996 budget. Because of his expertise in the area, Senate Majority Leader Bob Dole and Budget Committee Chairman Pete Domenici gave him considerable latitude in shaping GOP policy. Frist meticulously fought to preserve funding for medical and scientific research, knowing from his own experience in the lab that the investment would generate better health for all Americans in years ahead. A year later, in 1997, he repelled efforts to limit funds for the Ryan White CARE Act for AIDS patients, knowing costs would continue to grow at least until the medical community fully understood the disease. But these were not the costs fueling deficit growth. Medicare and Medicaid were growing at more than 10 percent annually, double the rate for the budget as a whole. For the first time, Medicare costs were exceeding funds coming into the Medicare Trust Fund. If limits were not imposed, the fund would be depleted within seven years. What to do? In 1995, Democrats were using GOP calls for "cuts" in Medicare (really calls for slowing the growth in spending) to brand Republicans as insensitive to the elderly, even while the *New York Times* and other liberal papers were confirming the seriousness of the problem of impending bankruptcy in their editorial pages. Frist recognized that political realities effectively precluded the resolution of the issue before 1997. In 1995, Dole appointed Frist chairman of the Medicare Working Group, a task force charged with developing policies to strengthen Medicare. The physician-Senator was the natural choice to appear in a GOP television ad to refute Democratic charges that Republicans were cutting Medicare and to reassure seniors that the truth was that Republicans were cutting the growth rate of expenditures in order to save and strengthen Medicare.

Frist played an even larger role in drafting and enacting the 1996 Kassebaum-Kennedy-Frist health insurance bill. While a Republican Congress and a Democratic president were not likely to agree on any broad-based health care proposal, particularly in an election year, both parties were interested in passing some incremental health insurance measures. He worked to limit the power of insurers to deny coverage for preexisting conditions and to ensure portability of insurance from one job to another. These were causes dear to his heart. A thirty-eight-year-old lawyer whose heart Frist had replaced found it virtually impossible to move to better-paying law firms because insurers for those firms would not cover him. In addition, it came naturally for Frist to push for a feature inserting information about organ donation into the tax return envelopes of more than seventy million Americans.

Furthermore, he saw to it that the bill allowed for the testing of medical savings accounts (MSAs) in some group insurance plans. These allowed employers to set aside funds for health care benefits in IRA-like savings accounts from which employees could spend as the need arose. While some Republicans deemed MSAs the salvation of America's health care system, Frist was too experienced to see MSAs as a panacea. To him, they formed a small but definite improvement that would empower consumers, spending directly from their own personal accounts, to seek a better value for their health care dollar. To more conservative Republicans, it was the inclusion of the MSA proposal that swung them to join the rest of their colleagues in approving a key piece of legislation by a rare vote of 100–0.

The same year, Frist noted that health maintenance organizations and insurance companies, eager to minimize costs, were going too far by forcing many women after giving birth to leave hospitals before physicians felt they were ready. To Frist, these "drive-by deliveries," as he termed them, were antithetical to both the mother's and baby's health and the primacy of the doctor-patient relationship in determining length of stay. While he could not go along with a bill letting mothers alone determine the length of their stay, he did join with New Jersey Democrat Bill Bradley to craft and spearhead the enactment of a maternity stay bill which created a forty-eight-hour safe haven during which insurers must cover the costs of maternity services. The safe haven allowed doctors and mothers—not insurance companies—to once again make the decision of when mother and baby could go home. Frist, though warning repeatedly against the slippery slope of legislating by "body part," nevertheless believed this legislation to be necessary because HMOs had begun to sacrifice quality of care for women to achieve cost savings.

The Republican Party recognized the value of Frist's voice in health care. He was one of four Senators not in an official leadership capacity who were chosen to speak at the 1996 Republican national convention in San Diego—his topic, health care.

Frist broadened his activities during the 105th Congress. He added a seat on the Foreign Relations Committee and, later in the year, was appointed to the National Bipartisan Commission on the Future of Medicare. His scientific background and chairmanship of the Subcommittee on Science, Technology and Space led him to sponsor such legislation, ultimately signed by the President, as the Next Generation Internet bill and the Commercialization of Space.

At the outset of 1997, he ascended to the chairmanship of the Public Health and Safety Subcommittee and took a position as vice chairman of the Alliance for Health Reform, a bipartisan caucus formed several years earlier by West Virginia Democrat Jay Rockefeller to provide a forum on the Hill for debate and discussion of health care issues. Together, they introduced a Medigap bill to require insurers to cover people with preexisting conditions who don't qualify for Medicaid but aren't old enough for Medicare. They also introduced a bill letting local provider sponsored organizations (PSOs) contract directly with Medicare to offer health care services. This bill allowed networks of physicians and facilities, not just large insurance companies, to participate in the emerging managed care market in Medicare, thus increasing competition and bringing to the table those most naturally focused on quality. The Frist-Rockefeller bill set strict standards of quality for PSOs, but also allowed physicians to proceed with treatments without checking with insurers, thus eliminating paperwork and other costs. Frist and Rockefeller inserted the PSO Act in the balanced budget agreement of 1997, a deal reached only after President Clinton yielded to longstanding GOP pressure for cuts in the growth of Medicare spending which had truly been driving the deficit.

Senator Baker told Frist that he would love getting to know the people all across Tennessee, and how right he was. Frist travels to each of the ninety-five counties at least once each Congress, holding his "Listening Town Meetings." Legislatively, he has been an advocate for strong public elementary and secondary education, chairing the Budget Committee's task force on education and authoring the popular Frist-Wyden "Ed-Flex" bill signed into law in 1999. He championed improved air service in small and medium-sized communities, like Chattanooga, the Tri-Cities, and Jackson, to promote job development and economic growth. As a scientist, he is pushing legislation to double federal research and development, and his voice was heard when it came time to decide to place the Spallation Neutron Source in Oak Ridge. Frist and Fred Thompson joined forces to save TVA $300,000 a day for the next ten years by arranging refinancing of a large portion of the TVA debt. His love for the Smoky Mountains, where he and his family hike and camp, translated to increased funding for the trails.

Frist continues to use his medical skills far more frequently than he had contemplated. He regularly gives up part of a day to see patients at a free clinic in Washington, D.C., or a school clinic, or a rural hospital in Tennessee. In 1998 he spent two weeks in Africa as a medical missionary. In case of an emergency, he keeps a fully equipped medical bag in the top of his closet in his Washington office. His first medical emergency which captured considerable attention on Capitol Hill came on September 14, 1995. Graeme Sieber, who ran a home for troubled boys in Cleveland, Tennessee, was lobbying Senators to limit cuts proposed for facilities like his when his heart stopped beating outside of Senator John Chafee's office in the Dirksen Building. As soon as Sieber collapsed, one Chafee aide attended the patient, and another ran down the hall for the doctor Frist. To the astonishment of passers-by, Frist rushed out of his office, down the hall, and immediately began mouth-to-mouth cardiopulmonary resuscitation. On his knees, he inserted a plastic tube through Sieber's windpipe directly into his lungs, injected drugs directly into his veins, and, with a defibrillator brought by the Capitol physician's office, successfully shocked Sieber's heart back to life. When Frist visited Sieber in the hospital a few days later, Sieber expressed gratitude to the Senator who had saved his life, but quickly reminded him why he had come to Washington. "Remember, doc, I want you to help my boys back at home."

It took a senseless act of violence to bring Frist's surgical acumen to national attention. In the mid-afternoon of Friday, July 24, 1998, he learned that something terrible had occurred at the Capitol. He called the Capitol physician's office and was told that two people had been shot. Frist immediately sprinted to the Capitol. Soon, he learned that there were four victims. The first person he reached in the Capitol building was Officer Jacob J. ("J. J.") Chestnut, who had been fatally shot in the head. Frist, monitoring Chestnut's heart, evacuated him by stretcher and initiated CPR in the ambulance when Chestnut's heart stopped. After other medics and physicians took over CPR, Frist ran back into the Capitol to the scene of the shooting to treat the next patient, who unbeknownst to him, was the alleged assassin. For Frist, the man's identity was immaterial. "I am trained to take care of the patient," he told reporters later. "I'm not the judge. I'm not the jury. I'm the physician." Frist managed the patient's multiple wounds and kept his heart and lungs working until they arrived at D.C. General Hospital.

While I have never observed one of Bill Frist's operations, I can attest to his bedside manner. The day the Senator called to invite me to collaborate with him on this project was the day of my father's funeral. I'd been up late the night before planning the service, getting the next day's lecture to a substitute, and writing the eulogy. I wasn't answering when he called, and he, upon hearing the message, was sensitive enough to the circumstances to hang up without leaving his name or number. Once I awoke, I used the *69 feature on my phone to redial a Washington number I did not know. Having met the Senator only once, I did not recognize his voice when he answered. I indeed thought I may have reached a friend of my dad's or an irate parent of one of my less successful students. I went on to explain to him the *69 feature. Being accustomed to beepers, he still thought he had not called. Then I told him who I was, and I heard a man with a boyish southern drawl shout back, "LEE! This is Bill Frist. Did Ah hear your message right? Did your dad die yesterday?" "Yessir," I replied in a weary tone. "Well," he replied, "you're going to be in our prayers tonight."

Even though he and I do not agree on every issue, Frist's words showed me a mature and sensitive perspective on the important things in life. It's one

I suspect that will keep him providing *pro bono* medical services as long as he stays in another line of work. And it's one that will keep him in search of different challenges for the rest of his life. How can he best serve others, he will continue to ask, and he will come to different conclusions over the next quarter century. Stay tuned!

Epilogue

Before any Tennessee Senators of today—or *tomorrow*—can answer the pressing questions of the present, he or she must first understand the history of our past—the strength and substance of our leaders, the character and quality of our people—and the relevance both have to our future.

In many ways, we Tennesseans are not unlike millions of other Americans who have made our Nation special—men and women who, while they may never realize their own dreams, are nevertheless content to reinvest those dreams in their children.

Yet it is precisely those dreams and that spirit that not only characterizes our past but distinguishes our citizens right up to the present day. For Tennessee is a place where family still counts, community is still important, and that distinctive yet tangible quality known as the American spirit still exists, nourished by long tradition and carried on by the countless, everyday heroes of American life—neighbors who help neighbors, parents who sacrifice for their children, church and community volunteers who care for the needy and nurse the sick. It is a place where people are proud of their past and optimistic about their future.

Not surprisingly, Tennesseans have sent to Washington people who represent those hopes and dreams, and characterize that spirit.

It is a spirit exemplified by the independence and principled courage of Luke Lea, the persistent energy and integrity of Kenneth McKellar, the vision and example of Will Brock, the idealism of Cordell Hull, the hard-working drive and humility of Tom Stewart, the honest sincerity and frontier fighting spirit of Estes Kefauver, the simple virtue of Herbert Walters, the practical politics of Bill Brock, and the homespun common sense of Fred Thompson.

Together, they—and all who have represented Tennessee over the last hundred years—paint the history of a people who represent the heart and soul and essence of America.

Bernard Baruch once wrote that America has never forgotten things that brought her into being and that light her path. Those "nobler things" live on and prosper in Tennessee, thanks in no small measure to the men who have represented her in the U.S. Senate.

My job, and that of my contemporaries, is to carry that precious legacy forward into a new century and a new millennium so that all future generations of Tennesseans may sing as we do today.

From the Smokie Mountain Mornings to the Mississippi shores
Let's take time to remember those who went before
Whose lives made a difference in the work for you and me
Their courage, faith and vision are the Pride of Tennessee.

—"The Pride of Tennessee"
by Fred Congdon, Thomas Vaughn, and Carol Elliott
Adopted as Tennessee official state song in 1996

Sources

Two reference volumes which served as valuable sources and guides to our research were *Senators of the United States: a historical bibliography: a compilation of works by and about members of the United States Senate, 1789–1995*, compiled by Jo Anne McCormick Quatannens and Diane B. Boyle (editorial assistant), and prepared under the direction of Kelly D. Johnston, Secretary of the Senate (1995, U.S. Government Printing Office); and *Guide to Research Collections of former United States Senators, 1789–1995: a listing of archival repositories housing the papers of former senators, related collections, and oral history interviews*, compiled by Karen Dawley Paul (Senate Archivist) and Diane B. Boyle (editorial assistant), and prepared under the direction of Kelly D. Johnston, Secretary of the Senate (1995, U.S. Government Printing Office).

Another valuable reference has been *The Tennessee Encyclopedia of History and Culture*, Carroll Van West, editor-in-chief (Tennessee Historical Society, Nashville, 1998).

We've relied upon the *Congressional Quarterly*, the weekly that has chronicled congressional activities since 1945, and the *Congressional Record*. On more recent Senators, we've used the fourteen biennial editions of Michael Barone's and Grant Ujifusa's *The Almanac of American Politics* and the eight editions of *Congressional Quarterly*'s equally authoritative *Politics in America*. In addition, we've found most useful the collections of clippings of newspaper articles stored in the Hamilton County Bicentennial Library in Chattanooga (largely of the *News-Free Press* and the *Times*), the Franklin County Library in Winchester, the Lawrence County Library in Lawrenceburg, the Lawson-McGhee Library in Knoxville (largely of the *News-Sentinel* and the now defunct *Journal*), the Senate Historical Office in Washington, the main Shelby County Library in Memphis (largely of the *Commercial Appeal* and the *Press-Scimitar*), the Nashville Room of the main Davidson County Public Library in Nashville (largely of the *Banner* and the *Tennessean*), the Tennessee State Library and Archives, and the *Washington Star* collection in the Martin Luther King, Jr. Library in Washington, D.C.

For those envisioning more concentrated research on one or more of our sub-jects, we heartily recommend these depositories as starting points.

Works we've used for our introduction include Taylor Branch, *Parting the Waters: America in the King Years, 1954–63* (New York, 1988); Robert E. Cor-lew, *Tennessee: The Volunteer State* (Northridge, 1989); Pete Daniel, *The Shadow of Slavery: Peonage in the South, 1901–1969* (Urbana, 1972) and *Breaking the Land: The Transformation of Cotton, Tobacco, and Rice Cultures since 1880* (Urbana, 1985); Wilma Dykeman, "Too Much Talent in Tennessee," *Harper's Magazine* 210 (March 1955), 48–53; David Halberstam, *The Children* (New York, 1998); Charles W. Johnson, "War Comes to Wheat," Wali R. Kharif, "School Desegregation in Clinton, Tennessee," and George C. Webb, "Origins of the Scopes Trial," thus in Larry H. Whiteaker and W. Calvin Dickinson (eds.), *Tennessee in American History* (Needham Heights, 1991); Jeanette Keith, *Country People in the New South: Tennessee's Upper Cumberland* (Chapel Hill, 1995); Jack Temple Kirby, *Rural Worlds Lost: The American South, 1920–1960* (Baton Rouge, 1987); Bill C. Malone, *Country Music, U.S.A.* (Austin, 1985); Aldon D. Morris, *The Origins of the Civil Rights Movement: Black Communities Organizing for Change* (New York, 1984); Gunnar Myrdal, with the assistance of Richard Sterner and Arnold Rose, *An American Dilemma: The Negro Prob-lem and Modern Democracy* (New York, 1944); W.B. Ragsdale, "Three Weeks in Dayton," *American Heritage* 26, no. 4 (June 1975), 38–103; George O. Robin-son, *The Oak Ridge Story: The Saga of a People Who Share in History* (Kingsport, 1950); Carl T. Rowan with a New Introduction by Douglas Brinkley, *South of Freedom* (Baton Rouge, 1997); Harvard Sitkoff, *The Struggle for Black Equality* (New York, 1981); Robert Sobel, *They Satisfy: The Cigarette in Ameri-can Life* (Garden City, 1978); James Summerville, *Educating Black Doctors: A History of Meharry Medical College* (University, Alabama, 1983); George B. Tin-dall, *The Emergence of the New South, 1913–1945* (Baton Rouge, 1967); Twelve Southerners, *I'll Take My Stand: The South and the Agrarian Tradition, by Twelve Southerners* (New York, 1930); Pat Watters, *The South and the Nation* (New York, 1969); John R. Vile and Mark Byrnes, eds., *Tennessee Government and Politics* (Nashville, 1998); and C. Vann Woodward, *The Origins of the New South, 1877–1913* (Baton Rouge, 1951).

HOWARD H. BAKER, JR.

For the chapter on Howard Baker, documentation can be found in J. Lee Annis, Jr., *Howard Baker: Conciliator in an Age of Crisis* (Lanham, MD, 1995), and "Howard H. Baker, Jr.: A Public Biography" (unpublished Ph.D. dissertation, Ball State University, 1985). The material we've added can be found in the recently opened papers of Senator Baker at the University of Tennessee, Knoxville, and those of Howard Liebengood, his longtime aide, at the Library of Congress. Per-haps the best account of Howard's wedding to Nancy Kassebaum can be found in "United State," *People* (Dec. 23, 1996).

ROSS BASS

The papers of Ross Bass have been destroyed, although there are some tapes of campaign commercials and a commemorative dinner stored at the Martin Methodist College library in Pulaski. For accounts of the two Bass campaigns for the Senate, see Annis on *Howard Baker* and Lee S. Greene, *Lead Me On: Frank Goad Clement and Tennessee Politics* (Knoxville, 1982).

GEORGE L. BERRY

Material on George Berry is scattered, but the most complete accounts of his work in the labor movement can be found in Elizabeth Faulkner Baker, *Printers and Technology* (New York, 1957) and Jack Mooney, *Printers in Appalachia: The International Printing Pressmen and Assistants' Union of North America, 1907–1967* (Bowling Green, Ohio, 1993). We've scanned the contemporary accounts of the 1924 Democratic convention in the *New York Times*, but the most complete account of that melee can be found in Robert K. Murray, *The 103rd Ballot* (New York, 1976). Other short references to Berry can be found in the unpublished chapter for Kenneth McKellar's first edition of this work stored in the McKellar Papers in the Memphis Public Library; Bernard Bellush, *The Failure of the NRA* (New York, 1975); Irving Bernstein, *The Lean Years: A History of the American Worker, 1920–1933* (Boston, 1960); Alan Brinkley, *The End of Reform: New Deal Liberalism in Recession and War* (New York, 1995); Donald Davidson, *The Tennessee*, Vol. 2. *The New River: Civil War to TVA* (New York, 1948); James A. Hodges, *New Deal Labor Policy and the Cotton Textile Industry* (Knoxville, 1986); William E. Leuchtenburg, *Franklin D. Roosevelt and the New Deal, 1932–1940* (New York, 1963); William R. Majors, *The End of Arcadia: Gordon Browning and Tennessee Politics* (Memphis, 1982); George Martin, *Madam Secretary, Frances Perkins* (Boston, 1976); John Dean Minton, *The New Deal in Tennessee* (New York, 1979); Ronald Radosh, *American Labor and United States Foreign Policy* (New York, 1969); Martha H. Swain, *Pat Harrison: The New Deal Years* (Jackson, Miss., 1978); Arthur M. Schlesinger, Jr., *The Politics of Upheaval* (Boston, 1978); Thomas T. Spencer, "Printer and Politician: The Political Career of George L. Berry, 1907–1948," *Tennessee Historical Quarterly* 17 (Fall 1997), 212–229; and Philip Taft, *Organized Labor in American History* (New York, 1964).

WILLIAM (WILL) E. BROCK

The best source of information on the first William E. Brock is the file of clippings on him in the Hamilton County Bicentennial Library in Chattanooga. Other information can be found in David Lee, *Tennessee in Turmoil: Politics in the Volunteer State, 1920–1932* (Memphis, 1979); James W. Livingood, *A History of Hamilton County, Tennessee* (Memphis, 1981); Nannie M. Tilley, *The R. J. Reynolds Tobacco Co.* (Chapel Hill, 1985); and George B. Tindall, *The Emergence of the New South, 1913–1945* (Baton Rouge, 1979).

WILLIAM (BILL) E. BROCK, III

The best sources on the congressional service of Bill Brock are Helene Lecar and Catherine Bell, *William E. Brock III* (New York, 1972), a work conducted by Ralph Nader's Congress Watch organization, and the oral history Brock recorded with the Former Members of Congress in February 1979 that is stored in the Library of Congress. See also Steven E. Ambrose, *Nixon: Ruin and Recovery, 1962–1972* (New York, 1991); Bill Brock, "Committees in the Senate," *American Academy of Political and Social Sciences* (Jan. 1974), 15–26; James Cannon, *Time and Chance: Gerald Ford's Appointment With History* (New York, 1994); Lee Edwards, *Goldwater* (Washington, 1995); and Bob Woodward and Carl Bernstein, *The Final Days* (New York, 1975). For Brock's work in building the Tennessee Republican Party, see J. Lee Annis, Jr., "Whiggery Redux: The Rise of the Tennessee Republican Party, 1945–1970" (forthcoming); Jack Bass and Walter DeVries, *The Transformation of Southern Politics: Social Change and Political Consequence Since 1945* (New York, 1976) and the interviews Bass and DeVries conducted with Brock and others in preparing that book, which are stored in the Southern Historical Collection at the University of North Carolina; Larry Daughtrey, "Tennessee," *New Republic* (Oct. 30, 1976), 19; Richard Harris, "How the People Feel," *The New Yorker* (July 10, 1971), 34–54; Alexander Lamis, *A Two Party South* (New York, 1984); Reg Murphy and Hal Gulliver, *Southern Strategy* (New York, 1970); Neil R. Peirce, *The Border South States; People, Politics, and Power in the Five Border South States* (New York, 1975); "Tennessee: Moderates and Wallace-Voters-to Brock or Gore?," *Ripon Forum* (July 8, 1970), 33–36; and "Tennessee's William Brock," *Time* (Nov. 16, 1970), 18–19. For his work as Republican Party National Chairman, see Ken Bode, "Mating Dance," *New Republic* (May 6, 1978), 6–9; Lou Cannon, *Reagan* (New York, 1982); Alan Crawford, *Thunder on the Right* (New York, 1980); "Everyone's Second Choice," *Time* (Jan. 24, 1977), 19; Morton Kondracke, "Is Ronnie Going Soft," *New Republic* (July 5–12, 1980), and "The GOP Gets Their Act Together," *New York Times Magazine* (July 13, 1980), 18–24; Lyn Nofziger, *Nofziger* (Washington, 1992); "Now Republicans Map a Comeback," *US News and World Report* (Jan. 31, 1977), 56; Joseph Persico, *Casey: From the OSS to the CIA* (New York, 1990), and "The GOP Renaissance Man," *Newsweek* (May 26, 1980), 34–37. For Brock's work as U.S. Trade Representative, see Steve Dryden, *Trade Warriors: USTR and the American Crusaders for Free Trade* (New York, 1995) and Clyde H. Farnsworth, "William Brock, Our Man for Trade," *New York Times Magazine* (Jan. 13, 1983), 126–140. For his transfer to the Labor Secretaryship, see the periodicals of the week of April 1, 1985, and Ed Rollins and Thomas W. DeFrank, *Bare Knuckles and Back Rooms* (New York, 1996). The best academic treatment of Brock's secretaryship can be found in William C. Buhl, "Transforming Leadership in a Political Environment: A Case Study of William Brock at the Department of Labor" (Ph.D. dissertation, University of Southern California, 1989), but see also Bill Brock, "Workforce 2000 Agenda Recognizes Lifelong Need to Improve Skills," *Monthly Labor Review* (Feb. 1988), 54–56. The best weekly coverage of the Labor Department during Brock's tenure can be found in *Business Week*. For his work as Bob Dole's campaign manager, see Jack Germond and Jules Witcover, *Whose Broad Stripes and Bright Stars? The Trivial Pursuit of the Presidency, 1988* (New York, 1989) and Peter Goldman, Tom Mathews and the *Newsweek* Special Election Team, *The Quest for the Presidency* (New York, 1989). For Brock's work with educational groups since 1988, see Gisela Bolte, "Will Americans Work for $5 A Day," *Time* (July 23, 1990), 12; Ray Marshall and Marc Tucker, *Thinking for a Living: Education and the Wealth of Nations* (New York, 1992); and John R. McKernan, Jr., *Making the Grade* (Boston, 1994). For Brock's Maryland Senate campaign, see the *Washington Post* for 1994.

WILLIAM (BILL) H. FRIST

For the chapter on Bill Frist, Lee Annis has used the usual array of clippings and snippets from *Congressional Record* and *Congressional Quarterly* as well as a multitude of documents from Frist's office files. Future researchers should begin their work with William H. Frist, *Transplant: A Heart Surgeon's Account of the Life-and-Death Dramas of the New Medicine* (New York, 1989), the Senator's nonfiction narrative that treats the ethical, social and economic issues of transplantation from the perspective of his personal training and practice as a heart and lung transplant surgeon; "Health Care Hall of Fame: Thomas F. Frist," *Modern Healthcare* (Sept. 10, 1990), David Beiler, "Surgical Precision. How Senate Power Jim Sasser was Stomped by a Political Novice in Tennessee," *Campaigns & Elections* (Apr. 1995); and, "Senator, Formerly a Researcher, Gets a Key Role in Setting U.S. Science Policy," *Chronicle of Higher Education* (Feb. 28, 1997). For further research on the Senate confirmation hearings of Henry W. Foster, Jr., M.D. the reader is directed to Dr. Foster's autobiography *Make a Difference*, with Alice Greenwood (New York, 1997).

ALBERT A. GORE, SR.

All research on Albert Gore, Sr., should start with his two semiautobiographical works, *Let the Glory Out; My South and its Politics* (New York, 1972) and *The Eye of the Storm: A Peoples Politics for the Seventies* (New York, 1970). Thereafter, one should turn to a splendid and thoughtful work by James Bailey Gardner, "Political Leadership in a Period of Transition: Frank G. Clement, Albert Gore, Estes Kefauver and Tennessee Politics, 1948–1956" (Ph.D. dissertation, Vanderbilt University, 1978). The 1976 interviews Dr. Gardner and Dewey Grantham conducted with the elder Gore are transcribed and maintained in the Southern Historical Collection at the University of North Carolina, as are a series of interviews Jack Bass and Walter DeVries conducted for their *The Transformation of Southern Politics: Social Change and Political Consequences Since 1945* (New York, 1976) that relate to Gore. The best lode of material on Gore can be found at the Gore Center at Middle Tennessee State University in Murfreesboro. We've found particularly valuable the transcripts of the weekly reports to his constituents Gore delivered over WSM Radio in the 1940s, the tape of a public television interview recorded on March 2, 1984, in which Gore shared his recollections, and that of a symposium commemorating the Senator's career held at MTSU on November 8, 1997. We encourage future researchers to consult with Jim Neal, the Gore Center's director, who has made that repository more user friendly than any other of its kind. Other works we've found helpful for understanding Gore are Louise Davis, "Tales of a Combative Hillbilly," *Nashville Tennessean Magazine* (March 22 and 29, 1970); Rowland Evans, Jr. and Robert D. Novak, *Nixon in the White House* (New York, 1972); Hugh D. Graham, *Crisis in Print: Desegregation and the Press in Tennessee* (Nashville, 1967); David Halberstam, "The End of a Populist," *Harper's* (Jan. 1971), 35–45; Richard Harris, "How the People Feel," *New Yorker* (July 10, 1971), 34–54; Harry McPherson, *A Political Education* (Boston, 1972); George Morris, "The Pride of Possum Hollow," *Colliers* (May 23, 1942), 23–24, 44; Dan Murph, "The Special Bond Between a Father and a Son," *Tennessee Monthly* (June 1996), 12–16; Richard Reeves, *President Kennedy: Profile of Power* (New York, 1993); Deborah Shapley, *Promise and Power: The Life and Times of Robert McNamara* (Boston, 1993); Richard Spohn and Charles McCollum, *The Revenue Committees* (New York, 1973); Tom Wicker, *JFK and LBJ: The Influence of Personality in Politics* (New York, 1968) and *One of Us: Richard Nixon and the American Dream* (New York, 1991); and Aaron Wildavsky, *Dixon-Yates: A Study in Power Politics* (New Haven, 1962).

ALBERT A. GORE, JR.

Research on Al Gore, Jr., should start with Hank Hillin, *Al Gore Jr.: His Life and Career* (Secaucus, 1992), a superb campaign biography. Gore and his wife Tipper have produced a book apiece. His is the best-seller *Earth in the Balance: Ecology and the Human Spirit* (Boston, 1992). Hers is *Raising PG Kids in an X-Rated World* (Nashville, 1987). Other works we consulted include Joseph Barnes, "Southern Strategy," *National Journal* (Dec. 5, 1987), 3078–3080; Tucker Carlson, "The Real Al Gore," *Weekly Standard* (May 19, 1997), 15–22; Jack Germond and Jules Witcover, *Whose Broad Stripes and Bright Stars? The Trivial Pursuit of the Presidency, 1988* (New York, 1989) and *Mad As Hell: Revolt at the Ballot Box, 1992* (New York, 1993); Alex S. Jones, "Al Gore's Double Life," *New York Times Magazine* (Oct. 25, 1992), 40–80; Daniel Klaidman and Karen Breslau, "The Trouble With Al," *Newsweek* (Sept. 22, 1997), 39–40; David Maraniss and Michael Weisskopf, *Tell Newt to Shut Up* (New York, 1996); Mary Matalin and James Carville with Peter Knobler, *All's Fair* (New York, 1994); Dick Morris, *Behind the Oval Office* (New York, 1997); Timothy Noah, "Albert the Brainiac," *US News and World Report* (Jan. 27, 1988), 38–44; William O'Rourke, *Campaign America '96: The View From the Couch* (New York, 1997); Dan Quayle, *Standing Firm* (New York, 1994); William Schneider, "Simon, Gore: What You See Isn't What You Get," *National Journal* (Dec. 5, 1987), 3095–3098; Strobe Talbott, "Trying to Set Himself Apart," *Time* (Oct. 19, 1987), 17–18; Karen Tumulty, "But Will It Hurt Al," *Time* (Apr. 28, 1997), 46–47; Martin Walker, *The President We Deserve: Bill Clinton: His Rise, Falls and Comebacks* (New York, 1996); Curtis Wilkie, "Every Which Way But Loose," *Southern* (Dec. 1988), 26–29, 60; E. Thomas Wood, "Al Gore: Boy Reporter," *Nashville Scene* (Sept. 17, 1992), 10–13;

and Bob Woodward, *The Agenda: Inside the Clinton White House* (New York, 1994) and *The Choice* (New York, 1996).

CORDELL HULL

Material on Cordell Hull is extensive. One must start with his two volumes of *Memoirs* (New York, 1948); Robert Dallek, *Franklin D. Roosevelt and American Foreign Policy, 1932–1945* (New York, 1979); Donald Drummond, "Cordell Hull" in Norman A. Graebner (ed.), *An Uneasy Tradition: American Secretaries of State in the Twentieth Century* (New York, 1961), 184–209, and Irwin Gellman, *Secret Affairs: Franklin D. Roosevelt, Cordell Hull and Sumner Welles* (Baltimore, 1995). Other helpful works include Alben Barkley, *That Reminds Me* (Garden City, New York, 1954); Will Brownell and Richard N. Billings, *So Close to Greatness: A Biography of William C. Bullitt* (New York, 1987); James MacGregor Burns, *Roosevelt: The Lion and the Fox, 1882–1940* (New York, 1956); Sean Dennis Cashman, *America, Roosevelt and World War II* (New York, 1989); Wayne S. Cole, *Roosevelt and the Isolationists, 1932–1945* (Lincoln, Nebraska, 1983); Margaret Coit, *Mr. Baruch* (Boston, 1957); Tom Connally as told to Alfred Steinberg, *My Name is Tom Connally* (New York, 1954); John Costello, *Days of Infamy* (New York, 1994); Robert A. Divine, *The Reluctant Belligerent: American Entry Into World War II* (New York, 1965); Herbert Feis, *The Road to Pearl Harbor* (Princeton, 1950); John Lewis Gaddis, *The United States and the Origins of the Cold War* (New York, 1972); Lloyd C. Gardner, *Economic Aspects of New Deal Diplomacy* (Boston, 1964); Philip A. Grant, Jr., "Tennesseans in the 63rd Congress, 1913–1915," *Tennessee Historical Quarterly* 29 (1970), 281–285; Waldo Heinrichs, *Threshhold to War* (New York, 1988); Walter Isaacson and Evan Thomas, *The Wise Men: Six Friends and the World They Made: Acheson, Bohlen, Harriman, Kennan, Lovett, McCloy* (New York, 1986); Manfred E. Jonas, *The United States and Germany: A Diplomatic History* (Ithaca, New York, 1984); Herbert S. Parmet and Marie B. Hecht, *Never Again: A President Runs for a Third Term* (New York, 1968); Thomas G. Paterson et al., *American Foreign Policy*, Volume II, Third Edition (Lexington, Massachusetts, 1988); Dexter Perkins, *The New Age of Franklin D. Roosevelt* (Chicago, 1957); Robert E. Sherwood, *Roosevelt & Hopkins* (New York, 1948); Gaddis Smith, *American Diplomacy During the Second World War* (New York, 1965); Henry Stimson and McGeorge Bundy, *On Active Service in Peace and War* (New York, 1947); and Randall Woods, *Fulbright: A Biography* (New York, 1995).

C. ESTES KEFAUVER

There are two superb biographies of Estes Kefauver. Charles Fontenay was a reporter friendly to Kefauver whose *Estes Kefauver, A Biography* (Knoxville, 1980) provides the most intimate portrait of Kefauver we are likely to see. Joseph Gorman's *Kefauver: A Political Biography* (New York, 1971) is equally good, even if its focus is strictly political. For Kefauver's role in Tennessee politics, the best source is Gardner's "Political Leadership in a Time of Transition." Kefauver presented his ideas on congressional reform in Kefauver and Jack Levin, *A Twentieth-Century Congress* (New York, 1947). Treatments of his investigation into organized crime can be found in Jack Anderson and Fred Blumenthal, *The Kefauver Story* (New York, 1956), a campaign biography; David Halberstam, *The Fifties* (New York, 1993); James Kirby Martin et al., *America and its Peoples: A Mosaic in the Making* (New York, 1997), and W. H. Moore, *The Kefauver Committee and the Politics of Crime* (Columbia, Missouri, 1974). Other works we've found beneficial include Sherman Adams, *Firsthand Report* (New York, 1961); Jeff Broadwater, *Adlai Stevenson and American Politics* (New York, 1994); Douglas Cater, "Estes Kefauver: The Most Willing of the Willing," *The Reporter* (Nov. 3, 1955), 14–18; Estes Kefauver, "How Boss Crump Was Licked," *Colliers* (Oct. 16, 1948), 24–25; Allen H. Kitchins, "Political Upheavals in Tennessee: Boss Crump and the Senatorial Election of 1948," *West Tennessee Historical Society's Publications* 16 (1962), 104–114; Richard McFadyen, "Estes Kefauver and the Tradition of Southern Progressivism," *Tennessee Historical Quarterly* 37 (Winter 1978), 430–443; Porter McKeever, *Adlai Stevenson: His Life and Legacy* (New York, 1989); Merle Miller, *Lyndon, An Oral Biography* (New York, 1980); Neil MacNeil, *Dirksen* (New York, 1970); John Bartlow Martin, *Adlai Stevenson and the World* (New York, 1977); Herbert Parmet, *Jack: The Struggles of John F. Kennedy* (New York, 1980) and *The Democrats: The Years After FDR* (New York, 1976); George E. Reedy, *The U.S. Senate* (New York, 1986); Richard Langham Riedel, *Halls of the Mighty: My 47 Years at the Senate* (Washington, 1969); Edward L. and Frederick H. Schapsmeier, *Dirksen of Illinois* (Urbana, Illinois, 1985); and Theodore H. White, "Kefauver Rides Again, *Colliers* (May 11, 1956), 26–29. We also direct those embarking on their own research of the life of Kefauver especially to the Kefauver papers at the UT Library in Knoxville.

LUKE LEA

Luke Lea is best treated in Mary Louise Lea Tidwell, *Luke Lea of Tennessee* (Bowling Green, 1993), a loving and scholarly portrait by his daughter. Although understandably one-sided in some respects, Mrs. Tidwell's book can be relied upon with entire confidence as to matters of objective fact. Other works we've found helpful include the previously cited Hull, *Memoirs*, Volume I; Lee, *Tennessee in Turmoil*, and Majors, *End of Arcadia*, as well as William T. Alderson (ed.), Luke Lea, "The Attempt to Kill the Kaiser," *Tennessee Historical Quarterly* 21 (Fall 1961), 222–261; Everett Robert Boyce (ed.), Ben W. Hooper, *The Unwanted Boy: The Autobiography of Governor Ben W. Hooper* (Knoxville, 1963); Don H. Doyle, *Nashville Since the 1920s* (Knoxville, 1985); Paul E. Isaac, *Prohibition and Politics; Turbulent Decades in Tennessee, 1885–1920* (Knoxville, 1965); Arthur S. Link, "Democratic Politics and the Presidential Campaign of 1912 in Tennessee," *East Tennessee Historical Society's Publications* 2 (1946), 107–130; John Berry McFerrin, *Caldwell and Company, A Southern Financial Empire* (Chapel Hill, 1939); J. Winfield Qualls, "Fusion Victory and the Tennessee Senatorship," *West Tennessee Historical Society's Publications* 15 (1961),

79–92; Joe Michael Shahan, "Reform and Politics in Tennessee, 1906–1914" (Ph.D. dissertation, Vanderbilt University, 1981); James Summerville, *The Carmack-Cooper Shooting: Tennessee Politics Turns Violent, November 9, 1908* (Jefferson, North Carolina, 1994); Oscar Cromwell Tidwell, "Luke Lea and the American Legion," *Tennessee Historical Quarterly* 28 (Spring 1968), 70–83. For those beginning their own study of the life of Lea, the microfilmed papers of Luke Lea at the Tennessee State Library and Archives will provide a tremendous amount of information and insight.

HARLAN MATHEWS

Material on Harlan Mathews is drawn almost entirely from the *Record, Congressional Quarterly* and newspaper clippings and interviews, but there are also references to him in Greene's *Lead Me On.* Newspaper clippings included Duren Cheek, "Mathews Picked to Fill Gore's Seat," *Tennessean* (Dec. 29, 1992); Larry Daughtrey, "Can Mathews Thrive Outside of the Backroom," *Tennessean* (Apr. 18, 1993); Carrie Ferguson, "Politicians, Business Leaders Approve," *Tennessean* (Dec. 29, 1992); and Kimberly C. Moore, "Mathews Disproves 'Yes' Man Tag, *Nashville Banner* (July 28, 1993).

KENNETH D. MCKELLAR

Easily the best starting points for research upon Kenneth McKellar are the forerunner and inspiration for this volume—McKellar's own *Tennessee Senators as Seen by One of Their Successors* (Kingsport, 1942); and Robert Dean Pope, "Senatorial Baron: The Long Political Career of Kenneth D. McKellar" (Ph.D. dissertation, Yale University, 1976), and "The Senator from Tennessee," *West Tennessee Historical Society's Publications* 22 (1968), 102–123. McKellar's voluminous papers are stored in the Shelby County Public Library on Front Street in Memphis, and we've merely sampled them, particularly his correspondence with Ed Crump. Other works strictly devoted to McKellar include a chapter in Allan A. Michie and Frank Ryhlick, *Dixie Demagogues* (New York, 1939); Edward Felsenthal, "Kenneth D. McKellar: The Rich Uncle of the TVA," *West Tennessee Historical Society's Publications* 20 (1966), 108–122; Russell Walter Menk, "Senator Kenneth McKellar and the TVA," (M.A. thesis, University of Maryland, 1966); and Robert Ellis Thiel's quite thorough "Kenneth D. McKellar and the Politics of the TVA, 1941–1946 (M.A. thesis, University of Virginia, 1967). For McKellar's relationship with Boss Ed Crump, see Lyle Dorsett, *Franklin D. Roosevelt and the City Bosses* (Port Washington, New York, 1977); William D. Miller, *Mr. Crump of Memphis* (Baton Rouge, 1964); and Alfred Steinberg, *The Bosses* (New York, 1974). For material on McKellar and TVA, see Wilmon Henry Droze, *High Dams and Slack Waters: TVA Rebuilds a River* (Baton Rouge, 1965); Preston J. Hubbard, *Origins of the TVA: The Muscle Shoals Controversy, 1920–1932* (New York, 1968); David E. Lilienthal, *The Journals of David E. Lilienthal,* Volume I, *The TVA Years* (New York, 1964); Thomas K. McCraw, *TVA and the Power Fight,*

1933–1938, (Philadelphia, 1971); Steven M. Neuse, *David E. Lilienthal: The Journey of an American Liberal* (Knoxville, 1996); and Marguerite Owen, *The Tennessee Valley Authority* (New York, 1973). Other works with valuable information on McKellar include Alben Barkley, *That Reminds Me* (Garden City, New York, 1954); Roger Biles, *Memphis in the Great Depression* (Knoxville, 1985); Allen Drury, *A Senate Journal, 1943–1945* (New York, 1963); the previously cited Gardner, "Political Leadership in a Time of Transition"; David Lee, *Tennessee in Turmoil: Politics in the Volunteer State, 1920–1932* (Memphis, 1979); William R. Majors, *The End of Arcadia: Gordon Browning and Tennessee Politics* (Memphis, 1982); Jennings Perry, *Democracy Begins at Home, The Tennessee Fight on the Poll Tax* (Philadelphia, 1944); Richard Langham Riedel, *Halls of the Mighty; My 47 Years at the Senate* (Washington, 1969); William S. White, *Citadel: The Story of the U.S. Senate* (New York, 1954); and T. Harry Williams, *Huey Long* (New York, 1969).

JAMES R. SASSER

The best sources on Jim Sasser are the usual ones: the *Record, Congressional Quarterly*, and the clipping collections in Tennessee libraries. Some material on his chairmanship of the Tennessee Democratic Party can be found in the interviews conducted by Jack Bass and Walter DeVries that are kept in the Southern Historical Collection at the University of North Carolina. Worthwhile on his election to the Senate are Larry Daughtrey, "Tennessee," *New Republic* (Oct. 30, 1976), 19 and "Tennessee: *Brock v. Sasser*," *Time* (Oct. 18, 1976), 39. Other sources we've found valuable include Ethan Bronner, *Battle for Justice: How the Bork Nomination Shook America* (New York, 1989; Jimmy Carter, *Keeping Faith* (New York, 1982); Lawrence J. Haas, "Cautious Populist," *National Journal* (Apr. 14, 1989), 914–918; George Hager, "True to Form, Sasser's Bid Required a Little Budging," *Congressional Quarterly* (June 11, 1994), 1495–1498; and Jim Wright, *Worth It All: My War for Peace* (Washington, 1993).

A. THOMAS (TOM) STEWART

Outside of the *Record*, the best mine of information on A. T. "Tom" Stewart lies in scrapbooks of clippings and campaign materials kept in the offices of Chancellor Jeff Stewart in Winchester and in the Stewart file of the correspondence of Hub Walters in the UTK Library. For material on the Scopes trial, see L. Sprague de Camp, *The Great Monkey Trial* (Garden City, New York, 1968); Paul K. Conkin, *When All the Gods Trembled: Darwinism, Scopes, and American Intellectuals* (Lanham, Md., 1997); Willard B. Gatewood, Jr. (ed.), *Fundamentalism, Modernism, and Evolution* (Nashville, 1969); Ray L. Ginger, *Six Days or Forever? Tennessee v. John Thomas Scopes* (Boston, 1958); Louis W. Koenig, *Bryan: A Political Biography of William Jennings Bryan* (New York, 1971); Edward J. Larson, *Summer for the Gods: The Scopes Trial and America's Continuing Debate Over Science and Religion* (New York, 1997). W. B. Ragsdale, "Three Weeks in Dayton," *American Heritage* 26, no. 4 (June 1975), 38–103; John T. Scopes and James

Presley, *Center of the Storm; Memoirs of John T. Scopes* (New York, 1967); Jerry R. Tompkins (ed.), *D-Days at Dayton: Reflections on the Scopes Trial* (Baton Rouge, 1965), and *The World's Most Famous Court Trial: State of Tennessee v. John Thomas Scopes* (New York, 1971). For a brief treatment of Stewart's position on the Japanese-American relocation issue, see Page Smith, *Democracy on Trial: The Japanese-American Evacuation and Relocation in World War II* (New York, 1995).

FRED D. THOMPSON

We are grateful to the office of Fred Thompson for allowing us the use of some biographical pieces that supplement the sources we've ordinarily relied upon. For Fred's role in the Watergate investigation, see his intriguing *At That Point in Time* (New York, 1975) as well as Annis, *Howard Baker* and Samuel Dash, *Chief Counsel* (New York, 1976). For his representation of Marie Ragghianti, see the film *Marie* or read Peter Maas, *Marie* (New York, 1982) and "Watergate Lawyer Fred Thompson Is Perfect for His Role in *Marie*; After All, He Plays Himself," *People* (Nov. 11, 1985), 119–120. For the Thompson Committee probe of the campaign financing abuses of 1996, we've relied upon the daily reporting of the *New York Times*, the *Washington Post*, and the *Washington Times* and Andrew Ferguson's pieces in the *Weekly Standard*. For other facets of Fred's career, see David R. Beiler, "The Senator from Central Casting," *Ripon Forum* (Jan.–Feb. 1995), 6–11; Howard Fineman and Michael Isikoff, "Now, the Role of a Lifetime," *Newsweek* (July 14, 1997), 30–34; Kent Jenkins, Jr., "What Is Thompson Aiming For," *U.S. News and World Report* (July 14, 1997), 18–21; Haynes Johnson and David S. Broder, *The System: The American Way of Politics at the Breaking Point* (Boston, 1996); Jill Lawrence, "Senator Style: Is White House Next? Don't Bet Against Him, Many Say," *USA Today* (Feb. 14, 1997); and Karen Tumulty, "Perfectly in Character," *Newsweek* (Dec. 9, 1996), 41–42.

HERBERT ("HUB") S. WALTERS

The best storehouse for information on Herbert "Mr. Hub" Walters is his papers at the University of Tennessee, Knoxville, but we also consulted Howard L. Hill's hagiographic *The Herbert Walters Story* (Kingsport, 1963). And as with so many matters of Tennessee's not-too-distant past, we advise scholars in the next few years to consult Howard Baker, who served as CEO of Colonial Gas while Walters was its chairman of the board, and Bob Clement, who looked upon Walters as virtually a third grandfather.

Photo Credits

The following photographs were provided courtesy of the U.S. Senate Historical Office: Howard H. Baker, Jr.; Ross Bass; George L. Berry; William E. Brock; William E. Brock, III; Albert A. Gore, Sr.; Albert A. Gore, Jr.; Cordell Hull; C. Estes Kefauver; Luke Lea; Harlan Mathews; Kenneth D. McKellar; James R. Sasser; A. Thomas Stewart; Herbert S. Walters.

The photographs of Fred D. Thompson and William H. Frist were provided courtesy of the Senators.

Appendix I

Tennessee
U.S. Senators

Class One: *The Cocke Seat*

Congress	Senator	Party	Commencement of Term	End of Service	Remarks
4th	William Cocke	R	Aug. 2, 1796	March 3, 1797	Appointed by governor to fill vacancy
5th	William Cocke	R	April 22, 1797	Sept. 26, 1797	Resigned from office
5th	Andrew Jackson	R	Sept. 26, 1797	April 1798	Appointed by governor to fill vacancy
5th	Daniel Smith	R	Oct. 6, 1798	March 3, 1799	Appointed by governor to fill vacancy
6th–10th	Joseph Anderson	R	March 4, 1799	March 3, 1809	
11th	Joseph Anderson	R	March 4, 1809	April 10, 1809	Appointed by governor to fill vacancy
11th–13th	Joseph Anderson	R	April 11, 1809	March 3, 1815	
14th–15th	George W. Campbell	R	Oct. 10, 1815	April 20, 1818	Resigned from office
15th–16th	John H. Eaton	R	Sept. 5, 1818	Oct. 8, 1819	Appointed by governor to fill vacancy
16th–21st	John H. Eaton	R, JR, J	Oct. 9, 1819	March 9, 1829	Resigned from office
21st–25th	Felix Grundy	J, D	Oct. 19, 1829	July 4, 1838	Resigned from office to become Attorney general of the United States
25th	Ephraim H. Foster	W	Sept. 17, 1838	March 3, 1839	
26th	Felix Grundy	D	Dec. 14, 1839	Dec. 19, 1840	Died while in office
26th–27th	Alfred O. P. Nicholson	D	Dec. 25, 1840	Feb. 7, 1842	Appointed by governor to fill vacancy
28th	Ephraim H. Foster	W	Oct. 17, 1843	March 3, 1845	
29th–31st	Hopkins L. Turney	D	March 4, 1845	March 3, 1851	
32nd–34th	James C. Jones	W, OP	March 4, 1851	March 3, 1857	
35th–37th	Andrew Johnson	D	Oct. 8, 1857	March 4, 1862	Resigned from office to become military governor of Tennessee during the Civil War. Vacancy until July 24, 1866, when Tennessee was readmitted to the Union.
39th–40th	David T. Patterson	U, D	July 24, 1866	March 3, 1869	
41st–43rd	William G. Brownlow	R	March 4, 1869	March 3, 1875	

Class One: *The Cocke Seat (Continued)*

Congress	Senator	Party	Commencement of Term	End of Service	Remarks
44th	Andrew Johnson	D	March 4, 1875	July 31, 1875	Died while in office
44th	David M. Key	D	Aug. 18, 1875	Jan. 19, 1877	Appointed by governor to fill vacancy
44th–46th	James E. Bailey	D	Jan. 19, 1877	March 3, 1881	
47th–49th	Howell E. Jackson	D	March 4, 1881	April 14, 1886	Resigned from office
49th	Washington C. Whitthorne	D	April 16, 1886	March 3, 1887	Appointed by governor to fill vacancy
50th–59th	William B. Bate	D	March 4, 1887	March 9, 1905	Died while in office
59th–61st	James B. Frazier	D	March 21, 1905	March 3, 1911	
62nd–64th	Luke Lea	D	March 4, 1911	March 3, 1917	
65th–82nd	Kenneth D. McKellar	D	March 4, 1917	Jan. 2, 1953	
83rd–91st	Albert A. Gore, Sr.	D	Jan. 3, 1953	Jan. 2, 1971	
92nd–94th	William E. Brock, III	R	Jan. 3, 1971	Jan. 2, 1977	
95th–103rd	James R. Sasser	D	Jan. 3, 1977	Jan. 2, 1995	
104th–106th	William H. Frist	R	Jan. 3, 1995		

Class Two: *The Blount Seat*

Congress	Senator	Party	Commencement of Term	End of Service	Remarks
4th–5th	William Blount	R	Aug. 2, 1796	July 8, 1797	Expelled from office
5th	Joseph Anderson	R	Sept. 26, 1797	March 3, 1799	
6th–8th	William Cocke	R	March 4, 1799	March 3, 1805	
9th–11th	Daniel Smith	R	March 4, 1805	March 31, 1809	Resigned from office
11th–12th	Jenkin Whiteside	R	April 11, 1809	Oct. 8, 1811	Resigned from office
12th–13th	George W. Campbell	R	Oct. 8, 1811	Feb. 11, 1814	Resigned from office
13th–14th	Jesse Wharton	R	March 17, 1814	Oct. 10, 1815	Appointed by governor to fill vacancy
14th	John Williams	R	Oct. 10, 1815	March 3, 1817	
15th	John Williams	R	March 4, 1817	Oct. 1, 1817	Appointed by governor during the recess of the legislature
15th–17th	John Williams	R	Oct. 2, 1817	March 3, 1823	
18th–19th	Andrew Jackson	JR	March 4, 1823	Oct. 14, 1825	Resigned from office
19th–23rd	Hugh Lawson White	J	Oct. 28, 1825	March 3, 1835	
24th–26th	Hugh Lawson White	AJ, W	Oct. 6, 1835	Jan. 13, 1840	Resigned from office
26th	Alexander O. Anderson	D	Jan. 27, 1840	March 3, 1841	Vacancy from Mar. 4 to Oct. 16, 1843
28th–29th	Spencer Jarnagin	W	Oct. 17, 1843	March 3, 1847	
30th–32nd	John Bell	W	Nov. 22, 1847	March 3, 1853	
33rd–35th	John Bell	W, OP, AM	Oct. 29, 1853	March 3, 1859	
36th	Alfred O. P. Nicholson	D	March 4, 1859	March 3, 1861	Retired. Seat vacant until July 24, 1866.
39th–41st	Joseph S. Fowler	UU, R	July 24, 1866	March 3, 1871	
42nd–44th	Henry Cooper	D	March 4, 1871	March 3, 1877	
45th–55th	Isham G. Harris	D	March 4, 1877	July 8, 1897	Died while in office
55th	Thomas B. Turley	D	July 20, 1897	Feb. 1, 1898	Appointed by governor to fill vacancy
55th–56th	Thomas B. Turley	D	Feb. 2, 1898	March 3, 1901	
57th–59th	Edward W. Carmack	D	March 4, 1901	March 3, 1907	

Class Two: *The Blount Seat (Continued)*

Congress	Senator	Party	Commencement of Term	End of Service	Remarks
60th–62nd	Robert L. Taylor	D	March 4, 1907	March 31, 1912	Died while in office
62nd	Newell Sanders	R	April 8, 1912	Jan. 24, 1913	Appointed by governor to fill vacancy
62nd	William R. Webb	D	Jan. 24, 1913	March 3, 1913	
63rd–68th	John K. Shields	D	March 4, 1913	March 3, 1925	
69th–71st	Lawrence D. Tyson	D	March 4, 1925	Aug. 24, 1929	Died while in office
71st	William E. Brock	D	Sept. 2, 1929	Nov. 3, 1930	Appointed by governor to fill vacancy
71st	William E. Brock	D	Nov. 4, 1930	March 3, 1931	
72nd	Cordell Hull	D	March 4, 1931	March 3, 1933	Resigned from office to become Secretary of state of the United States
73rd	Nathan L. Bachman	D	March 4, 1933	Nov. 6, 1934	Appointed by governor to fill vacancy
73rd–75th	Nathan L. Bachman	D	Nov. 7, 1934	April 23, 1937	Died while in office
75th	George L. Berry	D	May 6, 1937	Nov. 8, 1938	Appointed by governor to fill vacancy
75th–80th	A. Thomas Stewart	D	Jan. 16, 1939	Jan. 2, 1949	
81st–88th	C. Estes Kefauver	D	Jan. 3, 1949	Aug. 10, 1963	Died while in office
88th	Herbert S. Walters	D	Aug. 20, 1963	Nov. 3, 1964	Appointed by governor to fill vacancy
88th–89th	Ross Bass	D	Nov. 4, 1964	Jan. 2, 1967	
90th–98th	Howard H. Baker, Jr.	R	Jan. 3, 1967	Jan. 2, 1985	
99th–103rd	Albert A. Gore, Jr.	D	Jan. 3, 1985	Jan. 2, 1993	Resigned from office having been elected Vice president of the United States
103rd	Harlan Mathews	D	Jan. 3, 1993	Dec. 1, 1994	Appointed by governor to fill vacancy
103rd–104th	Fred D. Thompson	R	Dec. 2, 1994	Jan. 2, 1997	
105th–107th	Fred D. Thompson	R	Jan. 3, 1997		

Appendix II

U.S. Senate Election Results

Class One: *The Cocke Seat*

Year	Party/Candidate	Primary Votes	Primary Percent	General Votes	General Percent
1915	Democrat				
	Kenneth D. McKellar	42,547	37.2		
	Malcolm R. Patterson	39,380	34.4		
	Luke Lea	32,571	28.4		
1915	Democrat	Run-Off			
	Kenneth D. McKellar	55,694	62.1		
	Malcolm R. Patterson	33,927	37.9		
1916	Democrat				
	Kenneth D. McKellar			143,718	54.4
	Republican				
	Ben W. Hooper			118,174	44.8
	Socialist				
	H. H. Mangum			2,193	0.8
1922	Democrat				
	Kenneth D. McKellar	102,692	64.0	151,523	68.0
	Guston T. Fitzhugh	47,627	29.7		
	Noah W. Cooper	9,480	5.9		
	T. W. Sims	619	0.4		
	Republican				
	Newell Sanders	36,581	66.7	71,200	32.0
	Harry B. Anderson	18,239	33.3		

Class One: *The Cocke Seat (Continued)*

Year	Party/Candidate	Primary Votes	Primary Percent	General Votes	General Percent
1928	Democrat				
	Kenneth D. McKellar	120,298	63.3	175,431	59.3
	Finis J. Garrett	64,470	33.9		
	John R. Neal	3,510	1.8		
	George Casey	1,908	1.0		
	Republican				
	James A. Fowler			120,289	40.7
1934	Democrat				
	Kenneth D. McKellar	212,226	84.0	195,430	63.4
	John R. Neal	40,463	16.0		
	Republican				
	Ben W. Hooper	64,409	100.0	110,401	35.8
	Independent				
	C. W. Hoisington			2,443	0.8
1940	Democrat				
	Kenneth D. McKellar	230,033	91.5	295,440	70.8
	John R. Neal	14,653	5.8		
	Claude C. Toler	6,671	2.7		
	Republican				
	Howard H. Baker, Sr.			121,790	29.2
	Independent				
	John R. Neal			35	0.0
1946	Democrat				
	Kenneth D. McKellar	188,805	62.0	145,654	66.6
	Edward W. Carmack, Jr.	107,363	35.2		
	John R. Neal	3,130	1.0		
	Herman H. Ross	2,995	1.0		
	Byron Johnson	2,495	0.8		
	Republican				
	William B. Ladd	30,756	100.0	57,238	26.2
	Independent				
	John R. Neal			11,516	5.3
	Herman H. Ross			4,303	2.0
1952	Democrat				
	Albert A. Gore, Sr.	334,957	56.5	545,432	74.2
	Kenneth D. McKellar	245,054	41.4		
	John R. Neal	7,181	1.2		
	Herman H. Ross	4,950	0.8		
	Pat Sutton	288	0.1		
	Republican				
	Hobart F. Atkins	25,061	65.7	153,479	20.9
	Richard J. Demere	6,858	18.0		
	Robert C. Gregory	5,380	14.1		
	C. W. Moore, Jr.	846	2.2		
	Independent				
	Richard M. Barber			22,169	3.0
	John R. Neal			14,132	1.9

Class One: *The Cocke Seat (Continued)*

Year	Party/Candidate	Primary Votes	Primary Percent	General Votes	General Percent
1958	Democrat				
	Albert A. Gore, Sr	375,439	59.7	317,324	79.0
	W. Prentice Cooper	253,191	40.3		
	Republican				
	Hobart F. Atkins	23,744	100.0	76,371	19.0
	Independent				
	Chester W. Mason			5,324	1.3
	Thomas Gouge, Jr.			2,646	0.7
1964	Democrat				
	Albert A. Gore, Sr.	401,163	84.7	570,542	53.6
	Sam J. Galloway	37,974	8.0		
	W. N. "Rube" McKinney	21,414	4.5		
	Charles G. Vick	11,059	2.3		
	John S. Wrinkle	2,183	0.5		
	Republican				
	Dan H. Kuykendall	72,376	100.0	493,475	46.4
1970	Republican				
	William (Bill) E. Brock, III	176,703	74.9	562,645	51.3
	Tex Ritter	54,401	23.0		
	James Durelle Boles	4,942	2.1		
	Democrat				
	Albert A. Gore, Sr.	269,770	51.0	519,858	47.4
	Hudley Crockett	238,767	45.2		
	Herman Frey	10,297	2.0		
	Stanford Andress	9,871	1.9		
	American				
	Dr. Cecil E. Pitard	872	100.0	8,691	0.8
	Independent				
	Dan R. East			5,845	0.5
1976	Democrat				
	James (Jim) R. Sasser	244,930	44.2	751,180	52.5
	John Jay Hooker, Jr.	171,716	31.0		
	Harry Sadler	54,125	9.8		
	David Bolin	44,056	8.0		
	Lester Kefauver	29,864	5.4		
	Edward Brown	4,695	0.8		
	William T. Hardison, Jr.	4,461	0.8		
	Republican				
	Bill Brock	173,743	100.0	673,231	47.0
	Independent				
	Mark-Clark Bates			5,137	0.4
	Willie C. Jacox			1,406	0.1
	Arnold J. Zandi			1,061	0.1
1982	Democrat				
	James R. Sasser	511,059	88.9	780,113	61.9
	Charles G. Vick	63,488	11.1		
	Republican				
	Robin L. Beard	205,271	91.4	479,642	38.1
	William B. Thompson, Jr.	19,277	8.6		

Class One: *The Cocke Seat (Continued)*

Year	Party/Candidate	Primary Votes	Percent	General Votes	Percent
1988	Democrat				
	James R. Sasser	332,560	100.0	1,020,061	65.1
	Republican				
	Bill Andersen	115,341	72.9	541,033	34.5
	Alice W. Algood	34,413	21.8		
	Hubert D. Patty	8,358	5.3		
	Independent				
	Khalil-Ullah Al-Muhaymin			6,042	0.4
1994	Republican				
	William (Bill) H. Frist	197,734	44.4	834,226	56.4
	Bob Corker	143,808	32.3		
	Steve Wilson	50,274	11.3		
	Harold Sterling	28,425	6.4		
	Byron Bush	14,267	3.2		
	Andrew (Buddy) Benedict, III	11,117	2.5		
	Democrat				
	James R. Sasser	402,610	100.0	623,164	42.1
	Independent				
	John Jay Hooker, Jr.			13,244	0.9
	Charles F. Johnson			6,631	0.4
	Philip L. Kienlen			3,087	0.2

Class Two: *The Blount Seat*

Year	Party/Candidate	Primary Votes	Percent	General Votes	Percent
1918	Democrat				
	John K. Shields	66,389	54.3	98,605	62.2
	Tom C. Rye	55,845	45.7		
	Republican				
	H. Clay Evans			59,989	37.8
1924	Democrat				
	Lawrence D. Tyson	72,496	41.8	147,821	57.3
	John K. Shields	54,990	31.7		
	Nathan L. Bachman	44,946	26.0		
	George L. Casey	791	0.5		
	Republican				
	H. B. Lindsay			109,863	42.6
	Independent				
	S. W. Williams			247	0.1
†1930	Democrat				
	William (Will) E. Brock	113,492	70.7	144,021	74.4
	John R. Neal	47,110	29.3		
	Republican				
	F. Todd Meacham			49,634	25.6

†Special election.

Class Two: *The Blount Seat (Continued)*

Year	Party/Candidate	Primary Votes	Primary Percent	General Votes	General Percent
1930	Democrat				
	Cordell Hull	140,802	62.9	154,071	71.3
	Andrew L. Todd	79,649	35.6		
	David W. Dodson	3,319	1.5		
	Republican				
	Paul E. Divine			58,550	27.1
	Independent				
	Sherman Bell			3,392	1.6
†1934	Democrat				
	Nathan L. Bachman	166,293	57.8	200,249	80.1
	Gordon Browning	121,169	42.2		
	Republican				
	Dwayne Maddox	45,325	100.0		
	Independent				
	John R. Neal			49,773	19.9
1936	Democrat				
	Nathan L. Bachman	217,531	82.9	273,298	76.4
	John R. Neal	44,830	17.1		
	Republican				
	Dwayne D. Maddox			67,238	18.8
	Independent				
	John R. Neal			14,627	4.1
	Socialist				
	Howard Kester			2,516	0.7
†1938	Democrat				
	A. Tom Stewart	174,940	48.9	194,028	70.5
	George L. Berry	101,966	28.5		
	J. Ridley Mitchell	70,393	19.7		
	John R. Neal	4,689	1.3		
	C. L. Powell	3,171	0.9		
	Edward W. Carmack, Jr.	2,536	0.7		
	Republican				
	Harley G. Fowler	11,760	100.0	72,098	26.2
	Independent				
	John R. Neal			9,106	3.3
1942	Democrat				
	A. Tom Stewart	136,415	51.9	110,432	69.2
	Edward W. Carmack, Jr.	116,841	44.4		
	John R. Neal	9,653	3.7		
	Republican				
	F. Todd Meacham			33,832	21.2
	Independent				
	John R. Neal			15,258	9.6

†Special election.

Class Two: *The Blount Seat (Continued)*

Year	Party/Candidate	Primary Votes	Primary Percent	General Votes	General Percent
1948	Democrat				
	C. Estes Kefauver	171,791	42.2	326,142	65.3
	A. Tom Stewart	129,873	31.9		
	John A. Mitchell	96,192	23.6		
	George W. Hardin	5,415	1.3		
	John R. Neal	1,876	0.5		
	John Hickey	1,534	0.4		
	Republican				
	B. Carroll Reece	82,522	81.7	166,947	33.4
	Allen J. Strawbridge	18,526	18.3		
	Independent				
	John R. Neal			6,103	1.2
1954	Democrat				
	C. Estes Kefauver	440,497	68.2	249,121	70.0
	Pat Sutton	186,363	28.8		
	E. L. (Ed) Brown	9,644	1.5		
	John R. Neal	9,446	1.5		
	Republican				
	Ray H. Jenkins	45,015	81.7		
	Robert C. Gregory	10,053	18.3		
	Thomas P. Wall			106,971	30.0
1960	Democrat				
	C. Estes Kefauver	463,848	64.6	594,460	71.8
	Andrew T. Taylor	249,336	34.7		
	Jake Armstrong	4,867	0.7		
	Republican				
	A. Bradley Frazier	16,633	58.8	234,053	28.2
	Hansel Proffitt	11,667	41.2		
†1964	Democrat				
	Ross Bass	330,213	50.8	568,905	52.1
	Frank G. Clement	233,245	35.9		
	M. M. Bullard	86,718	13.3		
	Republican				
	Howard H. Baker, Jr.	93,301	84.9	517,330	47.4
	Dr. Charles Moffett	10,596	9.6		
	Hubert D. Patty	5,947	5.4		
	Independent				
	Melvin B. Morgan			4,853	0.4
1966	Republican				
	Howard H. Baker, Jr.	112,617	75.7	483,063	55.7
	Kenneth Roberts	36,043	24.2		
	Democrat				
	Frank G. Clement	384,322	51.2	383,843	44.3
	Ross Bass	366,079	48.8		

†Special election.

Class Two: *The Blount Seat (Continued)*

Year	Party/Candidate	Primary Votes	Primary Percent	General Votes	General Percent
1972	Republican				
	Howard H. Baker, Jr.	242,373	97.0	716,539	61.6
	Hubert D. Patty	7,581	3.0		
	Democrat				
	Ray Blanton	292,249	76.4	440,599	37.8
	Don Palmer	40,700	10.6		
	Herman S. Frey	18,814	4.9		
	Ron Stinnett	15,804	4.1		
	Raymond P. Gibbs	14,941	3.9		
	Independent				
	Dan East			7,026	0.6
1978	Republican				
	Howard H. Baker, Jr.	205,680	83.4	642,644	55.5
	Harvey D. Howard	21,154	8.6		
	James Boles	8,899	3.6		
	Hubert D. Patty	3,941	1.6		
	Dayton Seiler	3,831	1.6		
	Francis Tapp	2,994	1.2		
	Democrat				
	Jane Eskind	196,156	34.5	466,228	40.3
	Bill Bruce	170,795	30.1		
	J. D. Lee	89,939	15.8		
	James Boyd	48,458	8.5		
	Walter Bradley	22,130	3.9		
	Douglas Heinsohn	17,787	3.1		
	James Foster	10,671	1.9		
	Virginia Nyabongo	7,682	1.4		
	Charles G. Vick	4,414	0.8		
	Independent				
	Thomas J. Anderson			45,908	4.0
	Fern L. Keasler			2,243	0.2
1984	Democrat				
	Albert A. Gore, Jr.	345,527	100.0	1,000,607	60.7
	Republican				
	Victor Ashe	145,774	86.5	557,016	33.8
	Jack McNeil	17,970	10.7		
	Hubert D. Patty	4,777	2.8		
	Independent				
	Ed McAteer			87,234	5.3
	Khalil-Ullah Al-Muhaymin			3,179	0.2

Class Two: *The Blount Seat (Continued)*

Year	Party/Candidate	Primary Votes	Primary Percent	General Votes	General Percent
1990	Democrat				
	Albert A. Gore, Jr.	479,961	100.0	530,898	67.7
	Republican				
	William R. Hawkins	54,317	38.9	233,703	29.8
	Ralph Brown	53,873	38.5		
	Patrick K. Hales	31,515	22.5		
	Independent				
	William Jacox			11,191	1.4
	Charles G. Vick			8,021	1.0
†1994	Republican				
	Fred D. Thompson	235,386	64.2	885,998	60.4
	John Baker	131,431	35.8		
	Democrat				
	Jim Cooper	375,615	100.0	565,930	38.6
	Independent				
	Charles N. Hancock			4,169	0.3
	Charles M. Moore			2,219	0.2
	Terry L. Lytle			1,934	0.1
	Kerry Martin			1,719	0.1
	Jon Walls			1,532	0.1
	Hobart R. Lumpkin			1,184	0.1
	Don Schneller			1,150	0.1
1996	Republican				
	Fred D. Thompson	266,549	94.1	1,091,554	61.4
	Jim F. Counts	16,715	5.9		
	Democrat				
	Houston Gordon	156,704	63.5	654,937	36.8
	Ashley M. King	89,887	36.5		
	Independent				
	John Jay Hooker, Jr.			14,401	0.8
	Bruce Gold			5,865	0.3
	Robert O. Watson			5,569	0.3
	Greg Samples			4,104	0.2
	Philip L. Kienlen			2,173	0.1

†Special election.

Appendix III

Appendix Abbreviations and Sources

ABBREVIATIONS–APPENDIX I

AM	American (Know-Nothing)
AJ	Anti-Jackson
D	Democrat
J	Jacksonian
JR	Jackson Republican
OP	Opposition
R	Republican
U	Unionist
UU	Unconditional Unionist
W	Whig

SOURCES–APPENDIX I

Biographical Directory of the American Congress, 1774–1996: the Continental Congress, September 5, 1774, to October 21, 1788, and the Congress of the United States from the First through the 104th Congresses, March 4, 1789 to January 3, 1997. Editor, Joel D. Treese. CQ Staff Directories, Inc., Alexandria, Virginia, 1997.

Guide to Research Collections of former United States Senators, 1789–1995: A Listing of Archival Repositories Housing the Papers of Former Senators, Related Collections, and Oral History Interviews, compiled by Karen Dawley Paul (Senate Archivist) and Diane B. Boyle (editorial assistant), and prepared under the direction of Kelly D. Johnston, Secretary of the Senate, U.S. Government Printing Office, 1995.

Senate Manual containing the Standing Rules, Orders, Laws and Resolutions Affecting the Business of the United States Senate, Declaration of Independence, Articles of Confederation, Ordinance of 1787, and the Constitution of the United States. Prepared by Lana R. Slack, under the direction of Grayson Winterling, Staff Director, U.S. Government Printing Office, 1996.

Senators of the United States: a Historical Bibliography: A Compilation of Works by and about Members of the United States Senate, 1789–1995, compiled by Jo Anne McCormick Quatannens and Diane B. Boyle (editorial assistant), and prepared under the direction of Kelly D. Johnston, Secretary of the Senate, U.S. Government Printing Office, 1995.

SOURCES—APPENDIX II

America Votes; A Handbook of Contemporary American Election Statistics. Volumes 1–22, Richard M. Scammon, Congressional Quarterly Inc, Washington, D.C., 1956-1996.

"Begin Canvass of Senatorial Vote," *Nashville Banner,* December 31, 1915, p.12. (results of Democratic primary runoff on December 15, 1915)

Congressional Quarterly's Guide to U.S. Elections, Third Edition, Congressional Quarterly, Inc., Washington, D.C., 1994.

Fifty Years of Tennessee Elections 1916–1966, compiled under the direction of Joe C. Carr, Secretary of State, by Shirley Hassler, State Election Coordinator, Nashville, 1967 or 1968.

Fifty Years of Tennessee Primary Elections 1918–1968, compiled under the direction of Joe C. Carr, Secretary of State, by Shirley Hassler, State Election Coordinator, Nashville, 1969 (?).

"Reports Indicate Light Vote To-Day," *Nashville Banner,* December 15, 1915, p.1. (results of November 20, 1915 Democratic primary)

Statistics of the Presidential and Congressional Elections. Available on the WWW page of the U.S. House Clerk at http://clerkweb.house.gov/histrecs/history/elections/elections.htm

Tennessee Blue Books, 1918–1998, Tennessee Secretary of State.

Tennessee Votes, 1799–1976, by Anne H. Hopkins, William Lyons, Bureau of Public Administration, University of Tennessee, Knoxville, 1978.

United States Congressional Elections, 1788–1997: The Official Results of the Elections of the 1st through 105th Congresses, Michael J. Dubin, McFarland & Company, Inc., Jefferson, North Carolina, 1998.

Index

About the Authors

WILLIAM H. FRIST, M.D.—heart surgeon, teacher, scientist, author, and U.S. Senator—was elected to the Senate in 1994, becoming the first physician elected to that body in almost seventy years. A citizen-legislator in the truest sense, he graduated from Princeton University, where he studied at the Woodrow Wilson School of Public and International Affairs. He began his twenty-year medical career at Harvard Medical School and received his postgraduate training at Massachusetts General Hospital and Stanford University Medical Center. He returned to his hometown of Nashville to found the Vanderbilt University Multiorgan Transplant Center. Senator Frist's Tennessee roots go back four generations, his family being among the initial fifty-three families who settled Chattanooga. He and his wife, Karyn, are the parents of three sons.

J. LEE ANNIS, Jr., is associate professor of history and political science at Montgomery College in Rockville, Maryland. He received his undergraduate degree in history from Hanover College and his master's and doctorate in history from Ball State University.